A STUDY OF WRITING

A STUDY OF
WRITING

REVISED EDITION

I. J. GELB

THE UNIVERSITY OF CHICAGO PRESS
CHICAGO & LONDON

TO THE MOKSTADS

SBN: 226-28605-3 (clothbound); 226-28606-1 (paperbound)

THE UNIVERSITY OF CHICAGO PRESS, CHICAGO 60637
The University of Chicago Press, Ltd., London

PREFACE

THE book contains twelve chapters, but it can be broken up structurally into five parts. First, the place of writing among the various systems of human inter-communication is discussed. This is followed by four chapters devoted to the descriptive and comparative treatment of the various types of writing in the world. The sixth chapter deals with the evolution of writing from the earliest stages of picture writing to a full alphabet. The next four chapters deal with general problems, such as the future of writing and the relationship of writing to speech, art, and religion. Of the two final chapters, one contains the first attempt to establish a full terminology of writing, the other an extensive bibliography.

The aim of this study is to lay a foundation for a new science of writing which might be called grammatology. While the general histories of writing treat individual writings mainly from a descriptive-historical point of view, the new science attempts to establish general principles governing the use and evolution of writing on a comparative-typological basis. The importance of this study lies in its being the first systematic presentation of the history and evolution of writing as based on these principles. Some specific results of the new reconstruction are: Elimination of the so-called 'word writings' and their replacement by the word-syllabic type; assignment of the so-called 'Semitic alphabet' to the syllabic type; placing the so-called 'Maya and Aztec writings' not under writings proper but under forerunners of writing; conclusion that the mysterious 'Easter Island inscriptions' do not represent writing but formal designs for magical purposes.

Let it be clearly understood from the start that the work here presented is not a comprehensive history of writing. This work is concerned only with those writings that are representative of certain types or are crucial for the understanding of certain developments. One would look in vain, therefore, in this study for a discussion of Latin writing through ancient, medieval, and modern times, because that system represents nothing new and important for the theory of writing. Generally speaking, we write to-day the way the ancient Romans did, and the ancient Latin writing is identical in principle with that of the Greeks, from whom it was borrowed.

Much of the theoretical reconstruction of writing as presented in this study may sound heretical to some scholars, especially to those philologists who, being imbued with sacred traditions in their narrow fields of specialization, feel reticent about accepting conclusions drawn from a comprehensive view of writing. Indicative of this attitude is the request of one of my colleagues not to quote his name in acknowledgement for help I had received from him in matters pertaining to Chinese. It is with a certain degree of self-assurance that I refer to that scholar's reluctance to be associated with 'heretics', since I hope to see him go to Canossa when he sees the light.

The study relies chiefly on internal structural evidence, placing in secondary position arguments that can be drawn from external formal evidence. Thus there is plenty of room in a future study of similar nature to work out thoroughly the formal aspects of the typology and evolution of writing. Subjects which might receive more adequate treatment in the future pertain to writing materials, numbers, order of signaries, names of signs, and auxiliary marks, such as prosodic features, word division, etc.

This study has been in the making for slightly over twenty years. It includes parts in the chapter 'Writing and Civilization' which were taken over from a paper written in my college days as well as a chapter entitled 'Future of Writing' which was written only about two years ago. The major part of the study was composed in the few years immediately preceding the American entry into the Second World War. The long period of gestation, coupled with the heavy burden of scholastic and administrative duties that have fallen to me in the last few years, is mainly responsible for whatever unevenness in style and composition may appear in the final product. It is for the latter reason that I have been unable to utilize fully the scientific literature of the last two or three years. From among the important works on writing which have not received full justice in this study I should like to single out James G. Février, *Histoire de l'écriture* (Paris, 1948) and G. R. Driver, *Semitic Writing from Pictograph to Alphabet* (London, 1948).

In order to prevent misunderstanding on the part of some

linguists it should be pointed out that the term 'syllabic sign' is used here to denote a unit of writing which must contain a vowel (either by itself or flanked by consonants in front or in back of it) and which may or may not contain prosodic features (such as stress, tone, quantity, etc.); this definition in the field of writing differs, therefore, from that of a syllable, taken by some linguists to denote a speech unit which is characterized in the first place by prosodic features and which may or may not contain a vowel.

One of the most vexing problems in a study of such a wide range as this one is that of transliteration and transcription. Nobody realizes better than myself that (while striving to achieve uniformity) I have not succeeded in avoiding a number of inconsistencies. Especially unfortunate is, in my opinion, the use of $i̭$, j and y (for y in English 'yes'); the force of existing conventions in different languages and writings presented a problem for which no satisfactory solution could be found.

This study owes much directly and indirectly to many friends and colleagues both in this country and abroad. The whole manuscript was read and constructively criticized by my former teacher at the University of Rome, Professor Giorgio Levi Della Vida (when he was at the University of Pennsylvania), Professor Giuliano Bonfante of Princeton, Professor John Lotz of Columbia, Professor Thomas Sebeok of the Indiana University, Professor Ralph Marcus, Dr. Richard T. Hallock, Mrs. Erna S. Hallock, and my former student Mr. Byron E. Farwell, all of Chicago. Parts of Chapters I and IX were read by Professor Thorkild Jacobsen of Chicago, Professor Henri Frankfort and Mrs. Frankfort formerly of Chicago, now of London. Much help was received in the field of Sumerian from Professor Jacobsen, in the field of Egyptian from Professors William F. Edgerton, Keith C. Seele, and John A. Wilson of Chicago, and in the field of Chinese from Professors Ch'ên Mêng-chia and Têng Ssŭ-yü (when they were at the University of Chicago). Mr. Jørgen Laessøe of Chicago was kind enough to help me with many hand drawings in this study. To all these scholars and friends may I offer in this place my warmest thanks and appreciation.

I. J. G.

Chicago, Illinois.
June, 1951.

PREFACE TO THE SECOND EDITION

THE present edition of *A Study of Writing* is being issued to bring up to date the older editions, both American and British, which have completely disappeared from the market. In order not to disturb the format of the older edition unduly, only short revisions and those easy to incorporate without changing the pagination were made in the main body of the volume, while all the larger revisions, corrections, and additions were relegated to the Notes near the end of the book. Because of the numerous additions in that section, the Notes, Bibliography, and Index were completely reset and repaged. The present edition contains the same illustrations as the older editions with the exception of Figures 50, 51, and 69, which were replaced by more adequate illustrations.

I. J. G.

Chicago, Illinois
November 1962

ix

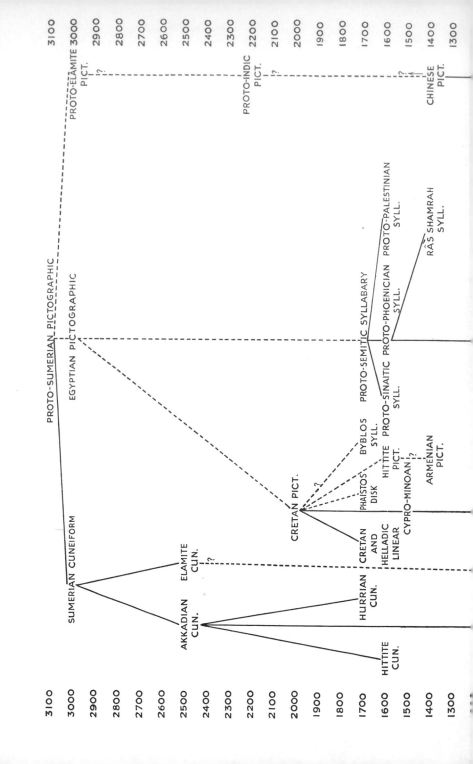

ORIGIN OF THE ALPHABET

CONTENTS

CONTENTS

LIST OF ILLUSTRATIONS

I

WRITING AS A SYSTEM OF SIGNS

WAYS OF COMMUNICATING IDEAS

THE two most important external characteristics of human behaviour are expression and communication. The first affects what we may call personal behaviour, the second social behaviour. Man has many ways, natural and artificial, of expressing his thoughts and his feelings. He can give expression in a natural way to his joy by laughing or humming and to his sorrow by weeping or moaning. He can express himself with the help of artificial means in a written poem, a painting, or any other piece of art. Man can try to communicate his feelings, thoughts, and ideas by means of conventional and generally understandable forms. What is the relation of expression to communication? Is there such a thing as pure expression or pure communication? Is it not rather that man, as a social being, the *zoon politikon* of Aristotle, finds himself or visualizes himself to be at all times in conditions in which he can express himself only by communicating? And, vice versa, are not all the great masterpieces of art or poetry forms of communication achieved through the personal expression of individuals? It seems to me that the aims of expression and communication are so closely intertwined with each other in all forms of human behaviour that normally it is impossible to speak about one without being forced at the same time to consider the other.

In order to communicate thoughts and feelings there must be a conventional system of signs or symbols which, when used by some persons, are understood by other persons receiving them. Communication under normal circumstances requires the presence of two (or more) persons, the one(s) who emit(s) and the one(s) who receive(s) the communication.

The process of communication is composed of two parts, emission and reception. As the means of emitting communication are too varied and numerous to allow for any systematic classification, our treatment must start from the point of view of reception. The reception of communication is achieved by means of our senses, of which sight, hearing, and touch play the most important roles. Theoretically, other senses, such as smell and taste, could also be taken into consideration, but in practice they play a very limited role and lead to no fully developed systems of signs.[1]

Visual communication can be achieved by means of gesture and mimicry.[2] Both are frequent companions of speech, although the intensity of their use differs with various individuals or social strata or folk groups. Some persons, more than others, use gesticulation or mimicry for oratorical effect or through natural impulse. In our society it is considered bad taste to 'talk with the hands'. It is a well-known fact that in Europe the southerners, like the Italians, use both gesticulation and mimicry to a much greater extent than, for instance, the Scandinavians or the British. A combination of language and gesture has played an important role in the ritual proceedings of all times and places. The restrictions imposed upon the use of language by natural and artificial conditions has resulted in the origin and development of systems of communication based on gesture and mimicry. Such are the systems developed for the use of deaf-mutes deprived by nature of the power of natural language. Here we may mention the gesture language of the Trappist monks, who, because of their vow of silence, were forced to develop a substitute system for speech. Systems of gesture language are often used among the Australian aborigines by widows who are not allowed to utter a word during the period of mourning.[3] And, finally, the system of gesture language used among the Plains Indians was introduced as the need grew for communication between tribes speaking various mutually incomprehensible languages.

Among other ways of communication appealing to the eye we should mention optic signals by means of fire, smoke, light, semaphores, etc.

One of the simplest forms of auditory communication is, for instance, whistling with the intention of calling someone. Hissing or applauding in the theatre are other simple specimens of this kind of communication. Sometimes artificial means, such as drums, whistles, or trumpets are used as acoustic signals.[4]

The most important system of auditory communication is the spoken language directed to the ear of the person receiving the communication. Language is universal. Within the span of human knowledge there has never existed a group of men who have not possessed a fully developed language.

Simple ways of communicating feeling by the sense of touch are, for instance, the handclasp, the backslap, the lovestroke. A fully developed system of communication by handstroking is used among blind deaf-mutes, for which the best-known example is provided by the case of Helen Keller, the American writer and educator.[5]

The means of communication mentioned above have two features in common: (1) They are all of momentary value and are therefore restricted as to time; as soon as the word is uttered or the gesture made, it is gone and it cannot be revived except by repetition. (2) They can be used only in communication between persons more or less in proximity to each other and are therefore restricted as to space.

The need for finding a way to convey thoughts and feelings in a form not limited by time or space led to the development of methods of communication by means of (1) objects and (2) markings on objects or any solid material.

Visual means of communication with the help of objects are unlimited. When a person sets up a pile of stones or a single stone monument on a grave, he intends to give expression to his feelings for the deceased and to perpetuate his memory in the days to come. The cross symbolizing faith or the anchor symbolizing hope are further modern illustrations. A modern survival is the rosary, each bead of which, according to its position and size, is supposed to recall one certain prayer. We might also mention here the so-called 'flower and gem languages', in which a certain flower or gem is supposed to convey a certain sentiment.

Systems of mnemonic signs to keep accounts by means of objects are known throughout the world. The simplest and the most common are the so-called 'counting sticks' to keep records of cattle; these are simple wooden sticks with carved notches corresponding to the number of cattle under the custody of a shepherd. Another simple device is keeping account of cattle with the help of little pebbles in a sack. A more complicated mnemonic system is represented among the Peruvian Incas by the so-called '*quipu* writing', in which accounts concerning objects and beings were recorded by means of strings and knots of various length and colour. All the reports about the alleged use of the *quipu* for the recording of chronicles and historical events are plain fantasy. Neither the Peruvian nor the modern knot writings in South America and on the Riukiu Islands near Japan have any other aim than that of recording simplest facts of statistical nature.[6]

Here, too, we may mention the *wampums* of the North American Indians, consisting of strings of shell beads, frequently tied together in belts, which served as money, ornaments, and also as means of communication. In their simplest form, coloured *wampum* strings were used to convey messages following the colour conventions of the American Indians (see p. 19): white beads for peace, purple or violet for war, etc.[7] The more complicated forms of *wampum* belts, representing full figures and scenes, may very well be assigned to the descriptive-representational stage discussed in Chapter II.

Objects are used as memory aids for recording proverbs and songs among the Ewe Negroes in a form quite similar to that which they achieved by means of written symbols (see pp. 48 ff.). Carl Meinhof[8] relates that a missionary found in a native hut a cord on which were strung many objects, such as a feather, a stone, etc. In answer to his query as to the meaning of the string with the objects the missionary was told that each piece was supposed to stand for a certain proverb. Another custom is related by Mary H. Kingsley[9] from West Africa about native singers who carry around in a net all kinds of objects, such as pipes, feathers, skins, birdheads, bones, etc., each of which serves the purpose of recalling a certain song. The songs are recited with pantomimes. Persons in the audience choose a certain object and before the recital they bargain about the price to be paid to the singer. In a way, the net of the singer can be considered the repertoire of his songs.

Cowrie mussels are frequently employed for communicative purpose. Thus, among the Yoruba Negroes[10] one cowrie mussel denotes 'defiance and failure', two placed together mean 'relationship and meeting', while two placed apart mean

4

'separation and enmity', and so on. Surprising is the development of the phonetic principle (see p. 66) evident in the following examples: six cowrie mussels mean 'attracted' because the word *efa* in the Yoruba language means 'six' and 'attracted'; a message consisting of a string with six mussels, when sent by a young man to a girl, therefore expresses: 'I feel attracted to you, I love you.' And since the word *eyo* means both 'eight' and 'agreed' the answer from the girl to the young man may be a message consisting of a string with eight mussels, saying: 'Agreed, I feel the same way as you do.'

A modern illustration of the use of objects for the purpose of communication is contained in the story from the Hungarian writer Jókai,[11] according to which a man sent a package of coffee to another man to warn him about danger from police. The story can be understood on the basis of the phonetic principle by noting that the Hungarian word for coffee is *kávé* and that it resembles in sound the Latin word *cave*, 'beware!'.

A most interesting usage from the comparative point of view is reported from the same Yoruba country, where the cowrie mussels are used so frequently for communicating messages. During an attack of a king of Dahomey upon a city of the Yoruba one of the natives was taken captive and, anxious to inform his wife of his plight, sent her a stone, coal, pepper, corn, and a rag, conveying the following message: the stone indicated 'health', meaning 'as the stone is hard, so my body is hardy, strong'; the coal indicated 'gloom', meaning 'as the coal is black, so are my prospects dark and gloomy'; the pepper indicated 'heat', meaning 'as the pepper is hot, so is my mind heated, burning on account of the gloomy prospect'; the corn indicated 'leanness', meaning 'as the corn is dried up by parching, so my body is dried and become lean through the heat of my affliction and suffering'; and finally, the rag indicated 'worn out', meaning 'as the rag is, so is my cloth cover worn and torn to a rag'.[12] An exact parallel to this usage is reported in the fourth book, section 131 ff., of Herodotus. 'The Scythian kings sent a herald bringing Darius the gift of a bird, a mouse, a frog, and five arrows. The Persians asked the bringer of these gifts what they might mean; but he said that no charge had been laid on him save to give the gifts and then depart with all speed; let the Persians (he said), if they were clever enough, discover the signification of the presents.

5

The Persians hearing and taking counsel, Darius' judgement was that the Scythians were surrendering to him themselves and their earth and their water; for he reasoned that a mouse is a creature found in the earth and eating the same produce as men, and a frog is a creature of the water, and a bird most like to a horse; and the arrows (said he) signified that the Scythians surrendered their weapon of battle. This was the opinion declared by Darius; but the opinion of Gobryas, one of the seven who had slain the Magian, was contrary to it. He reasoned that the meaning of the gifts was: 'Unless you become birds, Persians, and fly up into the sky, or mice and hide you in the earth, or frogs and leap into the lakes, you will be shot by these arrows and never return home." Thus the Persians reasoned concerning the gifts.' Those modern cultural historians who may object to some of my reconstructions based on comparisons between ancient peoples and modern primitive societies (see p. 21 f.) cannot easily overlook the weight of such parallel usages from ancient and modern times.

Still another parallel to the two stories given above is reported from East Turkestan and concerns a billet doux sent by a young native girl to a boy friend with whom she fell in love.[13] The loveletter consisted of a small sack containing various objects which were supposed to convey the following message: a lump of pressed tea, meaning 'I can drink tea no more'; a blade of straw, 'because I became wan from love for you'; a red fruit, 'I get red when I think of you'; a dried-out apricot, 'I became withered like the fruit'; a piece of charcoal, 'my heart burns of love'; a flower, 'you are handsome'; a piece of sugar candy, 'you are sweet'; a pebble, 'is your heart made of stone?'; a feather of a falcon, 'if I had wings I would fly to you'; a kernel of a walnut, 'I give myself to you.'

All these means of communication are sometimes called in German *Sachschrift* or *Gegenstandschrift*,[14] that is, 'object writing', but entirely without justification since they have nothing to do with writing as we normally understand it. The impracticability of using objects prevented the development of any full system, and the devices used are restricted to small geographic areas.

Writing is expressed not by objects themselves but by markings on objects or on any other material. Written symbols are normally executed by means of motor action of the hands in drawing, painting, scratching, or incising. This is reflected by the meaning and etymology of the word 'to write' in many different languages. The English word 'to write' corresponds to the Old Norse *rīta*, 'to incise (runes),' and modern German *reissen, einritzen* 'to tear, to incise'. The Greek word γράφειν, 'to write,' as in English 'graphic, phonography,' etc., is the same as 'to carve', German *kerben*. Latin *scribere*, German *schreiben*, English 'scribe, inscribe,' etc., originally meant 'to incise' as we can see from its connection with Greek σκαριφᾶσθαι, 'to incise, to scratch.' Gothic *mēljan*, 'to write,' at first meant 'to paint' as we see from the fact that the modern German word *malen* means 'to paint'. And, finally, Slavonic *pisati*, 'to write,' originally referred to painting, as shown by the connection with Latin *pingere*, 'to paint,' found also in our 'paint, picture, pictography', etc. [15] The same semantic development can be observed in the Semitic family of languages. Thus, the root *štr*, 'to write,' must originally have meant 'to cut', as can be deduced from the occurrence of the Arabic word *sāṭūr*, 'large knife,' and *sāṭir*, 'butcher'; the root *ktb*, 'to write,' meant originally 'to incise', as indicated by Syriac *makteᵇbā*, 'awl'; and the root *ṣḥf* or *šḥf* meant not only 'to write' but also 'to excavate, to hollow' in South Semitic languages.

The expressions just described give us illustrations for the mechanical background of writing, and at the same time point toward a very close connection between picture and writing. This is as it should be, since the most natural way of communicating ideas by means of visible markings is achieved by pictures. To the primitives a picture takes care in a crude way of the needs fulfilled in modern times by writing. In the course of time the picture develops in two directions: (1) pictorial art, in which pictures continue to reproduce more or less faithfully the objects and events of the surrounding world in a form independent of language; and (2) writing, in which signs, whether they retain their pictorial form or not, become ultimately secondary symbols for notions of linguistic value.

The cases of stable communication achieved by tactual reception—such as Braille—and auditory reception—such as phonograph records—are all secondary transfers (see next paragraph) developed from systems created on the basis of visual reception.

Figure 1 shows in the form of a chart some of the various means of communication available to human beings.

7

	Momentary Communication	*Stable Communication*
For visual reception.	Gesture; mimicry; mien, eye expression; lip reading; mimetic dancing; signalling by means of fire, smoke, light, or semaphores.	(a) Objects: cross or anchor; rosary; flower or gem language; counting sticks; pebbles; quipu; cowrie mussels. (b) Markings on objects: picture and sculpture; WRITING.
For auditory reception.	Whistling; singing and humming; applauding or hissing; SPEECH; signalling by means of drums, whistles, or trumpets.	Phonograph records or dictaphone cylinders.
For tactual reception.	Handclasp, backslap, or lovestroke; handstroking of blind deaf-mutes.	Reading with fingers of raised or incised inscriptions; Braille.

FIG. I. WAYS OF COMMUNICATING IDEAS

In discussing the various systems of human intercommunication we should be careful to distinguish between primary and secondary systems. We can best illustrate this difference by the following example. When a father calls his son by whistling he expresses, without the interference of any linguistic form, his desire to bring the boy to a certain place. His thought or feeling is directly and immediately conveyed in the whistle. This is a primary means of communication. But when a father tries to call his son by whistling the letters of the Morse code expressing *s-o-n*, he is doing so by means of a linguistic transfer. His desire to bring the son to a certain place is now conveyed in the whistle through the intermediary of a linguistic form. This is what we may call a secondary means of communication.

There is no limit to secondary transfers. The spoken word 'son', for instance, is a primary speech sign. In the written word 'son' we find a written sign used for a spoken sign. If this written word *s-o-n* were then transmitted by means of flashlight signals, the resulting flashes would be signs of signs of signs. And so on *ad libitum*.

There is no good English expression capable of covering all

8

the conventional means of human intercommunication through signs. The French linguists use *le langage* in this sense, while they call the auditory language *langage parlé*, *langage articulé*, or simply *la langue*. In Anglo-American usage 'speech' often stands for auditory language and 'language' for any system of signs. [16] For the general science of signs several terms have been proposed, of which the term 'semiotic', used by Charles Morris, may perhaps be the most appropriate. [17]

What lies at the basis of all human intercommunication? What do we mean when we say we are communicating our ideas, thoughts, or feelings? To take three concrete examples from daily life, what is communicated by a gesture of a speaker asking for silence, by the bugle sounding reveille, or by the warning stop sign in the road? To the linguists of the behaviourist school the answer is clear and simple: what we are communicating is language. According to them, language is the only medium through which all humans communicate with each other and all means of human intercommunication outside of language are nothing but secondary substitutes for language. [18] Even thinking or having ideas is to them nothing else but 'silent talk', which they believe is always accompanied by 'soundless movements of the vocal organs, taking the place of speech-movements, but not perceptible to other people'. But this is a point where one may diverge from the principal dogma of the linguists belonging to the behaviourist school. [19] Of course, silent talk plays an important role in all forms of thinking, especially in cases of intensive thinking. For instance, a meditated situation in which we intend to say 'get out!' to another person could very well be accompanied by a perceptible movement of lips, sometimes even clearly vocal. On the other side, we know from experience, supported by experiments in the field of psychology, that we can think without a silent flow of words [20] and that we can understand the meaning of things for which we have no word in mind. [21] Certainly at least the born deaf-mutes are quite capable of communicating among themselves without any vocal background; and while in their case intensive thinking may at times be accompanied by more or less perceptible motions of hands and face, such reflexes must be considered secondary and on a line with perceptible movements of lips in the case of 'silent talk' by persons capable of speaking normally. Many more examples of reception of communication without a linguistic background can be found everywhere in our daily life. When I jump from bed in the morning at the sound of reveille or when I see on the highway a warning sign to stop I seem to react to these signs immediately without the interference of any linguistic form; the sound of the bugle or the sight of the traffic signal speak directly to my mind.

There is frequently an enormous difference between the process of emitting and that of receiving the communication. While our slow writing may be accompanied by sub-vocal processes, these processes may be difficult, if not impossible, to detect in persons who can read silently two or three times as fast as they read aloud. It is an established fact that many persons can read visually without an intermediary flow of speech signs.

To be sure, almost all sign systems can be transferred into some linguistic form, simply because speech is the fullest and the most developed of all our systems of signs, [22] but to draw on that basis the conclusion that speech forms the background of all human intercommunication seems a fallacy. Nobody would say that everything in the world is money because everything in the world can (theoretically) be transferred into money.

The more conservative of the American linguists do not deny the existence of visual images, ideas, or concepts without a necessary speech-sign background. What they say is that in linguistics such 'disembodied words' mean absolutely nothing and that for a linguist 'les idées ne viennent qu'en parlant', to quote a French saying very much in vogue in this country. [23] This may be true of the 'linguistic science which deals first and last with the word, its only reality'. [24] Where they err, however, is in taking for granted the complete identity of speech and writing and in believing that as a linguist can operate only with speech symbols, so a historian of writing can use fruitfully only speech symbols and should relegate visual images or ideas without words to the wastebasket. But writing in the widest sense cannot be in all stages identified with speech, and a student of writing does not necessarily have to be a linguist. The symbolism of visual images in the earliest stages of writing, like that of gesture signs, can express meaning without the necessity of a linguistic garment and both can profitably be investigated by a non-linguist. It is only after the development of writing into a full phonetic system, reproducing elements of speech, that we can speak of the practical identity of writing and speech and of epigraphy or paleography as being subdivisions of linguistics.

This tremendous difference between the *semasiographic* stage of writing (expressing meanings and notions loosely connected with speech) and the *phonographic* stage (expressing speech) must be thoroughly emphasized here because of the controversies which are continuously taking place in the matter of the definition of writing. Those general linguists who define writing as a device for recording speech by means of visible marks,[25] and take the written language to be a point-by-point equivalent of its spoken counterpart,[26] show little appreciation of the historical development of writing and fail to see that such a definition cannot be applied to its early stages, in which writing only loosely expressed the spoken language. On the other hand, the philologists, who believe that writing even after the introduction of phonetization was used for the recording or transmission of both idea and sound,[27] fail to understand that once man discovered a way of expressing exact forms of speech in written signs, writing lost its independent character and became largely a written substitute for its spoken counterpart.

DEFINITION OF WRITING

An average person asked to define writing would more than likely give something like the following answer: 'Why, that is the easiest thing in the world. Every child knows that writing is part of the elementary three "R's" and that our expression "ABC" denotes the simplest rudiments of any subject in our knowledge.' The problem is not so simple, however.

Writing began at the time when man learned how to communicate his thoughts and feelings by means of visible signs, understandable not only to himself but also to all other persons more or less initiated into the particular system. In the beginning pictures served as a visual expression of man's ideas in a form to a great extent independent of speech which expressed his ideas in an auditory form. The relationship between writing and speech in the early stages of writing was very loose, inasmuch as the written message did not correspond to exact forms of speech. A certain message had only one meaning and it could be interpreted by the reader in only one way, but it could be 'read' that is, put into words in many different ways and even in many different languages.

In later periods systematic application of the so-called 'phonetization' enabled man to express his ideas in a form which could correspond to exact categories of speech. From then on writing gradually lost its character as an independent mode of expressing ideas and became a tool of speech, a vehicle through which exact forms of speech could be recorded in permanent form.

In every great human achievement can be observed one important and decisive step which entirely revolutionized its further progress. In talking about inventions, I refer elsewhere to the fact that although Watt did not 'invent' the steam engine, he did take the decisive step in first using steam in a practical way as motive power (p. 199). We must reckon with a similar step in the history of writing. Such a step of revolutionary importance is the phonetization of the script. If we believe that the steam engine first started with Watt, then we might also assume that writing began only when man learned to express in writing notions of linguistic value. This would mean that writing is, as some linguists assume, a device for the recording of speech and that all the stages in which writing does not serve this purpose are only feeble attempts in the direction of writing, but not real writing. [28] This restriction of the definition of writing is unsatisfactory, however, because it does not take into account the fact that both stages have one identical aim: human intercommunication by means of conventional visible marks. Furthermore, it is impossible to lump together all the early or primitive writings and consider them to be on the same low level of development. Even though all the early writings are inefficient in expressing speech adequately, some of them, like the Maya and Aztec writings, reached a level of systematization and convention which in some ways may be compared with such fully developed writings as Sumerian or Egyptian.

What, then, is writing? Writing is clearly *a system of human intercommunication by means of conventional visible marks*, but it is evident from what has been said that what the primitives understood as writing is not the same thing as what we do. The question of what lies at the basis of all writing—words or ideas— is clearly the same as the question of what lies at the basis of all human intercommunication (see pp. 9 ff.).

For the primitive Indo-Europeans, Semites, or Amerindians the needs of writing were fulfilled in a simple picture or series of pictures which normally had no clear connection with any linguistic form. As the pictures are *per se* understandable they do not have to correspond to any signs of the spoken language. This is what we call primitive semasiography.

To us, layman and scholar alike, writing is *written language*. Ask a man in the street and he will not even hesitate about giving this answer. The same definition is expressed poetically by Voltaire: 'L'écriture est la peinture de la voix; plus elle est ressemblante, meilleure elle est,' and by Brébeuf: 'Cet art ingénieux de peindre la parole et de parler aux yeux.' The French authors are in good company here because they can back their opinion with the authority of the reliable Aristotle, who centuries ago, in the introductory chapter of *De Interpretatione* of his Logic, said: 'Spoken words are the symbols of mental experience and written words are the symbols of spoken words.' [29]

I agree entirely with the linguists who believe that fully developed writing became a device for expressing linguistic elements by means of visible marks. Take, for example, such a sentence as 'Mr. Theodore Foxe, age 70, died to-day at the Grand Xing Station'. Although English writing, like Latin, is called alphabetic, it is clear that our sentence is not written in purely alphabetic characters. Besides such letters as *e, o, d* expressing their corresponding single sounds, we have a digram *th* for the spirant θ, the letter *x* for the two consonants *ks*, a word sign *70* for the word 'seventy', and the rebus-type symbol *X* plus alphabetic *ing* for the word 'Crossing'. Unsystematic as the writing is, still every sign or combination of signs in our sentence has its correspondence in a speech form. It seems absurd to see in the written '70' an ideogram in contrast to the phonographic 'died'—as is generally done by philologists—simply because the written '70' contains such different meanings as 'seven, zero, seventy, seventieth', etc. Both '70' and 'died' evoke the corresponding words for 'seventy' and 'died', and in both of them is inherent the idea of the number or death, respectively. The fact that '70' is written logographically and 'died' alphabetically can be explained simply as an accident of writing and is no more baffling than the various ways of writing other words, for instance, 'Mister' or 'Mr.,' 'compare' or 'cf.,' 'and' or '&'. In all cases a conventional use, or uses, of certain signs for certain speech forms can be observed.[30]

If under the term 'linguistic elements' we understand phrases, words, syllables, single sounds, and prosodic features, then the sentence discussed above includes only signs for words, single sounds, and prosodic features. Phraseograms or signs for phrases are rarely found in popular writings, but they form an integral part of all stenographic systems. Syllabic signs[31] are, of course, characteristic of syllabic writings. Of the prosodic features, such as quantity (or length), accent (or stress), tone (or pitch), and pauses, only the latter are partially expressed in our sentence by word division and punctuation marks in the form of commas. Normally, writing fails to indicate adequately the prosodic features. Thus, in such a sentence as 'are you going home?' the interrogation is indicated by the question mark, but it is left to the discretion of the reader to decide whether the emphasis is on the first, second, third, or fourth word. By contrast, scientific transliterations frequently employ special signs to denote characteristics of prosodic nature, by means of diacritic marks or numbers, as in the writing of *dêmos* to denote quantity and stress, or *ku₃* to denote tone. A full indication of tone or pitch has been developed only in the system of musical notation. Figure 2 shows in chart form the various ways of writing linguistic elements.

	Written Sign	*System of Signs*
Single Sound (phoneme)	Letter or Alphabetic Sign	Alphabet or Alphabetic Writing.
Syllable	Syllabogram or Syllabic Sign	Syllabary or Syllabic Writing.
Word	Logogram or Word Sign	Logography or Word Writing.
[Phrase	Phraseogram or Phrase Sign	Phraseography or Phrase Writing]
[Prosodic Feature	Prosodic Sign or Mark	Prosodic Writing]

FIG. 2. WAYS OF WRITING LINGUISTIC ELEMENTS

Writing can never be considered an *exact* counterpart of the spoken language. Such an ideal state of point-by-point equivalence in which one speech unit is expressed by one sign, and one sign expresses only one speech unit, has never been attained in writing. Even the alphabet, the most developed form of writing, is full of inconsistencies in the relations between sign and sound. The inconsistencies of phonetic writing are illustrated in Figure 3. At the same time, the chart is intended to point out the differences between the historical and functional characters of writing.

However, the general statement that full writing expresses speech should not be taken to mean that it expresses nothing else but speech. All writing—even the most developed phonetic writing—is full of forms which, when read aloud, are ambiguous and easily misunderstood. The existence of these so-called 'visual morphemes', that is, forms or spellings which convey the meaning only in writing, shows clearly that writing can sometimes function as a means of communication separately and in addition to speech. From among many examples of visual morphemes [32] we may quote the following: 'The *sea* is an ocean, and *si* is a tone, as you can readily *see*.' 'The danger is safely *passed*' or 'the danger is safely *past*'. 'How much *wood would a woodchuck chuck* if a *woodchuck would chuck wood*?'. '*Grey*' in 'she has lovely *grey* eyes' and '*gray*' in 'it was a *gray*, gloomy day'. Other pairs of this bifurcation of meaning in written words are *check—cheque, controller—comptroller, compliment—complement.* [33]

In modern usage we sometimes meet with signs which have no conventionally assigned speech forms. For instance, an arrow used as a symbol can have different meanings depending on the situation. On a sign along the road this arrow may mean something like 'follow in the direction of the arrow', but at the entrance to a cave it may mean 'enter here' or 'this is the entrance'. Such examples as there are of this sort of symbolism have many parallels in the semasiographic stage of writing in which meanings—not words or sounds—are suggested by signs. This symbolism is outside of our normal system of writing. As part of the phonetic system of writing an arrow sign would necessarily have developed in the course of time one or two unequivocal speech meanings, such as 'go (there), follow', or the like.

Here, too, belong certain symbols in our comic strips which

FIG. 3. INCONSISTENCIES OF PHONETIC WRITING

Alphabetic signs	function as single sounds	function as syllables	function as words
	i = i in 'dim'; = ay in 'dime'; = $ə$ in 'dirt' c = s in 'Caesar'; = k in 'cat' x = ks in 'fox'; = gz in 'exam'; = z in 'Xavier' th = $θ$ in 'thin'; = $ð$ in them; = t in 'Thomas'	l = $lə$ in the dialectal pronunciation of 'elm' as 'eləm' b = bi in rebus writing q = $kyuu$ in unusual writing of 'barbecue' as 'Bar-B-Q'	m = 'meter, mile, minute,' etc. $M.$ = 'Martin, Mary, Majesty, Master, Monday,' etc. $v.$ = 'see' $e.g.$ = 'for example, for instance' $No.$ or $N°$ = 'number' $α$ in Greek = 'one'

Syllabic signs	function as syllables	$ma = ma$ in Hittite syllabary
	function as single sounds	$ma = m$ in Hittite writing of ta-ma for tam
	function as words	$ma = mana$, 'mina' in Akkadian
Word signs	function as words	† = 'dead, died' 2 = 'two, second' ° = 'degree' & (originally Latin et) = 'and' &c = 'et $caetera$, and so forth, and so on,' and the like
	function as syllables	Picture of arrow = ti in Sumerian = syllabic value ti 7 = $septem$ in $7ber$ for 'September' & = et in medieval writing of $vidčlic$ & for $videlicet$
	function as single sounds	Picture of bee = b in rebus writing

are generally understood even though they have no conventional counterpart in speech. Such symbols, called 'sublinguistic ideographs' by Weston Labarre,[34] are, for example, a balloon encircling print signifying 'speaking', footprints for 'going', sawing wood for 'snoring, sleeping', light bulb with rays for 'idea', and]%!*/=# for 'unspeakable'.

Equally outside of our normal phonetic system of signs are the conventions employed in mathematics, logic, and some other sciences. Although in the writing of such a mathematical formula as :—

$$y \; (\lambda) \; = \; \prod_{i=1}^{n} \; \sum_{j=1}^{n} \; e^{\,a_{ij}} \; + \; \lambda \; b_{ij}$$

each single sign has or can have an exact correspondence in speech, the meaning is here conveyed by the sum of the signs in an order and form which do not follow the conventions of normal, phonetic writing.

Meaning can sometimes be conveyed within writing not only by conventional forms of signs but also by various auxiliary methods based on the descriptive device, colour, position, and context of situation.

The oldest Oriental systems of writing, such as Mesopotamian, Egyptian, etc., being fully phonetic, employ conventional signs with definite word or syllabic values. However, even in these fully phonetic writings the meaning is sometimes expressed not by conventional signs, but by drawings of scenes following the descriptive-representational device (see pp. 29 ff.). Thus, in Egyptian, in a written context describing the victories of Ramses II over foreign lands, Pharaoh's honorary title, 'he who binds the foreign peoples,' is not expressed by individual hieroglyphs but by a scene depicting the Pharaoh binding the foreign king with ropes.[35] In another written context, the formula, 'an offering which the king gives,' is expressed by a picture of a king holding a mat with a loaf of bread.[36] The meaning is conveyed in these two scenes in a form which we know so well from the earliest periods of Egyptian writing, as found, for example, on the Narmer palette, described in full below (see pp. 72 f.).

Colour does not seem to play an important role in our modern writing. Although colouring schemes are occasionally used to differentiate meaning, as in charts, it is normally the black or dark colour that predominates, whether in our handwriting or book print. In older times, when all writing was done by hand, colour differentiation was found more frequently. Both the old Mexican writings and the more modern writings of the American Indians frequently employ a method of colouring the signs. Among the Cherokee Indians white colour is used for peace or happiness, black for death, red for success or triumph, blue for defeat or trouble.[37] Finally, we may mention the Polychrome Bible in which colours are used to represent certain sources, and the modern developments in pasigraphy (see p. 244) giving to colour an important function of differentiating meaning. Outside of writing, colouring schemes are used on maps and in tattooing. Also the *quipu* system was used to record statistical facts by tying knots in strings of various colours. Colour characteristics in flowers and gems are often used to convey certain messages.

The meaning can sometimes be indicated by a device based on the so-called 'principle of position' or 'principle of positional value.' We know how important this principle is in mathematical systems as, for instance, in our writing of '32' and '3²'. While individually these numbers represent 'three' and 'two', respectively, the intended meaning is here expressed by placing the signs in a conventional position in respect to each other. An unusual application of the principle of position can be observed in the writing of the Egyptian word $m^x\underline{h}^xn^xw^x$, 'within,' by means of two signs placed one upon the other, the JAR sign upon the WATER sign. This gives syllabically $m^x(w^x)$, 'water,' plus $\underline{h}^x(r^x)$, 'under' (not expressed by any sign), plus n^xw^x, 'jar,' together $m^x\underline{h}^xn^xw^x$, 'within.'[38] A similar example in modern times is the writing of $\frac{\text{WOOD}}{\text{JOHN}}\ \frac{\text{AND}}{\text{MASS}}$ for 'John Underwood, Andover, Massachusetts', supposedly found as an address on a letter. Word division, frequently left unindicated in the older writings, is another important application of the principle of position, as anyone can judge for himself from the differences in meaning indicated in the writing of 'see them cat' or 'see the meat', and that of 'a nice box' or 'an icebox'.

Hand in hand with the principle of position goes the principle of context of situation, to use a term introduced lately by B. Malinowski in his study of the problem of meaning in primitive languages.[39] Thus, the query 'where is the pen?' is usually perfectly understandable to the listener, even though the word 'pen' may have such different meanings as that of a writing instrument, a play pen, or a small enclosure, simply because the query was uttered under certain conditions which make the interpretation unequivocal. Similarly, it can be interpreted without difficulty from the context that an abbreviation PG will stand for *Parteigenosse* in a report on the Nazi party, for *Panzergrenadier* in a statement on the German army, and for 'post-graduate' in university usage,[40] just as AO will be interpreted as standing for *Der Alte Orient* when found in an Orientalistic periodical and for *Auslandsorganisation* when mentioned in a report on Nazi activities outside of Germany. The principle of context of situation finds its application also in other systems of signs, for example, in those involving gestures: a man pointing his finger at the door in certain situations may want to express something like 'Get out!', while in others the same gesture may simply stand for 'there' or 'in that direction'. The import of the context of situation can be well illustrated by our modern cartoons; a political cartoon published some fifty years ago is well nigh incomprehensible to a young fellow who is not acquainted with the situation and conditions which served as the background for the cartoon. [41]

SOURCES OF INFORMATION

In trying to reconstruct the early phases of our culture we rely mostly on sources from the ancient East. This is perhaps more true of the history of writing than of any other great cultural achievement. There, in the lands of the Sumerians, Babylonians, Assyrians, Hittites, Canaanites, Egyptians, and Chinese, the spade of the excavator has unearthed within the last century thousands of documents which have immensely enriched our knowledge and opened entirely new avenues of research. It would be unthinkable even to try to sketch the history of writing without taking into consideration the written sources of the ancient East. But frequently we find great gaps in our knowledge. The further back we go in years the fewer sources we have at our disposal. The very interesting problem of the 'origins' of writing is shrouded in a cloud of darkness and is as hard to interpret as the 'origins' of art, architecture, religion, and social institutions, to name only a few of the important aspects of our culture.

Where ancient times fail to give us the clue to a certain development we must look elsewhere for light on our subject. We assume that there are to-day, or have lived within the last few centuries, primitive[42] societies on a cultural level which in some respects resembles the level of ancient cultures long since dead. The written remains of such primitive peoples as the American Indians, the African Bushmen, or the Australian aborigines, even though far removed from what we call writing to-day, offer valuable ground for understanding the way men learned to communicate with each other by means of visual markings. In our investigation we must not neglect the artificial writings created by natives under the influence of white men, usually missionaries. The history of these writings—the most interesting of which are the systems of the Alaska Eskimos, of the African Bamum, and of the Cherokee Indians—shows us the various stages through which they passed before they reached the final form. The sequence of these stages greatly resembles the history of writing in its natural development.

Another fruitful approach results from the study of child psychology. It has often been observed that the mental attitudes of infants and children sometimes resemble those of societies on the most primitive basis. One of the most important points of similarity is the tendency toward concrete specification.[43] Just as a child will draw a vertical line and explain it as the tree which grows in front of the house, so primitive men will frequently associate their drawings with concrete things and events in the surrounding world. This tendency in writing and drawing is an outgrowth of the character of their language which seeks expression in concrete and specific terminology. The observations made upon those primitive languages which do not use the word 'arm' or 'eye', but 'my arm' or 'right eye', according to the occasion, and which do not have a general word for 'tree', but individual words for 'oak, elm', etc., can be duplicated to a great extent by the study of children just emerging from the initial stage of language-learning. Another interesting point of contact can be established from the study of the direction and orientation of signs in children's drawings and primitive writings. It has been noted that children will draw individual pictures in undue proportion to each other and without any apparent sense of order or direction. Even a child learning how to write will frequently draw signs from left to right or from right to left without ever being aware of any difference in the two directions. Similar phenomena pertaining to the direction and orientation of signs can frequently be observed in almost all the primitive writings.

The tendency toward concrete specification noted among children and primitives has been observed recently in grown-up people afflicted by mental infirmities of the type called amnesic aphasia.[44] It was noted empirically that these persons will normally avoid general terms such as 'knife' and will use specific expressions such as 'bread knife, paring knife', or 'pencil sharpener'. The road taken by these persons in relearning the language is similar to the course of the natural linguistic development of children. Thus, a detailed study of the amnesic aphasiacs may yet furnish another fertile field for the study of the origins of language and writing.

STUDY OF WRITING

The investigation of writing from the formal point of view is the prime domain of the epigrapher and the paleographer. These terms are frequently interchangeable, but in good usage the two should be carefully distinguished. The epigrapher is interested chiefly in inscriptions incised with a sharp tool on hard material, such as stone, wood, metal, clay, etc., while the paleographer studies mainly manuscripts on skin, papyrus, or paper, written in drawn or painted characters. Generally speaking, epigraphy treats of older writings, while paleography is concerned with manuscripts from younger periods.

As a matter of fact, epigraphy and paleography do not exist as general scientific disciplines. There are no studies in either of the two fields which treat of the subject from a general, theoretical point of view. For example, a treatise which presents the formal development of signs from pictorial to linear or from round to angular taking in consideration all the writings of the world is unknown to me. What we have, instead, are narrow fields of study of the type Semitic epigraphy, Arabic paleography, Greek or/and Latin epigraphy or/and paleography, Chinese paleography, papyrology, etc., all limited to certain periods and geographic areas. In all cases these narrow fields of study form subdivisions of wider, but still specific, fields of study, such as Semitic or Arabic philology, classical philology, Assyriology, Sinology, and Egyptology.

As there is no general epigraphy or paleography, so there is no general science of writing. This statement may sound preposterous to anyone who remembers the dozens of various books which treat of writing in general. What should be noted, however, is that all these books are characterized by a common historical-descriptive treatment. Such a simple narrative approach to a subject does not make it into a science. It is not the treatment of the epistemological questions *what?*, *when?*, and *where?* but that of *how?* and, above all, *why?* that is of paramount importance in establishing the theoretical background of a science. Disregarding a few notable exceptions in the case of individual systems, such questions have rarely, if ever, been posited and answered in the general field of writing. However, the greatest shortcoming from the theoretical point of view of all the existing studies on writing is the general lack of systematic typology. Good studies on individual writings, such as Egyptian hieroglyphic or Greek alphabet, are not wanting. What we miss entirely is the theoretical and comparative evaluation of the various types of writing, such as discussions of various types of syllabaries, alphabets, word signs, and logo-syllabic writings. The present confusion in the typological classification of writing can be best illustrated by the term 'transitional'[45] given to such important writings as Mesopotamian cuneiform and Egyptian hieroglyphic, which lasted for over 3,000 years and whose exact place in the classification of writing can be established without great difficulties (see pp. 61 ff.).

The aim of this book is to lay a foundation for a full science of writing, yet to be written. To the new science we could give the name 'grammatology', following partially the term 'grammatography' which was used some years ago in a title of a book on writing published in England.[46] This term seems to me better suited than either 'graphology', which could lead to a misunderstanding, or 'philography' (a new term coined in contrast to 'philology'), which is not so exact as 'grammatology'.

The descriptive treatment of writing will be presented in the following four chapters, with separate discussions, usually at the end of each chapter, devoted to comparative evaluation. Chapter VI will deal with the historical evolution of writing from the earliest stages of semasiography to full phonography.

II

FORERUNNERS OF WRITING

UNDER Forerunners of Writing we shall discuss all those phases which, while they do not yet represent real writing, form the elements from which real writing gradually developed. The Germans have a good term, *Vorstufe*, which designates a stage before the first real stage in a certain development, something like prehistory in contrast to history. The word which I should have liked to coin for *Vorstufe* is 'forestage', but unfortunately this term cannot be used for our purpose because it already has the meaning 'forecastle' or 'a ship with a forecastle', even though only in obsolete English.

PRIMITIVE DRAWINGS

Naturally there was a time when man did not know how to write. If we define full writing as a device for expressing linguistic elements by means of conventional visible marks (see p. 12), then writing, in this sense, is no more than five thousand years old. But already in the earliest times, tens of thousands of years ago, man felt the urge to draw or paint pictures on the walls of his primitive dwelling or on the rocks in his surroundings. Primitive man is similar in this respect to a child, who no sooner learns to crawl than he begins to scribble on the wallpaper or to draw crude pictures in the sand.

All over the world man has left traces of his imaginative powers in drawings on rocks dating from the oldest paleolithic down to modern times. These drawings can be called petrograms if they are drawn or painted and petroglyphs if they are incised or carved. They usually depict man and animal in various relations to each other. Well known to everybody are the faithful reproductions of animal figures left by paleolithic man in Europe[1] and the graceful paintings of the South African

Bushmen (Fig. 4). An immense number of rock drawings and carvings have been found on this continent (Figs. 5–6), especially in the mountainous regions of North America.[2] These drawings have aroused popular fancy in support of the most fantastic reconstructions. Julian H. Steward, in an interesting and sober-minded article, derides all these interpretations that try to prove that 'Egyptians, Scythians, Chinese, and

FIG. 4.—ROCK PAINTING FROM
SOUTHERN RHODESIA DEPICTING RAIN
CEREMONY

From Leo Frobenius and Douglas C. Fox,
Prehistoric Rock Pictures in Europe and Africa
(New York, 1947), p. 47

a host of other Old World peoples, including the Ten Lost Tribes of Israel, whose fate continues to have absorbing interest to many persons, invaded America in ancient days . . . (that these drawings are) markers of buried treasure, signs of ancient astrology, records of vanished races, symbols of diabolical cults, works of the hand of God, and a hundred other things conceived by feverish brains'. He further states that 'devotees of the subject have written voluminously, argued bitterly, and even fought duels'.[3] In reality the drawings have a much simpler aim.

In most cases it is, of course, very difficult, if not impossible, to ascertain the purpose or the urge which stimulated man to draw or incise a picture, since we do not know the circumstances which led to its execution. Is the picture a manifestation of magic, religious, or aesthetic expression? Was it drawn for the purpose of securing good hunting or was it the result of the artistic impulse? It is not improbable that several urges may

FIG. 5.—PETROGLYPH FROM OREGON

From L. S. Cressman, *Petroglyphs of Oregon* (Eugene, 1937), p. 31

have been instrumental at the same time in the origin of a drawing. When a hunter returned from a successful chase, or a warrior from a military expedition, he felt the desire to record his experiences in a picture. The picture may have been drawn as the result of his artistic urge, but at the same time it may have served as a monument to commemorate past experiences. It could also have had the magic purpose of securing another good hunt or a successful razzia in the future. Such pictures do not represent writing because they do not form part of a conventional system of signs and can be understood only by the man who drew them or by his family and close friends who had heard of the event.

Just as speech developed out of imitation of sound, so writing developed out of imitation of the forms of real objects or beings. At the basis of all writing stands the picture. This is clear not only from the fact that all modern primitive writings are pictorial in character, but also because all the great Oriental systems, such as Sumerian, Egyptian, Hittite, Chinese, etc., were originally real picture writings.

FIG. 6.—PETROGLYPH FROM NORTH-WESTERN BRAZIL

From Theodor Koch-Grünberg, *Südamerikanische Felszeichnungen* (Berlin, 1907), pl. 5

To be sure, all these writings already have in their earliest stages signs which do not look like pictures of real objects, but rather like simple linear, geometric designs. Such geometric signs are found in all the areas of the world from prehistoric periods down to modern times. They are sometimes found on rocks, but are especially common on movable objects such as pots and weapons (*art mobilier*).

There is no doubt in my mind that such geometric designs do not represent abstract forms but are the result of a schematic development from real pictures. In Fig. 7 is given a series of drawings showing post-paleolithic examples of linear forms painted on rocks from Spain as compared with later forms from Mas d'Azil in France painted on small pieces of flint. Hugo Obermaier has shown in this series how pictures became schematized in the course of time until they reached a stage in which it is impossible to recognize what they were originally intended to represent.[4] The most striking and the most common of all the developments is the transition of the drawings of the so-called 'hallelujah man'—that is, a man in a praying position with the hands raised—into simple linear designs.

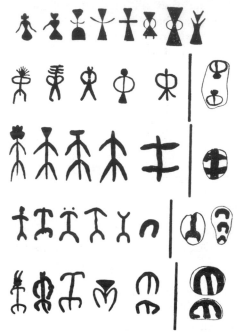

FIG. 7.—LINEAR DRAWINGS FROM SPAIN
AND FRANCE
From Ebert, *Reallexikon der Vorgeschichte*, vii,
pls. 114 f.

That the geometric designs are schematic developments from picture forms can be proved conclusively from the observation of the development of any writing in its historical stages. All of the well-known ancient writings, such as Sumerian, Egyptian, Chinese, etc., developed in the course of time a cursive, linear form usually so far removed from the original pictures that without knowledge of the intervening stages it would often be impossible to conclude that the linear form is a direct descendant of the picture form.

DESCRIPTIVE-REPRESENTATIONAL DEVICE

Among the forerunners of writing the most widely used class is that generally known by the misleading term of 'pictographic' or 'ideographic' writing. Such writing is best represented among the American Indians. Before entering into the difficult subject of definitions and terminology let us pause to glance at a few outstanding examples.

A simple communication of 'no thoroughfare' was found in New Mexico on a rock drawing placed near a precipitous trail, here presented as Figure 8.[5] The design warns horsemen that a mountain goat could climb up the rocky trail but a horse would tumble down.

FIG. 8.—INDIAN ROCK DRAWING
FROM NEW MEXICO
From Garrick Mallery, *Picture-Writing of the American Indians* (Washington, 1893), p. 354

More complicated examples of transmission of communication by the American Indians are contained in the three following illustrations.

Figure 9 represents a drawing, found on the face of a rock in Michigan on the shore of Lake Superior, which describes the course of a military expedition across the lake.[6] At the top, five canoes carrying fifty-one men, represented by vertical strokes, can be seen. The expedition is led by a chieftain named Kishkemunasee, 'Kingfisher,' whose totem or animal symbol, in the form of a water bird, is drawn above the first canoe. The trip lasted three days, as we can judge from the pictures of three suns under three arches, representing the celestial dome. After a happy landing, symbolized by the picture of a turtle, the expedition marched on quickly, as can be seen from the picture of a man riding a horse. The eagle, symbol of courage, embodies the spirit of the warriors. The description closes with pictures of a panther and a serpent, the symbols of force and cunning respectively, whom the chief invokes for help in the military expedition.

Figure 10 is a letter sent by mail from a Southern Cheyenne, named Turtle-Following-His-Wife, at the Cheyenne and Arapaho Agency, Indian Territory, to his son, Little-Man, at the Pine Ridge Agency, Dakota. It was drawn on a half-sheet of ordinary writing paper, without a word written, and was enclosed in an envelope, which was addressed to 'Little-Man, Cheyenne, Pine Ridge Agency,'

FIG. 9.—INDIAN ROCK DRAWING FROM MICHIGAN

From Henry R. Schoolcraft, *Historical and Statistical Information, Respecting the History, Condition, and Prospects of the Indian Tribes of the United States*, Part I (Philadelphia, 1851), pl. 57 B, opp. p. 406

in the ordinary manner, written by someone at the first-named agency. The letter was evidently understood by Little-Man as he immediately called upon Dr. V. T. McGillycuddy, Indian agent at Pine Ridge Agency, and was aware that the sum of $53 had been placed to his credit for the purpose of enabling him to pay his expenses in going the long journey to his father's home in Indian Territory. Dr. McGillycuddy had, by the same mail, received a letter from Agent Dyer, enclosing $53, and explaining the reason for its being sent, which enabled him also to understand the pictographic letter. With the above explanation it very clearly shows, over the head of the figure to the left, the turtle following the turtle's wife united with the head of a figure by a line, and over the head of the other figure, also united by a line to it, is a little man. Also

over the right arm of the last-mentioned figure is another little man
in the act of springing or advancing toward Turtle-Following-His-
Wife, from whose mouth proceed two lines, curved or hooked at the
end, as if drawing the little figure towards him. It is suggested that
the last-mentioned part of the pictograph is the substance of the
communication, i.e. 'come to me,' the larger figures with their name
totems being the persons addressed and addressing. Between the
above the two large figures are fifty-three round objects intended for
dollars. Both the Indian figures have on breechcloths, corresponding

FIG. 10.—CHEYENNE INDIAN LETTER
From Mallery, *Picture-Writing*, p. 364

with the information given concerning them, which is that they are
Cheyennes who are not all civilized or educated.[7]

Figure 11 is a letter written by an Ojibwa girl to a favoured
lover, requesting him to call at her lodge.[8] The girl is represented by the bear totem, the boy by that of the mud puppy.
The trail leads toward the lakes, shown by the three irregular
circles, whence it branches off in the direction of two tents.
Three Christian girls, indicated by the crosses, are encamped
there. From one of the tents protrudes the arm of the girl
inviting the Indian boy to call on her. Observe that this
drawing has some of the characteristic features of a map, such

as the trail and the lakes, side by side with such symbolic representations as the protruding hand expressing the idea of invitation.

Communication can sometimes be adequately expressed by means of a sequence of simple drawings in a manner which the Germans call *fortlaufende Illustration,* that is, 'continuous illustration.' In modern times good examples for this device are wordless comic strips of the Sad Sack type or even full-size novels, such as those composed in wood cuts by Lynd Ward (*Vertigo, God's Man, Madman's Drum,* etc.). While one picture in a cartoon is *per se* understandable, the meaning is conveyed only by the sequence of all the pictures in a certain order.

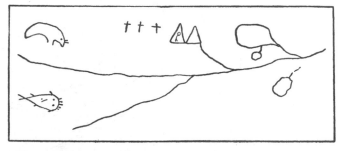

FIG. 11.—LETTER FROM AN OJIBWA GIRL TO HER LOVER
From Mallery, *Picture-Writing,* p. 363

Another, older, example of this kind is the proclamation issued by the governor of Van Diemen's Land (Tasmania) to the natives illustrating 'retributive justice for the edification of parrots, 'possums, and Black fellows'[9] (Fig. 12). The first register shows the state of peace in which both white and dark men should live. The second confirms the peace concluded between the official parties. The third register states that if a native kills a white man, the former will be punished by hanging; finally, the fourth sets the same punishment for a white man who kills a native.

Our other examples, in which pictures follow upon each other in a certain logical order corresponding to the continuity of the ideas which are to be conveyed, all come from Alaska. Native Alaskans use drawings to inform their visitors or friends of their departure for a designated purpose. The drawings are depicted upon strips of wood pointing in the direction taken by the departed men and placed in conspicuous places near the doors of their habitations.

The following is an explanation of the characters in Figure 13.[10]

a, the speaker, with the right hand indicating himself and with

FIG. 12.—PROCLAMATION FROM VAN DIEMEN'S LAND (TASMANIA)

From James Bonwick, *The Last of the Tasmanians* (London, 1870), pl. opp. p. 84

the left pointing in the direction taken; *b*, holding a boat-paddle, going by boat; *c*, the speaker holding the right hand to the side of the head, to denote sleep, and the left elevated with one finger erect to signify one night; *d*, a circle with two marks in the middle, signifying an island with huts upon it; *e*, same as *a*; *f*, a circle to denote another island where they touched; *g*, same as *c*, with an additional finger elevated, signifying two nights; *h*, the speaker, with his harpoon . . . ; *i* represents a sea-lion which the hunter, *j*, secured by shooting with bow and arrow; *k*, the boat with two persons in it, the paddles projecting downward; *l*, the winter habitation of the speaker.

Another pertinent example is given in Figure 14.[11] Alaskan hunters, who had been unfortunate in their hunt and were

FIG. 13.—ALASKAN NOTICE OF HUNT

From Mallery, *Picture-Writing*, p. 332

suffering from hunger, drew some characters on a piece of wood and placed the lower end of the stick in the ground on the trail where there was the greatest chance of its being discovered by other natives. The stick was inclined toward their shelter. The following are the details of the information contained in the drawing: *a*, canoe, showing double projections at bow, as well as the two men, owners, in the boat; *b*, a man with both arms extended signifying nothing, corresponding to the gesture for negation; *c*, a person with the right hand to the mouth signifying

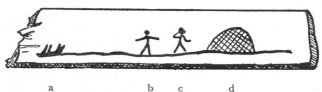

FIG. 14.—ALASKAN SIGNS OF DEPARTURE

From Mallery, *Picture-Writing*, p. 353

the act of eating, the left hand pointing to the house occupied by the hunters; *d*, the shelter. The whole thing means that the two men have nothing to eat in the house.

What are these drawings intended to represent? Are they pictures or are they writing? These questions are not difficult to answer. The drawings attempt to communicate a certain message by certain persons in a way that could be understood by the people for whom the message was intended. It is clear that the drawings do not serve the purpose of pictures in the normal sense, since they were drawn for the purpose of communication and not for the purpose of artistic-aesthetic expression. But the differences between pictures and our drawings lie not only in the divergent aims, but also in the form of the execution. Our drawings, like all drawings for the purpose of communication, are characterized by stereotyped execution as well as by omission of all details (grass, mountains, etc.) not necessary for the expression of the communication. In short, our drawings lack all the embellishment, the artistic effect, evident in pictures representative of art.

It has been said before (see p. 29) that all those means of human communication described above are known by the misleading term of 'pictographic' or 'ideographic' writing. The term 'pictographic', meaning 'picture writing', is not appropriate because there are other systems, such as Egyptian, early Sumerian, etc., also expressed in picture form, but entirely different in inner structure from such primitive systems as those used by the American Indians. Furthermore, the term 'pictography' implies characteristics of outer form, not of inner development of the system. Although problems of outer form should not be neglected in a treatise on writing, I personally am inclined toward a reconstruction of the history of writing based more on the inner characteristics. For that reason I should like to use terminology indicating this development. We could, of course, invent new terms to distinguish between the primitive picture writings of the American Indians and the advanced picture writings of the Egyptians, etc., in a way parallel to that taken by Arthur Ungnad who calls the former *Bildschrift* and the latter *Bilderschrift*, [12] but terminology of this sort is difficult to remember and sounds too artificial.

Objections similar in nature to those raised against 'pictography' can be made against the term 'ideography'. This term, too, has been extended outside of the sphere of primitive systems, sometimes to cover cases in which it is entirely misappropriate. The Orientalists who use the term 'ideogram' for the simple word sign or logogram have been so sinful in this respect that the term 'ideography' has become a real opprobrium in linguistic circles. Because of this double meaning of 'ideography' I prefer to avoid the term entirely in this study.

In searching for a correct term to cover the means of

expressing ideas discussed in this chapter we must once more give attention to the purposes for which they are used and to the way in which they are achieved. The examples quoted above all serve to communicate men's ideas by means of pictures, each of which separately, or their sum total, suggests the intended meaning. For this reason this stage of writing has sometimes been called *Gedankenschrift* ('thought writing'), *Vorstellungschrift* ('representational writing'), or *Inhaltschrift* ('content writing') by the Germans.[13] The picture or a series of pictures describe to the eye what the eye sees in a way parallel to that achieved by the picture originated under the artistic-aesthetic urge. To be sure, there are differences between the schematic execution of pictures intended to convey one's ideas and that of pictures made for artistic reasons, but the general similarities between the two entirely overshadow the existent divergences. This stage of the forerunners of writing could therefore be called the 'descriptive' or 'representational' stage, using a term which points toward a close connection in the technique of expression in writing and in art.

IDENTIFYING-MNEMONIC DEVICE

Let us permit ourselves to speculate a little as to other possibilities of human intercommunication which may have served as the basis for the ultimate evolution of full writing. Suppose that a primitive man drew on his shield a picture of a panther. This drawing originally may have had the magic purpose of transmitting the strength or the swiftness of the panther to the man who owned the shield. But in the course of time the panther on the shield became also a symbol which communicated to everyone the fact that the shield was owned by a certain person. The symbol of the panther therefore became a property mark, whose aim was that of utilitarian writing. The drawing of a panther as a property mark is, of course, not yet real writing, even though it stands for a personal name and may be habitually associated with one certain person, because it does not yet form a part of a well-established and conventional system. But it is an important step in the direction of writing.

A specialized system of this kind is found in the heraldic symbols used by the nobility as identification marks. In the same class are the military insignia of rank and branch of service and the symbols for various professions and crafts very popular even in modern Europe, such as a key for a locksmith, a pair of glasses for an optician, or a trumpet for a post office.

Simple linear, geometric designs are frequently found on objects of daily use, such as pots, utensils, weapons, bones,

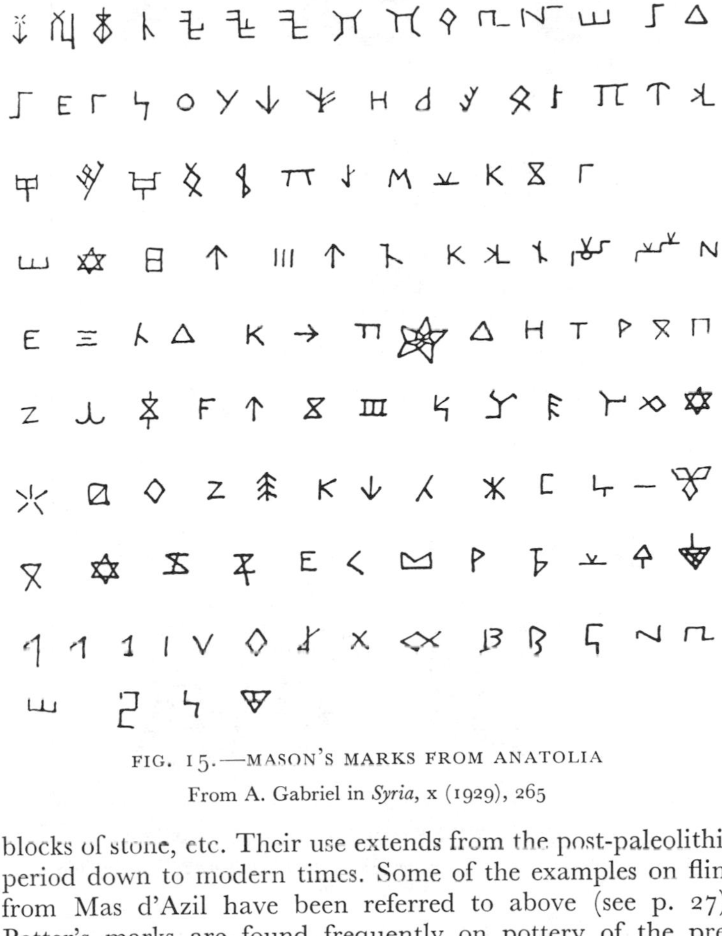

FIG. 15.—MASON'S MARKS FROM ANATOLIA

From A. Gabriel in *Syria*, x (1929), 265

blocks of stone, etc. Their use extends from the post-paleolithic period down to modern times. Some of the examples on flint from Mas d'Azil have been referred to above (see p. 27). Potter's marks are found frequently on pottery of the pre-dynastic and historical periods from Egypt. Figure 15 gives examples of mason's marks found on Turkish buildings in Anatolia. Examples of potter's and mason's marks and similar

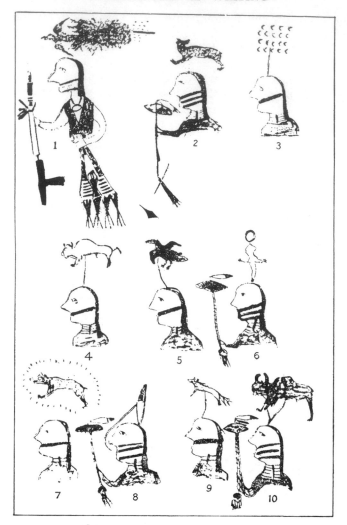

FIG. 16.—NAMES FROM THE OGLALA ROSTER

From Mallery, *Pictographs of the North American Indians* (Washington, 1886), pl. lii

types from all parts of the world could be multiplied *ad libitum.* The custom of branding animals belongs to the same class. The designs serve in all cases to identify either the owner of a certain object or its maker.

FIG. 17.—NAMES FROM THE RED-CLOUD'S
CENSUS
From Mallery, *Pictographs*, pl. lix

The identifying method of recording proper names includes also the various ways in which the American Indians designate personal and tribal names. It will be noted that an individual can be called either by his real or tribal name or by a totem.

In Figure 16 we reproduce part of the so-called 'Oglala Roster' which includes the names of eighty-four heads of families in the band or perhaps the clan of Chief Big-Road, belonging to the Northern Oglala tribe.[14] Each chief and sub-chief holds the insignia of his office in his right hand. The name appears in each case above the head of the man. Following is the interpretation of some of the names: (1) Chief Big-Road, represented by a road with tracks. The flying bird indicates the rapidity of travel which a good road allows; the chief was often called 'Good-Road' because a road that is big or broad and well travelled is good. (2) Bear-Looking-Behind. (3) Brings-Back-Plenty. (4) White-Buffalo. (5) The-Real-Hawk (6) Shield-Boy. (7) The-Bear-Stops. (8) Wears-The-Feather. (9) Dog-Eagle. (10) Red-Horn-Bull.

More personal names, in Figure 17, are taken from the so-called 'Red-Cloud's Census'.[15] The census was prepared about 1884 under the direction of Red-Cloud, chief of the

FIG. 18.—INDIAN TRIBAL DESIGNATIONS

From Mallery, *Picture-Writing*, pp. 380 ff.

Dakotas at Pine Ridge Agency, Dakota Territory. The 289 individuals enumerated were the adherents of Red-Cloud and did not represent all the Indians at that agency. Owing to some disagreement the agent refused to acknowledge that chief as head of the Indians at the agency and named another as the official chief. The Indians, however, manifested their allegiance to Red-Cloud by signing their names to seven sheets of ordinary manila paper, which were then sent to Washington. Following is the interpretation of the individual names: (1) Chief Red-Cloud. (2) Top-Man. (3) Slow-Bear. (4) He-Dog. (5) Little-Chief. (6) Red-Shirt. (7) White-Hawk. (8) Cloud-Shield. (9) Good-Weasel. The symbol of goodness is expressed by two wavy lines passing upward from the mouth in imitation of the gesture sign for 'good talk'. (10) Afraid-Eagle (no interpretation

known). Many more personal names are to be found in another
book by Mallery.[16]

The examples of tribal designations reproduced in Figure 18
are taken from winter counts discussed on the following pages.[17]
(1–3) The Crows are symbolized by pictures of persons (or *pars
pro toto*, only of the head) with the characteristic arrangement
of hair brushed upward and slightly backward. (4) The
Arapaho, in the Dakota language meaning 'blue cloud', are
represented by a circular cloud drawn in blue in the original,
enclosing the head of a man. (5) The Arikara or Ree are
symbolized as an ear of corn because these Indians are known
as 'corn shellers'. (6) The Assiniboin or Hohe are designated by
a picture showing the vocal organs (upper lip, roof of mouth,
tongue, lower lip, chin, and neck), based on the fact that Hohe
means 'the voice', or, as some say, 'the voice of the musk ox.'
(7) The Kayowa are pictured by a sign of a man shaking his
hands in a circular motion, symbolizing 'rattlebrained' or 'crazy
heads'. The sign is taken over from an Indian gesture for
craziness made by a circuitous movement of the hand around
the head. (8) The Omaha are designated by a human head
with cropped hair and red cheeks.

Of similar nature to those discussed above are the examples
of forerunners of writing expressed by means of mnemonic signs.
Also for this device we find ample illustration among the
American Indians in their use of symbols for recording time
and songs.

The Dakota Indians use a method of recording time by
means of winter counts[18] named after an important event in the
previous year in a manner identical with that of the ancient
Sumerians and Babylonians, who also named their years after
outstanding events. The Dakotas count their years by winters,[19]
which may be due to the fact that in the regions inhabited by
them the cold season generally lasts more than six months.
Contrast this custom with that of the Poles who count years by
summers. The way a certain event was chosen for a certain
year is described as follows by Mallery :—

Probably with the counsel of the old men and authorities of his
tribe, Lone-Dog [the Dakota Indian who was responsible for the
systematization of the recording of the winter counts] ever since his
youth has been in the habit of deciding upon some event or
circumstance which should distinguish each year as it passed, and

when such decision was made he marked what was considered to be its appropriate symbol or device upon a buffalo robe kept for the purpose. The robe was at convenient times exhibited to other Indians of the [Dakota] nation, who were thus taught the meaning and use of the signs as designating the several years, in order that at the death of the recorder the knowledge might not be lost. . . . It was also reported by several Indians that other copies of the chart in its various past stages of formation had been known to exist among the several tribes, being probably kept for reference, Lone-Dog and his robe being so frequently inaccessible.

The different editions of the Dakota winter counts extend from the winter 1775–76 to 1878–79. The chief edition, represented by the Lone-Dog buffalo robe, covers the years 1800–1801 to 1876–77. Although Lone-Dog is described as a very old Indian, he probably was not old enough in the year 1800–1801 to begin the recording of events then. As suggested by Mallery:—

Either there was a predecessor from whom he received the earlier records or obtained copies of them, or, his work being first undertaken when he had reached manhood, he gathered the traditions from his elders and worked back so far as he could do so accurately. . . .

The following is a discussion of examples taken from the Dakota winter counts. In each case I, II, III refers to different editions of the same text.

In Figure 19 the year 1800–1801 is named after the fact that thirty (or thirty-one) Dakotas were killed by Crows. The device consists of thirty parallel lines in three columns, the outer lines being united. Black lines always signify the death of Dakotas killed by enemies. (On the significance of colour, as in using black for death, etc., see above, p. 19.) The year 1801–1802 signifies that many died of smallpox. The device is the head and body of a man covered with red blotches. The year 1802–1803, symbolized by a horseshoe, is named after the first shod horses seen by Indians or, following a different Indian tradition, after the theft by the Dakotas of some horses having shoes (then first seen by the Indians).

The next three years give examples of different forms of pictures as noted in different editions. Observe the bow in different positions in the picture for the year 1815–16 and the divergent positions of the chimney and of the tree in the picture

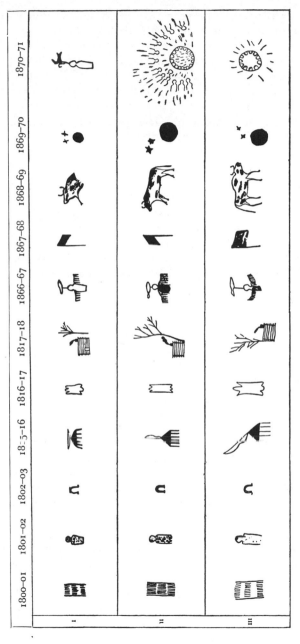

FIG. 19.—DAKOTA WINTER COUNTS

From Mallery, *Pictographs*, pls. ix, xiv, xxxi, and xxxii

for the year 1817–18. The year 1815–16 is named after a large dirt lodge made by the Sans Arc Dakotas. The bow over the lodge may have been drawn in allusion to the tribe Sans Arc, without any sign of negation, however. It is also possible that we should interpret the bow as a feather in allusion to Crow-Feather who was the chief of the Sans Arc tribe. The year 1816–17, represented by a buffalo hide, indicates the time when buffaloes were very plentiful. The year 1817–18 marks the building of a trading store with dry timber; the dryness of the wood is shown by the dead tree.

The year 1866–67, named after the death of Swan the Dakota chief, is represented by the picture of a man with the totem of a swan in the water. The year 1867–68, represented by the flag, records the peace made with General Sherman and others at Fort Laramie. The year 1868–69 is named either after the issue of beef by the Government to the Indians or after the Texas cattle brought into the country. Observe the abbreviated form of the animal in edition I. Similar abbreviations in form are found in the pictures for other years, as in the year 1864–65, where only the heads of men are drawn instead of the full bodies.

Sometimes there is disagreement as to the choice of the event after which a year should be named. Thus, while in edition I the year 1870–71 is named after the killing of the Flame's son, editions II and III record a battle between the Uncpapas and the Crows.

Of similar mnemonic character are drawings on birch bark made by the Ojibwa Indians for the purpose of recording their songs.[20] According to Mallery, these songs are in general connected with religious ceremonies, and are chiefly used in the initiation of neophytes into secret religious orders. The words are invariable, even to the extent that by their use for generations many of them have become archaic and form no part of the colloquial language. Indeed, they are not always understood by the best of the Shaman singers. But no Indian can change the wording of the ancient songs because in doing so he would cause loss of the power which such songs are alleged to possess.

In Figure 20 we give a collection of the Songs of the Meda (priest) with the explanations of the first four groups by Mallery:— [21]

FIG. 20.—OJIBWA SONGS

From Mallery, *Pictographs*, pl. iv

No. 1.—A medicine lodge filled with the presence of the Great Spirit who, it is affirmed, came down with wings to instruct the Indians in these ceremonies. The meda, or priest, sings, 'The Great Spirit's lodge—you have heard of it. I will enter it.' While this is sung, and repeated, the priest shakes his shi-shi-gwun, and each member of the society holds up one hand in a beseeching manner.

FIG. 21.—OJIBWA SONGS

From Mallery, *Picture-Writing*, pl. xvii

All stand, without dancing. The drum is not struck during this introductory chant.

No. 2.—A candidate for admission crowned with feathers, and holding, suspended to his arm, an otter-skin pouch, with the wind represented as gushing out of one end. He sings, repeating after the

46

priest, all dancing, with the accompaniment of the drum and rattle: 'I have always loved that that I seek. I go into the new green leaf lodge.'

No. 3 marks a pause, during which the victuals prepared for the feast are introduced.

No. 4.—A man holding a dish in his hand, and decorated with magic feathers on his wrists, indicating his character as master of the feast. All sing, 'I shall give you a share, my friend.'

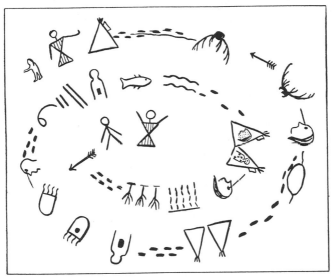

FIG. 22.—ALLEGED INDIAN WRITING

From William Tomkins, *Universal Indian Sign Language of the Plains Indians of North America* (San Diego, California, 1927), p. 82

In Figure 21 a group of songs pertaining to the ceremony of initiating new members into the *Midē'wiwin* or Grand Medicine Society is offered.[22]

In connection with the American Indian writings I should like to call attention to a type represented by about half a dozen illustrations, all published as a sort of appendix to a book on the sign language of American Indians.[23] One of them, reproduced here as Figure 22, is explained as follows by Tomkins: 'An Indian and his wife had a quarrel; he wanted to go hunting and she did not want to go. He gave the sign of negation, would not do what she wanted, and he took his bow and arrows and started into the forest. A snowstorm came upon him and he looked for shelter. He saw two teepees, went over to them, but found that they contained two people who were sick, in one teepee a boy with the measles, in the other teepee a man with the smallpox. He ran away as fast as he could and shortly came to a river. He saw some fish in the river, so he caught a fish, ate it, and rested there for two days. After that he started out again and saw a bear. He shot and killed the bear and had quite a feast. Then he started on again and saw an Indian village, but as they proved to be enemies he ran away until he came to a little lake. While walking around the lake he saw a deer. He shot and killed it and dragged it home to his teepee, to his wife and his little boy.' The story begins with the signs for Indian and his wife in the centre and continues spirally and counter-clockwise to the end in the upper left corner marked by the signs for woman and child. One glance at the illustration is sufficient to see that this pictography has no parallels among the American Indian writings which were discussed above on pp. 29 ff. and 39 ff. To be sure, most of the symbols may have been taken from some Indian system, but the whole arrangement of the symbols and the writing of 'two days' by means of the number '2' plus the symbol for 'day' (near the upper left corner) instead of two symbols for 'day', [24] evoke the suspicion that the author may have concocted freely the illustrations. This is supported by the cavalier fashion in which the whole book was written for the use of 'our young friends, the boy-scouts', and it should have been a warning to Jacques van Ginneken against taking these inscriptions too seriously in his treatment of the American Indian writings. [25]

The Ewe Negroes of Togo, in Africa, are able to record proverbs by means of mnemonic signs in a way similar to that of the Ojibwa Indians. Figure 23 gives the following examples: [26] The picture of the needle with the thread represents the proverb 'the thread follows the needle' (not vice versa) and resembles in its meaning the English saying 'a chip off the old block', or 'like father, like son'. The picture of a threaded needle and cloth means 'the needle sews great cloth', in other words, that small things can achieve greatness, parallel to the English 'great oaks from little acorns grow'. The proverb 'two opponents cannot last' (because sooner or later one of them must retreat) is expressed by pictures of two men armed with bows and arrows. The proverb 'whatever is found and whatever is mine

48

is not the same' implies that things found should be returned to the owners and is in opposition to the English saying 'finders keepers, losers weepers'. The Ewe proverb is expressed by the picture of a man pointing at his chest, meaning 'mine', and of another man holding in his left hand the object found. The proverb 'the world is like a baobab tree'—so great that it is impossible to embrace it—is expressed by the picture of a man trying in vain to stretch his arms between the tree and the world (symbolized by a circle). The proverb 'the chameleon says, even if you move fast, you must die just the same' (therefore it moves

FIG. 23.—EWE PROVERBS

From C. Meinhof in *Zeitschrift für ägyptische Sprache*, xlix (1911), pl. i b opp. p. 8

slowly) is expressed with some difficulty by the picture of a big man (who can move fast), a straight line symbolizing moving, and an animal with wings symbolizing death. The divinity of death must be a fast-moving one since people can die at the same time in different parts of the country.

The use of written symbols as memory aids for recording proverbs is also known from the Congo region. [27] On the parallel use of objects for the same purpose see the discussion on pp. 4 ff.

There is one great difference in the use of pictorial signs by the American Indians and the Africans. The American Indians have reached a stage of systematization and standardization entirely unknown among the African Negroes. As Mallery[28] puts it:—

One very marked peculiarity of the drawings of the Indians is that within each particular system, such as may be called a tribal system, of pictography, every Indian draws in precisely the same manner. The figures of a man, of a horse, and of every other object delineated, are made by everyone who attempts to make any such figure with all the identity of which their mechanical skill is capable, thus showing their conception and motive to be the same.

Among the American Indians the signs drawn by one person of a tribe are generally understood by other members of the same tribe. Among the Africans the signs are understandable only to the person who drew them or at most to some of his nearest friends acquainted with the meaning of the signs.

Besides the identifying-mnemonic systems discussed above there are others which have had limited use in various parts of the world. Among them we should mention the system of the Cuna Indians in Panama,[29] of the Aymara Indians in Bolivia and Peru,[30] the inscriptions discovered at Sicasica in Peru,[31] the *Nsibidi* system used by the natives in Nigeria,[32] and perhaps the symbolism of the Dogon, Bambara, and other tribes of Sudan.[33]

The symbols discussed in this chapter are supposed to represent a stage of writing which Meinhof calls *Satzschrift*, that is, sentence or phrase writing. I feel that this is an entirely inappropriate term. The individual symbols are not used for actual sentences or phrases as parts of speech[34] but stand as mnemonic devices for remembering year dates or songs. The picture of a horseshoe in the year 1802–03 discussed above (see p. 42) does not in itself represent the sentence 'this is the year in which shod horses were first seen by the Indians', but it is a symbol to help remember the particular event. For this reason I prefer to call this class of forerunners of writing the 'mnemonic' or the 'recording' stage.

Systems of mnemonic signs by means of objects are used throughout the world for the purpose of keeping records (see pp. 3 ff.). The ancient Sumerians, too, felt the necessity of keeping records by means of mnemonic signs, but instead of using the objects themselves they chose the method of drawing the accounts on tablets. This important innovation, discussed fully in Chapter III, led to the ultimate development of real writing.

LIMITED SYSTEMS

In addition to the systems described in the preceding pages there are a few, mostly on the American continent, which should be discussed in this chapter. Chief among them are the system of the Aztecs in central Mexico and that of the Mayas in Yucatan, Salvador, British Honduras, and Guatemala. It may shock some scholars to find the highly elaborate inscriptions of Central America classified with the primitive systems of the North American Indians and the African Negroes. Still, the result cannot be otherwise if we look at the problem from an unprejudiced point of view. No matter how elaborate in form the beautiful manuscripts and stone inscriptions of the Aztecs and Mayas may appear, in inner structure they are not on a much higher level of development than are the primitive systems of North America and Africa. What can be clearly understood in the Central American inscriptions are first and above all the mathematical and astronomical systems of notation. Outside of these, some inscriptions or parts of inscriptions are understandable but only in the sense that the North American pictures are *per se* intelligible without the conveyance of any linguistic form. Although the beginnings of phonetization can be observed among both the Aztecs and the Mayas neither even approximately reached the phonetic stage of writing which we find so well developed already in the oldest Sumerian inscriptions. However, before we make any more aprioristic statements let us glance at some typical Central American inscriptions.

Figure 24 gives a page from the so-called 'Codex Boturini' dealing with the migrations of the Aztecs.[35] The scene on the left shows four Aztec tribes (with their 'names' marked by signs above their heads) moving (shown by footprints) in the direction of a place called *Tamoanchan*, 'Place of Descent' (marked by a broken tree and an altar), to take leave of eight kindred tribes. At this place, while the members of the Aztec and kindred tribes are engaged in a feast and a religious ceremony (two scenes at right bottom), their respective leaders are deciding about the departure. The two men depicted just above

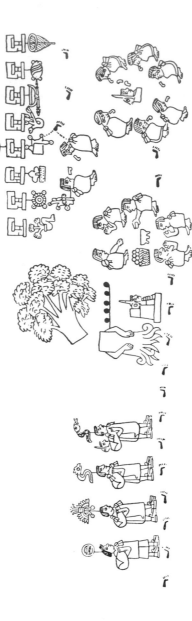

FIG. 24.—AZTEC INSCRIPTION, EXEMPLIFIED BY A PAGE FROM THE CODEX BOTURINI

From Eduard Seler, *Gesammelte Abhandlungen zur amerikanischen Sprach- und Alterthumskunde*, ii (Berlin, 1904), 35 the feast and ceremonial scenes are, on the left, the chief of the Aztecs (marked by the word 'Aztlan' in the form of the water-plus-pillar sign) and, on the right, the chief of the kindred tribes who belongs to one of the eight tribes noted in the upper right by the pictures of houses with the respective 'names'

FIG. 25.—AZTEC INSCRIPTION, EXEMPLIFIED BY A PAGE FROM THE CODEX HAMBURGENSIS

From Theodor-Wilhelm Danzel, *Handbuch der präkolumbischen Kulturen in Latein-amerika* (Hamburg und Berlin, 1927), p. 51

attached below. The chief on the right is shown crying by the sign for water extending from his left eye to the ear. The ceremony takes place at night, as can be seen from the picture of the sky with stars above the names of the eight kindred tribes. The departure of these tribes is indicated by the footprints moving in the opposite direction from the centre.

Another illustration of Aztec writing is given in Figure 25 [36] showing in symmetrical arrangement the following: 1–20 stands for 20 days (an Aztec year consists of 13 months of 20 days each); 21–24 mark the divinities of the four cardinal points, that is, *Xochipilli*, the flower-prince, marked by a flower in his left hand (21); *Mictlantecutli*, the prince of the underworld, marked by the skull (22); *Chalchiuhtlicue*, the water-goddess, marked by water (with snails) flowing from her shoulders (23); and *Tlaloc*, the weather-god, holding in his left hand a lower jaw as a symbol of this power to crush everything (24); 25–40 represent the 16 chiefs with their names expressed in rebus-form signs; 41 depicts *Mayauel*, the goddess of the agave plant and of fertility.

Such examples of phonetic writing as are found are conspicuous by their rarity and by their occurrence almost exclusively in the writing of proper names. For example, the Aztec geographic name *Quauhnauac*, 'near the forest', composed of the words *quauh*, 'tree, forest,' and *nauac*, 'near,' is written with the signs for 'tree' (*quauh*) and for 'speech' (*naua-tl*); the word *Teocaltitlan*, 'temple personnel,' is written with the signs for 'lips' (*te-n-tli*), 'road' (*o-tli*), 'house' (*cal-li*), and 'teeth' (*tlan-tli*), omitting only the syllable *ti*. [37] The sporadic occurrences of phonetization cannot be taken as evidence of a high level of the Central American systems since the principle of phonetization appears sometimes among primitive peoples without any prospects of developing into a full phonetic system (see p. 5).

Much less understood than the Aztec writing is the system used by the Mayas (Fig. 26). [38] In spite of many and various attempts to decipher the Maya writing, the only sure result is that whatever is clearly understood in this system is limited to signs of mathematical and astronomical nature. Besides these, a few more signs for divinities and other terms are known, some of which were apparently expressed by a phonetic method, as among the Aztecs.

In whatever light we understand the statement of the Spanish bishop Diego de Landa in his book published in the middle of the sixteenth century, that a Mayan alphabet of twenty-seven signs was used in Yucatan in his time, one thing is clear: nobody has ever succeeded in deciphering the Maya inscriptions on the basis of de Landa's alphabet. [39] Even if we

FIG. 26.—MAYA INSCRIPTION FROM COPAN

From S. G. Morley, *An Introduction to the Study of the Maya Hieroglyphs* (Washington, 1915), pl. 7 opp. p. 167

admit that this alphabet was composed in the sixteenth century under Spanish influence and had a limited use in some areas of Yucatan, it does not follow that it reproduces the systems of the pre-Columbian Indians.

The best proof that the Maya writing is not a phonetic system results from the plain fact that it is still undeciphered. This conclusion is inescapable if we remember the most important principle in the theory of decipherment: *A phonetic writing can and ultimately must be deciphered if the underlying language is known.* Since the languages of the Mayas are still used to-day, and therefore well known, our inability to understand the Maya system means that it does not represent phonetic writing.

Another proof that neither of the Central American systems can be called phonetic is evident from the analysis of the following inscription. Figure 27 represents a catechism composed some time in the sixteenth century under white influence for the use of Mexicans converted to Catholicism. [40] Although it contains a number of signs which correspond to words of the language, the inscription cannot be read in the way phonetic writings are normally read. The signs and groupings of signs merely suggest the meaning, which can be reconstructed only on the basis of independent knowledge of the Catholic catechism. The character of the text will be better understood if we try to analyse some of its parts. Seven Articles of Faith pertaining to Jesus begin with the second group of the second line marked by the picture of the cross with instruments of torture as the sign for Jesus. Article I, stating 'God's only son, conceived by the Holy Ghost, born of the Virgin Mary' is expressed by the number 'one', a picture of a piece of paper to designate the article, God (recognizable by the characteristic crown and beard), the Holy Ghost (symbolized by a bird), and finally Mary with the child Jesus at her bosom. The second article is found in the first group of the third line, since the writing is boustrophedon, and it expresses simply 'crucified and buried'. Starting with the second group of the fifth line the Ten Commandments are given. The first, 'Thou shalt love God above all other things,' is expressed by the picture of a man with a heart in his hand. The fifth, 'Thou shalt not kill,' is shown by pictures of a man with a sword and of a man in a defending attitude. The rest of the text can be deciphered in the same way with the help of the Catholic catechism and without any knowledge of the Aztec and Maya languages and writings. The analysis of this Mexican catechism shows clearly that it is not written in a phonetic system of writing but in a device amply exemplified in the systems discussed above among the forerunners of writing. If, therefore, the Aztecs and the Mayas did not succeed in evolving a phonetic system by the sixteenth

FIG. 27.—AZTEC CATECHISM

From Seler, *Gesammelte Abhandlungen zur amerikanischen Sprach- und Alterthumskunde*, i (Berlin, 1902), pl. opp. p. 289

century in spite of the Spanish influence, it is difficult to argue that they had had such a system in pre-Columbian days.

Would it not be surprising, somebody may ask, if the pre-Columbian Indians, who produced a culture frequently compared with the fully developed cultures of the ancient Near East, did not have a writing of the same stature as the systems found in the Orient? The answer I would give is that the Amerindian cultures cannot properly be compared with the cultures of the Near East. Not being quite at home in the field of American archæology I cannot pretend to be able to give a competent answer in the matter of comparing cultures of such diverse origin. But I cannot help expressing my views, or rather my feelings, on this subject. The pre-Columbian cultures in America—characterized as they are by scarcity of metals, poverty of tools and weapons, limited agriculture and almost no domestication of animals, lack of the wheel and consequently of carts and wheel-made pottery, extensive human sacrifices and cannibalism—cannot stand comparison with the Oriental cultures which almost from the oldest historical stages have a fully developed copper and bronze metallurgy with an abundance of tools and weapons, full agriculture and domestication of animals, the potter's wheel and carts, almost no human sacrifices, and no trace of cannibalism. The highly developed calendar system is the most conspicuous feature of the Amerindian cultures and it stands out as a unique achievement among the dearth of other cultural accomplishments. Such a high level of development in a specialized field is surprising, but not unique. The wonderful works of the Luristan bronze makers stand out against the background of the general cultural poverty of the Zagros Mountains, just as the high ethical and religious ideas of the biblical Hebrews tower over their mediocre achievements in the political, economic, and technological spheres.

It is not true that the Amerindian cultures were 'nipped in the bud' at the time of the conquest, as is claimed by some scholars who believe that Amerindian writings were on the right way towards developing into full systems. Many Mayan towns were found in ruins by the Spanish conquistadors, showing that at least the Mayan culture was in a declining state.[41] Furthermore, even a superficial knowledge of the inscriptions of the Aztecs and Mayas is enough to convince oneself that they could never have developed into real writing without foreign influence. The features of the written forms, stagnant for about seven hundred years,[42] the creation of the grotesque head-variant forms with their characteristic superabundance of unnecessary detail—a cardinal sin in writing from the point of view of economy—are all indications of a decadent, almost baroque, development.

One more remark should be added in connection with our

classification of the Aztec and Maya systems among the fore-runners of writing. This is necessary to make it clear that we do not wish to imply by this classification that the Central American systems are on the same low level of development as their North American counterparts, discussed at the beginning of this chapter. Even to an outside observer the systematization of the formal aspect of the writing will appear considerably more progressed among the Aztecs and Mayas than among the North American Indians. In addition, we may note in Central America the existence of phonetization, entirely unknown among the comparable systems in the north and, above all, the highly developed numerical system, in comparison with which anything produced in the north looks childish and primitive. The Central American method of writing numbers and things counted as, for example, in the writing of '5 men' by means of the number '5' and the sign for 'man', is identical with that of the Oriental writings and is totally different from the method employed in the north, where the expression '5 men' would have to be written by means of five separate pictures of 'man' [43] All these characteristics point toward a higher level of writing in Central America than in North America, but they can in no way lead to the conclusion that the Central American systems are identical in general structure with any of the Oriental writings. The similarity in the use of the descriptive-representa-tional device among both the North and Central Americans, on the one hand, and the general lack of *systematic* phonography among the Indians, on the other, are two chief characteristics which divide sharply all Amerindian systems from those in the Old World. I find myself thus in complete accord with the opinions of two eminent Americanists as expressed in the following: 'No native race in America possessed a complete writing';[44] 'the Maya hieroglyphs are by no means a real writing in our sense, and no counterpart to the Egyptian hieroglyphs.'[45]

III

WORD-SYLLABIC SYSTEMS

FULL systems of writing originated for the first time in the Orient—that vast mass of land extending from the eastern shores of the Mediterranean Sea to the western Pacific. For historical as well as practical reasons, Egypt and the adjacent areas in Africa and, at least in the pre-Hellenic period, the areas surrounding the Aegean Sea, should also be included within the orbit of the Oriental civilizations.

In the large area thus defined we find seven original and fully developed systems of writing, all of which could *a priori* claim independent origin:—

Sumerian in Mesopotamia, 3100 B.C.–A.D. 75.
Proto-Elamite in Elam, 3000–2200 B.C.
Proto-Indic in the Indus Valley, around 2200 B.C.
Chinese in China, 1300 B.C.–present.
Egyptian in Egypt, 3000 B.C.–A.D. 400.
Cretan in Crete and Greece, 2000–1200 B.C.
Hittite in Anatolia and Syria, 1500–700 B.C.

The fact that we know of exactly seven Oriental systems—a number so sacred to occultists, cabbalists, and universalists—is due simply to coincidence. The Orient is full of writings which await discovery and every few years some new writing comes to light through the efforts of the excavators. To be sure, at the present time there are no likely candidates to be added to the list of the seven original Oriental systems. The Proto-Armenian inscriptions, which have recently been discovered in great numbers in Armenia, are too little known to allow any safe conclusions.[1] The undeciphered Phaistos and Byblos writings are most likely syllabic and thus fall under the classification of writings which will be discussed in Chapter IV. The mysterious Easter Island inscriptions, on which so much effort has been wasted by so many imaginative minds, are not even writing in the most primitive sense of the word as they probably represent nothing else but pictorial concoctions for magical purposes.[2] Finally, the Amerindian systems of the Mayas and the Aztecs do not represent full writing since even in their most advanced stages they never attained the level of development characteristic of the earliest phases of the Oriental systems (see pp. 51 ff.).

Inasmuch as three of the seven Oriental systems—namely, Proto-Elamite, Proto-Indic, and Cretan—are as yet undeciphered or only partially deciphered, we can deal constructively in this chapter only with the remaining four writings, whose systems we can understand fully. Of these, Sumerian is the oldest and the only one in which ample illustration is available for the reconstruction of the earliest stages. For that reason our discussion of the Oriental systems of writing will start first with a full presentation of the Sumerian system; next will come the discussion of the Egyptian, Hittite, and Chinese writings, followed by short sketches of the salient points of the three undeciphered or partially deciphered systems; and finally we shall try to review the common characteristics of all the Oriental systems of writing.

SUMERIAN SYSTEM

The home of the cuneiform writing is in Mesopotamia, in the basin of the Tigris and Euphrates rivers. The term 'cuneiform' means literally 'wedge-form', from Latin *cuneus*, 'wedge', plus *forma*, 'form', and owes its origin to the wedgelike appearance of the little strokes in the signs of the Mesopotamian writing. The decipherment of cuneiform, initiated in the first half of the last century by the German Georg Friedrich Grotefend and the Englishman Henry Rawlinson, progressed so much in the following years that by the end of the century it was possible to read with relative ease the various forms of cuneiform in which many different languages of the ancient Near East were written. Chief among these were Sumerian, spoken in southern Mesopotamia by a people of unknown ethnic and linguistic affiliation, and Akkadian, a Semitic language spoken in northern Mesopotamia, which includes two main dialects, Babylonian and Assyrian. Toward the end of the third millennium B.C. the Sumerian language died out, giving way to Akkadian.

Discoveries in Mesopotamia in the nineteenth century soon

made it apparent that, although the term 'cuneiform' could well be applied to the major part of the life of this writing, it was not applicable to its earliest stages. It was noted that the signs on early tablets brought to light in the course of excavations in southern Mesopotamia did not have the cuneiform appearance, and before long it was found that the older the tablet was the more its signs resembled plain pictures as they are found in many other pictographic systems, such as Egyptian hieroglyphic, for example. Thus, as it became clear that the Mesopotamian cuneiform writing had developed from a pictographic stage, attempts were soon made to reconstruct in detail the various phases of development. The task was considerably lightened by the recent discovery at Uruk (biblical Erech, Greek Orchoe, modern Warka) in southern Mesopotamia of

FIG. 28.—EARLIEST PICTOGRAPHIC TABLETS FROM
URUK

From A. Falkenstein, *Archaische Texte aus Uruk* (Berlin, 1936),
pl. 1

about a thousand tablets which give a rather clear picture of the development of the Mesopotamian writing in its earliest stages.[3]

The Sumerian writing owes its origin to the needs arising from public economy and administration. With the rise in productivity of the country, resulting from state-controlled canalization and irrigation systems, the accumulated agricultural surplus made its way to the depots and granaries of the cities, necessitating keeping accounts of goods coming to the cities, as well as of manufactured products leaving the cities for the country.

The earliest known Sumerian records were found at Uruk in what is usually called 'Uruk IV stratum'. The exact dating of this stratum, like the dating of all early remains in the Near East, is still in the realm of fantasy, with the extreme dates differing by as much as one thousand years. Thus, while one scholar places the beginning of the Proto-literate period between the end of the forty-first and the middle of the thirty-eighth century B.C.,[4] others assign it to the beginning of the third millennium B.C.[5] Lacking concrete evidence there is nothing that I can say about this or that date except to express my opinion that to a historian of writing the lowest possible date would seem to be the most acceptable. The span of over one thousand years between the beginning of Sumerian writing at the start of the fourth millennium and the establishment of full writing around 2500 B.C., postulated by the 'high' chronologists, has always seemed to me out of proportion with the realities of Sumerian epigraphy. For that reason I have felt rather in sympathy with the 'low' chronologists who proposed to reduce this span to about 400 or 500 years, yielding a reconstruction which was much similar to that of my own based on the observation of the inner and outer development of the Sumerian writing. There is a limit, however, below which we cannot possibly go, and that is the date of the earliest Egyptian hieroglyphic inscriptions. If it is true, as generally assumed, that the Egyptian writing originated under the stimulus of the Sumerian writing (see pp. 214 ff.), and if the date of the earliest Egyptian inscriptions is set at about 3000 B.C., then the earliest Sumerian writing cannot be dated after 3000 B.C. There is nothing set, however, about the earliest dates of Egyptian chronology, and it is possible that further studies may result in the reduction by a few centuries of the date of the First Egyptian Dynasty and, with it, of the introduction of writing in Egypt. If this is impossible, then in the light of the facts outlined above, the date of the earliest Sumerian writing should be set tentatively at about 3100 B.C.

In assigning the earliest known Mesopotamian records to the Sumerians we must guard against the easy assumption that the Sumerians were the real 'inventors' of the Mesopotamian writing. In fact, as it has become ever more clear in the last few years that an ethnic element different from the Sumerians (which for want of a better term I call 'the X element') inhabited Mesopotamia alongside, or perhaps even before, the Sumerians, it is not at all excluded that this 'X element' and not the Sumerians may have been responsible for first introducing what became known later as the Sumerian writing.

The simplest forms of Sumerian records are represented by tags or labels showing perforations with traces of strings by which they were originally attached to an object or group of objects. Such tags, usually made of clay, more rarely of gypsum, contained nothing more than the impression of a cylinder seal, that is, the property mark of the person who sent the objects, plus (sometimes) marks giving the number of objects sent, but no signs which in any way would indicate what objects were sent.[6] The limitations of this system are obvious; although the recipient of the goods knew at the time what objects were involved, since the tags came with the objects, once the tags were detached from the objects the connection was gradually lost and forgotten. A further limitation was involved in the fact

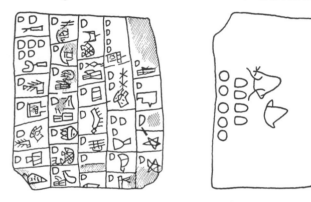

FIG. 29.—LEDGER TABLET FROM URUK

From Falkenstein, *Archaische Texte aus Uruk*, pl. 31, No. 339

that by this method it was possible to record the names of only those persons who owned cylinder seals.

All these limitations led quickly to the enlargement of the system by drawing the signs for the objects and substituting written signs for the seals. Although the small tablets in Figure 28[7] are rather difficult to interpret, it is clear that the signs can stand for nothing else but objects and persons. More developed and easier to interpret is Figure 29,[8] a ledger tablet with many little cases on the obverse, each giving a number in the form of semicircles and a personal name expressed by one or more signs. What is being sent or recorded is stated on the reverse, reading clearly 54 ox cow, that is, '54 oxen (and) cows' or '54 cattle'. It evidently made no difference to the recorder whether oxen or cows were connected with individual persons,

64

and there is nothing to indicate whether the cattle were brought in by different persons or sent out to them.

In saying that the substitution of seal impressions by written personal names was an important factor in the development of Sumerian writing, it must be emphasized that I strongly disagree with the opinion that the Sumerians came upon the idea of writing through their use of the cylinder seal or that the immediate ancestor of Mesopotamian writing was the cylinder seal. [9] It seems to me that the aims of the seal and of writing and the form in which these aims are achieved are so different throughout the whole course of their history that it is difficult to see how the use of seals could have ever influenced the origin of the writing. The purpose of the seal as a mark of ownership in both its utilitarian and magical aspects is the identification of the owner, that of writing is the transmission of communication. The seal depicts scenes taken from religious and legendary spheres, showing no direct relationship to the owner of the seal, while writing uses signs, that is, pictures and non-pictorial symbols, for the purpose of communicating a message by the writer. Even the forms of the individual drawings in the early Uruk writing frequently differ greatly from those found on contemporary seals, as one can readily see from a comparison of the signs for ox and sheep in the Uruk writing with the drawings of these two animals on the seals.

The signs used in the earliest Uruk writing are clearly word signs limited to the expression of numerals, objects, and personal names. This is the stage of writing which we call logography or word writing and which should be sharply distinguished from the so-called 'ideography'. [10] The differences can be easily grasped by anybody who would take the trouble to compare any of the early Uruk inscriptions with the primitive devices of the American Indians, discussed above on pp. 29 ff. [11]

In the most primitive phases of logography it is easy to express concrete words, such as a sheep by a picture of a sheep, or the sun by a picture of the sun, but soon a method must be evolved whereby pictures can express not only the objects they originally depict but also words with which they can be secondarily associated. Thus, a picture of the sun can stand secondarily for the words 'bright, white', later also 'day'; similarly, a picture of a woman and a mountain can stand for 'slave girl'—a

65

combination derived from the fact that slave girls were normally brought to Babylonia from the surrounding mountains.

Logography of this kind has, of course, its drawbacks in its inability to express many parts of speech and grammatical forms; this is not very serious, however, since the intended meaning can frequently be understood through the 'context of situation', to use a term introduced by B. Malinowski in his study of the meaning in primitive languages[12] (see p. 19). Much more serious are the limitations of the system in respect to the writing of proper names. The primitive device of the American Indians for expressing personal names (see pp. 39 ff.) may have been sufficient for tribal conditions but it certainly could not satisfy the requirements of large urban centres like those in Sumer. In an Indian tribe, where everybody knows everybody else, it is normal for every individual to have an exclusive name.

FIG. 30.—WRITING OF PERSONAL NAMES IN THE URUK PERIOD
From Falkenstein, *Archaische Texte aus Uruk*, p. 24

In large cities, in spite of the proximity of living conditions, people do not know each other and many different persons bear the same names. Therefore, in documents, persons with the same name have to be further identified by their paternity and place of origin. Furthermore, names of the Indian type, such as 'White-Buffalo' or 'Big-Bear', which can be expressed in writing with relative ease and are found perhaps in our Figure 30, were relatively rare among the Sumerians, while common Sumerian names of the type 'Enlil-Has-Given-Life' were difficult to express by the Indian device.

The need for adequate representation of proper names finally led to the development of phonetization. This is confirmed by the Aztec and Maya writings, which employ the phonetic principle only rarely and then almost exclusively in expressing proper names (see p. 54). That the need for indicating grammatical elements was of no great importance in the origin of phonetization can be deduced from the fact that even after the full development of phonetization writing failed for a long time to indicate grammatical elements adequately.

Phonetization, therefore, arose from the need to express words and sounds which could not be adequately indicated by pictures or combinations of pictures. Its principle consists in associating words which are difficult to express in writing with signs which resemble these words in sound and are easy to draw. The procedure involved may result in a full phonetic transfer, as in a drawing of knees to express the name 'Neil' (from 'kneel'), of the sun for the word 'son', or even together in a drawing of knees plus the sun to express the personal name 'Neilson'.[13] Partial phonetic transfer is involved in the drawing of the bear in the coat of arms of Berlin or of the monk in that of the city of Munich. Phonetic indicators are normally used when it is imperative to differentiate words which are similar in meaning and which theoretically could be expressed by one and the same sign. Thus, while a picture of two women facing each other may stand through association of ideas for the words 'discord, quarrel, litigation', in order to express the word 'discord' pictures of two women and of a cord may be used, because the final syllable of the word 'discord' resembles, or in this case is identical with, the sound 'cord' expressed by the picture of a cord. Of course, the word 'discord' could also be written through the process of phonetic transfer by means of two signs, one representing a disk, the other a cord.

Although most of the Uruk inscriptions are as yet unreadable we can safely assume that the principle of phonetization was evolved very early. Falkenstein himself quotes as an example of phonetization the case of the ARROW sign, which is found in the second oldest stage of the writing (the so-called 'Uruk III stratum').[14] This sign stands in Sumerian for the word *ti*, 'arrow', and also for the word *ti*, 'life'. But since in the oldest stage of the writing (the so-called 'Uruk IV stratum') we find *men*, the word for 'crown' in Sumerian, written with the sign for 'crown' plus the phonetic indicator *en*,[15] and since possibly the divine name Sin, originally Suen, Suin, is written phonetically as *su-en*,[16] it is probable that examples of this kind will be greatly increased when we reach a better understanding of the earliest stages of the Uruk writing.

Once introduced, the principle of phonetization spread rapidly. With it entire new horizons were opened to the expression of all linguistic forms, no matter how abstract, by means of written symbols. The establishment of a full system of writing required conventionalization of forms and principles. Forms of signs had to be standardized so that everybody would draw the signs in approximately the same way. Correspondences of signs with definite words and meanings had to be established, and signs with definite syllabic values had to be chosen. Further regulation of the system had to take place in the matter of the orientation of signs and the direction, form, and order of the lines. The order of signs had in general to follow the order of forms in the spoken language, in contrast to the convention of the descriptive-representational device, as known among the North American Indians (see pp. 29 ff.), the Aztecs (see pp. 51 ff.), and the Egyptians (see pp. 72 ff.); it should be remembered, however, that for aesthetic or practical reasons (see p. 230) the sign order may be changed within words and short expressions.

Conventionalization of the system of writing required not only the setting-up of the rules but also the actual learning of the forms and principles of writing. The few school tablets found in the Uruk IV stratum giving lists of signs [17] testify to the educational and scientific activities of the Sumerians, fields in which they became so proficient in the later course of their history.

Some time in the first half of the third millennium B.C. the system of the Sumerian writing was taken over first by the Semitic Akkadians and a little later by their eastern neighbours, the Elamites. In the second millennium it was the Hurrians of northern Mesopotamia and the Hittites of Anatolia who borrowed the writing from the Akkadians. That was the period in which the Akkadian language, as the *lingua franca* of the Near East, reached its greatest period of cultural expansion. The Urartians of Armenia, who used the Mesopotamian writing for their language in the first half of the first millennium, were the last nation to borrow the cuneiform system from Mesopotamia.

Outside of the cuneiform systems just mentioned, reference should be made to Ugaritic (see pp. 129 f.) and Persian (see pp. 172 ff.), both of which were independent local creations, whose only connection with the Mesopotamian cuneiform was the notion that signs could be made in the form of wedges.

Throughout its history the material par excellence of the Mesopotamian writing was clay. As the rounded forms of pictures could not easily be incised on clay with a stylus the signs perforce acquired in the course of time an angular form executed by means of a few separate strokes of the stylus. Due to natural pressure of the stylus in one of its corners the strokes acquired the appearance of wedges, resulting in the development of cuneiform writing. This writing was later used on other materials, such as stone and metal. The development of some of the Sumerian pictographic signs into cuneiform is shown in the table in Figure 31. This is the usual interpretation of the origin of cuneiform writing, but it should be noted that there are some indications pointing towards the use of wood as a writing material in Mesopotamia. Wood, even more than clay, would have necessitated the development of rounded into angular and square forms. The Chinese, too, had a 'square script' around the time of Jesus, which may have arisen as a result of the difficulties in incising rounded forms on wood. Even the Hebrew *scriptura quadrata* may owe its origin to similar causes.

The Sumerian syllabary and the systems derived from it consist of signs which usually represent monosyllables ending in a vowel or a consonant, more rarely dissyllables of the same structure.

At no time did any of the Mesopotamian syllabaries (see p. 130) contain signs for all the possible syllables existing in the languages for which they were used. The principle of economy aiming at the expression of linguistic forms by the smallest possible number of signs, resulted in various economizing measures. No Mesopotamian system distinguishes between voiced, voiceless, and emphatic consonants in the case of signs ending in a consonant. Thus, the sign IG has the value *ig*, *ik*, and *iq*, just as the sign TAG can stand for *tag*, *tak*, and *taq*. In addition, some older systems, such as Old Akkadian and Old Assyrian, do not even indicate the quality of the consonant in signs beginning with a consonant. Thus, in these systems the sign GA has the value of *ga*, *ka*, and *qa*. In all cuneiform systems many signs ending in *i* may stand also for those ending in *e*, as in the sign LI with the values *li* and *le*. In the case of syllables which are not represented by a sign in the syllabary, signs with similar consonants can be used as, for

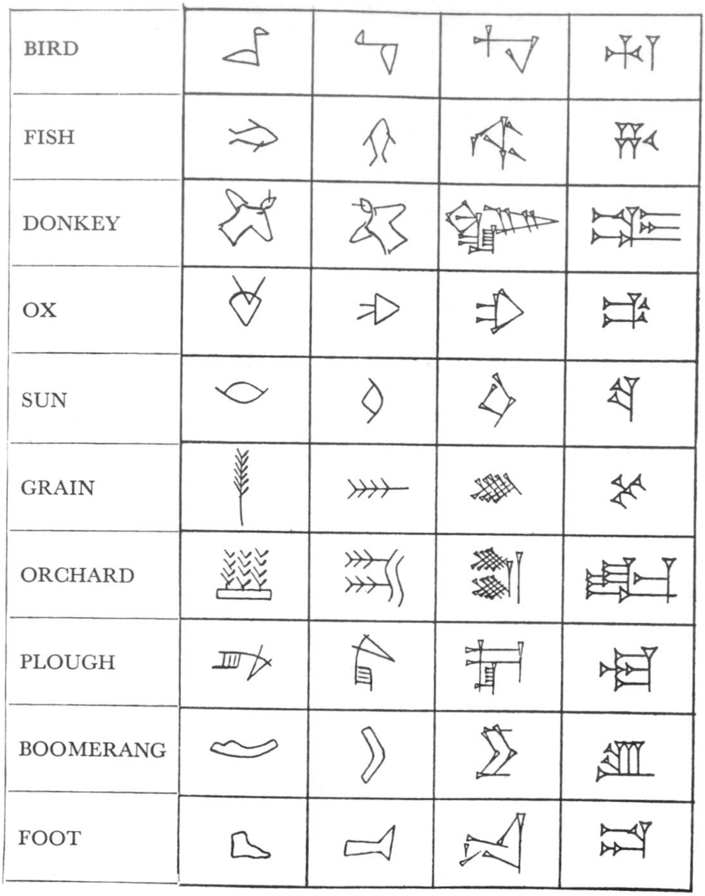

FIG. 31.—PICTORIAL ORIGIN OF TEN CUNEIFORM SIGNS
Oriental Institute Photo No. 27875 (after A. Poebel)

instance, in writing the syllable *rin* by means of the sign which has a normal value *rim*. Syllables for which no signs with similar consonants can be found are written in a way which developed uniquely in Sumerian and finds no parallels in any other syllabic system with the possible exception of the Chinese system (see pp. 87 f.). Thus, in the Mesopotamian system the syllable *ral*, for which no separate sign exists, is written as *ra-al*, while in other known syllabic systems this syllable would be written *ra-l(a)*, *ra-l(e)*, or the like. This method of writing syllables, for

which we have the first documentation in the spelling of
Ti-ra-áš for *Tiraš* at the time of Ur-Nanše (about 2500 B.C.),
invaded the Mesopotamian system of writing to the extent that
in the course of time it became one of the two normal ways of
writing monosyllables consisting of a consonant plus a vowel
plus a consonant. The Mesopotamian writing of *ral* as *ra-al* may
be explained by the principle of reduction (pp. 105 and 182 f.).
In cases of polyphonous signs, such as the sign which may be
read as *gul* or *sun*, the writing *gul-ul*, composed of the basic sign
gul plus the phonetic complement or indicator *ul*, was used to
show that the sign should be read as *gul* and not *sun*. The
spelling *gul-ul* may then have been conceived as *gu(l)-ul*, with
the result that the *gul* sign was now considered to stand for *gu*
alone, while the *ul* sign supplied the remainder of the required
gul.

The normal Mesopotamian syllabic writing contains signs of
the type *da, du, dam, dum,* etc., each of which indicates exactly
the required vowel. But besides these there are signs such as
WA which has the value of *wa, wi, we,* and *wu,* in other words,
the consonant *w* plus any vowel.[18] Still another sign is the A'or
'A sign which contains the weak consonant ' and any required
vowel. The early Assyriologists frequently transliterated the
former sign as *w*, and the latter even in modern practice is still
commonly transliterated as ' by persons who have not yet
grasped clearly the difference between syllabic and alphabetic
writings. This latter sign developed from an older form which
had the value of *aḫ, iḫ, eḫ,* and later also *uḫ.* In addition, it has
recently been proved that the sign IA can in some periods have
the value of the consonant *y* plus any vowel. Then there are
signs such as ḪAR or LAḪ, which can be read with any medial
vowel, and many more signs such as LI/LE, IG/EG, LAB/LIB,
DIN/DUN, etc., in which readings with more than one vowel are
possible.

Remembering that the Mesopotamian writing often inadequately indicates the consonants in having identical signs
for voiced, voiceless, and emphatic consonants (see p. 69), we
can observe two methods in play. One procedure is to indicate
the consonant correctly but not the vowel (the sign WA, WI,
WE, WU), and the other to indicate the vowel correctly but not
the consonant (the sign GA, KA, QA or the sign AG, AK, AQ).
Of these methods it is the second which is by far the more

important in Mesopotamian. Thus, the Mesopotamian syllabic writing is the result of the amalgamation of two processes both aiming at the effective expression of the language by means of the smallest possible number of signs. This is the principle of economy, which may be observed in many other syllabic systems, such as Egyptian, which indicates the consonant correctly but not the vowel, or Hittite, Cypriote, and older Japanese, none of which indicates the distinction between voiced, voiceless, emphatic, or aspirate consonants.

If we try now to reconstruct the two Mesopotamian methods of creating syllabic signs in accordance with the principle of economy we can draw the following picture:—

Method I	*Method II*
One sign expresses *ga* or *ka* or *qa*	One sign expresses *wa* or *wi* or *we* or *wu*
One sign expresses *gi* or *ki* or *qi*	One sign expresses *ya* or *yi* or *ye* or *yu*
One sign expresses *ge* or *ke* or *qe*	One sign expresses *aḫ* or *iḫ* or *eḫ* or *uḫ*
One sign expresses *gu* or *ku* or *qu*	One sign expresses *ḫar* or *ḫir* or *ḫer* or *ḫur*

FIG. 32.—THE TWO MESOPOTAMIAN METHODS OF CREATING SYLLABIC SIGNS

EGYPTIAN SYSTEM

The name of the hieroglyphic writing of the Egyptians is derived from the Greek ἱερογλυφικὰ γράμματα and owes its origin to the belief that this kind of writing was used chiefly by the Egyptians for sacred purposes and on stone (ἱερός means 'sacred' and γλύφειν 'to incise', namely, on stone). By 1822 the hieroglyphic writing was successfully deciphered by the Frenchman François Champollion chiefly on the basis of comparison with the Greek inscription on the famous Rosetta stone.

The origins of the Egyptian writing are not as clear as those of Sumerian. At the beginning of the history of Egyptian writing we have a number of slate palettes from Hieraconpolis, situated about fifty miles south of the ancient town of Thebes

FIG. 33.—THE NARMER PALETTE

From J. E. Quibell in *Zeitschrift für ägyptische Sprache*, xxxvi (1898), pls. xii f.

in Upper Egypt. The best of these for the purpose of our discussion is the 'Narmer palette' (Fig. 33), so named because of the belief that the two central symbols in the uppermost register on both the obverse and reverse represent signs which in later Egyptian could be read something like 'Narmer'. As the

73

name 'Narmer' is otherwise unknown in later Egyptian history, the syllabic reading of the symbols as well as the proposed identity of Narmer with Menes, the founder of the First Dynasty of Egypt, are purely hypothetical.

Let us now glance at the reverse side of our palette. The central scene shows an Egyptian king in the process of smiting an enemy to his knees. The scene to the right depicts a falcon, probably symbolizing the king as the god Horus, leading on a string a man from the Delta Land, symbolized by the head of a man plus six papyrus reeds. The whole is supposed to record a conquest of the Lower Land (Delta) by Menes, the founder of the Upper Egyptian kingdom, an event which presumably took place around 3000 B.C. In addition, we find symbols scattered throughout the palette, as in the uppermost register between the two heads of Hathor and near the heads of the subjugated enemy, all of which, no matter what their reading or interpretation, can hardly stand for anything else but proper names or titles. The whole structure of the record, different as it is from what we have seen in the earliest stages of Sumerian writing, finds striking parallelism in comparable examples of the Aztec writing (Fig. 25 and p. 54). In both cases the record is achieved by means of the descriptive-representational device by depicting an event and, as in art, by disregarding entirely the main object of full writing, which is to reproduce language in its normal word order.

The proper names on the Narmer palette, as also on several other examples from Hieraconpolis, are evidently written in the rebus-form device which we have found in use among the Amerindians (see pp. 39 ff.) and perhaps also among the early Sumerians (see pp. 66 ff.).

Soon after Menes a full phonetic system of writing developed in Egypt, perhaps under the Sumerian stimulus (see p. 214 f.). After a short transitory period in which the phonetically written inscriptions still offer great difficulties of interpretation, a fully developed system appeared which in principle remained unchanged to the very end of the history of Egyptian writing. Throughout all of its history Egyptian was a word-syllabic writing.

The hieroglyphic form of writing, used chiefly for public display purposes, was not the writing of everyday practical life. For such purposes the Egyptians developed two forms of cursive

writing, first the hieratic and then the demotic (Fig. 34). The
development of the forms of some of the signs in hieroglyphic,
hieratic, and demotic is shown in Figure 35.

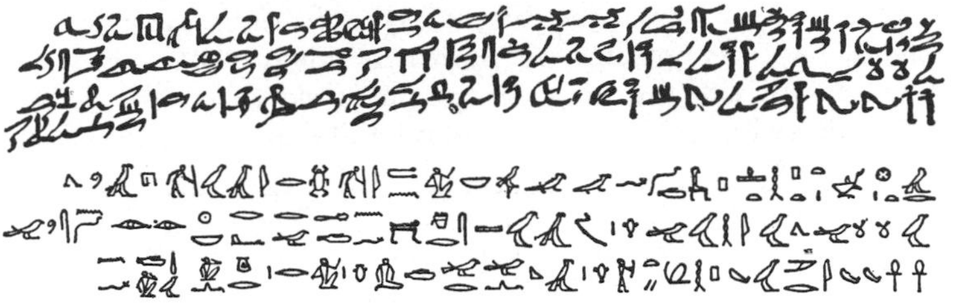

LITERARY HIERATIC OF THE TWELFTH DYNASTY (*Pr.* 4, 2-4),
WITH TRANSCRIPTION

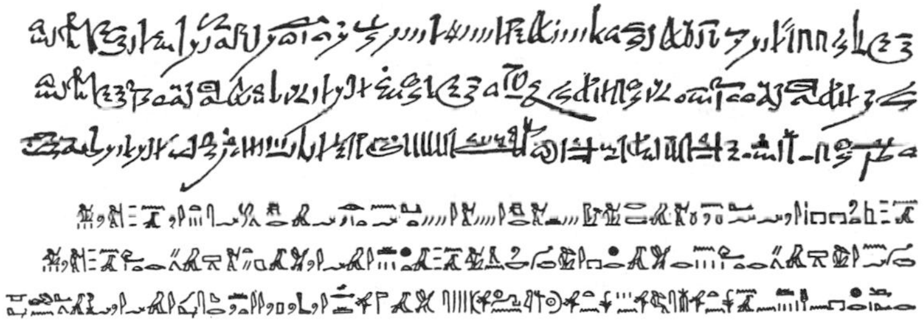

OFFICIAL HIERATIC OF THE TWENTIETH DYNASTY (*Abbott* 5, 1-3),
WITH TRANSCRIPTION

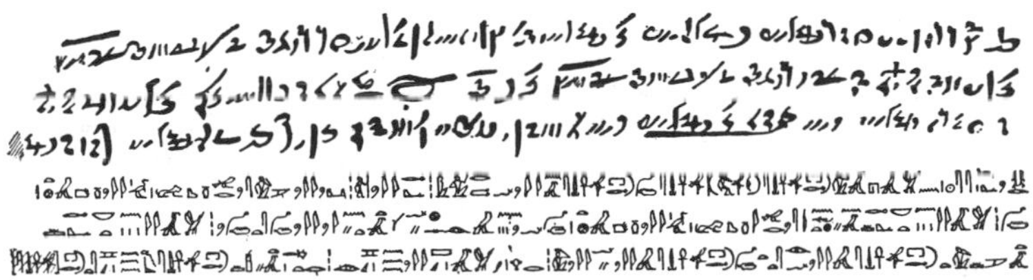

LITERARY DEMOTIC OF THE THIRD CENTURY B.C. (*Dem. Chron.* 6, 1-3),
WITH TRANSCRIPTION

FIG. 34.—SPECIMENS OF HIERATIC AND DEMOTIC WRITING WITH
HIEROGLYPHIC TRANSLITERATIONS IN A MODERN EGYPTOLOGICAL
HAND

From A. H. Gardiner, *Egyptian Grammar* (2nd ed.; Oxford, 1950), pl. ii

The Egyptian syllabary consists of about twenty-four signs,
each with an initial consonant plus any vowel, such as the sign
m^x with the value m^a, m^i, m^e, m^u, and $m^{(x)}$ (Fig. 36), and of
about eighty signs, each with two consonants plus any vowel(s),

75

such as the sign $t^x m^x$ with the value $t^a m^a$, $t^i m^i$, $t^e m^e$, $t^u m^u$, $t^a m^i$, $t^e m^i$, $t^a m^{(a)}$, $t^e m^{(e)}$, $t^{(a)} m^a$, etc. (Fig. 37).

The name 'syllabary' given here to the Egyptian phonetic, non-semantic signs must be understood in its simplest sense, that is, as a system consisting of syllabic signs. This simple terminology has nothing to do with the ideas of those Egyptologists who divide the Egyptian 'phonetic' signs into two classes: Alphabetic signs of the type m and syllabic signs of the type tm. [19]

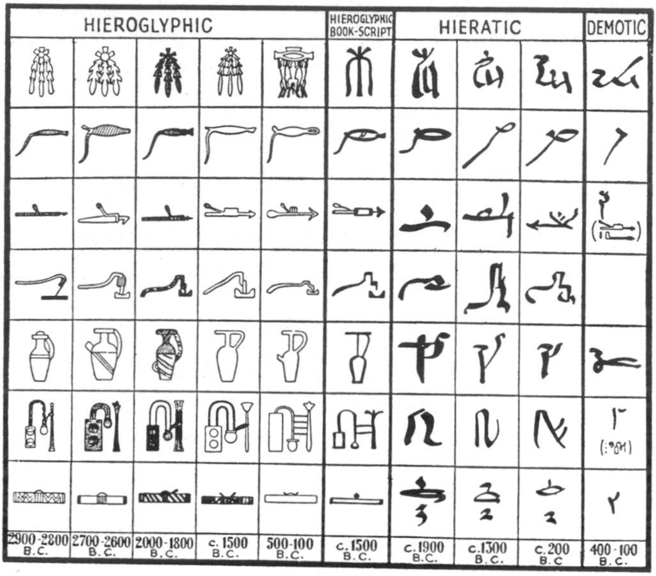

HIEROGLYPHIC					HIEROGLYPHIC BOOK-SCRIPT	HIERATIC			DEMOTIC
2900-2800 B.C.	2700-2600 B.C.	2000-1800 B.C.	c. 1500 B.C.	500-100 B.C.	c. 1500 B.C.	c. 1900 B.C.	c. 1300 B.C.	c. 200 B.C.	400-100 B.C.

FIG. 35.—FORMAL DEVELOPMENT OF SOME OF THE SIGNS IN HIEROGLYPHIC, HIERATIC, AND DEMOTIC

From G. Möller in *Zeitschrift des Deutschen Vereins für Buchwesen und Schrifttum*, ii (1919), 78

As justly observed by Kurt Sethe, the distinction is not real since both types are identical in structure, except that the first contains one consonant, the second two consonants. [20] For that reason Sethe and almost all modern Egyptologists include the non-semantic signs of Egyptian, whether uniconsonantal or multiconsonantal, under consonantal writing. The problem, therefore, as posed in the following, is not whether the Egyptian non-semantic signs are alphabetic and syllabic, as taken originally by Erman, but whether they are all consonantal, as taken generally by Egyptologists, or syllabic, as proposed by myself.

There is no difference between the Egyptologists on the one hand and myself on the other in the belief that the non-semantic signs indicate fully the consonants but do not indicate differences in vowels. I agree entirely with Sethe, for example, that the

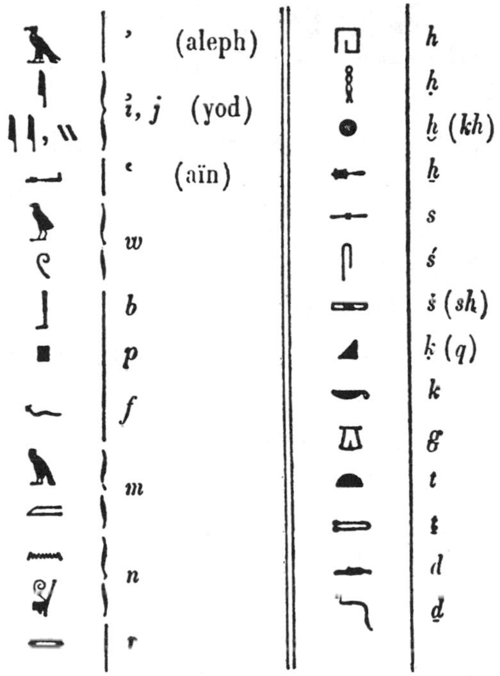

	' (aleph)			h
	i, j (yod)			$\dot{h}$
	' (aïn)			$\underline{h}$ (kh)
				$\underline{h}$
	w			s
				$\acute{s}$
	b			$\check{s}$ (sh)
	p			$\dot{k}$ (q)
	f			k
				g
	m			t
				$\underline{t}$
	n			d
				$\underline{d}$
	r			

FIG. 36.—EGYPTIAN UNICONSONANTAL
SYLLABARY

From C. Fossey, *Notices sur les caractères étrangers* (Paris, 1927), p. 4

sign transliterated as *mn* by the Egyptologists stands for *mắn, mĭn, mĕn, mūn, mŏn* of later Coptic, [21] implying that some such vowels must have been inherent in the words of ancient Egyptian in which the sign *mn* was used. Also, from the practical point of view, there seems to be no difference between the traditional transliteration as *mn*, [22] taking this writing to be consonantal, and the transliteration $m^x n^x$, $m^x n(^x)$, $m(^x) n^x$, etc.,

77

if we take the writing to be syllabic in the sense that it shows correctly the consonants (*m* and *n*) and does not indicate the vowels (*ᵃ*). However, from the point of view of the theory of

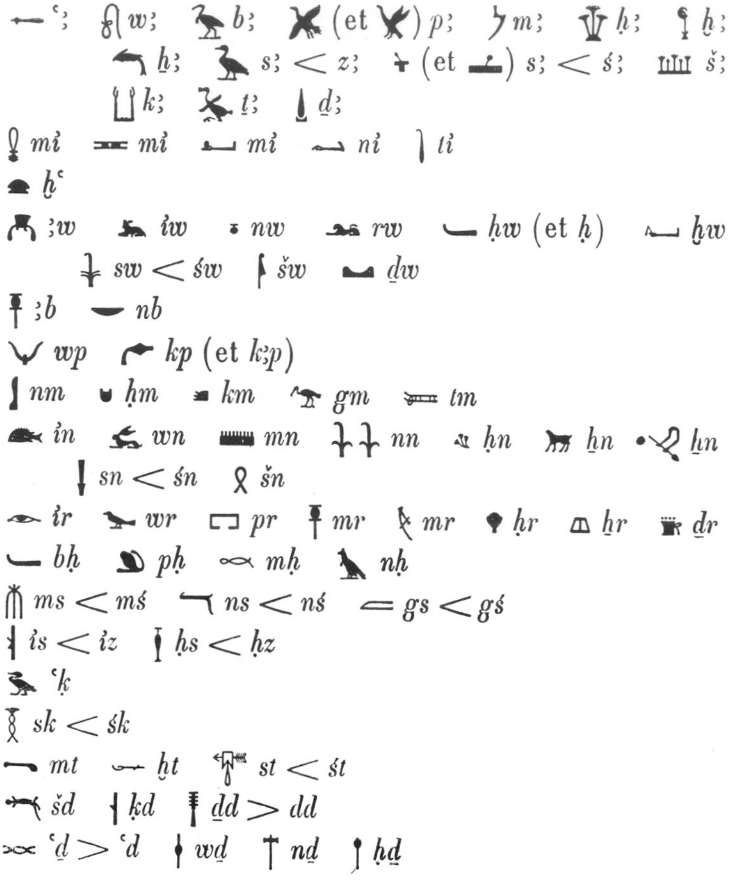

FIG. 37.—EGYPTIAN BICONSONANTAL SIGNS

From G. Lefebvre, *Grammaire de l'Égyptien classique* (Le Caire, 1940), pp. 12 f.

writing, the difference is enormous. *The Egyptian phonetic, non-semantic writing cannot be consonantal, because the development from a logographic to a consonantal writing, as generally accepted by the Egyptologists, is unknown and unthinkable in the history of writing, and because the only development known and attested in dozens of various systems is that from a logographic to a syllabic writing.* [23]

The attested development in the ancient Oriental systems, such as Sumerian, Hittite, and Chinese, as well as in some modern writings created by American Indians and African Negroes under foreign impulse, such as Cherokee, Bamum, and many others, is from a logographic to a syllabic stage. From the psychological point of view this is the most natural development. The first step in the analysis of a word is to divide it into its component syllables, not into its component single sounds or consonants. In fact, when we consider that almost all the native American Indian and African writings stopped at the syllabic stage without further developing into alphabetic systems, we can deduce that these natives encountered difficulties in abstracting words into their component single sounds. Thus, in taking the Egyptian non-semantic writing to be consonantal, we should not only face a development entirely unique in the history of writing, but also we should have to grant to the Egyptian writing a stage of abstraction which—as will be proved—was not achieved until thousands of years later, in the Greek alphabet.

No matter whether we consider the Egyptian non-semantic signs as syllabic or consonantal, one fact stands out clearly, and that is that the vowels are not indicated in the writing. At first glance this looks like a unique development since all other writings known to us—with the exception of Semitic writings which descend directly from Egyptian—regularly indicate the vowels. Nevertheless, the phenomenon is not entirely unique if we remember that a number of signs in the Mesopotamian cuneiform systems never indicate the vowels and many others indicate them only inadequately (see pp. 69 ff.). Thus, in these systems the sign normally called WA can be read as *wa, wi, we,* and *wu,* in other words, as the consonant *w* plus any vowel, just as the sign LI can be read as either *li* or *le* and the sign LAB as *lab* or *lib.* In the Mesopotamian systems, besides signs which either never indicate the vowels or indicate them inadequately, there are others which do not indicate adequately the consonant, as in the sign AG with the values of *ag, ak, aq,* or GA with those of *ga, ka, qa.* Of these two methods of creating syllabic signs the second plays by far the more important role in cuneiform. By contrast, in the Egyptian system the first method was chosen as the basis for the formation of its syllabary. *In both cases the underlying idea is the principle of economy, which strives for the effective expression of language by means of the smallest possible number of signs* (see p. 72).

If one should ask why Egyptian and its Semitic derivates omit systematically the indication of vowels, the answer is that usually given by Orientalists who are at home in the Semitic field. The Egyptian language—as is well known—belongs in the widest sense to the Semitic group, and one of the chief morphological characteristics of these languages is the retention of consonants and variability of vowels. Thus, for instance, the abstract root *ktb*, 'to write,' has *katab* for 'he wrote', *kātib* for 'writer', *kitb* for 'book', and many more forms all retaining the basic consonants *ktb*. It is not that 'the vowels are less important in the Semitic languages than in the Indo-European' or that 'the vowels play a more prominent role in Greek than in Semitic', as is often suggested by some philologists, because writing without vowels can be read with relatively equal ease or equal difficulty in both groups of languages. 'n rdng ths sntnc y wll fnd th bst prf tht 'ls th 'nglsh lngug cn b wrttn withut vwls.[24] The truth is rather that the Indo-European languages usually indicate morphological and semantic differences by endings, while the Semitic languages indicate these differences chiefly by internal vowel variations in a form occasionally found in the Indo-European languages, as in the German *brechen, brach, bräche, brich, gebrochen, Bruch, Brüche* or in the English sing, sang, song, sung. Thus, the relative stability of consonants and variability of vowels in the Semitic languages may truly have been the main reason why the Egyptians created a syllabary based on signs which indicated the consonants correctly while sacrificing the vowels.

For more evidence in favour of the syllabic character of the Egyptian non-semantic writing see the discussion on the West Semitic syllabary (pp. 147 ff.). As the West Semitic writing is clearly a direct descendant of the Egyptian syllabic writing, and as the two writings are fully identical from the point of view of inner structural characteristics, any evidence brought forth in favour of the syllabic character of the so-called Semitic 'alphabet' can be used also as proof in favour of the syllabism of the Egyptian non-semantic writing.

It was stated above (p. 75) that the Egyptian phonetic signs, whether uniconsonantal or multiconsonantal, always began with a consonant. This statement is in disagreement with the opinion of some Egyptologists who believe that the Egyptian phonetic writing was consonantal, with each sign representing one or more consonants plus any vowel, initial, medial, or final, as the sign MOUTH representing *ră, rā, rĕ, rē, ăr, ār, ĕr, ēr,* etc., or the sign HOUSE standing for *par, pĕr, āpr, epr, epra,* etc.[25] The reconstruction of Egyptian signs as representing vowel plus consonant is based seemingly on the observation that a number of Egyptian forms appear with or without an initial weak consonant, as in the case of the prepositions *iˣmᶻ* or *mᶻ,* 'in, from, with,' *iˣrˣ* or *rˣ,* 'as to,' of many imperatives such as *iˣd̲ˣd̲ˣ* or *d̲ˣd̲ˣ,* 'say!', and of other verbal forms. From the interchange of such spellings it was implied that some sort of (weak consonant plus) vowel was inherent in the shorter spellings, leading to the assumption that the first sign in the shorter spellings stood for a vowel plus consonant. There is no need, however, for a *graphic* interpretation, as in all cases, the prosthetic *ʾāleph* can be explained on a *phonetic* basis as a secondary element introduced before two contiguous consonants in order to facilitate their pronunciation.[26] This explanation may be confirmed by such parallels in Semitic languages as *ʾemna* or *min,* 'from,' *ʾuqtul,* or *qutul < *qtul,* 'kill!', and many others. The interpretation of Egyptian phonetic signs as representing vowel plus consonant could be accepted only if it could be proved that original initial vowels, like those in the name of Amon and Osiris, could be freely omitted in the classical Egyptian writing.

HITTITE SYSTEM

The decipherment of the Hittite hieroglyphic writing was achieved only in the thirties of this century through the combined efforts of scholars of such diverse origin as Helmuth T. Bossert (Germany), Emil O. Forrer (Switzerland), Bedřich Hrozný (Czechoslovakia), Piero Meriggi (Italy), and the present writer. As yet, the decipherment of Hittite has not progressed so far as to enable us to place our knowledge of Hittite on the same level as that of Sumerian or Egyptian. Although the general system of the writing is reasonably clear, much remains to be done in the interpretation of individual signs.[27]

The term 'hieroglyphic' used for the Hittite writing was taken over from the Egyptian and it simply implies that the Hittite writing, like the Egyptian, is a picture writing. Under no circumstances does it imply that the Hittite hieroglyphic system was borrowed from the Egyptian hieroglyphic or that it is in any way related to it.

FIG. 38.—SPECIMEN OF EARLY
HITTITE HIEROGLYPHIC WRITING

From I. J. Gelb, *Hittite Hieroglyphic Monuments* (Chicago, 1939), pl. lxxiv

The Hittite hieroglyphic writing was in use from about 1500 to 700 B.C. in a large area extending from central Anatolia to northern Syria. Its language is related to, but by no means identical with, the so-called 'cuneiform Hittite', so named from the fact that this language is preserved in the cuneiform writing borrowed from Mesopotamia. Both of these languages and writings were used simultaneously in the Hittite Empire, but while cuneiform Hittite was limited to the area around Boğazköy, the capital of the empire, and died out soon after 1200 B.C., hieroglyphic Hittite was used throughout the empire and continued as a living tongue up to about 700 B.C.

The beginnings of the Hittite hieroglyphic writing are still rather obscure, but all indications point toward the Aegean cultural area as its source of origin (see pp. 216 f.). The pictorial character of the signs of the earlier stages (Fig. 38) is preserved in the formal inscriptions of the classical period and is still recognizable even in the cursive form of the latest period (Fig. 39, translated on p. 114).

FIG. 39.—CURSIVE FORM OF HITTITE
HIEROGLYPHIC WRITING
From Gelb, *Hittite Hieroglyphic Monuments*, pl. xxxvii

The structure of the word signs is identical with or similar to that of other logo-syllabic writings. The normal Hittite syllabary consists of about sixty signs of the type *pa, pi, pe, pu,* each representing a syllable beginning with a consonant and ending in a vowel (Fig. 40). In agreement with the principle of economy no distinction is made between voiced, voiceless, and aspirated consonants. The normal Hittite syllabary is the one used in Syria at the beginning of the first millennium B.C. Syllabaries used in Anatolia at the same time contain a number

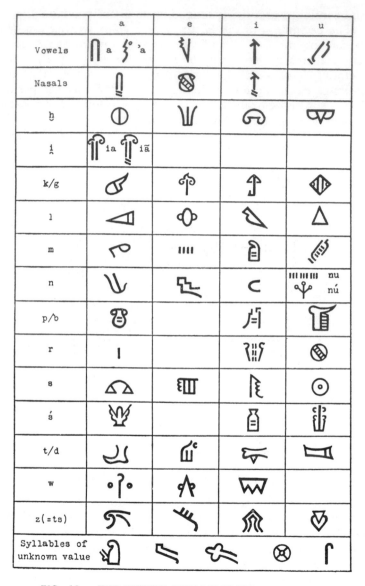

FIG. 40.—THE HITTITE HIEROGLYPHIC SYLLABARY

From Gelb, *Hittite Hieroglyphs*, iii (Chicago, 1942), Frontispiece

of signs which developed locally, just as the older syllabaries
from the period before 1200 B.C. contain some syllabic signs
which fell into disuse in later periods. Besides syllables of the
type *pa*, there is a small number of rebus signs used syllabically,
such as the signs *tra* and *ara*.

CHINESE SYSTEM

Of the four main Oriental writings, Chinese is the only one
which did not have to be deciphered in modern times, as its

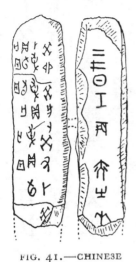

FIG. 41.—CHINESE
ORACLE TEXT ON
ANIMAL BONE

From F. H. Chalfant in
*Memoirs of the Carnegie
Museum*, iv (1906), 33

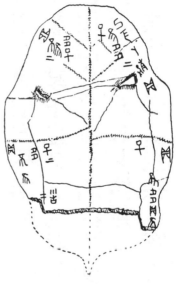

FIG. 42.—CHINESE ORACLE
TEXT ON TORTOISE SHELL

From F. H. Chalfant in *Memoirs of
the Carnegie Museum*, iv, 32

knowledge has passed traditionally from generation to generation up to the present day. The Chinese writing makes its
appearance about the middle of the second millennium B.C.
during the Shang Dynasty, as a fully developed phonetic
system. To be sure, in its outer form the writing has changed
greatly in the course of its long history, but from the point of
inner characteristics the oldest inscriptions hardly differ from
those of recent times.

85

The oldest Chinese inscriptions are the oracle texts on animal bones (Fig. 41) and tortoise shells (Fig. 42), and some short texts on bronze vessels, weapons, pottery, and jade. The signs in the Shang period are limited in number—no more than about 2,500—and in the majority of them the pictorial character is still clearly recognizable. But the signs soon develop

彊克其萬年子子孫孫永寶用
唆臣天子克其日易休無
口口口降克多福眉壽永令
其用朝夕享于皇且皇且考其
用獻于師尹朋友昏遘克
不顯魯休揚用作旅盨克
田人克拜稽首取對天子
令尹氏友史𧺫典善夫克
吉庚寅王才周康穆宮王
惟十又八年十又二月初

FIG. 43.—MODERN CHINESE WRITING

From C. F. Kelley and Ch'en Meng-chia, *Chinese Bronzes from the Buckingham Collection* (Chicago, 1946), p. 155

a linear form to the extent that in later writings it is impossible to recognize the pictures they originally represented (Fig. 43).

The Chinese writing does not have a full syllabary which could be compared with the syllabaries in the other three Oriental systems. As the words of the Chinese language are regularly expressed by word signs it is only in the writing of foreign words and names that the necessity arose to use word signs in a syllabic function. Thus, the name 'Jesus' is written as *Yeh-su*, 'English' as *Ying-chi-li*, 'French' as *Fa-lan-hsi*, 'telephone' as *tê-li-fêng*, etc. There are no set word signs for certain syllables, as there are in the Near Eastern systems; for example, the name 'Jesus' could also be written *Ya-su*, the word 'telephone' *tê-lu-fung*. The characteristic tendency of Chinese toward abbreviation can be noted in the use of *Ying* for 'English' (besides *Ying-kuo-jên* for 'Englishman', that is, 'English-country-man'), *Fa* for 'French' (besides *Fa-kuo-jên*), or *Lo* for 'Roosevelt' (besides *Lo-ssu-fu*). Frequently words spelled out syllabically acquired in time a logographic spelling as, for example, the above-mentioned *tê-li-fêng*, 'telephone,' nowadays usually written as *tien-hua*, meaning 'electricity talks'. The great attachment of the Chinese for their logographic writing shows itself in the spelling of foreign names in which the individual signs stand not only for the respective syllabic values, but are frequently so chosen as to convey a meaning either inherent in the name borne by the person or otherwise thought to be characteristic of him. Thus, the name 'Stuart' can be written *Ssu-t'u* by means of two phonetic signs which at the same time stand for a Chinese word for an official corresponding to the English 'steward'. Similarly, the name 'Woodbridge' can be written *Wu-pan-chiao*, in which *Wu* stands for the surname, while *pan-chiao* means actually 'wood-bridge'. Here, too, I should like to quote the Chinese name which a Chinese scholar, in a jocular mood, gave to me: it is *Kê-er-po*, in which *Kê* stands for the surname and *er-po* means something like 'refined, learned'. [28]

As far back as the fifth or sixth century of our era cases of syllabic writing based upon the so-called *'fan-ch'ieh* principle' appear for the first time in Chinese. This principle, originally employed only sporadically to help in the reading of rare and difficult word signs, was developed at the beginning of the twentieth century into a full system which for a while enjoyed a certain amount of success in the province of Hopei and to some extent also in Shantung. [29] The syllabary (Fig. 44) consists of sixty-two signs, divided into fifty initial and twelve final signs. The simple signs *p'u*, *pu*, *mu*, etc., are used naturally for the corresponding syllables *pu*, *bu*, *mu*, etc., but when the need arises to express a syllable which has no corresponding sign in the syllabary the *fan-ch'ieh* principle is employed. Such a syllable is written by two signs existing in the syllabary, one

(a) 50 Initial Signs

才	卜	才	夫	五	叉	ㄨ	十	土	厂
樸	卜	木	夫	五	皮	必	米	土	癨
p'u	*pu*	*mu*	*fu*	*wu*	*p'i*	*pi*	*mi*	*t'u*	*ts'u*

刀	夕	中	二	才	才	入	七	又	干
初	蘇	書	粗	都	朱	入	盧	奴	辞
ch'u	*su*	*shu*	*tsu*	*tu*	*chu*	*ju*	*lu*	*nu*	*ts'e*

了	幺	忄	牛	川	幺	寸	日	乙	匕
姿	絲	德	特	遲	之	詩	日	低	題
tse	*sse*	*tê*	*t'ê*	*ch'ih*	*chih*	*shih*	*jih*	*ti*	*ti*

ㄌ	亻	匕	女	口	屮	尸	勹	干	厶
勒	訥	尼	女	呂	趨	居	須	于	離
lê	*na*	*ni*	*nü*	*lü*	*ch'ü*	*chü*	*hsü*	*yü*	*li*

上	卄	ㄨ	く	才	刂	厂	弋	丩	才
基	其	希	衣	孤	剖	乎	戈	科	禾
chi	*ch'i*	*hsi*	*yi*	*ku*	*k'u*	*'hu*	*ko*	*k'o*	*ho*

(b) 12 Final Signs

了	)	一	乙	一	㇏
阿	敖	安(先)	亢	哀	爺
a	*ao*	*an (en)*	*ang*	*ai*	*eh*

刁	丨	ㄥ	刁	㇏	儿
危(灰)	樞(幽)	恩(金)	翁(東)	我	兒
ei (ui)	*ou (u)*	*ên (in)*	*êng (ung)*	*o*	*erh*

FIG. 44.—CHINESE FAN-CH'IEH SYLLABARY

From A. Forke in *Mitteilungen des Seminars für Orientalische Sprachen*, vol. ix, Abt. 1 (1906), p. 404

initial and the other final. Thus, the syllable *ming* is written with the signs *mi-eng*, *yu* with *yi-u*, *chiao* with *chi-ao*, etc. The syllabic signs, as can be seen from Figure 44, represent clearly simplified forms of the standard Chinese writing.[30]

PROTO-ELAMITE, PROTO-INDIC, AND CRETAN SYSTEMS

The common feature of the three systems is that they are all still undeciphered or only partially deciphered. Because of it we must limit our discussion to straight facts and try to avoid speculations in connection with the inner characteristics of the systems.

The Proto-Elamite writing first appears at Susa, the capital of ancient Elam, and it can be dated roughly to the so-called 'Jemdet Nasr period' after 3000 B.C.

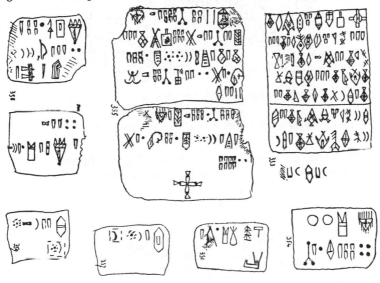

FIG. 45.—EARLIEST TYPE OF PROTO-ELAMITE WRITING

From V. Scheil, *Mémoires de la Mission Archéologique de Perse*, tome xxvi (Paris, 1935), pl. xl

The earliest type of writing occurs on several hundred clay tablets, evidently of an economic nature (Fig. 45). Not even one of the several hundred signs of this writing can as yet be read safely. The only relatively sure result of the decipherment is the interpretation of some number signs and the determination of the existence of a decimal system. A more developed form of Proto-Elamite writing, also undeciphered, occurs on about a dozen stone inscriptions from the Old Akkadian period dated to about 2200 B.C. Figure 46 gives a portion of a presumably bilingual inscription written in Old Akkadian and Proto-

Elamite.[31] The new type of writing consists of a very limited number of signs—only fifty-five have been discovered up to now—differing greatly in form from those of the previous period.

FIG. 46.—PROTO-ELAMITE INSCRIPTION OF OLD AKKADIAN PERIOD

From V. Scheil, *Délégation en Perse, Mémoires*, tome vi (Paris, 1905), pl. 2, No. 1

Seals with peculiar signs, which have aroused intense interest throughout the world, have been found sporadically during the past fifty years at various sites in the Indus Valley. It was not until 1924, however, when the Archaeological Department of

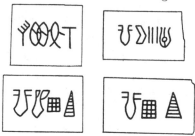

FIG. 47.—PROTO-INDIC WRITING

From John Marshall, *Mohenjo-Daro and the Indus Civilization*, iii (London, 1931), pls. cxvii f.

the Government of India undertook the first systematic excavation of the ancient sites to-day called Harappa and Mohenjodaro, that a considerable number of texts were discovered. In the following years more inscriptional material of the same nature was uncovered at Chanhudaro. At these sites cultures of great antiquity were unearthed, about which, strangely enough, Indic tradition tells us nothing. The still undeciphered writing consists of about 250 signs found on short seal inscriptions, pottery, and copper tablets (Fig. 47).[32] The dating of this Proto-Indic writing is established by comparative

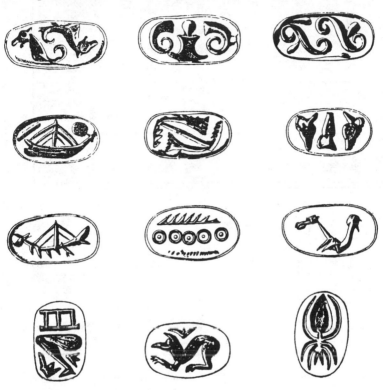

FIG. 48.—CRETAN HIEROGLYPHIC A WRITING
From A. J. Evans, *Scripta Minoa*, i (Oxford, 1909), p. 149

stratigraphy with the help of Mesopotamian finds. The writing made its appearance in the second half of the third millennium B.C. and, after a short-lived duration of a few centuries, it disappeared as suddenly as it had appeared.

The origin and development of the Cretan writing are best illustrated by the epigraphic finds made some sixty years ago by Sir Arthur Evans at Knossos, in Crete.[33] Other sites in Crete

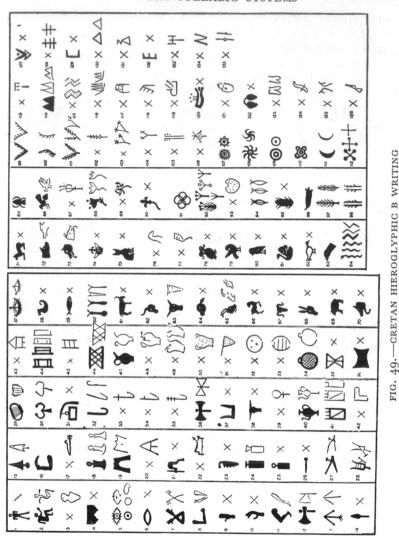

FIG. 49.—CRETAN HIEROGLYPHIC B WRITING
From Evans, *The Palace of Minos*, i (London, 1921), p. 282

(Mallia, Hagia Triada, etc.), in Greece (Mycenae, Orcho-
menos, Pylos, Thebes, Tiryns, etc.), and in the Aegean islands,
have yielded epigraphic material which is of great help in
filling the gaps in our knowledge as reconstructed from the
Knossos material. Although the Cretan writing is still only
partially deciphered, we can follow rather well its main line

No.	Ref	Value	B-ref	No.	Ref	Value	B-ref	No.	Ref	Value	B-ref
1	(L 30)	da	[B 1]	28	(L 78)	ti	[B 37]	55	(L 91)	qe	[B 78]
2	(L 22)	ro	[B 2]	29	(L 44)	e?	[B 38]	56	(L 101)	zu	[B 79]**
3	(L 2)	pa	[B 3]	30	(L 56)	pi	[B 39]	57	(L 95)	ma	[B 80]
4	(L 92)	te	[B 4]	31	(L 28)	wi	[B 40]	58	(L 98)	ku	[B 81]
5	(L 39)	to	[B 5]	32	(L 102)	de	[B 45]	59	(L 66)		[B 87?]
6	(L 26)	na	[B 6]	33	(L 81)	je??	[B 46]	60	(L 72 e 94 b)***		
7	(L 51)	di	[B 7]	34	(L 64)	pu	[B 50]	61	(L 83)		
8	(L 52)	a	[B 8]	35	(L 93 e L 24)	du	[B 51]	62	(L 50)		
9	(L 77)	se	[B 9]	36	(L 100)	no	[B 52]	63	(L 61)		
10	(L 97)	u	[B 10]	37	(L 75)	wa	[B 54]	64	(L 79)		
11	(L 21)	po	[B 11]	38	(L 25)	já?? nu??	[B 55?]	65	(L 88)		
12	(L 7)	so?	[B 12]	39	(L 1)	pà?	[B 56]	66	(L 63)		
13	(L 84)	me?	[B 13]	40	(L 32)	ja	[B 57]	67	(L 82)	wá??	
14	(L 17)	do?	[B 14]	41	(L 59)	su	[B 58]	68	(L 65)		
15	(L 62)	pá (ba)	[B 16]	42	(L 74)	ta	[B 59]	69	(L 36)		
16	(L 23)	za	[B 17]	43	(L 53)	ra	[B 60]	70	(L 37)		
17	(L 10)	zo?	[B 20]	44	(L 87)	o	[B 61]	71	(L 73)		
18	(L 67)		[B 22?]	45	(L 96 e L 68)		[B 65?]	72	(L 85)		
19	(L 27 e L 38)	mu?	[B 23]	46	(L 86)	tá	[B 66]	73	(L 49)		
20	(L 57)	ne?	[B 24]	47	(L 103)	ki	[B 67]	74	(L 43)		
21	(L 55)	ru	[B 26]	48	(L 6)	tu	[B 69]	75	(L 71)		
22	(L 54)	re	[B 27]	49	(L 45)	ko	[B 70]	76	(L 41)		
23	(L 34)	pú?	[B 29]	50	(L 90)	pe?	[B 72]	77	(L 9)		
24	(L 60)	ni	[B 30]	51	(L 76)	mi	[B 73]	78	(L 68 b)		
25	(L 31)	sa?	[B 31]	52	(L 94)	we	[B 75]	79	(L 33)		
26	(L 12)	qo?	[B 32]	53	(L 58)	rá	[B 76]	80	(L 14)		
27	(L 69)	di	[B 34]	54	(L 29)	ka	[B 77]				

FIG. 50.—CRETAN LINEAR A WRITING
From G. Pugliese Carratelli in *Annuario della Scuola Archeologica di Atene*, xiv–xvi (1952–54), 21

of development. Seals with representations of objects and living beings make their appearance in the very earliest stages of the Early Minoan period. Gradually at the beginning of Middle Minoan I (about 2000–1900 B.C.) the first pictorial form of writing begins to appear. This is what Evans calls 'Class A' of the hieroglyphic writing (Fig. 48), which in Middle Minoan II

93

	KN	PY	MY			KN	PY	MY			KN	PY	MY	
1				da	31				sa	61				o
2				ro	32				qo	62				pte
3				pa	33				ra³	63				
4				te	34				ai²	64				
5				to	35				"	65				
6				na	36				jo	66				ta²
7				di	37				ti	67				ki
8				a	38				e	68				ro²
9				se	39				pi	69				tu
10				u	40				wi	70				ko
11				po	41				si	71				
12				so	42				wo	72				pe
13				me	43				ai	73				mi
14				do	44				ke	74				ze
15				mo	45				de	75				we
16				pa²	46				je	76				ra²
17				za	47					77				ka
18					48				nwa	78				qe
19					49					79				
20				zo	50				pu	80				ma
21				qi	51				da	81				ku
22					52				no	82				
23				mu	53				ri	83				
24				ne	54				wa	84				
25				a²	55				nu	85				
26				ru	56					86				
27				re	57				ja	87				
28				i	58				su	88				
29				pu²	59				ta	89				
30				ni	60				ra					

FIG. 51.—CRETAN LINEAR B WRITING

From Emmett L. Bennett, Jr., *The Pylos Tablets* (Princeton, 1955), p. 201

(about 1900–1700 B.C.) is succeeded by 'Class B' of the hieroglyphic writing (Fig. 49). The progress of economic life contributed to the further development of Cretan writing. In
Middle Minoan III (about 1700–1550 B.C.) there appear a
cursive 'Linear A' writing (Fig. 50), which is used up to about
1450 B.C., and a cursive 'Linear B' writing (Fig. 51), which is

94

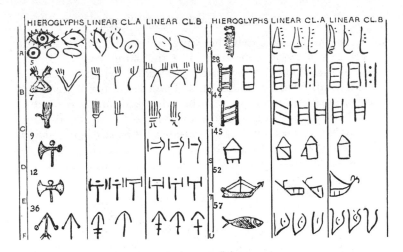

FIG. 52.—DEVELOPMENT OF SOME CRETAN HIEROGLYPHIC SIGNS
INTO LINEAR FORMS

From Evans, *The Palace of Minos*, i, p. 643

used up to about 1200 B.C. The development of some hieroglyphic signs into linear forms is illustrated in Figure 52. A
typical inscription in Linear B writing is shown in Figure 53.
The recent publication of extensive materials in Linear B writing has led to their successful decipherment by a young English architect, Michael Ventris. The decipherment is based on
a set of postulates which can be summed up as follows: The
tablets are inventories, accounts, or receipts. The writing contains an indeterminate number of 'ideograms' (really logograms, which normally serve the function of determinatives-
classifiers), which can be interpreted from their pictorial
representation or from the way in which they are grouped and
differentiated. From the fact that the writing contains about
eighty-eight different 'phonetic' signs it can be assumed that it
represents a syllabary of the Cypriote and hieroglyphic Hittite
type, in which each sign expresses a vowel or a consonant plus
a vowel. The frequency count yielded a number of very frequent signs which Ventris (following Kober and Ktistopoulos)
assumed represented vowels. By observing variation in the
final syllabic signs of a sign group representing words, he
reached the conclusion that the writing expressed inflection
of the type shown in Latin bo-*ni*, bo-*no*, bo-*nae*, etc. This assumption enabled Ventris to draw a tentative grid with rows

95

of signs containing either the same consonant and a varying vowel or a varying consonant and the same vowel. On the basis of these postulates Ventris proceeded experimentally to assign syllabic values to the signs. The road was not easy, and several attempts made in this direction ultimately proved to be wrong. But a happy strike in the interpretation of some geographic names, such as *A-mi-ni-so, A-mi-ni-si-io, A-mi-ni-si-ia* (corresponding to the Greek 'Aμνισό-, 'Aμνισίο-, 'Aμνισία-) and *Ko-no-so, Ko-no-si-io, Ko-no-si-ia* (corresponding to Κνωσό-,

FIG. 53.—LINEAR B INSCRIPTION FROM KNOSSOS

From Evans, *The Palace of Minos*, iv, p. 703

Κνωσίο-, Κνωσία-) provided him with the reading of a number of signs; while the inflectional endings occurring in these and other names led him to the conclusion that the underlying language was Greek.[34]

While, typologically speaking, the Linear B syllabary belongs together with Cypriote and hieroglyphic Hittite, the following divergent characteristics of Linear B should be noted: non-expression of *i* in the diphthongs *ai*, etc., while *u* in the diphthongs *au*, etc., is expressed; non-expression of syllable-final *m, n, l, r,* and *s;* existence of the row of signs for the voiced *d,* while those for *g* and *b* are missing.

The decipherment of Linear B writing raises hopes for the success of the decipherment of other types of Cretan writing, especially Linear A. This writing consists of about eighty syllabic signs, of which roughly one-half correspond formally to the signs of Linear B, plus a limited number of logograms. It may almost certainly be assumed that Linear A expresses a non-Greek language. For other related writings, see pages 153 ff.[35]

SIGNS IN GENERAL

The great majority of signs in the Sumerian, Egyptian, Hittite, and Chinese systems of writing are simple pictures of objects found in the surrounding world. But the creators of the signaries rarely drew the signs as an artist would draw them. The original object of writing is the creation of symbols which stand for words of the language and is achieved through economizing measures resulting in the omission of all details which are not necessary for the understanding of the symbol. An artist would not draw water, a mountain, or a house in the form in which we find them in writing, just as he would rarely allow himself to draw heads for full figures, following the *pars pro toto* convention so frequently utilized in the Sumerian and Hittite writings (Fig. 54).

A limited number of signs did not grow out of imitation of real objects but out of gradually evolved arbitrary conventions. Such are certain geometrical forms, such as strokes, circles, and half-circles for numbers and other abstract expressions, and in more modern times the symbols used in mathematics, such as the plus, minus, or root signs.

All four systems of writing in time developed cursive, linear forms which became so abbreviated and changed through frequent use in daily life that in the great majority of cases it is impossible to recognize in them the underlying pictures. But while the Sumerian and Chinese cursive systems succeeded in changing even their monumental forms into non-pictorial writings, the Egyptian and Hittite monumental systems retained their pictorial character to the very end.[36]

When, after an initial period of organization, a system of writing becomes stabilized (see p. 115 ff.), the number of signs is closed and new signs are normally created only through formal changes and differentiations or through new combinations of existing signs. Instructive in this respect is the sign for

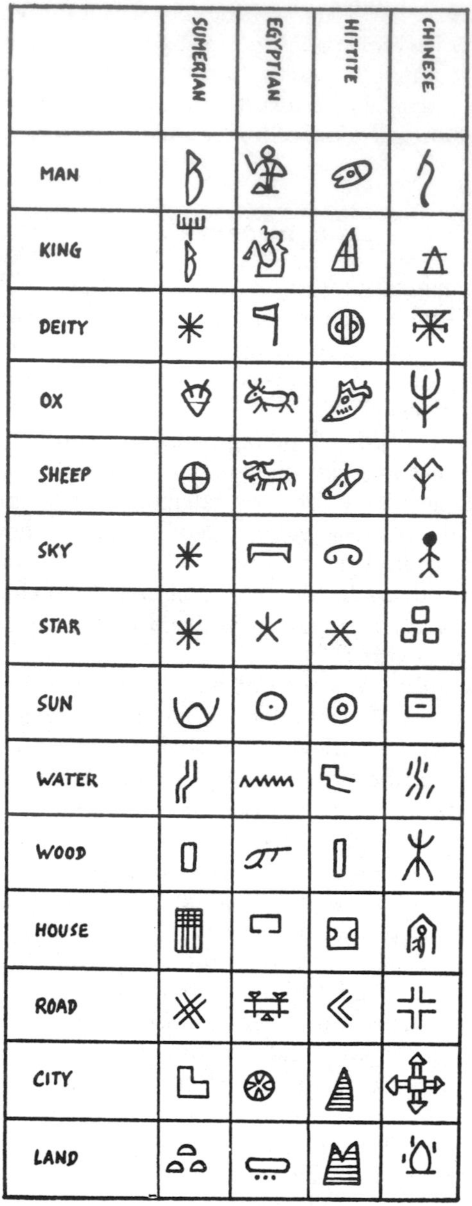

	SUMERIAN	EGYPTIAN	HITTITE	CHINESE
MAN				
KING				
DEITY				
OX				
SHEEP				
SKY				
STAR				
SUN				
WATER				
WOOD				
HOUSE				
ROAD				
CITY				
LAND				

FIG. 54.—PICTORIAL SIGNS IN THE SUMERIAN, EGYPTIAN, HITTITE, AND CHINESE WRITINGS

camel ANŠE.A.AB.BA, literally 'donkey of the sea', introduced in the cuneiform system after the camel had become known to the Mesopotamians, and the sign for telephone TIEN.HUA, literally electricity talks', introduced in recent times in the Chinese writing.

The fully developed systems of the four writings discussed above are characterized by three classes of signs:—

(1) Logograms, that is, signs for words of the language.

(2) Syllabic signs, developed by the rebus principle from logograms.

(3) Auxiliary marks, such as punctuation marks and, in some writings, classifiers, determinatives, or semantic indicators.

WORD SIGNS

Logograms, or signs for words, are created by means of various devices. We can distinguish six different classes (Fig. 55) which partially agree with the traditional classification of word signs in Chinese.[37] It is impossible to divide the signs rigorously within the classes because some signs may belong to different classes or they may be formed by means of more than one device.

The first three classes include word signs created by means of devices so simple and natural that they are found also among all the primitive forerunners of writing.

In the primary device concrete objects and actions are represented by pictures of objects or of a combination of objects.

The second, the associative class, includes signs which express words connected with the original drawing by association of meanings. Thus, while a picture of the sun expresses first directly the word 'sun', it can also have the secondary meaning of 'bright' or 'day'. Similarly, to the Sumerians living in the lowlands of South Mesopotamia, the sign for mountain could stand for 'foreign country', because almost all foreign countries were situated in the highlands from the point of view of the Sumerians.

The third class, called 'diagrammatic', contains signs which do not go back to original pictures, but are freely created from various geometric forms (p. 97). As stated above, the signs for numbers are usually derived from geometric forms—if not

	Sumerian	Egyptian	Hittite	Chinese
1. Primary	SUN 'sun', STAR 'star', MOUNTAIN 'mountain', MAN+BREAD 'to eat'	SUN 'sun', STAR 'star', MAN+BOWL 'to drink'	SUN 'sun', HEAD 'head', AX 'ax', MAN+BREAD 'to eat'	SUN 'sun', TOWER 'tower', SKY+DROPS 'rain'
2. Associative	SUN 'white; day', STAR 'deity', MOUNTAIN 'foreign country', MALE.MOUNTAIN 'male slave'	SUN 'day', STAR 'hour', COW LOOKING BACK AT CALF 'to rejoice'	HEAD 'chief', AX 'to cut', MAN.MAN 'to agree' or the like	SUN 'day', TOWER 'high', SUN.MOON 'bright', WOMAN.CHILD 'love, good', WOMAN.BROOM 'wife', WOMAN.WOMAN 'quarrel', WOMAN.WOMAN.WOMAN 'falsehood'
3. Diagrammatic	SEMICIRCLE 'one', CIRCLE 'ten', CIRCLE 'totality; all', HORIZONTAL LINE.HORIZONTAL LINE 'to add', GREEK CROSS 'to break'	VERTICAL LINE 'one', ST. ANDREW'S CROSS 'to break', VERTICAL LINE.SEMICIRCLE 'to cut off', CIRCLE 'to go round'	VERTICAL LINE 'one', HORIZONTAL LINE 'ten', VERTICAL LINE.SEMICIRCLE 'to return'	HORIZONTAL LINE 'one', LATIN CROSS 'ten', VERTICAL LINE.HORIZONTAL LINE 'up', HORIZONTAL LINE.VERTICAL LINE 'down', SEMICIRCLE.SEMICIRCLE 'to divide'

4. Semantic indicator	CITY.*Aššur* '(city) Aššur' and DEITY.*Aššur* '(deity) Aššur' WOOD.PLOW 'plow' and MAN.PLOW 'plowman'	LORD.MAN '(human) lord' and LORD.-DEITY '(divine) lord' $d^ūm^ᵃʔᵢ$.TOWN 'town' and $d^ūm^ᵃʔᵢ$.HAND 'to reach'	DEITY.PIGEON '(deity) Kupapaš' BEEHIVE.CITY '(city) Malatya?'	SQUARE.WOOD 'board' and SQUARE.EARTH 'district' (both *fang*) THUMB.WOOD 'village' compared with THUMB 'thumb' (both *ts'ung*)
5. Phonetic transfer	ARROW 'arrow; life' (*ti*) ONION 'onion; to give' (*šum*)	DUCK 'duck; son' ($s^{aⁱaⁱ}$) BASKET 'basket' ($n^ūb^ᵃʔᵃ$); 'lord' ($n^ūb^ᵃⁱ$)	SEAT 'seat; to complete?' (*asa-*)	WHEAT 'wheat; to come' (*lai*) SCORPION 'scorpion; ten thousand' (*wan*)
6. Phonetic indicator	CROWN.*en* 'crown' (*men*) EAR.*giš.tuk* 'wise; wisdom' (*geštuk*)	$s^ᵃ$.MAN 'man' ($s^ᵃ$) $n^ū$.BASKET.$b^ᵃʔᵃ$ 'basket' ($n^ūb^ᵃⁱᵃ$) $r^ūč̣ᵃ$.MAN 'person' ($r^ūm^ᵃč̣ᵃ$)	LORD.*ni-s*(*a*) or LORD.*na-ni-s*(*a*) 'lord' (*nanis*)	EYE.*ku* 'blind' (*ku*) HAND.*kung* 'to carry' (*kang*) WATER.*kung* 'river' (*kiang*)

FIG. 55.—TYPES OF WORD SIGNS IN WORD-SYLLABIC WRITINGS

created by the process of phonetic transfer (see later). For that reason the explanation of the Egyptian signs for fractions used in measuring grain (see Fig. 56) as derived from an ancient myth, according to which the eye of the falcon-god Horus was

torn into fragments by the wicked god Seth, cannot possibly hold water.[38] It is not that the fragments of the eye of Horus led to the creation of the signs for fractions, but rather that these signs, originally presumably geometric, may have been arranged secondarily by some ingenious scribe in such a way as to form the sacred eye.[39] Some signs geometric in form may owe their origin to imitation of signs in gesture language, as the written sign for 'all' drawn in the form of a circle may well go back to a gesture sign made by a circular motion of the hand.[40]

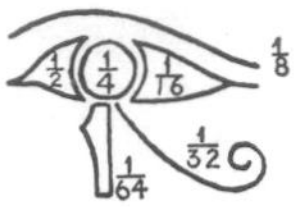

FIG. 56.—SIGNS FOR FRACTIONS IN EGYPTIAN

From A. H. Gardiner, *Egyptian Grammar* (Oxford, 1927), p. 197

These three simple devices for creating word signs may have been capable of taking care of the modest requirements of primitive systems but they certainly were not sufficient in systems which required the expression of more exact nuances of language. The full systems of writing, searching for new ways to express words by signs, evolved three new devices achieved by the use of (1) semantic but non-phonetic elements, (2) phonetic transfer, and (3) phonetic but non-semantic elements.

The first of these new devices, the fourth in our Figure 55, is achieved by means of semantic indicators, that is, semantic and non-phonetic elements, frequently called 'determinatives' in the case of ancient Oriental writings, which are attached to the basic signs to determine their exact reading. Thus, in cuneiform, while the writing *Aššur* can stand for both the city Aššur and the god Aššur, an unpronounced determinative in the form of the city sign may be added when the city Aššur is involved, and the deity sign when the god Aššur is intended. In the course of time these determinatives were attached to any word of a certain class, without respect to whether this word had one meaning or more or whether it was written logographically or syllabically. For example, in Mesopotamian cuneiform the name of the deity Ištar is written either logographically as *deity Ištar*, where the divine determinative is added to help in interpreting the word sign as the name of a deity, or syllabically as *deity*$Iš$-*tar*, which can, of course, be read only as *Iš-tar* and interpreted only as the name of the well known Mesopotamian goddess. In the three Near Eastern writings— namely, Mesopotamian, Egyptian, and Hittite—the semantic indicators or determinatives, which originally were used only in the case of signs with more than one possible meaning, developed in time into classifiers, that is, signs which marked the word to which they were attached as belonging to a certain class or category. In the three Near Eastern systems each class of words for persons, deities, animals, metals, stones, plants, cities, lands, mountains, rivers, etc., is marked by a different classifying determinative. Only Chinese, because of its aversion to expressing a word by means of a sign composed of more than two elements, has retained the old character of the determinatives and has never developed real classifiers.

In the three Near Eastern writings the semantic indicators developed in the course of time another characteristic which set them farther away from their original function. These signs, originated as semantic helps to the interpretation of word signs, developed in time into unpronounced auxiliary marks whose function was to facilitate in general the interpretation of the text. In fact, from the regularity of the appearance of the determinatives in Egyptian, some scholars have drawn the conclusion that these determinatives effect the practical function of dividing sentences into their component words, [41] that is, they serve as word separators. [42] There is no doubt that also in the Mesopotamian and Hittite writings the existence of determinatives helps greatly in the breaking-up of the sentence into individual words and thus facilitates the general interpretation of the text. This is of great importance especially in writings which do not regularly indicate word separation either by special marks or spacing.

The four devices discussed up to now have wide possibilities for creating signs for words but even they are not sufficient to achieve a full system of writing. Logographic writing thus limited can never hope to be able to express all the existing words of a language, let alone all the proper names and newly introduced words. The failure of the writings introduced among American Indians in modern times either directly by missionaries or under their influence (see pp. 206 ff.) is the best evidence of the inadequacy of such limited logographic systems. It was the invention of the phonetic principle that was instrumental in opening new horizons in the history of writing.

With the introduction of phonetization a new device was created by means of phonetic transfer, called 'rebus' in modern times, involved in expressing word signs which are difficult to draw by signs which are easy to draw and express words which are identical or similar in sound. Thus, the Sumerian word *ti*, 'life,' which is hard to draw in a sign, can be expressed through this device by the ARROW sign, which stands for *ti*, 'arrow,' in Sumerian.

Finally, the last device consists of adding a phonetic but non-semantic element to a sign as a help in its exact reading. Thus, in Chinese, while the sign HAND could theoretically stand for the words 'hand, to handle, to reach, to carry', etc., in order to express the word *kang*, 'to carry,' the syllable *kung* is added to the HAND sign to indicate that it is to be read *kang*. These phonetic indicators are called 'phonetic complements' in the Near Eastern writings. While they are not absolutely necessary in the writing of a word, in the fully developed systems it is indeed seldom that a word sign is found without its phonetic complements. Phonetic complements can precede or follow the word sign, although specific conventions and predilections are at work in the various systems. While in Egyptian the phonetic complements can be built around the word sign, in Mesopotamian and Hittite they usually follow it. Also, in respect to the length of the phonetic complements, various conventions can be observed. While in Egyptian and Hittite the phonetic complements can repeat the word sign fully, in the Mesopotamian system partial phonetic complements are definitely in the majority. In Chinese the situation is slightly different. There a phonetic complement or indicator, once added to a word sign, remains with it always to form one word sign composed of two elements. The great majority of Chinese word signs belong to this class. The creation of many signs in this class was facilitated by the preponderantly mono-syllabic character of the Chinese language and the resulting shortness of phonetic indicators. The phenomenon is not entirely unique in the history of writing. Also in Sumerian we find a few signs which regularly appear composed of the basic and phonetic elements, as in the case of the sign represented by an animal head which, when the syllabogram *za* is added, is read *aza*, 'bear,' but with *ug₅* expresses the word *ug*, 'lion'.

The so-called 'phonetic complements' started as phonetic indicators which were attached to a basic sign to facilitate its reading, as in the writing of *gul^{ul}* or *gul-ul* for *gul* in Sumerian and *ṭâb^{ab}* or *ṭâb-ab* for *ṭâb* in Akkadian. From this secondary position phonetic complements rose to a position of equal standing with the signs to which they were attached, resulting finally in reducing the basic signs to shorter values, such as *gu(l)* or *gu* and *ṭa(b)* or *ṭa* respectively. This is the principle of reduction discussed elsewhere on pp. 71 and 182 f. In Egyptian the attachment of full phonetic complements to logograms changed in the course of time the value of these basic logograms to that of semantic determinatives. This is what the Egyptologists call 'specific determinatives', as in the case of *^{ẜ}s^{ẜ}ḫ^{ẜ}* REAP, where the determinative REAP occurs only in the word '(to) reap', in contrast to generic determinatives, such as GO, which occur with all sorts of words expressing movement.

Only in borrowed systems of writing do we find a class of signs which are not based on any of the six classes discussed above. This class of signs, which I call 'allograms', includes logographic, syllabic, or alphabetic signs or spellings of one writing when used as word signs or even phrase signs in a borrowed writing. Thus, for example, the Sumerian sign *lugal*, 'king', stands for Akkadian *šarrum*, 'king'; similarly, the Sumerian spellings *in-lá-e*, 'he will weigh out' *in-lá-e-ne*, 'they will weigh out,' were accepted as standing for *išaqqal, išaqqalū*, 'he/they will weigh out,' respectively, in the Akkadian writing, just as the Sumerian *igi-lú-inim-inim-ma* was taken to stand for Akkadian *ina maḫar šíbī*, 'before witnesses.' There are hundreds of examples of this type of word and phrase signs, which may very well be called Sumerograms[43] whenever they stand for Sumerian writings. Similarly, Akkadian spellings are used regularly for the same purpose in the cuneiform Hittite system of writing. Among hundreds of examples we may quote Akkadian *id-din* standing for Hittite *pešta*, 'he gave,' Akkadian *a-na a-bi-ia* for Hittite *atti-mi*, 'to my father,' etc. A mixed type is represented by the spelling *dingir-lum*, where the Sumerian *dingir*, 'god,' plus the phonetic indicator *-lum* corresponds to Akkadian *ilum*, 'god', and the whole stands for the Hittite word *šiwanniš* with the same meaning. These so-called Sumerograms and Akkadograms find their parallel in a much later period in the use of Aramaeograms in the Persian Pehlevi writing, where, for instance, the Aramaic spelling *malkā*, 'king,' stands for Persian *šāh*, 'king.' In still later usage we find a similar type of writing in our interpretation of 'etc.' as 'and so on, and so forth', or the like. Another good parallel is the spelling 'god' in Latin characters for the word *agaiyun* with the same meaning in one of the writings introduced recently among the Alaska Eskimos. [44]

The meaning can sometimes be indicated not only by word signs formed through different devices, but also through the so-called 'principle of position' and 'principle of context of situation' which were discussed fully elsewhere (see p. 19 f.).

It is evident from this short discussion of the various classes of word signs that one sign can and actually does express many different words. One sign can stand not only for a group of words all related in meaning but also, with the emergence of phonetization, for words similar in sound but with no relation in meaning. This is pure and simple logography. In contrast to semasiography, in which such a sign as SUN conveys the meaning of 'sun' and of all of its related ideas, such as 'bright, light, clear, shining, pure, white, day,' or even 'the sun is shining, the day has come,' etc., in logography the sign has only as many meanings as there are words which are habitually and conventionally associated with it. Thus, in Sumerian, the SUN sign expresses at least seven words, all related to the basic meaning of 'sun', but in Chinese the SUN sign alone stands only for the words 'sun' and 'day', while the word *ch'ing*, 'pure, clear', is expressed by a combination of the sign for 'sun' with the sign for 'colour'; the word *ming*, 'bright, shining,' by that of 'sun' and 'moon'; and the word for 'white' by a sign of unknown interpretation evidently having no connection with the sun. Similarly, in Egyptian, the words for 'sun, day, white, light' are expressed by the picture of the sun, but the word *t͟ḫ͟n͟*, 'shining,' is written by a sign different from that for the sun. [45] There are no logographic systems in which a sign can stand for a certain idea with all of its related ramifications, just as there are practically no cases in these systems of signs which when written down are not intended to express words or when read or interpreted do not correspond to words of language. Almost all such cases, claimed by a majority of philologists to be 'ideography' (see pp. 13 f.), turn out upon investigation to be false. When a writer intends to express a word by means of a word sign which can stand for many words he will usually try through all the means available to him to make sure that the reader will read in this sign only the intended word. Addition to the basic word sign of semantic and phonetic indicators, use of the principle of position and context of situation are all devices leading to the achievement of this aim.

In connection with the controversy 'ideography versus logography' which is now raging in philological-linguistic circles (see pp. 13 f.), it may be worth while to note the following: All the Sumerian and Akkadian grammars use the term 'ideography', with Falkenstein, Friedrich (see p. 65), and Poebel (orally) forming a small but notable group of objectors to that term. The Egyptologists, as one man, favour 'ideography'.[46] In the Hittite field I myself used 'ideogram',[47] but later gave it up in favour of 'logogram'.[48] In the field of Chinese it is interesting to note that as far back as 1838 the ingenious Franco-American scholar Du Ponceau defined Chinese writing as 'logographic' or 'lexigraphic', and not 'ideographic'.[49] H. G. Creel's use of 'ideography'[50] was criticized by Peter A. Boodberg.[51]

SYLLABIC SIGNS

Although with the introduction of phonetization all sounds of language can be expressed in writing, the rebus way of writing is inadequate in practical use. Systems which would allow the expression of the word 'mandate' either by pictures of a man plus a palm date, or by those of a man plus a palm tree, or even by pictures of a man plus a boy-and-girl combination, may be considered quite right in our modern rebus compositions with their elements of mental gymnastics, but they are clearly not adequate in a practical system of writing, where speed and accuracy in reading are most essential. For that reason the convention soon had to be established to write identical syllables of various words with identical signs. Thus, a single sign would be chosen from among many possibilities to stand for the syllable *man*, no matter whether it occurred in the words 'man, mankind, mandate, woman,' etc., just as one sign would be chosen for the syllable *date*, no matter whether it occurred in the words 'date, mandate, candidate', etc. To be sure, each of these words could still be expressed by a word sign, if such existed in the system, but syllabically these words could be written only with signs taken from a conventionally used syllabary.

There are no such things as 'standard' Sumerian, Egyptian, Hittite, or Chinese syllabaries. What we actually have are various Sumerian, Egyptian, Hittite, and Chinese syllabaries, all limited to certain periods and areas. Thus, in Sumerian, out of some twenty-two different signs all read as *du* but each corresponding to a different word of the language, at one time one sign was picked which was conventionally used as the syllable *du* in all cases of non-semantic writing. Syllabic signs thus chosen formed part of a syllabary which may have been limited in its employment to a certain period and to a certain area. In another place and at another time a different sign *du* may have been chosen to stand for this syllable. The inter-mixture of influences may sometimes have provoked the existence of more than one sign for the same syllable. But such occurrences as occur are relatively rare before the latest periods, in which the writing started on its downward course of degeneration (see pp. 202 f.).

This categorical statement will seem fantastic to anyone who is even superficially acquainted with the Mesopotamian sign lists and who remembers the great number of homophonous signs listed in them. The existence of an almost unlimited homophony would, of course, be true for the *whole* Mesopotamian syllabary, but it certainly is not in the case of individual, area and period syllabaries. Anyone who would take the trouble to count the individual signs with syllabic values in one limited area and period—as I actually did in several cases—could easily reach the conclusion that identical syllables normally are expressed by only one sign. As evidence, let the syllabaries of the Old Assyrians and the Old Babylonians speak for themselves. The latter syllabary, taken from the Hammurapi Law Code, is presented here in transliteration in the form of a chart showing only uniconsonantal values (Fig. 57). The multiconsonantal values are, of course, very rarely homophonous. The use of more than one sign for a single sound, as in the case of sibilants, is due to the transitory nature of the

Old Babylonian syllabary of the Hammurapi period. The reader does not have to be reminded that the principle of economy in writing—so frequently invoked in this book—

a	i	e	ú				
ba	bi	be	bu	ab	ib	eb = ib	ub
da	di	de = di	du	ad	id	ed = id	ud
ga	gi	ge = gi?	gu	ag	ig	eg = ig	ug
ḫa	ḫi	ḫe = ḫi	ḫu	aḫ	iḫ = aḫ	eḫ = aḫ	úḫ
ia	ii = ia	ie = ia	iu = ia	—	—	—	—
ka	ki	ke = ki?	ku	ak = ag	ik = ig	ek = eg	uk = ug
la	li	le = li	lu	al	il	el	ul
ma	mi	me	mu	am	im	em = im	um
na	ni	ne	nu	an	in	en	un
pa	pí = bi	pé = bi	pu = bu	ap = ab	ip = ib	ep = eb	up = ub
qá = ga	qí = ki	qé = ke	qú = ku	aq = ag	iq = ig	eq = eg	uq = ug
ra	ri	re = ri	ru	ar	ir	er = ir	ur / úr
sa / sà = za	si / •sí = zi	se = ?	su / sú = zu	ás = áš	is = iz	es = ?	ús = uš
ša	ši	še	šu	aš	iš	eš	uš
ṣa — za	ṣi = zé / ṣí = zi	ṣe = zé	ṣú = zu	aṣ = az	iṣ = iz	eṣ = ez	uṣ = uz
ṭa	ṭi	ṭe	ṭu	aṭ — aḏ	iṭ — id	eṭ = ed	uṭ — ud
ṭa = da	ṭi = di / ṭì = ti	ṭe₄ = te	ṭú = tu	aṭ = ad	iṭ = id	eṭ = ed	uṭ = ud
wa	wi = wa	we = wa	wu = wa	—	—	—	—
za	zi	zé	zu	az	iz	ez = iz	uz

FIG. 57.—UNICONSONANTAL SIGNS OF THE OLD BABYLONIAN SYLLABARY

speaks unequivocally against the existence of uncontrolled homophony of signs.

What is true of the Mesopotamian syllabaries is also true of the other Oriental systems. The classical hieroglyphic Hittite syllabary, for instance, used in Syria around 800 B.C., lacks entirely a number of sign values which occur in the earlier inscriptions from Anatolia. The compactness of the Egyptian state prevented such great differentiation, but in Egypt, too, we find syllabaries limited in use to certain periods and areas. It is even more difficult to speak of a standard Chinese syllabary.

As a matter of fact, it is not only impossible to speak about 'standard' syllabaries in the logo-syllabic writings, but even an unqualified statement about the various period and area syllabaries is open to question. The people who used logo-syllabic writings certainly did not distinguish between the logographic and syllabic signs in the manner we do. What they knew about their writing was that all signs stood originally for words of their language and that under certain conditions some of these signs could also be used as syllables. That the users of logo-syllabic writings seemingly did not bother to compile special lists of syllabic signs does not mean, however, that in actual practice they did not distinguish carefully between word signs used logographically only and those used both logographically and syllabically. For that reason the negligence which modern philologists have been showing in not distinguishing clearly between logographic and syllabic uses is inexcusable. Only in the field of hieroglyphic Hittite lists of syllabic values have been compiled from the earliest stages of decipherment.[52] In the field of cuneiform there are now several lists of syllabic values used in Akkadian, but there is as yet no such list for Sumerian.[53] The confusion is quite evident in Egyptian manuals[54] which list under 'phonograms' (as contrasted with 'ideograms') not only the uniconsonantal and biconsonantal signs, which belong there, but also the triconsonantal signs which—with some 'sportive' exceptions—are used in Egyptian logographically only. Even in Chinese some convention must exist as to the choice of word signs for syllabic use if foreign proper names of the type reproduced below on p. 118 can be transliterated into Chinese and read correctly.

Syllabic signs clearly originated from word signs. This is a relatively easy matter in preponderantly monosyllabic languages, like Chinese or Sumerian, where the choice of monosyllabic signs from monosyllabic words is easy. Thus, in Sumerian, the syllable *a* originated from the word sign A for 'water', *ti* from the word sign TI for 'arrow' or 'life', *gal* from the word sign GAL for 'great'. In Egyptian it was relatively simple to create syllabic signs containing two consonants, as in the syllabogram $m^x n^x$ from the word sign $m^x n^x$, 'draughtboard', or $w^x r^x$ from the word sign $w^x r^x$, 'swallow, great.' There were difficulties, however, in creating monosyllabic signs with one consonant, because the language contained very few such monosyllabic words. These difficulties were overcome by choosing monosyllabic words ending in a so-called 'weak' consonant, such as ', y, w, or the feminine ending -t, which could be disregarded in the value of the sign. Thus, the word sign r^{xox}, 'mouth,' acquired the syllabic value r^x, just as the word $n^x t^x$, 'water,' led to the origin of the syllabic sign n^x. In the case of the syllabic signs $\underline{d}^x$ from $\underline{d}^x t^x$, older $*w^{xox}\underline{d}^x i^x t^x$, 'snake,' and perhaps d^x from $*i^x d^x$, 'hand,' we must probably reckon with the omission of an initial w or y, quite frequent in the Semitic languages.

The widely accepted idea that syllabic values originated frequently through the acrophonic principle, whereby the signs acquired the value of the beginning of the whole word, can hardly be true in the case of the Oriental systems of writing. In spite of Sethe's assertion,[55] there is no evidence for acrophony in Sumerian or Mexican writings. The existence of the syllabic sign tu beside the word tud, 'to bear,' does not mean that tu developed by the acrophonic principle from tud, but that the original word tud could, and actually did, acquire by a phonetic process the pronunciation tu, from which the shorter syllabic value tu was derived. Normal Egyptian writing has no traces of acrophony; only in the late period of degeneration have some examples of acrophony been found in the case of the Egyptian enigmatic writings.[56] For the sake of completeness, it should be mentioned that in the Hittite writing, besides such normal cases as the HAND sign, meaning pi-, 'to give,' for the syllable pi or the SEAL sign, meaning $\acute{s}iya$-, 'to seal,' for the syllable $\acute{s}i$ there are some other syllabic signs which are not attested as logograms. An unusual way of creating syllabic signs is shown in the Hittite sign mu, represented by a combination of the u and me signs. Finally, we should refer to pages 141 ff., where the alleged existence of acrophony in the West Semitic syllabary is discussed and rejected.[57]

The standardization of the syllabaries took different roads in the various Oriental writings (Fig. 58). The Sumerian

	Sumerian		Egyptian		Hittite		Chinese	
Open Mono-syllables	a	ta	ꜣ^a	t^a	a	ta	a	ta
	i	ti	ꜣ^i	t^i	i	ti	i	ti
	e	te	ꜣ^e	t^e	e	te	(e)	tê
	u	tu	ꜣ^u	t^u	u	tu	(u)	tu
	—	—	—	—	—	—	o	to
Close Mono-syllables	at	tam (or ta-am)	ꜣ^{a}b$^{(a)}$ (or ꜣ^a-b$^{(a)}$)	t^{a}m$^{(a)}$ (or t^a-m$^{(a)}$)	(a-t(a))	(ta-m(a))	an	man
	it	tim (or ti-im)	ꜣ^{i}b$^{(i)}$ (or ꜣ^i-b$^{(i)}$)	t^{i}m$^{(i)}$ (or t^i-m$^{(i)}$)	(i-t(i))	(ti-m(i))	(ih)	min
	en	men (or me-en)	ꜣ^{e}b$^{(e)}$ (or ꜣ^e-b$^{(e)}$)	t^{e}m$^{(e)}$ (or t^e-m$^{(e)}$)	(e-t(e))	(te-m(e))	ên	men
	ut	tum (or tu-um)	ꜣ^{u}b$^{(u)}$ (or ꜣ^u-b$^{(u)}$)	t^{u}m$^{(u)}$ (or t^u-m$^{(u)}$)	(u-t(u))	(tu-m(u))	(uh)	kun
	—	—	—	—	—	—	(oh)	(foh)
Open Dis-syllables	aka (very rare) (or a-ka)	bala (very rare) (or ba-la)	ꜣ^{x}b^x (or ꜣ^x-b^x)	t^{x}m^x (or t^x-m^x)	—	(a-ta)	— (a-ta)	(ta-ma)

FIG. 58.—TYPES OF SYLLABIC SIGNS IN WORD-SYLLABIC WRITINGS

syllabary and the systems derived from it consist of signs which usually represent monosyllables ending in a vowel or a consonant, more rarely dissyllables. The Egyptian system, like the Mesopotamian, contains signs for both monosyllables and dissyllables, but in contrast to Mesopotamian it does not indicate vowels. The Hittite syllabary is limited to signs for monosyllables ending in a vowel. The Chinese syllabary is similar to the Mesopotamian one, but it expresses only monosyllables ending in a vowel or a consonant. None of the systems contains signs for syllables with two or more contiguous consonants such as *amt*, *tma*, etc. It should be noted that the *ng* combination in such Chinese words as *ming*, *kung*, etc., does not express two contiguous consonants, but a nasal sound *ŋ*. In order to express syllables with contiguous consonants a circumventive way had to be used; thus *amt* can be written as *am-t(a)*, *a-m(a)-t(a)*, or the like, while *tma* can be expressed as *t(a)-ma*, or the like.

AUXILIARY MARKS

In addition to word and syllabic signs a third class of signs, found in all four Oriental systems, consists of the auxiliary marks, or signs, such as punctuation marks, and, in some systems, the determinatives or the classifiers (see pp. 103 f.). Their main characteristic is that in writing or reading these marks have no definite correspondences in speech but are used as helps to make easier the understanding of a sign or a group of signs or of the context in general.[58]

A systematic study of auxiliary marks in the Oriental systems is lacking and as this matter would lead us away from our main line of investigation it seems preferable to omit it entirely from our discussion.

WORD-SYLLABIC WRITING

All four Oriental systems are alike in having preserved throughout their long history a mixture of logographic and syllabic spellings. They differ, however, in some specific characteristics which we may now discuss.[59]

The normal Sumerian writing consists of both word and syllabic signs, but while the former are used chiefly to express nouns and verbs, the latter are more in evidence in the writing of proper names, pronouns, and grammatical formatives. This usage is, however, by no means general. The vernacular *eme-sal* dialect of Sumerian is written almost exclusively with syllabic signs. The emphasis upon the syllabic side is equally in evidence among some cuneiform writings derived from the Sumerian as, for example, in the Old Akkadian and Old Assyrian systems.

Egyptian, too, retained its logo-syllabic character to the very end. As in cuneiform, its usage varied from period to period. For example, the early Egyptian writing of the Pyramid texts shows greater preference for syllabic spellings than most of the later Egyptian writings. Then, again, we have a number of texts from the Saite period in the middle of the first millennium B.C. which, by an almost total suppression of word signs and multiconsonantal syllabic signs, give the appearance of a uniconsonantal syllabic writing which is almost identical with the West Semitic syllabary.[60]

The syllabic character asserted itself so strongly in the later Hittite writing that word signs were almost entirely eliminated. For example, the short inscription from Erkilet in Figure 39 (see p. 83) is written exclusively with syllabic signs in a form which is fully identical with Cypriote. In view of the fact that Hittite hieroglyphic has only recently been deciphered it may be of interest to give here a full transliteration and translation of the text so that scholars may judge for themselves the progress achieved in the decipherment:

i-wa	*ɔa-la-n(a)*	name	*ɔA-s(a)-ta-wa-su-s(a)*	*tu-t(e)*
ī(n)-wa	*ɔalan*		*ɔAsta-wasus*	*tut*
This	monument		*ɔAsta-wasus*	placed;

i-pa-wa-te	*ni ki-a-s(e)-ḫa*	*sa-ni-a-ta*
ī(n)-pawa-te	*ni-kiasḫa*	*saniata*
it then	nobody	should damage!

FIG. 59.—HITTITE HIEROGLYPHIC INSCRIPTION FROM ERKILET

The normal Chinese writing in contrast to that of the three other Oriental systems is almost exclusively logographic. Only foreign proper names and occasionally words of foreign origin are written by means of syllabic spellings (see pp. 117 ff.).

In closing our discussion of the Oriental systems of writing we may refer to a chart (Fig. 60) showing statistically the relationship of word signs to syllabic signs:—

	Total Number of Signs	*Syllabic Signs*
Sumerian	about 600	about 100–150
Egyptian	about 700	about 100
Hittite	about 450 +	about 60
Chinese	about 50,000	[62 in *fan-ch'ieh*]

FIG. 60.—RELATIONSHIP OF WORD SIGNS TO SYLLABIC SIGNS IN WORD-SYLLABIC WRITINGS

It is estimated that the earliest Sumerian writing (Uruk IV–II) consisted of close to 2,000 different signs, while in the later Fara period the number is only 800, to be further scaled down to 600 in the Assyrian period. This process is well illustrated by the reduction of thirty-one various signs for 'sheep' in the early Uruk period to one single form in later times. The diminishing number of signs follows the principle of convergence whereby a number of word signs are eliminated and are replaced by other spellings. Comparative statistics for early Egyptian, Hittite, and Chinese writings are lacking, but it is quite clear that the Hittite writing at least used in its early stages a number of signs which later disappeared entirely. The process may have been similar in the earliest stages of Chinese but in subsequent periods we have the following picture: about 3,000 signs around 200 B.C., 9,353 signs around A.D. 100, and close to 50,000 signs in modern times. This growing number of signs following the principle of divergence seems at first glance to be the reverse of the process in Sumerian; in reality, however, the two developments are not antithetic. The 50,000 Chinese signs do not represent 50,000 different pictures which can be contrasted with the 600 Sumerian signs, each of which originally represented a different picture. I do not know the exact number of basic pictures in the 50,000 Chinese signs or whether

Sumerian

STROKE.Ha-am-mu-ra-bi	BREASTS	STROKE.STAR.EN.ZU-mu-bal-li-it	CROWN.MAN
$Hammu$-rapi	damu	Sin-muballit	lugal
Hammu-rapi,	the son	of Sin-muballit,	the king

GATE.STAR.TA.LAND	HOUSE	STAR.$Marduk$	mu-PEG
Babilim	e	Marduk	mudu
of Babylon,	the temple	of Marduk	built.

Egyptian

$H^{x^{?}x}.^{?}e^{x}$-m^{x}-$m^{x}i^{x}$-r^{x}-$p^{x?x}$.THROWSTICK.SEMITE	n^{x} B^{x}-b^{x}-r^{x}.FOREIGN-LAND	CHIEF
$Hxmxrxpx$	nx Bxbxrx	uxrx
Hammurapi,	of Babylon,	the king

S^{x}-i^{x}-n^{x}.MOON.GOD-m^{x}-$m^{x}i^{x}$-b^{x}-r^{x}-d^{x}.THROWSTICK.- [SEMITE	DUCK.STROKE	EMBLEM.HOUSE.t^{x}.BUILDING	$n^{x}i^{x}$	M^{x}-$m^{x}i^{x}$-r^{x}-d^{x}-k^{x}.GOD
$Sxnxmxbxrxdx$	$sx^{?}x$	hxtx-nxtxrx	nxtx	Mxrxdxkx
of Sinmubalid,	the son	the temple	of	Marduk.

WALL.MAN.$q^{x}d^{x}$
gxdx
built

116

Hittite

STROKE.Ḫa-mu-ra-pí-s(a)	STROKE.Si-mu-pa-li-i(i)-ša-s(a)	HAND.ni-mu-wa-i-s(a)		
Ḫamurapiš	*Sinmupalitaš*	*nimuwaiš*		
Ḫammurapiš,	of Sinmupalitaš	the son,		

Pa-pí-li-wa-ni-s(a).LAND	TIARA-ta-s(a)	EMBLEM.Ma-ru-ta-ka-ša-s(a)	EMBLEM.HOUSE-za	WALL.HAND-me-i(i)
Papiliwaniš	*. . . . tas*	*Marutakaš*	*. . . . ḫaza*	*. . . . met*
the Babylonian	king,	of Marutakaš	the temple(s)	built.

Chinese

Ha-mu-lai-pí'i	Ḫsin-mu-pa-li-lē	chih	BOY	Ma-er-to-kê	chih	TEMPLE
Hamulaip'i	*Ḫsinmubalit*	*chih*	*tsu*	*Martok*	*chih*	*miao*
Hamulaipi,	of Ḫsinmubalit		the son,	of Mardok		the temple.

Pa-pí-lun	chih	KING	BUILD	chih	TEMPLE
Papilun	*chih*	*wang*	*chien*	*chih*	*miao*
of Babylon		the king,	built,		the temple.

FIG. 61.—ONE SENTENCE AS SPELLED IN WORD-SYLLABIC WRITINGS

117

anybody has ever taken the trouble to calculate it. There are to-day 214 keys according to which Chinese signs are classified, a number which was reduced from 540 keys used in an old Chinese lexicon called *Shuo-wên* (about A.D. 100). The number of keys in *Shuo-wên* may approximately reproduce the number of basic signs in the Chinese writing. All the additional signs do not stand for new pictures but represent either combinations of basic signs or, more commonly, combinations of basic signs plus phonetic indicators. Contrary to the practice in the Near East, where signs with many different phonetic indicators (complements) are counted as one sign, in China signs with different phonetic indicators are counted as separate signs. This is as if in one system the writing of †s (that is, the word sign for 'cross' plus the phonetic indicator *s* for the word 'cross') and †d ('dead') were counted as one sign, that is, †, and in another as two signs, that is, †s and †d. Therein lies the reason for the extraordinary number of Chinese signs.

By way of illustration of the word-syllabic writing, Figure 61 shows one sentence, as spelled in Sumerian, Egyptian, Hittite, and Chinese. In each case the first row gives sign-by-sign transliteration, the second approximate transcription, and the third word-by-word translation. Semantic elements, such as word signs and determinatives, are transliterated in capital roman characters, while phonetic elements are in italics. The Egyptian and Chinese sentences were composed with the help of Professors William F. Edgerton and Ch'ên Mêng-chia respectively. In connection with the Chinese part it should be stated that when I submitted the English sentence to a scholar of Chinese, asking him to put it into Chinese characters, he refused my request, saying that the Chinese transliteration of proper names would be totally incomprehensible due to the logographic character of Chinese writing. I then asked Professor Ch'ên to make the transliteration and one year later as a test submitted the sentence in Chinese characters to another Chinese scholar, Professor Têng Ssŭ-yü. The latter understood correctly the whole sentence and read exactly all the proper names, including some, such as *Hsin-mu-pa-li-tê*, of which he had never heard before. That does not prove, of course, that the process of transliterating a foreign sentence into Chinese characters was as easy as that in the other logo-syllabic writings. What it means is that the Chinese writing, in spite of its extreme logographic character, has a limited number of word signs which can be used in a definite syllabic function to express foreign words and names (cf. p. 110).[61]

IV

SYLLABIC WRITINGS

ROM the seven Oriental writings discussed in the previous chapter originated four types of syllabic systems: cuneiform syllabaries, such as Elamite, Hurrian, etc., from Mesopotamian cuneiform; West Semitic syllabaries, such as Sinaitic, Proto-Palestinian, Phoenician, etc., from Egyptian hieroglyphic; the Cypriote syllabary, and perhaps also the as yet little known Phaistos and Byblos writings, from Cretan; and, finally, the Japanese syllabary from Chinese. Our discussion will first be concerned with a descriptive presentation of the various syllabic systems, to be followed by a general résumé of their main structural characteristics.

CUNEIFORM SYLLABARIES

In the discussion of the Mesopotamian writing the observation was made that in certain periods or areas this writing had more of the characteristics of a syllabic than a logo-syllabic system (see p. 114). Thus, for instance, the Old Akkadian inscriptions, the *eme-sal* dialect of Sumerian, and the Cappadocian texts of the Old Assyrian merchants were written to a great extent with syllabic signs, while the few word signs which were used were confined to some of the most common expressions of the language. The derived cuneiform syllabaries which will be discussed in this chapter are not much different in character, although the use of syllabic signs is considerably expanded and systematized. In the strict sense of the word there is no cuneiform syllabary which could be compared, for example, with the Phoenician or Cypriote syllabic writing. What we actually have are different cuneiform syllabaries all used in company with a more or less limited number of word signs.

Among the derived cuneiform syllabaries we may include the Elamite, Hurrian, Urartian, Hattic, Luwian, and Palaic writings. All of these systems were borrowed from the Mesopotamian cuneiform by foreign peoples living in the areas to the north and north-west of the Valley of the Two Rivers.

When, in the middle of the third millennium B.C. the Elamites gave up their own Proto-Elamite writing (see p. 213) in favour of a system borrowed directly from cuneiform, they introduced a writing consisting of some 131 syllabic signs, twenty-five word signs, and seven determinatives.[1] However, it should be noted that the proportion of 131 syllabic signs to thirty-two word signs and determinatives in the sign lists does not even approximately express the preponderance of syllabic spellings in the actual texts. It would be just as wrong to draw the conclusion that in our own writing the proportion of alphabetic to word spellings is something like twenty-six to ten because there are twenty-six alphabetic signs and ten numbers (= word signs) in the English writing. The late Elamite cuneiform system is even more simplified, as it consists, according to Weissbach, of only 113 signs, of which 102 are syllabic and eleven are word signs and determinatives.[2] The emphasis upon syllabic spellings can be attested to a very large degree in the Hurrian writing used in northern Mesopotamia, Syria, and eastern Anatolia in the middle of the second millennium B.C. Even a superficial glance at the letter of the Mittannian king Tušratta[3] will show how rarely word signs are used in comparison with syllabic spellings: no more than one to three word signs are found scattered among hundreds of syllabic spellings. The Urartian or Vannic inscriptions from Armenia dated to the first half of the first millennium B.C. appear to have a slightly larger proportion of word signs than the Hurrian writing. The Hattic, Luwian, and Palaic texts discovered in the archives of Boğazköy, the capital of the Hittite Empire, use almost exclusively syllabic signs. These little-known languages were spoken by peoples living in various parts of central Anatolia.

Among the writings borrowed from Mesopotamia by foreign peoples the only one which closely followed its prototype in retaining a large number of word signs is the so-called 'cuneiform Hittite' writing. This is the writing of the thousands of cuneiform tablets discovered at Boğazköy and used for a language which with hieroglyphic Hittite was one of the two official languages of the Hittite Empire. The close adherence of the cuneiform Hittite writing to its Mesopotamian prototype may well be due to the existence at Boğazköy of a scribal tradition greatly under the influence of the Mesopotamian civilization.

WEST SEMITIC SYLLABARIES

In the following discussion the term 'Semitic' (writing, alphabet, syllabary) stands exclusively for West Semitic and applies to various writings used by peoples speaking North-west Semitic (Phoenician, Hebrew, Aramaic, etc.) and South-west Semitic (North Arabic, South Arabic, Ethiopic, etc.) languages. In place of East Semitic the term 'Akkadian', with its Assyro-Babylonian branches, is used throughout.

Before we enter into the discussion of the character and origin of the Semitic syllabaries we should first acquaint ourselves with the various systems of writing which originated in the second millennium B.C. in the vast Semitic area extending from the Sinai Peninsula to northern Syria.

In the winter of 1904–5 several stone inscriptions in a new type of writing were discovered by the English archaeologist, Sir William M. Flinders Petrie, near the locality of Serābīṭ el-Ḥādem, on the Sinai Peninsula. The discoveries aroused immediate interest in the scientific world, as a result of which several expeditions were sent to Sinai to search for more inscriptions of the same type. The total number of inscriptions discovered up to now is limited to a few dozens. The dating of these inscriptions is still a moot question, although most scholars seem now to agree that they originated around 1600–1500 B.C., a date reconstructed chiefly on the archaeological basis. Non-specialists are warned not to confuse these Proto-Sinaitic inscriptions with the much younger 'Sinaitic' script, which is considered to be the link between the Nabatean and Arabic writings.

The Proto-Sinaitic inscriptions are found on stone, frequently statues of female divinities, and were evidently made by the Semites who worked the copper and turquoise mines in the area of Serābīṭ el-Ḥādem. The English Egyptologist, Alan H. Gardiner, laid the foundations for the decipherment of the writing by suggesting that the four signs found on some of the statues (as in our Fig. 62) should be read as *B'lt*.[4] This reading of the name of the famous Semitic goddess Ba'lat seemed to have found support in the fact that the temple of the Egyptian goddess Hathor, with whom Ba'lat could have been identified, was discovered in the ruins of Serābīṭ el-Ḥādem. However, the progress of the decipherment of the Proto-Sinaitic inscriptions since Gardiner has been so negligible as to make even Gardiner's basic decipherment look suspicious. To some extent progress was hampered not only by the scarcity of comparative material but also by some rather fantastic reconstructions

FIG. 62.—PROTO-SINAITIC INSCRIPTION

From Martin Sprengling, *The Alphabet* (Chicago, 1931), p. 28

of scholars who tried to read into these inscriptions the names of Jahweh and Moses and the story of the Hebrew peregrinations! In reality the texts cannot contain anything more complicated than simple votive inscriptions. A recent study by W. F. Albright[5] takes us a good deal farther on the road toward the final decipherment of Proto-Sinaitic. For the sake of completeness we should mention here two fragmentary inscriptions from Sinai using signs which do not resemble those of the standard Proto-Sinaitic inscriptions.[6]

A list of signs found in the Proto-Sinaitic inscriptions is given as Figure 63 after Leibovitch.[7]

Moving northward from Sinai we enter Palestine, where, too, discoveries of great importance for the history of writing have been made. At such scattered places as Beth Shemesh, El-Ḥaḍr, Gezer, Lachish, Megiddo, Shechem, Tell el-Ḥesī, Tell eṣ-Ṣārem, and perhaps Jerusalem and Tell el-'Ajjūl were found various objects, chiefly pots and sherds, with short inscriptions containing signs sometimes resembling those on the Proto-Sinaitic inscriptions, sometimes entirely different.[8] As less than a dozen of these inscriptions are known the importance of the Palestinian finds lies not in the number of inscriptions; it is rather the number of localities in which the texts have been discovered that leads to the important conclusion that the writing was used rather extensively in Palestine centuries before the Hebrew invasion. One glance at the extant inscriptions

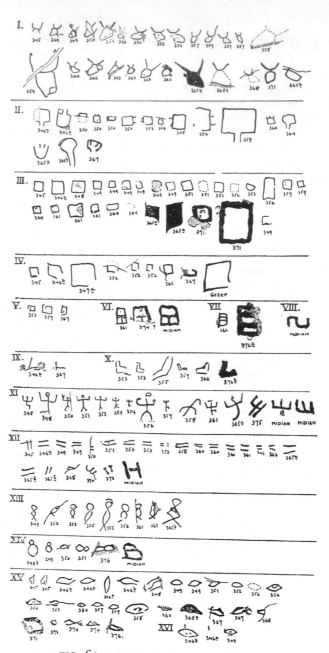

FIG. 63.—PROTO-SINAITIC WRITING

From J. Leibovitch, *Mémoires présentés á l'Institut d'Egypte*, xxiv (1934),
pls. iv–vi

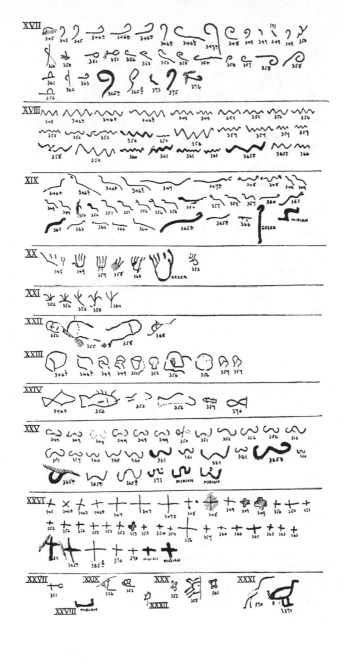

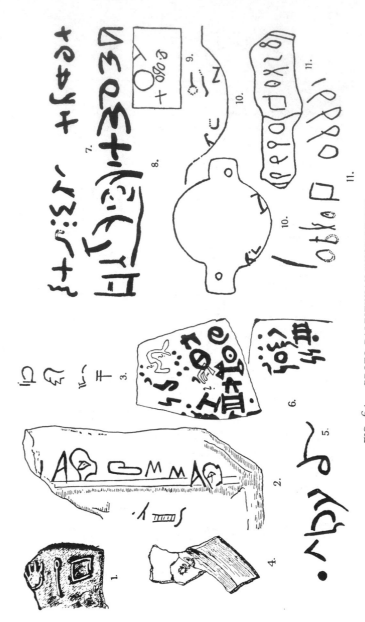

FIG. 64.—PROTO-PALESTINIAN INSCRIPTIONS

From D. Diringer in *Journal of the American Oriental Society*, lxiii (1943), 25–7

(Fig. 64) is sufficient to show that they must belong to different periods. The exact dating is still impossible, of course, but we may not be too far off if we assign the Gezer and Shechem fragments (Nos. 1–2) to about 1600–1500 B.C. and some of the Lachish inscriptions (Nos. 7–8, 10–11) to about 1300–1200 B.C.[9] There is no complete sign list and it cannot even be ascertained

FIG. 65.—ENIGMATIC INSCRIPTIONS FROM KAHŪN IN FAYYŪM (EGYPT)

From W. M. Flinders Petrie in *Ancient Egypt*, vi (1921), 1

whether the Proto-Palestinian inscriptions represent one or more systems of writing.[10]

Some inscriptions from the second millennium B.C., discovered outside of Palestine and as yet unreadable, should be mentioned here because they may very well constitute one of the many attempts to create systems which everywhere in this period began to spring up like mushrooms after a rain.

Among these in the first place belong the mysterious short

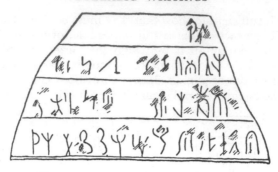

FIG. 66.—ENIGMATIC INSCRIPTION ON A STELE
FROM BALŪʻAH IN TRANSJORDAN

From G. Horsfield and L. H. Vincent, in *Revue Biblique*, xli
(1932), 425

inscriptions found in Kahūn in Fayyūm (Fig. 65), supposedly
dated to the end of the Twelfth Dynasty of Egypt, that is,
from the first half of the second millennium B.C. [11]

Another unreadable inscription on a stele of black basalt was
recently discovered at Balūʻah in Transjordan[12] (Fig. 66).
According to Étienne Drioton, its date is later than Ramses III
(about 1200–1168 B.C.). [13]

FIG. 67.—ENIGMATIC INSCRIPTION FROM BYBLOS
IN SYRIA

From M. Dunand, *Byblia grammata* (Beyrouth, 1945), p. 136

An enigmatic inscription containing three lines of writing was found on a stone fragment in Syrian Byblos[14] (Fig. 67). A similar type, represented by the Byblos syllabic writing and presumably developed under Aegean influence, is discussed elsewhere (see pp. 157 ff.). Another unreadable writing was discovered on a statuette from Byblos.[15]

One of the greatest archaeological finds of all times was made about twenty years ago in the obscure little village of Râs Shamrah, situated a few miles north of Latakiya (ancient Laodicea), in Syria. The accidental discovery in 1928 of a subterranean tunnel by a local peasant subsequently led to systematic excavations of the site which yielded the ruins of the ancient and prosperous town of Ugarit. From the point of view of the history of writing the most important discovery consisted of a number of clay tablets inscribed in a peculiar kind of cuneiform (Fig. 68) entirely unlike any other known cuneiform writing. As the writing is composed of a limited number of signs and the division of words is marked by a special sign, the decipherment presented no difficulties whatsoever. In fact, the system was deciphered in-

FIG. 68.—RÂS SHAMRAH TABLET

From C. Virolleaud in *Syria*, xxi (1940), 250

dependently by Hans Bauer, E. Dhorme, and Ch. Virolleaud within a few weeks after publication of the first texts—one of the shortest cases of decipherment on record. The Ugaritic writing consists of thirty signs, of which twenty-seven are of the usual Semitic type, expressing a consonant plus any vowel. Exceptional in a Semitic system is the use of the three signs expressing 'a, 'i, and 'u respectively (Fig. 69). The writing is dated to about the fourteenth century B.C. and is used for a

Semitic language closely akin to Phoenician and Hebrew, and also for the Hurrian language which in this period was widely spoken throughout vast areas in North Syria and Mesopotamia.[16]

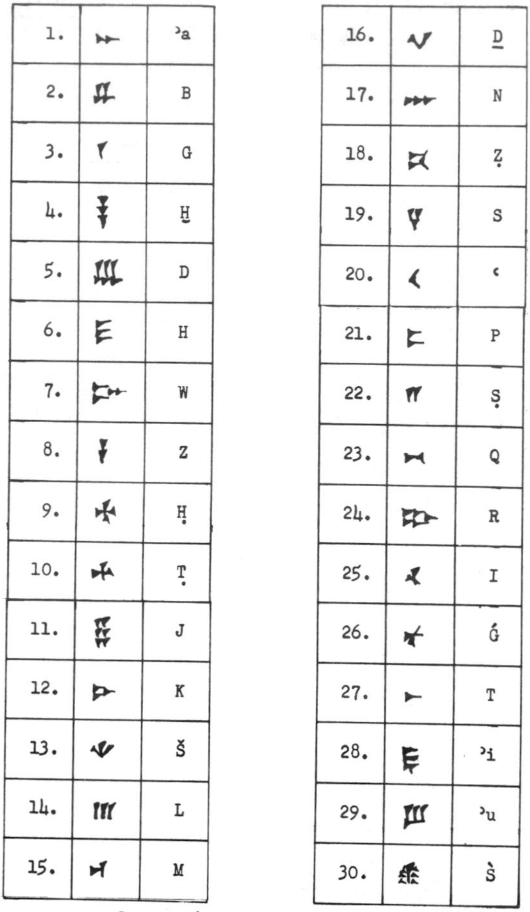

1.	▸▸—	ʾa		16.	∿	D̠
2.	𝛺	B		17.	▸▸▸	N
3.	𝖸	G		18.	𝇇	Ẓ
4.	𝖸	Ḫ		19.	𝖸	S
5.	𝍑	D		20.	◀	ʿ
6.	𝖤	H		21.	𝖤	P
7.	𝖻▸▸	W		22.	𝖶	Ṣ
8.	𝖸	Z		23.	▸◀	Q
9.	▸𝖸	Ḥ		24.	𝖻▸	R
10.	▸𝖸	Ṭ		25.	◀	I
11.	𝖶	J		26.	▸𝖸	Ǵ
12.	𝖻▸	K		27.	▸—	T
13.	⩔	Š		28.	𝖤	ʾi
14.	𝖶	L		29.	𝍑	ʾu
15.	▸◀	M		30.	𝖶	ṡ

FIG. 69.—RÂS SHAMRAH SYLLABARY

A variation of Ugaritic writing has recently been discovered on two inscriptions from Beth Shemesh and Mt. Tabor in Palestine, suggesting that a type of cuneiform similar to that of Ugaritic may have been used in Palestine in the middle of the second millennium B.C. [17]

Until about the middle of the 1920's the oldest Semitic inscription, preserved in the so-called 'alphabetic' writing, was thought to be the famous Moabite stone of King Meša', dated to the middle of the ninth century b.c. Since then our knowledge of Semitic epigraphy has increased greatly, thanks chiefly to new finds at Byblos, which allow a more exact chronological classification of the extant inscriptional material from the earliest periods.

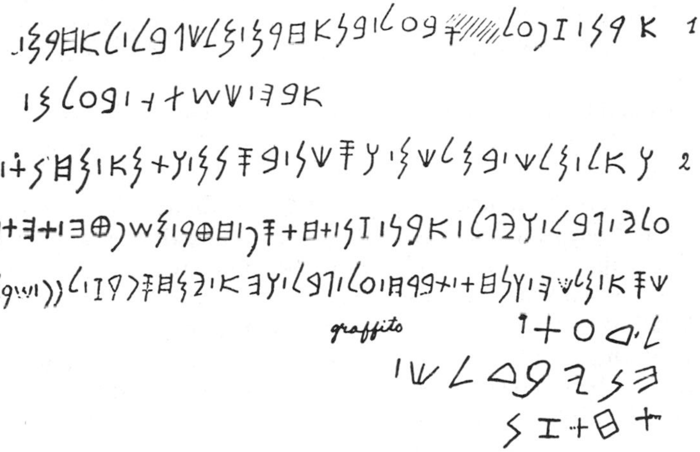

FIG. 70.—AḤĪRÂM INSCRIPTION FROM BYBLOS

From R. Dussaud in *Syria*, v (1924), p. 137, fig. 2, and p. 143, fig. 4'

At the present time the oldest of the Semitic inscriptions in the new form of writing is the inscription on the Aḥīrâm sarcophagus with the graffito incised on one of the walls of the tomb of Aḥīrâm, discovered at Byblos (Fig. 70).[18] The usual dating of the Aḥīrâm inscriptions to the thirteenth century b.c. rests solely upon stratigraphic reconstructions based on comparison with Egyptian materials (see later). Epigraphically younger are the inscriptions of 'Azarba'al[19] and Yeḥīmilk[20] from Byblos and the bronze arrowhead from Ruweiseh, in Lebanon.[21] Finally, from about the tenth century are the inscription of Abība'al,[22] dated historically to the time of the Egyptian king Sheshonq I (about 945–924 b.c.), and that of Elība'al,[23] dated to the time of Osorkon I (about 924–895 b.c.), son of Sheshonq I. Dunand's dating of the inscriptions of

Šapaṭbaʿal and ʿAbdaʾa to the eighteenth and seventeenth centuries [24] is without foundation. [25]

A note of warning is necessary in connection with the dating of the earliest Phoenician inscriptions. The epigraphic differences between the oldest inscriptions—like those of Aḥirâm—and the younger ones—like those of Abibaʿal and Elibaʿal—are so negligible that one may justifiably wonder how correct it is to assume the wide gap of three hundred years between them. As the dating of the Abibaʿal and Elibaʿal inscriptions to about the tenth century is beyond question, the lowering of the date of the Aḥirâm and related inscriptions by about two hundred years would seem to be much more satisfactory from the epigraphical point of view. [26]

On the basis of our knowledge of the earliest Semitic writings we can reconstruct the following picture:—

The Proto-Sinaitic inscriptions from about 1600–1500 B.C. are written in a system consisting of a limited number of signs of a definitely pictorial character. In other words, the pictures of each sign can in most cases be recognized without much difficulty. Exactly how many signs there are is unknown, since the number of thirty-one signs, counted by Leibovitch, may have to be reduced somewhat if we take into consideration the fact that some of the signs listed separately by him may be merely variants of the same sign.

From approximately the same period but extending up to about 1100 B.C. are the **Proto-Palestinian** texts from Gezer, Shechem, etc. Although some of the signs on the older inscriptions are pictorial in character, those on the later Proto-Palestinian inscriptions are mainly linear. The number of signs is unknown. Due to the limited material it is impossible to make any definite comparisons between the Proto-Sinaitic and Proto-Palestinian writings. The latter may represent one or more attempts to create a system identical in inner structure, but still formally different in the choice of signs from that of the Proto-Sinaitic inscriptions.

The as yet totally undeciphered inscriptions from Kahūn, Balūʿah, and Byblos may represent a few more attempts to create systems similar in inner structure to those of the Proto-Sinaitic and Proto-Palestinian inscriptions. The signs are everywhere linear in character.

The Ugaritic writing from the fourteenth century B.C. consists of cuneiform signs and is therefore linear in form. The attempts of some scholars to derive the Ugaritic system from either the Proto-Sinaitic writing[27] or Mesopotamian cuneiform[28] have not been successful. Although foreign influence may have been instrumental in the choice of some signs, in the majority of cases the forms of the Ugaritic signs are the result of free individual creation.

Finally, around 1000 B.C. come the earliest Byblos inscriptions (Aḥīrâm, etc.) written in a system composed of twenty-two signs purely linear in appearance. Of all the various Semitic attempts made in the second millennium B.C. to create a new writing this one was by far the most successful. From it directly, both from the structural and formal point of view, are derived

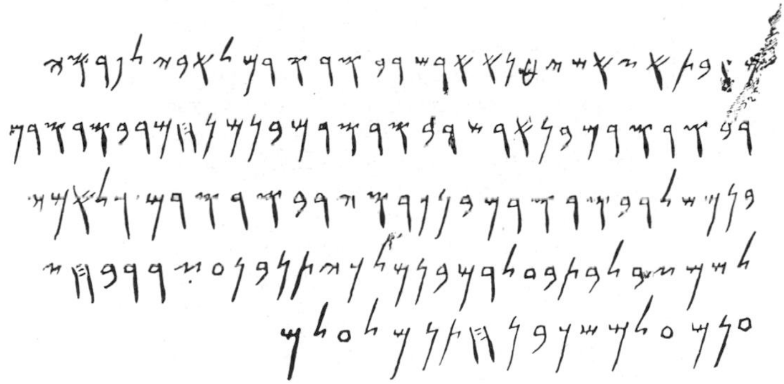

FIG. 71.—PHOENICIAN INSCRIPTION FROM CYPRUS
From Mark Lidzbarski, *Handbuch der nordsemitischen Epigraphik*, pl. vi, 2

three of the four main subdivisions of the Semitic writing represented by the Phoenician (Fig. 71), Palestinian (Fig. 72), and Aramaic (Fig. 73) branches. The fourth subdivision, represented by the South Arabic branch (Fig. 74), can only indirectly be derived from the Phoenician prototype. The South Arabic writings seem to have made their appearance in the first half of the first millennium B.C., although both earlier and later dates have been proposed by some scholars.[29] The writing consists of twenty-nine signs, a number which is almost identical with that of the Ugaritic writing, but exceeds by seven the number of signs in the Phoenician writing. The forms of the South Arabic writing are all linear; while a few are identical with those of the Phoenician writing, most of them were independently created.

133

The chart in Figure 75 attempts to bring together the signs of the most important Semitic writings with their corresponding values. Note the great similarity of form and number of signs

FIG. 72.—CANAANITE INSCRIPTION OF MEŠA'
KING OF MOAB

From Lidzbarski, *Handbuch der nordsemitischen Epigraphik*, pl. i

in the Phoenician, Palestinian, and Aramaic systems. The larger number of signs in the Ugaritic, South Arabic, Ethiopic, and Arabic systems is due to the fact that these languages contain a larger number of sounds than the other Semitic languages.

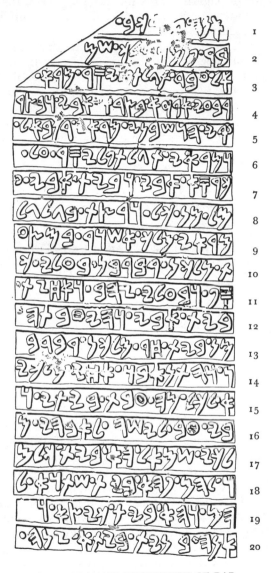

FIG. 73.—ARAMAIC INSCRIPTION OF BAR-
RĀKIB FROM ZINCIRLI

From Lidzbarski, *Handbuch der nordsemitischen
Epigraphik*, pl. xxiv, 1

In the case of Ugaritic also the necessity of transliterating Hurrian sounds, foreign to Semitic, may have stimulated the creation of additional signs.

In saying that the Byblos writing from Aḥîrâm on may be called the prototype of all the subsequent Semitic systems, we do not wish to imply that this writing was necessarily invented in Byblos or even in Phoenicia. It so happens that the earliest extant inscriptions of this new form of writing come from Byblos and Phoenicia, but nobody can deny the possibility that almost any site in the vast Semitic area extending from Sinai

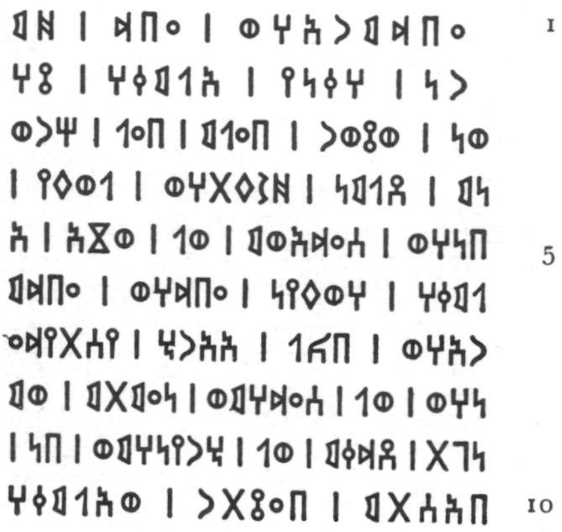

FIG. 74.—SOUTH ARABIC
INSCRIPTION
From K. Conti Rossini, *Chrestomathia Arabica Meridionalis Epigraphica* (Roma, 1931), p. 46, No. 29

to northern Syria could (at least theoretically) be considered the birthplace of the prototype of all the Semitic writings.

This is, in short, the story of the origins of the Semitic writings, from the various attempts in the middle of the second millennium B.C. to the creation of a full system which after 1000 B.C. conquered the Semitic world. Our next problem is to investigate the origin of this Semitic writing. As this is one of the most discussed subjects in the field of Oriental studies, it would be possible without much difficulty to write a whole book on the question. The mere listing of the various opinions would require a large chapter entirely beyond the scope of the present study. Suffice it to mention, therefore, that there is hardly a writing in the Near East, and even beyond that area, which has not been taken into consideration by one scholar or another as the archetype of the Semitic writing. From among the many

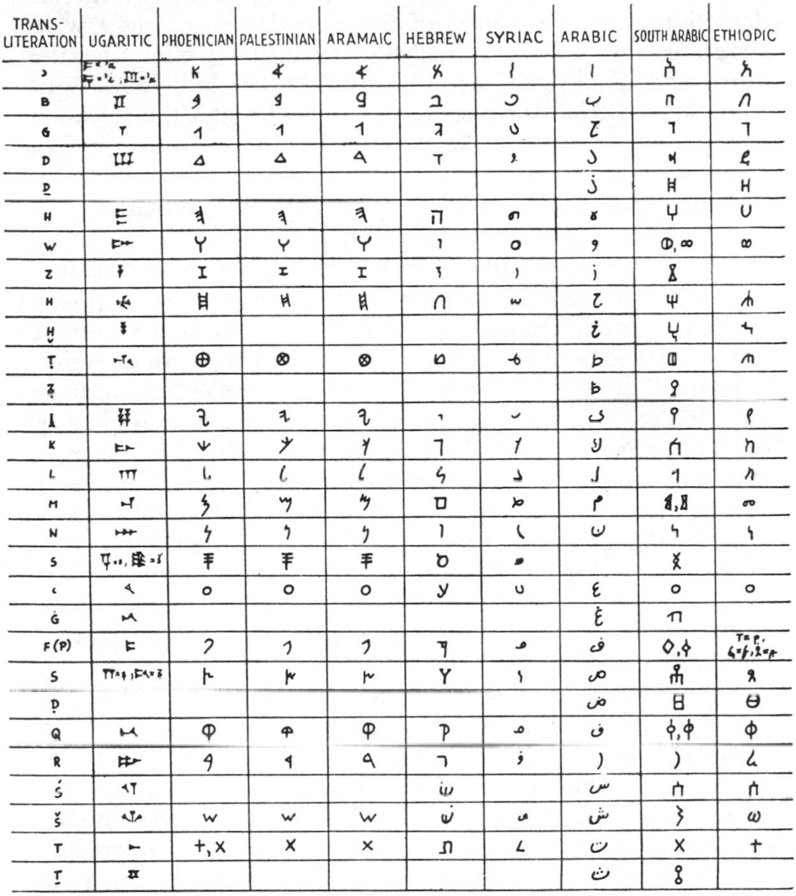

TRANS-LITERATION	UGARITIC	PHOENICIAN	PALESTINIAN	ARAMAIC	HEBREW	SYRIAC	ARABIC	SOUTH ARABIC	ETHIOPIC
ʾ					א		ا		አ
B					ב		ب		በ
G					ג		ج		ገ
D					ד		د		ደ
Ḏ							ذ		
H					ה		ه		ሀ
W					ו		و		ወ
Z					ז		ز		
Ḥ					ח		ح		ሐ
Ḫ							خ		ኀ
Ṭ					ט		ط		ጠ
Ẓ							ظ		
Y					י		ي		የ
K					כ		ك		ከ
L					ל		ل		ለ
M					מ		م		መ
N					נ		ن		ነ
S					ס		س		
ʿ					ע		ع		ዐ
Ġ							غ		
F (P)					פ		ف		
Ṣ					צ		ص		ጸ
Ḍ							ض		ፀ
Q					ק		ق		ቀ
R					ר		ر		ረ
Ś					שׂ		ش		ሠ
Š					שׁ		ش		ω
T					ת		ت		ተ
Ṯ							ث		

FIG. 75.—COMPARATIVE CHART OF THE MOST IMPORTANT SEMITIC WRITINGS

derivations which have been proposed we should note at least Egyptian in its three forms (hieroglyphic, hieratic, and demotic) Assyrian, Babylonian, Sumerian, Cretan, Cypriote, Hittite, South Arabic, and Germanic runes. Of these the Egyptian theory has enjoyed by far the most popular reception. In all cases the approach was quite similar, as it was based almost exclusively on formal comparisons. This is the usual interpretation: First, the forms of the Semitic writing were derived directly from the forms of Egyptian (hieroglyphic, hieratic, or demotic); next, the values of the Egyptian word signs were translated into a Semitic language, resulting in names for the signs; and, finally, the Semitic values of the individual signs were derived from the respective names through the so-called 'acrophonic principle'. Thus, for instance, first the Egyptian sign for 'house' was taken over by the Semites; next the Egyptian word p^xr^x for 'house' was translated into Semitic *bêth* (or the like) and became the name of the letter; and finally, the sign *bêth* received the value *b* according to the acrophonic principle. The derivation of the Semitic writing from Egyptian received a certain amount of support from the evidence brought forth by various scholars that both the Egyptian and Semitic 'alphabets' are identical in respect to the 'vowellessness' of their signs.[30] That it was necessary to prove this self-apparent identity only shows how blinded scholars were by the alleged importance of formal comparisons, neglecting entirely the evidence of inner structural value. Further impetus to the Egyptian theory was given by the discovery of the Proto-Sinaitic inscriptions written by Semites living in a territory controlled by Egypt, a fact which easily lent itself to the conclusion that the Proto-Sinaitic signs were the long-sought 'missing link' between the Egyptian and later Semitic forms.[31]

Thus matters stood until about fifteen years ago when the origins of the Semitic writing began to be investigated by a group of scholars with a different approach to the problem. Their chief idea was that, in the study of various systems of writing, formal comparison of signs was given undue importance at the expense of inner structural characteristics. This approach was not entirely new. Already in the days of the First World War and a little later, both A. Hertz[32] and C. F. Lehmann-Haupt[33] expressed this idea and brought forth evidence from many writings created among primitives, all showing forms of signs freely invented but with inner structural characteristics which could have been developed only under the stimulus and influence of white men. But it was not until recently that a series of articles by Johannes Friedrich,[34] René Dussaud,[35] and Hans Bauer[36] began to give weight to the new approach.[37] Of these the most pertinent to the question of the origin of the Semitic writing is the clear and logical presentation in the posthumous work of Bauer, which will serve as the basis for the following discussion. It is indeed a sad commentary upon the conservative attitude of some scholars in the Oriental field that out of about a dozen articles published in this country in the last few years on the subject of the origins of the Semitic writing, not one takes account of the new revolutionary approach.

It has been stated above that the basic tenet of the older school of investigators of the origin of the Semitic writing is that the classical Semitic writing (from Aḥīrâm on) is composed of a certain number of signs, all formally borrowed from some other system of writing. It should be remembered that even though of the various Oriental systems Egyptian seems at present to be favoured, there is no such agreement as to which form of Egyptian—hieroglyphic, hieratic, or demotic—should be taken as the prototype of the Semitic forms. Even if the problem could be limited by general agreement to one of these forms—let us say hieroglyphic still the question would remain as to which of the few hundred hieroglyphic signs should serve as the basis from which the twenty-two Semitic signs are derived. It is clear therefore that all the derivations of the Semitic signs from this or that Oriental writing, or from any form of Egyptian, or from any group of signs within one form of Egyptian, have so many weaknesses as to prevent the general acceptance of any one of them. Compare the self-evident and generally accepted derivation of the forms of the Greek alphabet from a Semitic writing, of the Hurrian cuneiform writing from Mesopotamian cuneiform, of the Japanese syllabary from Chinese, or even of the Cypriote syllabary from Cretan. Many years ago I observed that wherever there is an extended discussion in a history of writing, involving dozens of divergent opinions on the formal derivation of a certain system, the basic assumption becomes suspicious. Either the discussion should be limited because the derivation is simple and generally accepted—as in the case of the derivation of the Greek writing from some form of Semitic—or the listing of many differing opinions only tends to prove that no correct interpretation of a formal derivation exists, as in the case of the Germanic runes. Thus, I concluded that when there is no agreement as to the formal derivation of a system, the signs are usually not borrowed from outside but freely and arbitrarily invented. How well founded such doubts were in the case of the Semitic writing may be seen from further evidence.

The signs of the Old Phoenician writing are said to have originally represented pictures: The ʾāleph sign is supposed to depict the form of an oxhead, the bêth sign that of a house, and so on down the list. But again, as in the case of the choice of the Egyptian signs, there is no agreement among scholars as to what picture each sign is supposed to represent.[38] For the benefit of non-Semitists, it should be emphasized that scholars do not interpret the ʾāleph sign as an oxhead because this sign resembles the form of an oxhead, but simply because its name,

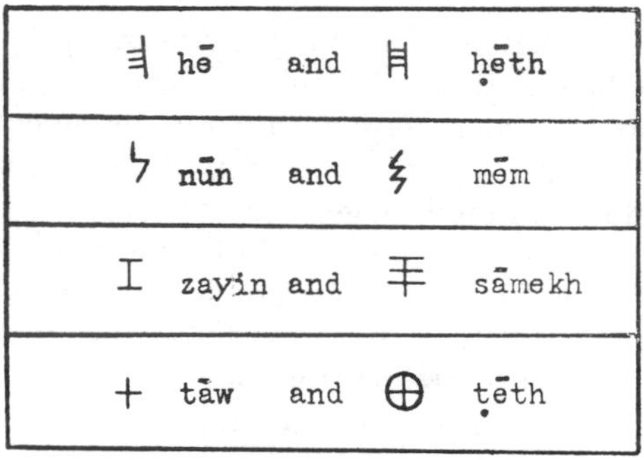

∃	hē	and	Ħ	ḥēth
ʬ	nūn	and	⟨	mēm
I	zayin	and	∓	sāmekh
+	tāw	and	⊕	ṭēth

FIG. 76.—FORMAL DIFFERENTIATION IN
SOME WEST SEMITIC SIGNS

ʾāleph, means 'ox' in Semitic languages, thus suggesting that the sign allegedly depicted the animal. None of the Semitic signs was drawn in a form which would immediately betray its pictorial character. The great difficulties in the interpretation of the signs as pictures will be apparent in the discussion of the following few examples. A number of signs, such as hē, ḥēth, ṭēth, ṣādhē, bear names which cannot be explained with the help of any Semitic language. Other names, such as gîmel, lāmedh, sāmekh, qōph, which may exist in the Semitic languages, cannot be interpreted easily as words fitting the pictures of the signs. A few signs seemingly bear more than one name in different periods or areas. Thus, the sign which in Canaanite bears the name nūn, 'fish' (to which it shows no resemblance), is called naḥāš, 'serpent,' in Ethiopic. Moreover, it was proposed that the sign *zayin*, 'weapon?,' originally had the name *zayit*, 'olive (tree),' because of Greek *zēta*, just as Greek *sigma* seems to favour something like *šikm*, 'shoulder,' for the sign usually called *šīn*, 'tooth.'[39] However, the best evidence that at least some of the signs do not originally represent pictures but are the result of free and arbitrary choice comes from the observation of pairs of similar forms noted in Figure 76. What these cases show is that the signs *hē* and *ḥēth*, for instance, did not originate as two independent pictures, but that out of one sign another sign with a similar value was arbitrarily developed by the addition or subtraction of a linear detail.[40]

Another fundamental point brought forth in favour of the Egyptian origin of the Semitic writing was that the Semites first named the signs obtained from Egyptian and then by the acrophonic principle derived the values of the signs from their names. In other words, the Semites were supposed to have named things before they had acquired any meaning! At least in the history of writing there are no parallels for any such development. In investigating various types of writings I have found the following conditions affecting the names of signs: Either the forms of the signs, their values, and their names are all directly borrowed by one system from another, as in the case of Greek from Semitic or Coptic from Greek; or the forms of the signs and their values are borrowed, as in the case of Latin from Greek or Armenian from Aramaic, and in subsequent years the names of the signs are freely invented and added; or finally the forms of the signs and their values are first freely invented and then the sign names are added, as in the case of the Slavonic Glagolitsa or the Germanic runes. The last case is especially instructive for the correct understanding of the situation in the Semitic writing. The names of signs of the Glagolitsa alphabet, called *azbuki* after the first two letters (*az*, 'I'; *buki*, 'letter'; *vedi*, 'knowledge'; *glagol*, 'speech'; *dobro*, 'good,' etc.), and of the Anglo-Saxon runes, called *fúthorc* after the initials of the first five names (*feoh*, 'money'; *ūr*, 'aurochs'; *thorn*, 'thorn'; *ōs*, 'god'; *rād*, 'voyage'; *cēn*, 'torch,' etc.), all have one characteristic in common: There is no apparent relation between the forms of the signs and their names. Worthy of note also is the fact that the names of the signs in the Anglo-Saxon alphabet are sometimes different from those in the Norse runic system, where we find the third letter called *thurs*, 'giant,'

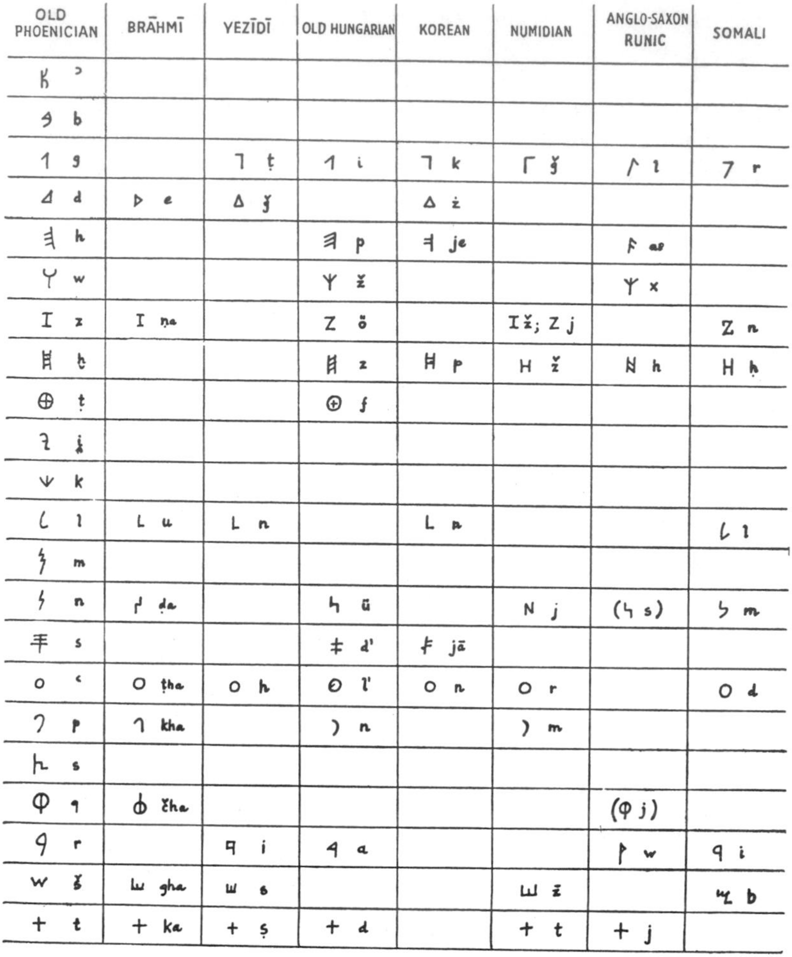

OLD PHOENICIAN	BRĀHMĪ	YEZĪDĪ	OLD HUNGARIAN	KOREAN	NUMIDIAN	ANGLO-SAXON RUNIC	SOMALI
K ʾ							
϶ b							
⌐ g		˥ t̄	⌐ i	˥ k	Γ ǧ	ʎ ʔ	7 r
⊿ d	▷ e	∆ ǰ		∆ i̇			
⌐ h			∄ p	⊣ je		⸠ æ	
Ψ w			Ψ ž			Ψ x	
I z	I na		Z ö		Iǯ; Z j		Z n
ⴳ t̤			ⴳ z	H p	H ž	N h	H h
⊕ ṭ			⊕ f				
? i̧							
↓ k							
L l	L u	L n		L ?			L l
⸾ m							
⸾ n	rʹ da		ⴄ ü		N j	(4 s)	ⴄ m
丰 s			⧺ dʹ	千 jā			
o ʿ	O tha	O h	⊖ lʹ	O n	O r		O d
? p	? kha		) n		) m		
ⴄ ṣ							
Φ q	ⴲ ṭha					(φ j)	
9 r		ⵕ i	⬱ a			⸠ w	9 i
w š	ⵞ gha	ⵞ ḅ			ⵞ ž		ⵞ b
+ t	+ ka	+ ṣ	+ d		+ t	+ j	

FIG. 77.—FORMAL COMPARISON OF SIGNS OF WEST SEMITIC
WRITING WITH SEVEN DIFFERENT WRITINGS

instead of *thorn*, 'thorn,' the fifth *kaun*, 'tumor,' instead of *cēn*, 'torch,' etc. The choice of the respective names is apparently as free as in our own mnemonic device for teaching the alphabet to children: 'A is for apple, B is for bunny,' etc., or in another system: 'A is for ape, B is for bear,' etc. The same free choice is apparent in the names of signs used by the United States Army: 'able' for A, 'baker' for B, 'Charlie' for C, etc., or, formerly, in the British Navy: 'able' for A, 'boy' for B, 'cast' for C, etc.

If it can be proved that the signs of the Old Phoenician writing do not represent pictures, then it is useless to speak about the derivation of the sign values by the so-called 'acrophonic principle'. According to this principle the sign values originated by using the first part of a word expressed in the word sign and by casting off the rest, as if we chose, for example, a picture of a house to stand for *h* because 'house' starts with an *h*. We have seen before that, at least in the case of the Mesopotamian and Egyptian writings, the principle of acrophony has no application as a system and even the sporadic use of this principle in some other writings is conspicuous by its rarity and difficulty of interpretation (see p. 110 f.). In the case of the Semitic writing, if the signs do not originally represent pictures with logographic values it is impossible, of course, to argue that the syllabic or alphabetic values were derived by the acrophonic (or any other) principle from logographic values which did not exist.

Now that we have shown the weaknesses of the older and still generally accepted theory deriving the forms of the Semitic writing from Egyptian we shall try to present the solution suggested from the point of view of the new approach, described above on p. 138 f. In order to understand better the origin of the Semitic writing from the formal aspect we should first consider the various possibilities in writings of the world outside of the Semitic group:—

(1) The forms of the signs and their values are borrowed, as in the case of Greek from Phoenician.

(2) The forms are all borrowed, but the values assigned are partly borrowed, partly freely invented, as in the case of Meroitic from Egyptian.

(3) The forms and values are partly borrowed, partly invented, as in the case of South Arabic from some North Semitic writing.

(4) The forms are borrowed but the values given to the signs are new, as in the case of the Sauk or Fox writing and normally, of course, in cryptography in the so-called 'substitution cipher'.

(5) The forms are partly borrowed, partly invented, with

new values, as found, for example, in the case of the Cherokee writing, built chiefly upon the forms of the Latin alphabet.

(6) The forms are freely invented, with new values, as found in a large number of writings such as Balti, Brāhmī, Celtiberian, Korean, Glagolitsa, Hungarian, Numidian, ogham, runic, Yezīdī, and many others created in modern times chiefly among primitive societies (see pp. 206 ff.).

In view of what has been said in the preceding pages there is no need to discuss the possibility that the forms of the Semitic writing may have been borrowed from another system. Such formal resemblances between Semitic and other writings as have been brought out by various scholars can be due to nothing but accident. What fallacious results can be reached on the basis of uncritical comparison of sign forms can be well seen from our Figure 77, in which the signs of the Semitic writing

FIG. 78.—EXCERPT FROM A WRITING INVENTED BY
A SCHOOL CHILD
From H. Bauer in *Der Alte Orient*, xxxvi, 1/2 (1937), 36

are compared formally with the signs of seven other different writings, picked at random from among those which presumably used freely invented signs. While no common derivation of any of the eight systems listed can be proved, they all contain some signs which either are fully identical or show great resemblances to each other. The reason for this is rather obvious. Although theoretically there are no limits to the number of linear forms which could be used for signs, in practice simple forms of straight lines, triangles, squares, and circles are usually chosen, since these can be easily learned and remembered by the users of the system. The number of such geometric forms is rather limited. Thus, Petrie listed only about sixty forms found by him as markings or signs in various prehistoric and historic systems in the areas surrounding the Mediterranean basin.[41]

We may complete these remarks by giving in Figure 78 an excerpt from a writing invented by a school child for the purpose of secret intercommunication.[42] The forms of the

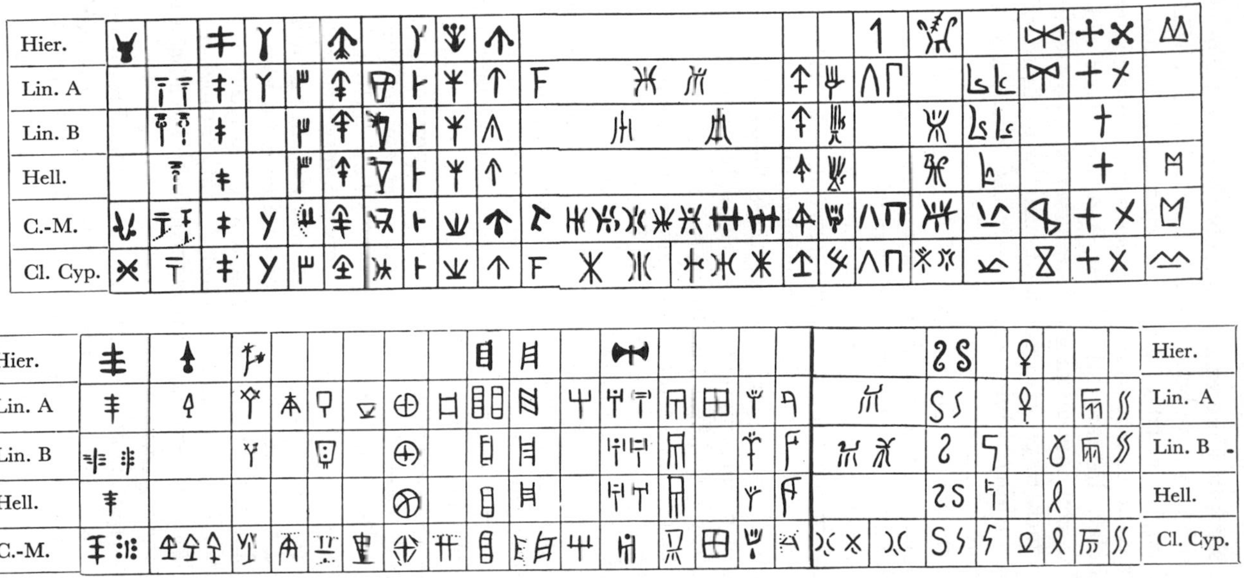

FIG. 79.—CYPRO-MINOAN CHARACTERS WITH MINOAN AND CLASSICAL CYPRIOTE PARALLELS

From J. F. Daniel in *American Journal of Archaeology*, xlv (1941), 254 and 286 geometric signs in some cases strikingly resemble those of the Semitic writing, yet nobody would dare to suggest that the child had any knowledge of Semitic epigraphy. Similar conclusions may be drawn from an experiment reported by the Dutch scholar, Johannes de Groot. [43] A nine year old girl requested to compose an original alphabet created twenty-six signs, of which seven corresponded exactly to those of the Phoenician writing, while others resembled Sinaitic, Cretan, and Cypriote forms.

Having eliminated the theory of foreign derivation of the Semitic signary and accepted that favouring original creation, we are still faced with the problem as to what forms—linear or pictorial—lie at the basis of the Semitic signary. The forms as they appear in the Semitic signary starting with Aḥīrâm are clearly linear. But were they linear when first introduced by the creators of this signary? Or are these linear forms rather the result of a development from originally pictorial forms? This much can be said safely: On the one hand, it is clear from Figure 76 that at least some of the signs of the Semitic signary developed not from pictures but from linear forms. In support of the linear origin, parallels from many writings listed under No. 6 on p. 144 can be quoted. On the other hand, we should remember the various Proto-Semitic systems in Sinai and in Palestine dated to the period before the Aḥīrâm writing, using to a great extent pictorial forms as signs. That pictures can in the course of time develop into linear forms is something quite normal in all systems of writing. But is there any connection in formal aspect between the Proto-Semitic signaries of Sinai and Palestine and the Semitic signary of Aḥīrâm and its descendants? This is a question which cannot be answered apodictically because of lack of comparative material. My own idea is that around the middle of the second millennium B.C. several writings, using either pictorial or linear forms, originated in the Semitic area. It is not at all excluded that, through mutual influence, both pictorial and linear forms may have been used in some of the systems.

The whole question of the formal aspect of the Proto-Semitic and Semitic writings is of secondary importance in comparison with that of the origin of the inner structure of these writings. Different as these various writings appear in outer form, they are all identical in their most important inner structural characteristic: They all consist of a limited number of signs (22–30) each of which expresses the exact consonant, but does not indicate a vowel. In the generally accepted reading of *B'lt* on Proto-Sinaitic stelae, of *Bl'* on a Proto-Palestinian sherd from Tell el-Ḥesī, or of *mlk* on the Aḥīrâm sarcophagus, this characteristic comes clearly to light. This is a system of writing which is normally called 'alphabetic', but which, as we shall try to prove in the following pages, is really a syllabic system of writing.

The first question is: where did the Semites get the idea of using signs which would indicate the consonants but not the vowels? The answer can be given without any difficulty. Of the three main groups of writing in the Near East which could be taken into consideration—namely, Mesopotamian cuneiform, Aegean, and Egyptian—only the last is identical with the Semitic writing in its failure to specify the vowels. Out of the complicated Egyptian system, composed of a few hundred word signs and other phonetic signs with one to three consonants, the Semites evolved a simple system of their own by throwing overboard all word signs and phonetic signs with two or more consonants and retaining only those with one consonant. Thus, the twenty-four simple signs of the Egyptian writing are identical in inner structure with the twenty-two to thirty signs of the various Semitic writings. The reason why the Semites chose the Egyptian system rather than cuneiform or Aegean as the prototype of their own writing may not be entirely due to the close cultural and commercial relations which existed in the second millennium B.C. between Syria and Palestine on the one hand and Egypt on the other. The main reason may lie rather in the fact that the genius of Egyptian writing was considered better suited to the expression of the Semitic languages than that of other Oriental writings. One should not forget that Egyptian belongs to the Hamitic languages, which in the widest sense should be considered a subdivision of the Proto-Semitic group of languages.

Once the identity of the Egyptian and Semitic systems is placed beyond the pale of doubt, the inevitable conclusion must be drawn that either they all represent alphabets, as is generally accepted, or syllabaries, as proposed in this study. Therefore, all the evidence brought together above in favour of the syllabic character of the Egyptian writing (see pp. 75 ff.)

may be used for the Semitic writing; and vice versa, whatever evidence can be found to prove the syllabic character of the Semitic writing should tend to support the conclusions drawn above in respect to Egyptian.

It is not surprising that scholars regard the Egyptian and Semitic systems as alphabets or really consonantal writings. Looking in any of the modern Semitic alphabets at the writing, for example, of *ba* by means of the *bêth* sign plus a diacritic, it seems natural to analyse the *bêth* sign as the consonant *b* and the diacritic mark as the vowel *a*. The result of this analysis of modern Semitic alphabets, therefore, is to construe the older Semitic writings, which do not use diacritic marks to indicate the vowels, as consonantal only. What seems not to have occurred to the scholars is the possibility that the modern Semitic alphabets may not be identical in structure with their earlier Semitic and Egyptian predecessors.

If the vowels are generally left unindicated in the older Semitic writings, still there are cases in which the quality of the vowel is expressed by means of the so-called 'weak' consonants. This is what is normally called *scriptio plena* or *plene* writing, which will be extensively discussed elsewhere (see pp. 166 ff.). In this writing the syllable *za*, for example, may be written with *zayin* plus *ʾāleph*, just as the syllable *ti* may be written with *tāw* plus *yodh*. Scholars who believe in the consonantal character of the Semitic writing do not hesitate to transliterate the two basic signs in the above examples as the consonants *z* and *t* respectively. What they overlook, however, is the fact that *scriptio plena* is not limited to the Semitic writings but that it occurs also in many other systems, definitely and clearly syllabic. We have referred above to a small number of signs in Mesopotamian cuneiform which express a consonant without indicating a vowel and thus are structurally identical with normal Egyptian and Semitic (see pp. 71 and 79 f.). Among these signs there is, for example, one containing *w* plus any vowel. This sign is not transliterated as *w*, as it would normally be transliterated in Egyptian or Semitic, but as *wa, wi, we, wu,* depending on the linguistic situation. This discrepancy appears even more clearly in cases in which a sign containing a vowel is attached to the sign *wa, wi, we, wu* to express the correct vowel as, for example, in the writing of *wa-a* for *wa*, *wi-i* for *wi*, etc., found regularly in Hattic, Hurrian, and Palaic texts from Boğazköy (p. 171).

Similarly, in transliterations of *ia-a* for *ya* or of *iu-ú* for *yu*, etc., occurring in Mesopotamian cuneiform, it is generally admitted that the cuneiform sign is *ia, ii, ie, iu,* and not the consonant *y* alone. The reason for this discrepancy is obvious. The cuneiform writings are syllabic; therefore the signs in question cannot be transliterated otherwise than *wa, wi, we, wu,* or *ia, ii, ie, iu* respectively. The Semitic writings are alleged to be alphabetic; therefore the signs of identical structure are transliterated there as consonants *w* or *y* alone. The incongruence of such transliteration from the point of view of the theory of writing is apparent. Since all the cases discussed above in the Semitic and cuneiform writings are identical in structure, the respective transliterations should be identical, that is, either syllabic or alphabetic. In view of the fact that the cuneiform writing is definitely syllabic, the resulting conclusion is that the identical Semitic spellings should also be considered syllabic and not alphabetic.

Another point in favour of the syllabic character of the so-called Semitic 'alphabet' results from the investigation of the *shewa* writing. When, under Greek influence, the Semites introduced a vocalic system into their writing they created not only some diacritic marks for full vowels, such as *a, i, e, o, u,* but also one mark called *shewa* which, when attached to a sign, characterizes it as a consonant alone or a consonant plus a very short vowel *ĕ* (introduced because of difficulties in pronouncing consonantal clusters). If the Semitic signs were originally consonantal—as is generally claimed—then there would simply be no use for the *shewa* mark. The fact that the Semites felt the necessity of creating a mark showing lack of a vowel means that to them every sign originally stood for a full syllable, that is, a consonant plus a vowel.

Even more important conclusions can be drawn from the Ethiopic and Indic writings. The Ethiopic writing is a formal development of South Arabic (see Fig. 75), and both of them are formally identical with the Semitic writings in the north. When, a few centuries after Christ, the Ethiopians decided to introduce into their writing a system of vowel notation, they invented not only special marks for the full vowels *ā, ī, ē, ū, ō,* but also one mark for the *shewa,* as in North Semitic. The most important feature, however, is that the basic sign, without any vowel marks, expressed not the consonant alone but a syllable consisting of a consonant plus the full vowel *a*! [44] Surely, if the Semitic writing were originally consonantal, one might legitimately have expected the basic sign, without any marks, to express the consonant alone and a special mark invented for the consonant plus the *a*-vowel. [45] The situation in the Indic systems is almost identical: special marks exist for the individual vowels, one mark indicates no vowel, but a syllable consisting of a consonant plus the vowel *a* is represented by the basic sign without any additional marks. The great similarity or even identity of the Ethiopic and Indic systems is due to the fact that structurally, if not formally, all the various Indic writings are derived from a Semitic prototype (see p. 187 f.).

From the fact that in the Indic and Ethiopic writings a consonant plus an *a*-vowel is represented by the basic sign without any marks a further conclusion may be drawn, namely, that in some Semitic writings the basic or rather the first value of all signs was a consonant plus the vowel *a*. The basic value of a consonant plus the vowel *a* developed in some systems into real sign names as, for instance, in Indic. The sign names in the Arabic writing are the result of a mixture of two systems: some Arabic names like '*alif*, *ǧīm*, *dāl*, *ḏāl*, *kāf*, *lām*, etc., are clearly borrowed from a North Semitic writing, while others like *bā*, *hā*, *za*, *ḥā*, *ḫā*, *ṭā*, etc., may attest to the existence in some Semitic writings of a system in which the sign names originated from the first values of the signs, namely, from a consonant plus the vowel *a*. However, this reconstruction may lose much of its strength if the Arabic names of the *bā*, *hā* type should prove to be later innovations, like the modern Ethiopic names *hā*, *lā*, etc., used in place of the older *hōi*, *lawe*, etc. [46]

The various names of the mark denoting the absence of the vowel furnish additional and important evidence in favour of the originally syllabic character of the Semitic and derived writings. Thus, the modern Hebrew name *shewa* is derived from a word *šāw'*, 'nothing,' while the older Hebrew expression *ḥiṭpā* goes back to the root *ḥṭp* meaning 'to take away'. The Arabic word corresponding to the Hebrew *shewa* is either *sukūn* from the root *skn*, 'to be quiet, to be without motion,' or *ǧezma*, from *ǧzm*, 'to cut, to cut off.' The Syriac word *marhᵉṭānā*, from the root *rhṭ*, 'to run,' is used not only to indicate the absence of the vowel but sometimes even that of a consonant which has disappeared from spoken usage as, for example, in the writing of $m^e d\bar{\imath}tt\bar{a}$ for the older $m^e d\bar{\imath}nt\bar{a}$ (with a $marh^e\underline{t}\bar{a}n\bar{a}$ stroke over the n sign). Finally, the derivation of the Sanskrit word $vir\bar{a}ma$ from the root ram, 'to bring to a stop, to rest,' parallels closely that of the Arabic $suk\bar{u}n$.[47] The implications which can be drawn, at least in the case of the names based on the roots $ht\underline{p}$ and $\check{g}zm$, are therefore that the $shewa$ sign is used to denote the cutting-off of the vowel value from the basically syllabic sign. The names based on the root meaning 'to rest' may similarly be taken to indicate the resting, that is, the non-pronunciation, of an inherent vowel.

To the question whether there is any evidence in favour of the theory here proposed in writings other than West Semitic, the answer cannot be given in dogmatic terms. Perhaps the following discussion will help to shed some light on the problem. It was observed long ago that the Late Assyrian and Babylonian texts frequently use abnormal spellings with vowels interpolated between consonants as, for example, na-ta-ku-lu for $natkul\bar{u}$, a-pa-ta-$la\underline{h}$ for $u\underline{p}talah$, li-qi-bi for $liqb\bar{\imath}$, i-$\underline{h}u$-bu-tu for $i\underline{h}butu$.[48] Especially important is the very frequent occurrence in this period of spellings with a non-functional vowel after a consonant at the end of the word as, for example, in ba-la-$\underline{t}a$ for $bal\bar{a}\underline{t}$, a-ra-ku for $ar\bar{a}k$, na-di-na for $n\bar{a}din$, ku-$\acute{u}$-mu for $k\hat{u}m$.[49] Both Sigurd Ylvisaker[50] and Thorkild Jacobsen[51] have tried to explain the interpolations as anaptyctic vowels introduced between any two consonants as a result of difficulties in pronouncing consonantal clusters. Theoretically, at least, there can be no serious objection against the development of anaptyxis in late Assyro-Babylonian, as this phenomenon is found in many languages of the world as, for instance, in our own dialectal 'eləm' for 'elm'. But even if we admit anaptyxis as the right interpretation for the vowels interpolated between consonants, still the problem of the spellings with final vowels is left unexplained. It seems to me that the question of vowels interpolated between two consonants and that of vowels added at the end of words should not be treated separately but as one problem. The main reason for this assumption is the fact that both phenomena seem to have made their appearance at the same time in the late Assyro-Babylonian period. Therefore, it appears that, as the question of the final vowels cannot be explained on a phonetic basis, so also the phonetic explanation of the interpolated vowels should be abandoned. Consequently, if the interpretation of both phenomena here discussed cannot be supported by phonetic arguments, the only other possibility is interpretation on a graphic basis.[52] Then again, there is nothing in the cuneiform system of writing which would support such an interpretation. Cuneiform writing is perfectly capable of expressing correctly words like *natkulū* or *balāṭ* as *na-at-ku-lu* or *ba-la-aṭ* respectively, leaving entirely unexplained the existence of such attested spellings as *na-ta-ku-lu* or *ba-la-ṭa*. But we should remember that it was not only the cuneiform writing that was used in Mesopotamia in the late Assyro-Babylonian period. This was the time when Aramaic influence began to be preponderant in large parts of the Near East. How strong this influence was, especially in Mesopotamia, is well attested by the numerous Aramaic inscriptions discovered in both Assyria and Babylonia, which clearly prove that the country was at that time bilingual and biscriptural. If, then, we understand the Aramaic writing, like other Semitic writings, to be a system of syllabic signs each expressing a consonant plus any vowel, we can explain the abnormal cuneiform spellings discussed above very simply as a reflection of the Aramaic system.[53]

In arguing in favour of the syllabic character of the Semitic writings I do not stand alone. Years ago Franz Praetorius, in comparing the Canaanite writing with the Cypriote syllabary, was forced to reach the conclusion that the former, too, was a syllabary.[54] Another scholar, for reasons which are not altogether clear, used the term 'Phoenician syllabary'.[55] S. Yeivin, in a short but stimulating article, identified both the Egyptian and the West Semitic writings as syllabaries.[56] David Diringer refers to the opinion of some scholars who believe that the Semitic alphabet cannot be considered a true alphabet because it does not possess vowels.[57] Relevant is the opinion of Eduard Schwyzer, who interpreted the older, syllabic, value *he* (besides *h*) of the Greek *ēta* 'als Rest der silbischen Geltung im phönikischen Alphabet'.[58] Here, too, should be mentioned the opinion of Professor Arno Poebel, of the University of Chicago, who regards the Semitic writing as a syllabary and not as an alphabet on the basis of evidence furnished by the character of the Ethiopic writing (see pp. 149 f.) and the Akkadian inter-polated vowels (see p. 151 f.).[59] However, Professor Poebel never thought of the Egyptian writing as being syllabic and he did not try to fit his interpretation into a general history of writing.

It was only after all this discussion was written down that a student in one of my classes called my attention to a remark in a recently published book by Edgar H. Sturtevant,[60] from which I learned that also the famous Danish scholar, Holger Pedersen, understood both the Egyptian and Semitic writings to be syllabic.[61] The interesting thing about this is that Pedersen was able to reach what I believe to be the correct solution of the problem not on the basis of any specific factual evidence but from a correct evaluation of the theoretical development of writing. To be sure, Pedersen still speaks of the 'Semitic alphabet' and places it among the 'alphabetical systems', but in his understanding of the 'Semitic alphabet' as 'a syllable-script, which to us may seem to be a consonant script',[62] he expressed an opinion that is quite near the one defended in this study.[63]

AEGEAN SYLLABARIES

Under the heading of Aegean syllabaries we include the Cypriote, Cypro-Minoan, Phaistos, and possibly the Byblos syllabaries, all of which originated under the direct or indirect influence of one or more of the Cretan writings. From the typological aspect the main characteristic of the Aegean syllabaries is the existence of syllabic signs expressing a vowel or a consonant plus a vowel.

At many sites on the island of Cyprus there have been discovered inscriptions in a system of writing which we call 'the Cypriote syllabary'. When this writing was deciphered in the second half of the past century it was found that most of the inscriptions were written in the Greek language while a few were in an ununderstandable autochthonous language of Cyprus. At first, nothing was known about the origin of this unique writing, which clearly had no connection with either the Greek or the Phoenician system.

In the course of time Enkomi, or old Salamis, and other sites in Cyprus yielded some short inscriptions in characters which could not be read. These Bronze Age inscriptions are now dated to about 1500–1150 B.C. and are thus considerably older than the Iron Age inscriptions in the Cypriote syllabary which was in use from about 700 to the first century B.C. The relatively long gap between the end of the Bronze Age writing and the beginning of the Cypriote syllabary is as yet difficult to explain.

Sir Arthur Evans proved, in my opinion convincingly, that these enigmatic Bronze Age signs, which he called 'Cypro-Minoan', are definitely related to the Cretan script.[64] In fact, as the Cretan influence on Cyprus is well attested for this period, he concluded that the Cypro-Minoan writing was a provincial offshoot of Cretan. Evans also proved that the signs of the later Cypriote syllabary can be linked formally with the Cretan characters by way of the intermediate Cypro-Minoan signs. The whole problem was restated in a full article by John Franklin Daniel.[65] Daniel reached the conclusion that there are some 101 extant Cypro-Minoan inscriptions, all on pottery, with sixty-three different signs plus ten additional signs for numbers. The ties between the Cypro-Minoan writ-

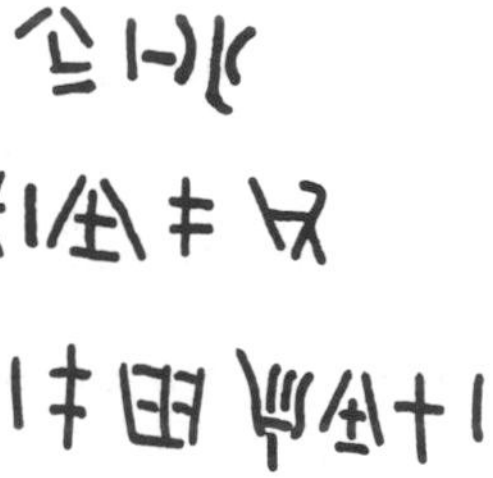

FIG. 80.—THREE SHORT TEXTS
FROM ENKOMI (CYPRUS)
From A. Evans, *The Palace of Minos*, iv
(London, 1935), 760

ing on the one hand and Cretan and later Cypriote on the other are shown in Figure 79. Figure 80 illustrates three short texts from Enkomi which, like other Cypro-Minoan inscriptions, are characterized by extreme brevity (1–8 signs).[66]

The classical Cypriote syllabary consists of fifty-six signs, each of which stands for a syllable ending in a vowel (Fig. 81). Double consonants, long vowels, pre-consonantal nasals, and distinction between voiced, voiceless, and aspirated consonants were not indicated in the writing. The syllabary was originally devised for a non-Greek language and was badly suited to express Greek, for which it was later adapted. The following examples best illustrate the difficulties: *to-ko-ro-ne* stands for τὸν χῶρον; *a-ti-ri-a-se* = ἀνδρίας; *sa-ta-si-ka-ra-te-se* = Στασι-κράτης; *a-ra-ku-ro* = ἀργύρῳ; *a-to-ro-po-se* = ἄνθρωπος or ἄτροπος

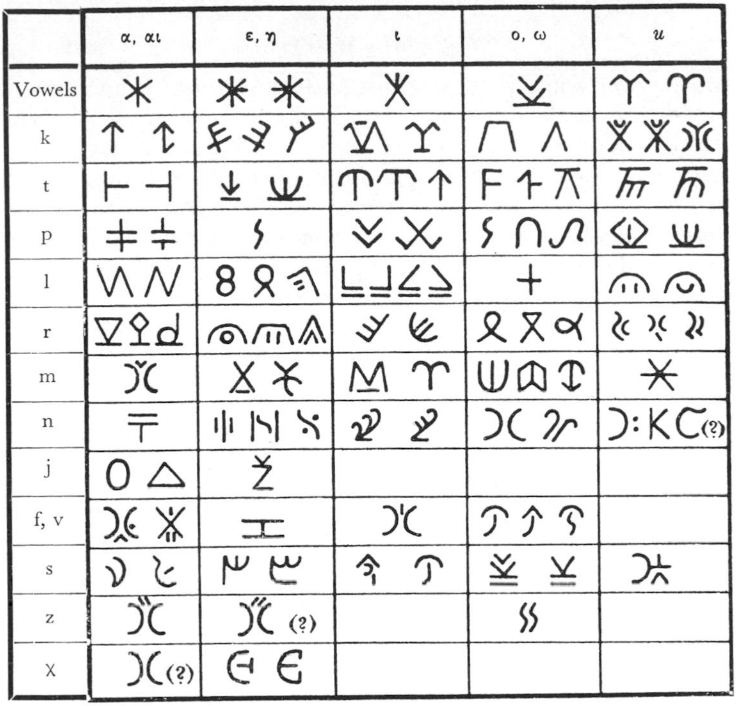

	α, αι	ε, η	ι	o, ω	u
Vowels					
k					
t					
p					
l					
r					
m					
n					
j					
f, v					
s					
z					
x					

FIG. 81.—CYPRIOTE SYLLABARY

From H. Jensen, *Die Schrift* (Glückstadt und Hamburg, 1935), p. 97

or ἄτροφος or ἄδορπος. A typical Cypriote inscription is shown in Figure 82.

Entirely unique is the clay disk from Phaistos, in Crete (Fig. 83), dated to the seventeenth century B.C. on the basis of stratigraphy. The lines of writing are arranged spirally. Since in most pictographic writings the pictures normally face toward the beginning of the line it is probably safe to assume that the writing starts at the outside of the disk, not in the

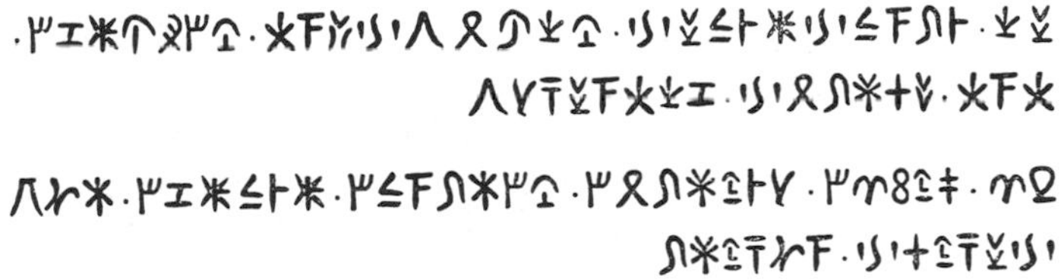

FIG. 82.—A CYPRIOTE INSCRIPTION FROM EDALION

From Fossey, *Notices sur les caractères étrangers*, p. 57

155

centre. The signs represent distinctly recognizable pictures of people, animals, objects of daily life, and buildings. The strange thing about these pictures is that even though some resemblances between them and the Cretan signs can be found, in general the forms are different. They clearly represent an individual development. There are only forty-five different signs used on the disk, but taking into consideration the relative brevity of the inscription we may assume that the complete system included about sixty signs. The number of signs used, and the fact that the words separated by vertical division lines consist of two to five signs, makes it safe to assume that the writing is syllabic, of the Aegean type.

Perhaps the most unusual feature of the Phaistos disk is the fact that the signs were not incised with a stylus, as could be

expected with writing on clay, but that the individual signs were made with stamps. This case of writing with movable type is unique in the Aegean cultural area, although parallels can be found in Mesopotamia from the much later Assyrian period. [67]

Another system which may very well belong to the Aegean group of syllabic writings was discovered recently in Syrian Byblos, where so many important archaeological discoveries have been made in the last few years. The first of the texts in the new writing came to light in 1929 in the form of a fragmentary stone stela with ten lines of writing (Fig. 84). Subsequently, nine more inscriptions were dug up in Byblos, among which were two bronze tablets, four spatulae, and three stone inscriptions. All these texts have now been published by Maurice

FIG. 83.—PHAISTOS DISK

From A. J. Evans, *Scripta Minoa*, i (Oxford, 1909), pls. xii f.

Dunand.[68] The writing has only recently been discussed by the distinguished French Orientalist Edouard Dhorme.[69]

According to Dhorme, there are fifty-three different signs in one inscription which has a total of 217 signs, and sixty-four different signs in another inscription which contains a total of 461 signs. However, Dunand refers to 114 different signs in the Byblos writing.[70] There seems to be a discrepancy here since from the existence of fifty-three and sixty-four different signs in two inscriptions of considerable length we should not expect the full syllabary to contain more than about eighty to ninety signs. Elsewhere, Dhorme calls the Byblos writing both syllabic and alphabetic, and even insists that there are certain syllabic signs which consist of a vowel plus consonant. These are

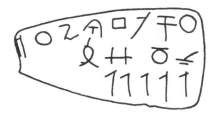

FIG. 84.—BYBLOS INSCRIPTION
From M. Dunand, *Byblia grammata*
(Beyrouth, 1945), p. 78

all facts which are incompatible with the type of syllabaries known to us from the Aegean area and force us to conclude that the Byblos writing may be of a character different from the Aegean syllabaries, unless, possibly, later revision and clarification by Professor Dhorme should remove some of the difficulties that stand in the way of an Aegean affiliation. The language of the Byblos inscriptions is taken to be Semitic and, more specifically, Phoenician.

The dating of the new inscriptions is still a moot problem. While Dunand assigned them to the last quarter of the third millennium or the first quarter of the second millennium, Dhorme lowered the date to the fourteenth century B.C. Important for the dating is to note that the other side of the spatula with the inscription of 'Azarba'al (see p. 131) contains signs which, according to Dunand himself,[71] find best parallels in the signs of the ten Byblos inscriptions discussed above. Thus, the date of the new Byblos writing may be considerably lower than hitherto thought.

JAPANESE SYLLABARY

After a few centuries of cultural and commercial contact between China and Japan the Chinese system of writing seems to have made its appearance in Japan some time in the fifth century of our era. The Chinese word signs were simply taken over by the Japanese and read not with their Chinese values but in Japanese. Thus, for example, the Chinese word sign *nan*, 'south,' was read in Japanese as *minami* with the meaning 'south'. The Chinese writing may have been well suited to a monosyllabic and isolating language in which grammatical forms are normally expressed by syntactical position rather than by special formatives. However, such a writing was not suited to Japanese, a language which is polysyllabic and agglutinative, and expresses grammatical forms by means of special formatives. Therefore, the custom soon developed of employing some of the Chinese word signs as syllabic signs to express the grammatical formatives of the Japanese language. Originally the choice of the syllabic signs was unsystematic, and it was not until about the ninth century that a stable syllabary with a limited number of signs made its appearance.

From the ninth century on, two formal types of the Japanese syllabary (the so-called *kana*, perhaps from *kanna* < *kari na*, 'borrowed names') developed:—

(1) The *katakana*, 'side *kana*,' also known as *Yamatogana*, 'Japanese *kana*' (*Yamato* = 'Japan,' *gana* = *kana*), developed usually from parts of the characters of the normal Chinese writing (*k'ai-shu*), and used chiefly in scientific literature and public documents (Fig. 85).

(2) The *hiragana*, 'simple *kana*,' developed from the cursive Chinese writing (*ts'ao-shu*), and used extensively in newspapers, belles-lettres, and in general in daily life (Fig. 86).

The Japanese syllabary consists of forty-seven basic signs. The *katakana* is a simple system and easy to learn because of the uniformity of the signs, while the *hiragana*, with its more than 300 variant forms and the difficulties which arise in joining the signs, offers a considerably more complex picture.[72]

The values of the Japanese syllabic signs are derived normally from Chinese, but frequently with their Japanese pronunciation: Chinese *nu*, 'slave,' is used for the syllable *nu*; Chinese *mao*, 'hair,' pronounced *mo* in Japanese, is used for the syllable *mo*;

k'ai-shu	kata-kana		k'ai-shu	kata-kana		k'ai-shu	kata-kana	
阿	ア	a	千	チ	*ti* (*chi*)	牟	ム	*mu*
伊	イ	i	閂 津	ツ	*tu* (*tsu*)	女	メ	*me*
宇	ウ	u	天	テ	*te*	毛	モ	*mo*
江	エ	e	土	ト	*to*	也	ヤ	*ya*
扵	オ	o	奈	ナ	*na*	勇 油	ユ	*yu*
加	カ	ka	仁 二	ニ	*ni*	與	ヨ	*yo*
幾	キ	ki	奴	ヌ	*nu*	良	ラ	*ra*
久	ク	ku	子	子	*ne*	利	リ	*ri*
个 計	ケ	ke	乃	ノ	*no*	流	ル	*ru*
己	コ	ko	八	ハ	*fa* (*ha*)	礼	レ	*re*
草 散 左	サ	sa	比	ヒ	*fi* (*hi*)	呂	ロ	*ro*
之	シ	*si* (*shi*)	不	フ	*fu*	曰	ワ	*wa*
須	ス	su	皿 邊	ヘ	*fe* (*he*)	慧	エ	*we*
世	セ	se	保	ホ	*fo* (*ho*)	伊	井	*wi*
曽	ソ	so	末	マ	*ma*	乎	ヲ	*wo*
多	タ	ta	三 美	ミ ミ	*mi*	—	—	—

FIG. 85.—JAPANESE KATAKANA WRITING COMPARED WITH CHINESE K'AI-SHU

From Jensen, *Die Schrift*, p. 156

Chinese *t'ien*, 'heaven,' pronounced *te(n)* in Japanese, is used for the syllable *te*. Sometimes the Chinese sign is given its Japanese value, as in Chinese *san*, 'three,' corresponding to Japanese *mi*, 'three,' giving rise to the syllable *mi*, or in Chinese *nü*, 'woman,' Japanese *me*, 'woman,' resulting in the syllable *me*.

JAPANESE SYLLABARY

In addition to the forty-seven basic signs of the *kana*, several marks were developed to indicate various phonetic features. Thus, the *nigori*-mark is used to differentiate voiced consonants from voiceless ones; the *maru*-mark, added to the syllables

Katakana

ア	カ	サ	タ	ナ	ハ	マ	ヤ	ラ	ワ		ガ	ザ	ダ	バ	パ
a	ka	sa	ta	na	ha	ma	ya	ra	wa		ga	za	da	ba	pa
イ	キ	シ	チ	ニ	ヒ	ミ		リ	ヰ		ギ	ジ	ヂ	ビ	ピ
i	ki	si	ti(tsi)	ni	hi	mi		ri	wi(i)		gi	zi	di	bi	pi
ウ	ク	ス	ツ	ヌ	フ	ム	ユ	ル			グ	ズ	ヅ	ブ	プ
u	ku	su	tu(tsu)	nu	hu	mu	yu	ru			gu	zu	du	bu	pu
ヱ	ケ	セ	テ	子	ヘ	メ	エ	✓	ヱ		ゲ	ゼ	デ	ベ	ヘ
e	ke	se	te	ne	he	me	ye	re	we (e)		ge	ze	de	be	pe
オ	コ	ツ	ト	ノ	ホ	モ	ヨ	ロ	ヲ		ゴ	ゾ	ド	ボ	ホ
o	ko	so	to	no	ho	mo	yo	ro	wo		go	zo	do	bo	po

ン (n)

Hiragana

わ	か	さ	た	ふ	は	ま	や	ら	わ		が	ざ	だ	は	ぱ
a	ka	sa	ta	na	ha	ma	ya	ra	wa		ga	za	da	ba	pa
い	き	し	ち	に	ひ	み		り	ゐ		ぎ	じ	ぢ	び	ぴ
i	ki	si	ti,(tsi)	ni	hi	mi		ri	wi		gi	zi	di	bi	pi
う	く	す	つ	ぬ	ふ	む	ゆ	る			ぐ	ず	づ	ぶ	ぷ
u	ku	su	tu,(tsu)	nu	hu	mu	yu	ru			gu	zu	du	bu	pu
ゑ	け	せ	て	ね	へ	め	え	れ	ゑ		げ	ぜ	で	べ	ぺ
e	ke	se	te	ne	he	me	ye	re	we (e)		ge	ze	de	be	pe
れ	こ	そ	と	の	ほ	も	よ	ろ	を		ご	ぞ	ど	ぼ	ぽ
o	ko	so	to	no	ho	mo	yo	ro	wo		go	zo	do	bo	po

ん (n)

FIG. 86.—JAPANESE KATAKANA AND HIRAGANA WRITINGS
From Fossey, *Notices sur les caractères étrangers*, first edition, p. 314

containing *h*, changes their value to *p;* the *tsu*-mark indicates the doubling of consonants; a special sign for *n, ng*, and *m* is used for syllables ending in these consonants and, finally, there are two different marks, one indicating the reduplication of a syllable and the other the reduplication of two or more syllables.

Even with their two fully developed syllabic systems the Japanese could not persuade themselves to give up the old Chinese logography. The syllabic writing is used normally in children's books; for all other purposes the Japanese use a type of writing called *Kanamajiri*, which consists of a mixture of word signs, called *kanji*, and of syllabic signs, called *kana*. While *kanji* is used mainly to express nouns, adjectives, and verbs, *kana* is used mainly to express names, foreign words, as well as grammatical formatives, particles, and other purely phonetic elements. The uses of the *kana* signs in conjunction with the main *kanji* sign as syllabic helps in the reading of difficult word signs are of two classes: *Okurigana* ('accompanying *kana*'), in which the signs are placed below the *kanji* sign to indicate grammatical formatives; and *hurigana* ('scattered *kana*'), in which the signs are placed to the right (very rarely to the left) of the *kanji* sign to indicate its pronunciation.

The efforts of some Japanese to simplify their writing by eliminating entirely the Chinese word signs have remained unsuccessful up to now. [73]

OBSERVATIONS

Of all the various systems of writing the syllabic writings are the easiest to evaluate. Actually our observations could be limited to this short statement: *All syllabic writings are either identical with, or simplified from, the respective syllabaries of the word-syllabic writings from which they are derived.* The following short discussion is presented here to bring out more sharply the existing similarities and divergencies.

The chart in Figure 87 shows the four types of syllabic writing, namely the cuneiform, Semitic, Cypriote, and Japanese syllabaries. The various cuneiform syllabaries of the Elamites, Hurrians, Urartians, etc., are all derived from the Mesopotamian cuneiform both from the formal and the structural point of view. The only difference is the lack of dissyllabic signs in the derived systems, a fact which should not surprise anyone who remembers that dissyllabic signs are rare even in the Mesopotamian system. The various Semitic syllabaries, different as they may be in their formal aspect, are all derived structurally from the Egyptian; but while Egyptian uses monosyllabic as well as dissyllabic signs, all ending in a

	Derived Cuneiform Syllabaries		*West Semitic Syllabaries*		*Cypriote Syllabary*		*Japanese Syllabary*	
Open Mono-syllables	a	ta	ʾ^{a}	t^{a}	a	ta	a	ta
	i	ti	ʾ^{i}	t^{i}	i	ti	i	ti
	e	te	ʾ^{e}	t^{e}	e	te	e	te
	u	tu	ʾ^{u}	t^{u}	u	tu	u	tu
	—	—	ʾ^{o}	t^{o}	o	to	o	to
Close Mono-syllables	at	tam (or ta-am)	— (ʾ^{a}-t$^{(a)}$)	— (t^{a}-m$^{(a)}$)	— (a-t(a))	— (ta-m(a))	— (a-t(o/u))	— (ta-m(o/u))
	it	tim (or ti-im)	— (ʾ^{i}-t$^{(i)}$)	— (t^{i}-m$^{(i)}$)	— (i-t(i))	— (ti-m(i))	— (i-t(o/u))	— (ti-m(o/u))
	en	men (or me-en)	— (ʾ^{e}-t$^{(e)}$)	— (t^{e}-m$^{(e)}$)	— (e-t(e))	— (te-m(e))	— (e-t(o/u))	— (te-m(o/u))
	ut	tum (or tu-um)	— (ʾ^{u}-t$^{(u)}$)	— (t^{u}-m$^{(u)}$)	— (u-t(u))	— (tu-m(u))	— (u-t(o/u))	— (tu-m(o/u))
	—	—	— (ʾ^{o}-t$^{(o)}$)	— (t^{o}-m$^{(o)}$)	— (o-t(o))	— (to-m(o))	— (o-t(o/u))	— (to-m(o/u))

FIG. 87.—TYPES OF SYLLABIC SIGNS IN SYLLABIC WRITINGS

vowel the Semitic syllabaries are restricted to monosyllables. The Cypriote syllabary, formally connected with the Cretan writing, consists only of open monosyllables with a clear indication of the final vowel, and thus represents the structural type well known in hieroglyphic Hittite and presumably in other writings of the Aegean group. The Japanese syllabary is formally derived from the Chinese writing. Structurally, however, it is farther removed from its Chinese prototype than are the Near Eastern syllabaries from their respective word-syllabic models. The creation of a syllabary consisting solely of mono-syllabic signs ending in a vowel may have been induced by the character of the Japanese language which generally requires open syllables as, for example, in the words 'mikado, Hirohito, Nagasaki', etc. Therefore, there may not be any need for assuming the influence of the Sanskrit writing upon the Japanese, as suggested by some scholars. [74]

The writing of close syllables in the derived syllabaries parallels generally the methods used in the syllabaries of the word-syllabic prototypes. Thus, the combination *tapta* would be written as *tap-ta* or *ta-ap-ta* in cuneiform, as t^a-$p^{(a)}$-t^a in Semitic, and as *ta-p(a)-ta* in Cypriote. In Japanese this would be written *ta-p(o)-ta* or *ta-p(u)-ta*, since in this system the consonant of a close syllable (usually in foreign words and names) is expressed normally by a syllable ending in *o* or *u*. It should be remembered, however, that Japanese close syllables ending in *n*, *ng*, and *m* are expressed by a special mark (see p. 161). The writing of a syllable ending in two contiguous consonants is similar to that of a syllable ending in one consonant. Thus, a combination *tapt* may be written as *tap-t(a)*, *ta-ap-t(a)*, *ta-pa-at*, or *ta-ap-at* in cuneiform, t^a-$p^{(a)}$-$t^{(a)}$ in Semitic, *ta-p(a)-t(a)* in Cypriote, and *ta-p(o)-t(o)* or *ta-p(u)-t(u)* in Japanese.

The following is a comparative table showing the number of signs as used in the four types of syllabaries:—

100–130 signs in the derived cuneiform syllabaries.

22–30 signs in the Semitic syllabaries.

56 signs in the Cypriote syllabary.

47 signs in the Japanese syllabary. [75]

Much more on the structure of the syllabic systems can be learned from the writings introduced among native societies under the stimulus of white men and briefly discussed below in Chapter VII. This is a subject which would require special treatment out of all proportion to the scope of the present study.

Only two of the four systems here discussed employ syllabic signs exclusively, namely the Semitic and the Cypriote writings. The derived cuneiform writings carry with them a limited number of word signs, taken over from the Mesopotamian cuneiform; and the Japanese syllabic system (*kana*) is used side by side with a number of Chinese word signs (*kanji*).

The respective similarities between the Mesopotamian, Egyptian, and Hittite writings on the one hand and the derived cuneiform, Semitic, and Cypriote syllabaries on the other are so striking that one naturally wonders about the reasons which prevented the word-syllabic systems from developing locally into full syllabic writings. How close some phases of the word-syllabic writings were to developing into full syllabic systems may very well be observed by comparing any of the Elamite, Hurrian, or Urartian texts with those of the Old Akkadian or Cappadocian period of the Mesopotamian writing ; or any West Semitic text with the late Egyptian texts discussed above in this study; or any Cypriote text with the Hittite inscription transliterated and translated above, all discussed above, p. 114. Still, near as some of the phases of word-syllabic writings were to the development of a full syllabary, they never quite reached it. The reason for this does not lie solely in the conservative attachment of a people for their own writing. It is rather the protection of vested interests of a special caste, religious (Egypt, Babylonia), or political (China), that frequently may have been responsible for maintaining a difficult and obsolete form of writing, making thus its general use by the people impossible. It is therefore foreign peoples, not bound by local traditions and religious or political interests of an alien group, that are frequently responsible for introducing new and important developments in the history of writing.

V

THE ALPHABET

I F the alphabet is defined as a system of signs expressing single sounds of speech, then the first alphabet which can justifiably be so called is the Greek alphabet. However, the new type of writing did not spring up suddenly on Greek soil as a new and strange blossom. We have had occasion on preceding pages to refer often enough to that important aspect of evolution which shows that for every new feature in a new type of writing parallels can be found in some older types. And so it happened with the Greek alphabet. Its roots and its background lie in the Ancient Orient.

ORIENTAL FORERUNNERS

The old Hebrew writing, like other West Semitic systems, used only syllabic signs beginning with a consonant and ending in any vowel. In order to indicate the exact character of a long vowel, syllabic signs beginning with a so-called 'weak consonant' were frequently added to the preceding syllable to form a unit which is known as *scriptio plena* or *plene* writing. Thus, the name 'David' was written in old Hebrew as $D^aw^id^{(i)}$ in *scriptio defectiva*, but as $D^aw^iy^id^{(i)}$ in *scriptio plena*. The sign y^i does not stand here for an independent syllable; its sole purpose is to make sure that the previous syllable w^i will be read as wi and not wa, we, wu, or wo. Similarly, the addition of w^u in the *plene* spelling of $^{\jmath}a^{š u}w^{u}r^{(u)}$, as contrasted with the defective spelling $^{\jmath}a^{š u}r^{(u)}$ for $^{\jmath}Aššur$, 'Assyria,' made it certain that at least the syllable $šu$ would be read with the correct vowel. These additional signs helping in the reading of the vowel of the preceding syllable are called *matres lectionis*, evidently a translation-borrowing from the Hebrew expression $^{\jmath}immōth haqq^er^{\bar{\imath}\jmath}āh$,

166

'mothers of reading.' According to the Hebrew scholar, David Qimḥi, there are ten vowels in Hebrew, five long (mothers) and five short (daughters) vowels, without the aid of which no letter can be pronounced.[1]

How old the biblical *plene* writing is cannot be ascertained because of the manifold difficulties with the dating of the Massoretic text. That the device was not freely invented by the Hebrews can be seen from the fact that many systems of writing, much older than even the oldest sources of the Bible, make extensive use of it.

The standard interpretation of the biblical *matres lectionis* is that they have developed from original diphthongs which were later contracted into long vowels.[2] Thus, the biblical spelling with w^z in $y^z w^z m^z$ for *yôm*, 'day,' is supposedly due to the fact that this word actually was pronounced at one time something like *yawm*, and only after it was contracted to *yôm* did the idea originate among the ancients that such full spellings could serve the purpose of vowel indication. Against this interpretation we may adduce the fact that the contraction of *aw* to *ô*, *ay* to *ê* took place in the middle of the second millennium B.C. long before the introduction of a full system of writing in Palestine and that *scriptio plena* occurs chiefly in the case of the plural ending *-îm*, *ôt*, and the 1st person pronominal suffix *-î*, which are not due to contraction. Furthermore, as we shall see later, the *scriptio plena* device occurs in many writings—Semitic and non-Semitic— where it could never be explained as originating from a diphthongal contraction.

If we disregard the doubtful occurrences of *plene* writing in the Ugaritic inscriptions from Râs Shamrah (see pp. 129 f.) and the earliest Phoenician inscriptions from Byblos (see pp. 131 f.), then the first sure evidence for the *plene* writing is found in the ninth century, in the Mešaᶜ inscription and in the earliest texts from Zincirli (see p. 133).[3] The *plene* writing at first is attested mainly in the final position, as in the spelling of $ᵓ^a b^i y^i$ for *ᵓabī*, 'my father,' or $w^a š^n m^u w^u$ for *wašâmū*, 'and they set.' In later times it is frequently found both in the final and medial portions. Compare, e.g., the spellings of $z^{a ᵓ a} t^{(a)}$ for *zât*, 'this,' (feminine) as against $z^{a t (a)}$; $z^e h^e$ for *zê*, 'this,' (masculine) as against z^e; $w^z y^z l^z k^u w^u$, 'they went,' as against $y^z z^z b^z h^u$, 'they will sacrifice'; $b^a n^i t^i y^i$ and $b^a n^i y^i t^i$ for *banîtī*, 'I built,' as against $b^a n^i t^i$.[4] Besides the signs *ᵓāleph*, *hē*, *wāw*, and *yōdh* also the signs *ḥēth* and *ᶜayin*[5] are used as *matres lectionis*, though only in late Semitic writings. In the course of years the device grew more common until it reached a rather high degree of systematization in the neo-Punic, Mandean, and other late Semitic systems of writing. To what extent this full Semitic device of vowel indication is the result of natural development and to what extent it may have been influenced by the classical writings (Latin or Greek) is rather difficult to decide.

The principle of vowel indication by means of *matres lectionis* which we found in the Semitic writings corresponds to what is known in Egyptian under the name of 'syllabic orthography'. Much as I agree with W. F. Albright[6] and his predecessors on the meaning and aims of the Egyptian 'syllabic orthography', I cannot accept this term. Since in my reconstruction the normal Egyptian phonetic, non-semantic writing is syllabic, the so-called 'syllabic orthography' with its *plene* writing represents a stage of writing in the process of developing from a syllabary toward an alphabet. However, this Egyptian system cannot be called an alphabet because the method of indicating vowels is still very inconsistent in comparison with full alphabets of the Greek type. For that reason I prefer to use the term '*plene* writing' taken over from the Semitic or even 'group writing' advocated by William F. Edgerton[7] following Alan H. Gardiner.

According to the evidence brought forth by Albright, the Egyptian *plene* or group writing made its appearance about 2000 B.C., during the Middle Kingdom, in the so-called 'execration texts' containing curses cast upon rulers of foreign lands. In subsequent centuries the device grew rapidly until it reached the apex of its development in the New Kingdom during the eighteenth and nineteenth dynasties, which ruled from the sixteenth to thirteenth centuries. From that period on the Egyptian *plene* writing proceeded on its downward course of corruption until it became completely amorphous by the tenth century B.C.[8] From the evidence adduced by Edgerton we know of some examples of *plene* writing going as far back as the Pyramid Texts of the first Egyptian dynasties.[9] That means that this device was not suddenly 'invented' around 2000 B.C., but was the result of a slow and gradual development fully comparable with that found in the Semitic writings. It is enough if we recall the rare use of the *plene* writing in the early

Semitic writings as compared with the fuller system of neo-Punic. In the case of the Egyptian *plene* writing, it may be suggested that the need to transliterate exactly the names of foreign rulers and lands during the periods of intensive foreign contacts which took place between the twelfth and nineteenth dynasties may have been the stimulus mainly responsible for the systematization of a device used only irregularly in previous periods.

Here are a few specific examples of *plene* writing in Egyptian: T^x-w^x-n^x-i^x-p^{x}^{x}-^{x} or T^x-w^x-n^x-p^x for the Syrian city Tunip; P^x-w^x-t^x-w^x-h^x-i^x-p^{x}^{x} for the name of the Hittite queen Putu-Hipa; D^x-^{x}-p^x-w^x-n^x-^{x} for the Canaanite geographical term Ṣapūna, Ṣapōn; Q^x-^{x}-$r^{(x)}$-q^x-^{x}-m^x-$š^x$-^{x} or Q^x-^{x}-r^x-i^x-q^x-^{x}-m^x-i^x-$š^x$-^{x} for the Syrian city Carchemish, old Karkamiša(š) or Karkamiš; N^x-^{x}-h^x-r^x-i^x-n^x-^{x}, N^x-h^x-r^x-i^x-n^x, N^x-h^x-r^x-i^x-n^x-^{x}, or N^x-h^x-^{x}-r^x-i^x-n^x-^{x} for Naharina or Nahrina, 'Mesopotamia'; Q^x-^{x}-d^x-^{x}-w^x-^{x}-d^x-^{x}-n^x-^{x}, Q^x-^{x}-d^x-w^x-^{x}-d^x-^{x}-n^x-^{x}, Q^x-i^x-d^x-^{x}-w^x-^{x}-d^x-^{x}-n^x-^{x} for the Anatolian country Kiz(zu)wat(a)na.

In the above examples we find the syllabic signs containing initial ', w, and i used as *matres lectionis*. The use of w^x and i^x in these examples to indicate the respective vowels u and i is self-evident. But besides the clear cases of the sign containing ' for the vowel a, as in the spelling of Nah(a)rīna, there are others in which this sign is used in group writings presumably requiring only a consonant. What is the reason for the final ^{x} in the names Tunip or Karkamiš? Even the argument that this sign may represent the vowel a of such old Semitic names as Qatna, Kassapa, Haṣūra, and many others, would still leave unexplained the spelling with i^x after r^x in the name Karkamiš. The correct interpretation of these anaptyctic vowels, medial and final, in the Egyptian group writing remains a problem to be tackled in the future by scholars interested in this subject.[10]

One does not have to be a trained Egyptologist to recognize that the Egyptian *matres lectionis* are functional in character. To the historian of writing the parallels from the Semitic and other systems alone prove the point conclusively. Of course, the system as reconstructed by Albright may not be true in all details, and there are many cases of inconsistent spelling which may speak against the interpretation of this or that reading. For instance, I feel very strongly that Albright's intrepretation of some sign groups as simple consonants, such as k or r, or as syllables beginning with a vowel and ending in a consonant, such as *an, in, un, ar, ir, ur,* will have to be revised. If it is accepted that the basic Egyptian phonetic, non-semantic writing consists only of syllabic signs beginning with a consonant (see pp. 75 ff.), then the group writing developed from it should have syllabic signs of identical structure. There is no need for transliterations of the type *r* or *ar* since parallels with such syllabic writings as hieroglyphic Hittite would allow transliterations as $r^{(x)}$, $r^{(a)}$, or the like for a syllable in which the final vowel is silent.[11]

In the article quoted above on p. 168, Professor Edgerton makes the statement that 'Albright's "syllabic" theory of Egyptian group-writing has certainly not been proved. The weight of evidence is clearly and strongly against it'; then after quoting some examples for which an interpretation as syllabic writing can be suggested, be it only 'a somewhat remote possibility', he concludes: 'It is my considered opinion that no Egyptian scribe of the Nineteenth Dynasty or earlier ever consciously attempted to represent a vowel sound in hieroglyphic or hieratic writing by any device whatever.'[12] This means, in short, that the addition of various signs in the Egyptian group writing has no function whatsoever, and is due simply to the whims of various scribal schools. Much as I respect the scholarly opinions of my good friend and colleague, this is a statement which I cannot leave unchallenged. Of course, there are many inconsistencies in the Egyptian writing due to personal whim, as there are in other writings or, for that matter, in all phases of human behaviour and culture. But the existence of these inconsistencies should not lead us to the blind denial of important principles or systems governing the majority of cases. To anybody who, like myself, has been brought up on the proposition that all life is governed by rules and principles, however inconsistently they may be applied in practice, a statement referring to the 'utterly unsystematic character of Egyptian writing' sounds almost like heresy. Such a statement can be challenged not only on general principle but, more than that, it can be proved to be most improbable in the case of Egyptian writing from comparison with many other systems. What should we say about such spellings as $n^x d^x r^x$, $n^{xc} d^x r^x$, and $n^x d^{xc} r^x$, 'vow'; $š^x m^{xc}$, $š^x m^{xɔx}$, $š^x m^x m^x$, and $š^{xc} m^{xɔx}$, 'he heard';[13] or $b^{xc} x l^x$ and $b^{xc} x l^{x)x}$, 'lord', all found in neo-Punic? Surely the existence of a general principle governing the indication of vowels by means of separate signs cannot be denied in the neo-Punic writing. That vowels are indicated in some places and not in others, or that they appear in places where we should not expect them normally, only shows how inconsistently or even erroneously this principle was applied in neo-Punic texts, but the validity of the principle is left unimpaired. If this principle is accepted for neo-Punic then, from the point of view of the theory of writing, it must apply also for the parallel system of vowel indication in the Egyptian group writing.

The system of vowel indication is found not only in writings which normally do not express the vowels, such as Semitic and Egyptian, but also in purely syllabic writings, such as cuneiform and Hittite hieroglyphic, which often fail to express the vowels adequately.

The normal way to indicate vocalic length in the Mesopotamian cuneiform writing in the later Assyrian periods is by the addition of a vowel sign to a preceding syllable ending in a vowel. Thus, *dâ* (*dā*) or *dî* (*dī*) are spelled *da-a* or *di-i*, in contrast to the spellings *da* or *di* which stand normally for short *da* or *di* respectively. However, in such spellings as ^{m}*Aš-šu-ra-iu-ú*,[14] 'Assyrian,' the combination *iu-ú* does not stand for *yû* (or *yū*) but for simple *yu*. Similarly, the spelling *liš-ʾa-a-lu*, 'may they ask,' frequently found in late Assyrian letters,[15] does not correspond to *lišʾālū*, but to *lišʾalū*. Even more indicative are the spellings *wa$_a$-ša-aḫ*, *at-ta-an-ni-wi$_i$-na*, *wu$_u$-la-a-ši-na*, and many others found in the Hattic, Hurrian, and Palaic cuneiform texts from Boğazköy.[16] Here the sign *wa, wi, wu* is written in its normal size, while the vowel signs *a, i,* and *u* are drawn much smaller and in a form making one unit with the preceding *wa, wi, wu* sign. It will be noted immediately that in all these cases the vowel signs are added to those syllabic signs which in the cuneiform system have the value of a consonant plus any vowel (see pp. 71 f.). As this vowel is not indicated, a device was created to eliminate this shortcoming of the cuneiform system by the addition of vowel signs.

We have seen in our discussion on pp. 69 ff. that the cuneiform system of writing usually indicated vowel differences by means of separate signs, as in the signs *da* and *du* for the syllables *da* and *du* respectively. Frequently, however, these vowels were indicated inadequately, as in the signs which can be read *li* or *ie, ri* or *re, ig* or *eg*, and in many others. This inadequacy, added to that of the signs which leave the vowel entirely unindicated, as in the sign representing *wa, wi, we*, or *wu*, led to a device of vowel indication which found its best expression in the Hurrian system of cuneiform writing as used in Mesopotamia in the second half of the second millennium B.C. (see p. 121). Thus, in the spelling of *i-i-al-le-e-ni-i-in* for *iyallenin*, the vowel sign *e* added to *li* insures that this sign will be read as *le* and not *li*, just as the vowel sign *i* added to *ni* indicates the pronunciation *ni* and not *ne*. To be sure, in the latter case the addition of *i* seems to be unnecessary because the reading of *ni* is already determined by the vowel of the sign *in*. Numerous cases of this type only show that, from a device which originally grew out of the necessity to indicate the vowels adequately, an enlarged system was gradually developed which allowed the regular addition of vowel signs even in cases where the vowels were clearly determined. But, as can be seen from such different spellings as *še-e-ḫa-la, še-ḫa-a-la*, or *še-ḫa-la-a*, this principle was used very inconsistently. [17]

Similar vowel indication is found also in systems which regularly indicate all vowel differences. In hieroglyphic Hittite the syllable *ta* in the word *ayata*, 'he will make,' is expressed by means of one syllabic sign *ta*. But besides *a-i-a-ta* also the spelling *a-i-a-ta-a* occurs. The final vowel sign is not used here to indicate the pronunciation *ayatā, ayataa*, or the like, but to show that the word is pronounced *ayata* and not *ayat*. This device was imperative in a system in which close syllables could be written only by means of syllabic signs consisting of a consonant and a vowel.

The Persian cuneiform writing was used between the sixth and fourth centuries B.C. during the period of the Achaemenid Dynasty. Being a cuneiform writing it could only have originated under the Mesopotamian stimulus, although the forms of the individual signs in the Persian system cannot be derived from any other system of cuneiform writing. As in the case of the Ugaritic system (see p. 129), the forms of the Persian signs are the result of free individual creation.

The Persian writing is a mixed system. It consists of only 41 signs, of which 36 are syllabic, four are signs for the words 'king, land, province', and 'Ahuramazda', and one is a word separator. Of the 36 syllabic signs, three different signs are used for the vowels *a*, *i*, and *u*, and six different signs for the syllables *da*, *di*, *du* and *ma*, *mi*, *mu*. Five signs stand for a consonant plus vowel *a* or *i* (*ga* = *gi*, *ka* = *ki*, *na* = *ni*, *ra* = *ri*, *ta* = *ti*), while five additional signs denote the consonant plus vowel *u* (*gu*, *ku*, *nu*, *ru* *tu*); two signs stand for a consonant plus vowel *a* or *u* (*ja* = *ju*, *wa* = *wu*) while two additional signs denote the consonant plus vowel *i* (*ji*, *wi*). In all other cases one sign stands for a consonant with any of the three vowels (*b*, *č*, *ç*, *f*, *h*, *ḫ*, *y*, *l*, *p*, *s*, *š*, *ṭ*, and *z* (Fig. 88).

In the Persian system simple consonants are expressed by syllabic signs ending in *a*, as in the writing *a-da-m*(*a*) for *adam*, but also, at least theoretically, for *adm* or *adma*. The long vowel *ā* is indicated by the addition of the vowel sign *a*, for example, in the spelling of *ha-ča-a* for *hačā*. But that this is a later development and that originally the addition of vowel signs did not serve to indicate vowel length can be deduced from such cases as *u-ta-a* = *uta*. From the parallels in the Hittite hieroglyphic writing just discussed we can judge that the sign *a* was added to *ta* to make sure that the whole word would be pronounced *uta* and not *ut*. Even more instructive is the comparison of some Persian spellings with those in the Hurrian system of writing. I refer to such spellings as *di-i* for *di* or *ku-u* for *ku*, in which apparently there is no need for writing the vowel signs *i* or *u*, since the vowels of the syllabic signs *di* and *ku* can be read in only one way. All these features indicate that the Persian writing was in the transition stage from a syllabic to an alphabetic system.

The main problem in connection with the origin of the Persian cuneiform writing is whether it was created suddenly as a full system or whether it was the result of a slow and gradual evolution. In favour of the first alternative we may refer to some traditional arguments supporting the creation of Persian writing during the time of Darius.[18] If this alternative be true, then a simple statement of fact would obviate any further speculation. The Persian cuneiform writing is a mixed system. Of the 22 consonants of Persian language, 13 are represented by 1 sign each, 7 by 2 signs each, and only 2 consonants are represented by 3 signs each. Thus, the Persian writing would seem to be a concoction based on two foreign systems. The structure of the 13 Persian signs expressing a consonant but not indicating the vowel would be identical in principle with that of the Egyptian

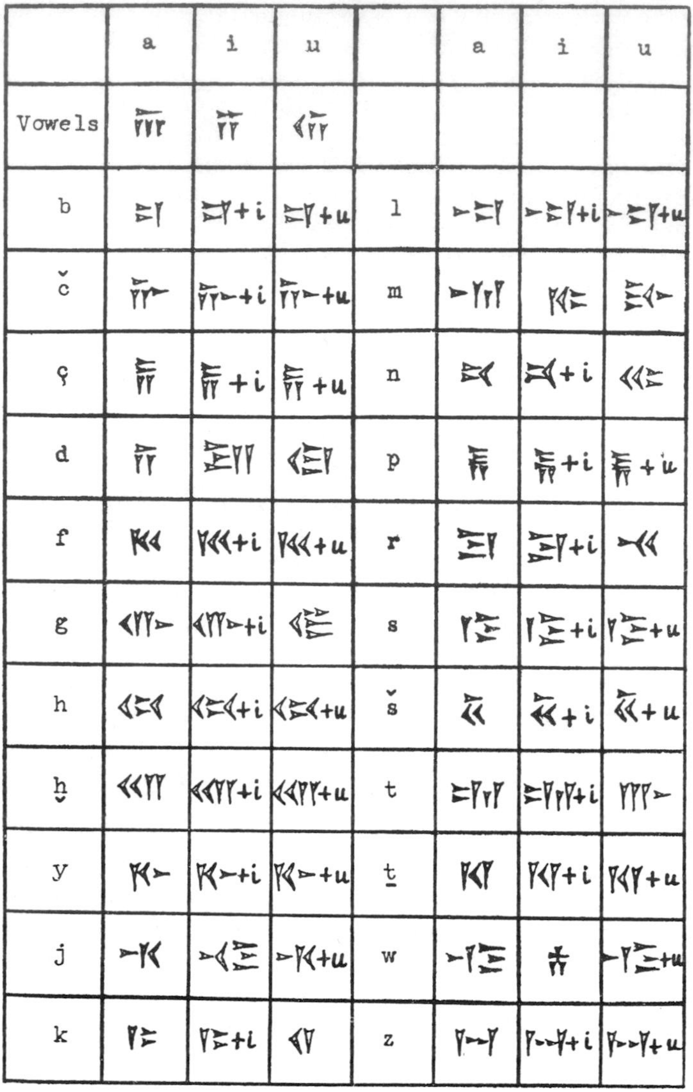

	a	i	u		a	i	u
Vowels	𒀀	𒄿	𒌋				
b		+i	+u	l		+i	+u
č		+i	+u	m			
ç		+i	+u	n		+i	
d				p		+i	+u
f		+i	+u	r		+i	
g		+i		s		+i	+u
h		+i	+u	š		+i	+u
ḫ		+i	+u	t		+i	
y		+i	+u	ṯ		+i	+u
j			+u	w			+u
k		+i		z		+i	+u

FIG. 88.—OLD PERSIAN SYLLABARY

and West Semitic writings; although some signs of the same structure exist also in the Mesopotamian cuneiform system, they are so few (see pp. 71 ff.) that it would be difficult to suggest

174

that they had formed the basis for this Persian development. The rest of the Persian signs, expressing a consonant and, more or less exactly, also the vowel, would then be formed on the pattern of the Mesopotamian writing. However, one must remember that there are some strong arguments against the thesis of a sudden creation of the Persian writing under Darius,[19] and consequently we may have to reckon with the possibility of a slow and gradual evolution. If this alternative be true, then it is possible to visualize two lines of evolution, depending on whether one takes the West Semitic or the Mesopotamian system as the prototype of the further Persian development. Taking the Semitic system as the basis, the original Persian writing should be reconstructed as consisting of 23 signs each expressing a consonant but not indicating the vowel, or possibly of 22 such signs plus three special vowel signs (as, e.g., in Ugaritic). To this basic system seven syllabic signs containing *i* and four containing *u*, and possibly the three vowel signs, would have been added in the course of time. The ultimate result of this line of development would have been a 69-sign syllabary of the *ma, mi, mu* type, in which each sign expressed exactly the consonant and the corresponding vowel. It does not have to be stressed here that this would have been an unusual development in the history of writing and that the principle of economy aiming at the expression of language by the smallest possible number of signs would speak unequivocally against it. Thus, it seems that the second line of evolution, taking the Mesopotamian cuneiform system as the basis of the Persian writing, offers more plausible possibilities of interpretation.

According to it, the original Persian writing would be a syllabary consisting of 69 signs of the *ma, mi, mu* type. From this basic system, in which each sign expressed the consonant and the corresponding vowel, a new system consisting of 36 signs was gradually evolved, in which vowels were indicated only partially. We may only speculate as to the reasons which may have led to this reduction of signs, and the best possibility which offers itself is an explanation based on the *plene* writing encountered in many other Oriental systems. Especially instructive is the comparison with the *plene* writing in such syllabaries as Mesopotamian cuneiform and Hittite hieroglyphic employing signs with full indication of vowels. A systematic employment of the *plene* writing in the Persian writing would have led gradually to the creation of a full alphabet along the lines of development clearly demonstrated in the case of the Bamum writing (see p. 209). Let the reader be warned that this is entirely a reconstructed picture and that the stages of development of Persian writing as proposed here to the best of knowledge cannot be tested on the basis of extant sources of Persian epigraphy.

GREEK ALPHABET

The Semitic origin of the Greek alphabet does not present much of a problem. The very Greek tradition in calling the Greek writing Φοινικήια γράμματα, or σημεῖα, that is, 'Phoenician writing',[20] shows clearly the direction in which the origin of this system should be sought. In addition, even a superficial investigation of the forms, names, and order of the Greek signs leads immediately to the conclusion that all these features must have been borrowed from a Semitic form of writing.

The formal derivation of the Greek signs from a Semitic prototype can be established without great difficulty. Even an uninitiated epigrapher cannot fail to observe the identity or great similarity of form in the signs of the Greek alphabet and those of the Semitic writings (Fig. 89).

While the names of the signs of the Greek alphabet cannot be explained with the help of the Greek language, they correspond almost exactly to those of the various Semitic writings. Thus, Greek *alpha, bēta, gamma, delta,* etc., correspond to Semitic *ʾāleph, bêth, gīmel, dāleth,* with the respective meanings of 'ox, house, camel(?)', and 'door'. Of the Semitic languages from which theoretically the names of the Greek signs could be derived, Phoenician is definitely to be preferred to Aramaic. It can be observed, for example, that Greek *alpha* is derived from *ʾāleph,* 'ox', a word which exists in Phoenician and Hebrew but not in Aramaic, while Greek *iōta, pī,* and *rhō* are nearer to the respective Phoenician or Hebrew words *yōdh,* 'hand,' *pē,* 'mouth,' and *rôš,* 'head,' than to Aramaic *yad, pum,* and *rêš.* As Theodor Nöldeke has pointed out,[21] the *a* ending of the Greek names *alpha, bēta,* etc., should not be derived from Aramaic since it can be best explained as a Greek addition resulting from the aversion of the Greek language to final consonants (with the exception of *n, r,* and *s*).

AHĪRĀM	RUWEISEH	AZARBA'AL	YEHIMILK	ABĪBA'AL	ELĪBA'AL	ŠAPATBA'AL	MEŠA'	ZINCIRLI	CYPRUS	SARDINIA	GREEK OLD	GREEK LATE	LATIN
K	K	⋌	K,K	⋌	⋌	⋌	⋋	⋋	⋋	⋋	⊅, A	A	A
⋎	⋎	⋎	⋎,⋎	⋎	⋎	⋀	⋎	⋎	⋎	⋎	⊋, ⋹	B	B
⋀			⋀	⋀	⋀	⋀,⋀	⋀	⋀	⋀	⋀	⋀, ⋀	Γ	C (& G REPLACING Z)
⋄	⊲		⋄		⋄	⋄	⊲	⋄	⋄,⋄	⋄	Δ	Δ	D
⋹		⋹				⋹	⋹	⋹	⋹	⋹, ⋹	E	E
Y		Y	Ψ		Y	Y	Y	⋎	⋎	⋎	⋹, Y, V	(Y AT END)	F (& U,V, Y AT END)
I		I	I		I	I	⋍	⋍	I		I	Z	(Z AT END)
⋈	B	B	H,B		B	B	⋈	⋈		B	B	H	H
⊕						⊖	⊗	⊕		⊕	⊗, ⊕	⊙	
⋌	⋌	⋌	⋌		⋌	⋌	⋌	⋌	⋌	⋌	⋌, ⋌	I	I
⋎	⋎	⋎	⋎	⋎	⋎	⋎	⋎	⋎	⋎	⋎	⋎, ⋎	K	K
⋎		⋎	⋎	⋎	⋎	⋎	⋎	⋎	⋎	⋎	⋎, √	Λ	L
⋎		⋎	⋎	⋎	⋎	⋎	ᵐ	ᵐ	⋎	⋎	ᵐ	M	M
⋎	⋎	⋎	⋎		⋎	⋎	⋎	⋎	⋎	⋎	⋎	N	N
Ŧ		Ŧ					Ŧ	Ŧ			Ŧ	Ŧ	(X AT END)
o	o	o	o	o	o	o	o	o	o	o	o	O	O
⋎		7:⋎	)		⋎	⋎	⋎	⋎	⋎	⋎	⋎, ⋎	π	P
	⋏		⋏	⋏			⋏	⋏		⋏	⋏, M	(M)	
		φ			φ	φ	φ	φ			φ, φ	(φ)	Q
⋌			⋌	⋌	⋌	⋌	⋌	⋌	⋌	⋌	⋌, P	P	R
w		w	w		w	w	w	w	w	w	⋎, ⋎, ⋎	Σ	S
I,X		+	×		⋌	I	X	⋌	⋌	X	T	T	T
												Y,Φ,X,Ψ,Ω	U, V, X, Y, Z

FIG. 89.—COMPARATIVE CHART OF GREEK AND WEST SEMITIC WRITINGS

Even the order of the letters of the two writings is the same, as can be seen from the names of the first letters quoted in the preceding paragraph. The Semitic signs *wāw*, *ṣādhē*, and *qōph*, which do not exist in classical Greek, occur in the older periods as *wau* or *digamma*, *san*, and *qoppa*. Furthermore, in later times these three signs continue to be used in the Greek numerical system, in which they have almost the same values as their counterparts have in the Semitic systems.

The direction of signs in writing varies greatly in the oldest Greek inscriptions, as it runs either from right to left or from left to right, continuing in boustrophedon fashion, alternately changing direction from line to line. Only gradually did the classical method of writing from left to right assert itself in the Greek system.

As there is no question that the Greeks borrowed their writing from the Semites, the problem is to establish from which Semitic system did the Greek writing originate. Theoretically, any of the writings used by the Semitic peoples living in the vast area stretching from south of Cilicia to north of Sinai could have formed the prototype of the Greek system. This was the area which was populated by the Amorites, Aramaeans, and Canaanites, including the Phoenicians. In reality, however, our search should be narrowed down to the Phoenicians, those sea-farers of antiquity who alone of the Semites dared to brave the

FIG. 90.—GREEK INSCRIPTION ON A DIPYLON VASE FROM ATHENS
From *Handbuch der Archäologie*, hrsg. von Walter Otto, i (München, 1939), p. 195, Abb. 8

Great Sea in search of new horizons. The Greeks did not come to the Asiatic coast to borrow the Semitic system; writings never pass from one people to another in this way. It was the Phoenicians, with trading posts scattered throughout the Greek world, who brought their writing to the Greeks. The Phoenician origin is supported not only by Greek tradition but also, as we have seen above on page 176, by the results derived from investigation of the names of the signs in the Greek and Semitic systems.

Our next problem to investigate is the time when the Greeks might have borrowed their writing from the Phoenicians. This is still a hotly discussed subject with differences of opinion varying by more than half a millennium. A. Mentz, for instance, advocates a date around 1400 B.C.,[22] B. L. Ullman the end of the Mycenean period or the Dark Ages which followed,[23] while Rhys Carpenter goes as far down as about 720 B.C.[24] If we do not wish to indulge in speculations based on circumstantial evidence, then the only safe approach to the problem of the introduction of the Phoenician writing among the Greeks is that starting with an investigation of the date of the earliest extant Greek inscriptions. At least the dating of these inscriptions does not vary by much more than one hundred years in extreme cases.

FIG. 91.—ROCK-CUT INSCRIPTIONS FROM
THERA

From R. Carpenter in *American Journal of Archaeology*, xxxvii (1933), p. 26, fig. 7

According to prevalent opinion among Greek epigraphers, the oldest known Greek inscription is that on the dipylon vase from Athens (Fig. 90)[25] dated to the early eighth[26] or early

Νι[κό]δεμος Φ[· · · ·]ίδες καταπύγον Λεο[· · · ·]δες ερι

FIG. 92.—SHORT LEGENDS ON GEOMETRIC POTTERY FROM MOUNT
HYMETTOS

From C. W. Blegen in *American Journal of Archaeology*, xxxviii (1934), 11

seventh[27] century B.C. Slightly later in date but still from the eighth or seventh century B.C. are the rock-cut inscriptions from Thera (Fig. 91),[28] short legends on geometric pottery from Mount Hymettos (Fig. 92),[29] and two inscribed sherds from Corinth (Fig. 93).[30]

Individual signs in these early Greek inscriptions frequently vary so much in form that it is clearly impossible to speak of a single Greek alphabet in this early period. One may assume, therefore, that the borrowing and adaptation of the Phoenician writing took place independently in the various areas of the Greek world.

Let us see now what conclusions, if any, can be reached as to the date of the introduction of the Greek writing from the point of view of Semitic epigraphy. The Phoenician writing developed only slightly from Aḥīrâm to Šapaṭbaʿal (about 1000–850 B.C.). Then for a few centuries we lose track of the Phoenician system in Phoenicia proper, but we can follow the development of the Semitic writing in various other areas. From the middle of the ninth century we have in the south the famous Mešaʿ inscription

FIG. 93.—INSCRIBED SHERDS FROM CORINTH

From A. N. Stillwell in *American Journal of Archaeology*, xxxvii (1933), 605

from Moab and slightly later in the north the first inscriptions from Zincirli (see p. 133). The earliest Phoenician inscriptions from Cyprus and Sardinia cannot be dated exactly but they, too, are probably from the ninth century. [31]

If we now look at the comparative table of Semitic and Greek signs (Fig. 89), several immediate observations can be made. The form of Greek *kappa* with its 'tail' is different from that of the Phoenician inscriptions up to Šapaṭbaʿal, but identical with that of the inscriptions dated from 850 B.C. on. Also the Greek *mu* sign looks much nearer to the corresponding forms of the Semitic inscriptions from about 850 B.C. on than to those of earlier inscriptions. On the other hand, the appearance of the Semitic *dāleth* sign with the 'tail' around 800 B.C. forces us to assume that the 'tailless' Greek *delta* was derived from a writing earlier than 800 B.C. The conclusions that can be drawn on the basis of these comparisons speak, therefore, in favour of the ninth century[32] as the most probable time of the borrowing of the Semitic writing by the Greeks. This date is fully in agreement with the dating of the earliest extant Greek inscriptions to the beginning of the eighth century B.C.

Passing from the problems of outward form to those of inner structure we can observe that the most important characteristic of the Greek writing, as contrasted with any of the Semitic writings, is a fully developed system of vowels. From the oldest period on all the vowels are written wherever they are expected. This can be recognized without difficulty from the transliteration of the old inscription on the dipylon vase from Athens (Fig. 90): ΗΟΣ ΝΥΝ ΟΡΧΕΣΤΟΝ ΠΑΝΤΟΝ ΑΤΑΛΟΤΑΤΑ ΠΑΙΖΕΙ ΤΟΤΟ ΔΕΚΑΝ ΜΙΝ, corresponding to classical ὃς νῦν ὀρχηστῶν πάντων ἀταλώτατα παίξει το⟨ῦ⟩το δεκᾶν μιν, 'whoever of the dancers makes merry most gracefully, let him receive this.'[33] Outside of sign forms, the only observable differences between the writing on the Athens vase and that of the later classical period are the following: The old writing fails to indicate accents and vowel and consonant quantity, and while the *spiritus lenis* is not indicated, the *spiritus asper* is expressed by the letter which later became *ēta*.

The generally accepted interpretation of the origin of the Greek vowel system is very simple. The Semitic writing had a number of signs expressing so-called 'weak consonants', which were not phonemic in Greek. What the Greeks allegedly did, therefore, was to convert these seemingly unnecessary signs into vowels. Thus the Semitic *'āleph* sign, expressing a soft breathing —something like the sound between *w* and *e* in 'however'—was changed to the vowel *a* of *alpha*; Semitic *hē* to Greek *e* of *epsilon*; Semitic *wāw*, used in older periods of Greek for the consonant *w* (*digamma*), also developed the vocalic value *u* of *upsilon*, placed near the end of the alphabet, after *tau;* Semitic *yōdh* became in Greek the vowel *i* (*iōta*); and finally the emphatic sound *ʿayin* of the Semites was converted into the vowel *o* (*omikron*).

There is nothing wrong with the usual derivation of individual Greek vowel values from the corresponding Semitic signs. The fact is, however, that the Greeks did not invent a new vowel system but simply used for vowels those signs which in the various Semitic systems of writing likewise can function as vowels in form of the so-called *matres lectionis* (see p. 167). The greatness of the Greek innovation lies, therefore, not in the invention of a new method of indicating vowels but in a methodical application of a device which the early Semites used only in an irregular and sporadic fashion. As we have seen, even the Semitic and other Near Eastern writings in the course of time developed this method of indicating vowels to such an extent that they, too, were on the way toward creating a full system of vowel signs and consequently an alphabet.

It seems very improbable that the full vocalic system attested in the earliest known Greek inscriptions was suddenly developed by an intelligent Greek on the basis of irregular parallels in the Semitic writings. I should rather favour the idea that the oldest Greek writing expressed the vowels in the same unsystematic fashion as did the Semitic, and that the full vocalic system was only gradually developed and systematized. Nothing would surprise me less than the discovery of early Greek inscriptions from the ninth century B.C., which would either not indicate any vowels at all or would indicate them only rarely in the manner of the Semitic *matres lectionis*.

The term 'full vocalic system' implies that vowels are regularly indicated in Greek, but it does not mean that the old vowel system is the same as that of the later classical period. In fact, the vowel system underwent considerable changes in the course of time, as already implied in the remarks on page 181. The older method did not attempt to indicate the vowel quantity. In the new system, as gradually evolved, only the *alpha* and *iōta* signs continued to be used for both short and long vowels. But when in some of the Greek dialects the consonant expressed by the Semitic *ḥēth* was lost, this sign acquired the value *ē* of *ēta*, differentiating it from *e* of *epsilon*. Similarly, a new sign *ōmega* was developed for *ō*, leaving only *o* for *omikron*. And finally, when the Greeks began to pronounce their old *u* of *upsilon* as *ü*, they were forced to use for the *u* sound the *omikron* plus *upsilon* combination originally reserved for the *ou* diphthong The gradual development of the Greek alphabet is further illustrated by the elimination of *digamma*, *san*, and *qoppa* and by the final addition of signs φ, χ, ψ which did not exist in the Semitic languages and were therefore arbitrarily created by the Greeks.

Once the six Semitic syllabic signs developed their vocalic values in Greek, the natural step was to analyse the remaining syllabic signs as consonants by the process of reduction. If in the writing t^iy^i the second sign is taken as a vowel i to help in the correct reading of the first sign which theoretically can be read as *ta, ti, te, tu*, or *to*, then the value of the first sign must be reduced from a syllable to a simple consonant. This is the principle of reduction, for which there are many precedents in the history of writing. For instance, the Sumerian sign representing female breasts stands for many related words, such as *dumu* 'son,' *banda*, 'boy,' and *tur*, 'small.' In order to differentiate between these words, phonetic complements or indicators were used, as in *banda-da*, where the phonetic sign *da* indicated the reading of the word sign as *banda*, and not *dumu* or *tur*. In the writing *banda-da*, since *da* was considered to be a full syllable, the value of *banda* was consequently reduced to *ban*. Similarly, from the Akkadian writing of *ṭâb-ab*, 'good,' the syllabic value *ṭa* was developed from the word sign *ṭâb* (see also pp. 71 and 105).

ALPHABET'S CONQUEST OF THE WORLD

The statement was made above (see pp. 181 ff.) that the introduction of the Greek vocalic system should not be regarded as a new and original creation in the Greek writing, but as a systematization of a device well known, though irregularly used, in many Oriental writings such as Semitic, Egyptian, Mesopotamian cuneiform, Hittite hieroglyphic, and Persian. This device consists of an addition of a syllabic sign containing a 'weak consonant' in the case of writings of the Egyptian-Semitic type, or of a vowel sign in the case of cuneiform and Hittite hieroglyphic writings, all for the purpose of making certain the reading of the vowel which was either totally unexpressed or inadequately expressed in the preceding syllabic sign. Any of the Oriental syllabic writings with this method of vowel indication could, at least theoretically, have developed into pure alphabetic systems. That such a writing of *mali* as *ma-a-li-i* in the cuneiform or hieroglyphic Hittite systems could have resulted in reduction of the syllabic signs *ma* and *li* to *m* and *l*, respectively, in the same way as the writing of this word as m^a-^ɔa-l^i-y^i in the Egyptian-Semitic writings ultimately led to the analysis of the syllabic signs as alphabetic in the Greek system, can be deduced from the development of the Bamum syllabic writing in the direction of an alphabet (see p. 209). That none of the Oriental systems independently developed an alphabet is due to their inconsistent use of vowel indication. It was, therefore, only the Greeks who, by regular use of a device borrowed from the Orient and by way of the principle of reduction, were able to achieve for the first time an alphabetic system of writing.

The development of a full Greek alphabet, expressing single sounds of language by means of consonant and vowel signs, is the last important step in the history of writing. From the Greek period up to the present, nothing new has happened in the inner structural development of writing. Generally speaking, we write consonants and vowels in the same way as the ancient Greeks did.

The use of vowel signs and the resulting analysis of writing as an alphabet passed in the course of time from the Greeks to the Semites, thus repaying the debt of the original borrowing. This is the alphabet that subsequently conquered the world. Much as the hundreds of alphabets used throughout the world may differ from each other in appearance, they all have characteristics of outer form, inner structure, or both, which first originated in the small area surrounding the eastern Mediterranean. In fact, if we exclude the various forerunners of writing scattered throughout the world, the small group of writings in eastern Asia which grew out of the Chinese system, and the chiefly syllabic systems introduced in modern times among primitive societies (which will be discussed in Chapter VII), there is only one system of writing in use to-day. And that is the alphabet of Semitic-Greek origin.

From the inner structural point of view the main characteristic of the alphabet is the existence of special signs for both consonants and vowels. As the signs for consonants are used in approximately the same way in all the alphabets of the world, the various types of alphabets can be distinguished only by their use of the vowel signs. In distinguishing three types of alphabets I should like to add that they are ideal types. In practice, numerous writings show so many mutual influences that it is frequently difficult to assign them to one certain type. The various types of vowel indication are shown in Fig. 94.

Type I, as represented by the Greek alphabet, is the simplest. Vowels are expressed by special signs on equal footing with

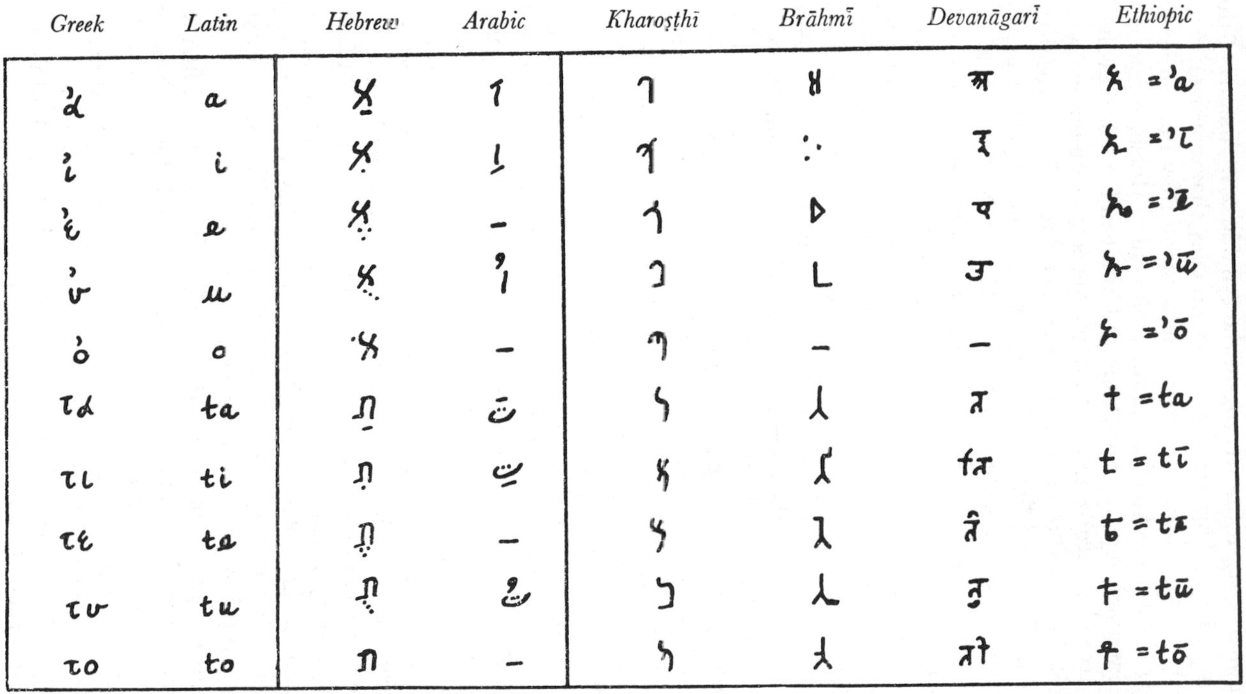

FIG. 94.—TYPES OF VOWEL INDICATION IN VARIOUS ALPHABETIC WRITINGS

consonants, as in the writing of the syllable *ta* by means of the signs *t* plus *a*. This type of vocalization is characteristic of all the Western writings no matter how much they may differ in outer form: Greek, Latin, runic, Slavonic, Morse, etc. Some Oriental writings like neo-Punic or Mandean have also evolved this type of vocalization, although never as systematically as Greek. It is hard to say whether the systematization of vocalization in these two Semitic systems should be regarded as the natural evolution of the *scriptio plena* device widely known in the Near East, or whether it is due to Latin[34] or Greek influence. In general, however, the Semitic writings are averse to introducing new vowel signs placed beside the consonant signs; instead, they prefer to place them above or below the consonant sign. When in the eighth century of our era the Greek vowel signs were introduced in the West Syriac or Jacobite writing, they were not placed beside the consonant sign as in Greek, but above or below it. Apparently in a similar way the Babylonian Jews originally used their weak consonants for vowels. There may be several reasons for this aversion of the Semites to placing vowel signs beside the consonants. One reason may be the attachment to the traditional spellings in the sacred books. And another, perhaps even more important, reason may lie in the fact that by leaving the consonantal structure intact and placing the vowel signs above or below the consonants the way was left open for anybody who wished to continue writing consonants alone without bothering about the vowels. It is a well known fact that even in modern times such Semitic writings as Arabic and Hebrew get along rather well, both in print and in handwriting, without the use of vowel signs. The unwillingness to have the consonantal structure obstructed by inserted vowel signs, which in Semitic are identical with the consonant signs, may truly have been the reason which finally led to the creation of a new type of vocalization expressed not by weak consonants but by special diacritic marks.

This is Type II of vocalization, probably introduced first in the East Syriac or Nestorian writing, whence it found its way into the Palestinian Hebrew and later into the Arabic writings. In all cases the vowels are indicated by small strokes, dots, or circles, placed either above or below the consonant sign.

Type III of vocalization, found in the Indic and Ethiopic writings, presents some difficult problems.

The Indic writings make their appearance as full systems in the third century B.C. in the famous edicts of Aśoka (who ruled from 272 to 231 B.C.), although there are indications that writing was known a few centuries earlier. We are leaving out of consideration the Proto-Indic writing, which was used in the third millennium B.C. (see pp. 90 f.), and is therefore too remote to have influenced the new Indic writings, which arose in the second half of the first millennium B.C. The Aśoka inscriptions were redacted in two types of writing: Kharoṣṭhī and Brāhmī.

The forms of the signs of the Kharoṣṭhī writing as well as the right-to-left direction are apparently derived from Aramaic. The basic sign always has the value of a consonant plus *a*, while other vowels are expressed by means of short strokes, in all cases attached to the sign with which they form one unit. Even the differences in vowels used initially (or syllabically) are indicated by the same diacritic marks. Thus, this type of vocalization is very similar to that noted above as Type II, with one important difference: while in Type II the vowel marks are written separately, in Type III they are always attached to the respective syllabic signs.

The Brāhmī writing goes one step further in its development. Vowel differences are normally noted in the same way as in the Kharoṣṭhī system, but a new set of signs was devised for the initial (or syllabic) vowels. The forms of the individual signs of the Brāhmī writing show no clear relationship with any other system, and were most probably freely invented. The direction of the Brāhmī writing is from left to right. All later Indic writings, including Devanāgarī, the writing of Sanskrit, are descended from Brāhmī, although the prevalent method of vocalization is represented by Type II.

From the formal point of view, the Ethiopic signs are derived directly from South Arabic (see pp. 149 f.). In conformity with other Semitic systems the oldest Ethiopic inscriptions were not vocalized. Then, around 350 of our era, a full system of vocalization made its appearance, which to all intents and purposes is identical structurally with that of the Kharoṣṭhī writing. The vowel differences are normally indicated by small diacritic marks attached to the signs. Ethiopic does have one additional feature, namely, the occasional modification of the form of the basic sign to express vowel differentiation. It does not seem plausible to suggest that such a method of vowel indication, as found in the Indic and Ethiopic writings, could have been independently devised in the two areas, especially since we know that the device of vowel differentiation is used nowhere else in this form. For that reason there is much in favour of Friedrich's suggestion that the Ethiopic vocalic system was devised following an Indic prototype.[35]

The main problem facing us in connection with the classification of the Indic and Ethiopic writings is: Are they syllabaries or are they alphabets? Basically, there is not much difference in the vowel notation between the writings of the Semitic type on the one side and those of the Indic-Ethiopic type on the other. Whether the diacritic marks are written separately, as in Hebrew and Arabic, or attached to the sign, as in older Indic and Ethiopic, still their function in all cases is to indicate vowel differentiation. But what shall we do with instances in Ethiopic and Indic writings in which a syllable is expressed by means of a sign without a diacritic mark, as in the case of signs ending in *a*? How shall we classify the signs in Ethiopic and in many stenographic systems which denote vowel variation by modifying the form of the basic sign? In stenographic systems the basic sign expressing a consonant is, of course, a consonant sign, and therefore an alphabetic sign, but the heavy form of this sign expressing, for instance, *ka* is not an alphabetic but a syllabic sign. Still, one would hardly call stenographic systems syllabic.[36] And how shall we classify the modern Semitic writings, such as Arabic and Hebrew, which although well able to express vowel differentiation, neglect it frequently by writing only consonants? It would hardly seem proper to call them syllabic in the sense in which this term was used for the older Semitic writings, which did not know how to express vowel differentiation. These are all disturbing problems, which must be left to the future theory of writing to speculate upon; with sharper typological definitions it should be possible to clear up the difficulties facing us at present in the classification of some writings.

The formal development of the alphabet from the Greek stage on is beyond the scope of the theory of writing. The best we can do is refer the reader interested in this subject to good treatments of the history of writing by Hans Jensen,[37] David Diringer,[38] and James G. Février.[39] Unfortunately, since the antiquated publication of Isaac Taylor[40] there is nothing that can be recommended in the English language. The English book published recently by Diringer[41] fills only partially the need, since it lacks the scientific apparatus. Useful reproductions of the various writings plus short discussions can be found in a book edited by Charles Fossey.[42] Basic for the history of writing, especially in its sociological aspect, is the recent book by Marcel Cohen.[43]

VI

EVOLUTION OF WRITING

STAGES OF DEVELOPMENT

HAVING treated writing in the preceding four chapters from the descriptive and comparative points of view I shall try in the following to sketch the history of writing in its evolution from the earliest stages of *semasiography*, in which pictures convey the desired meaning, to the later stage of *phonography*, in which writing expresses language. The various stages of the development of writing are shown in chart form in Fig. 95. Absurd as it may appear at first glance to designate the three main stages of writing as No Writing, Forerunners of Writing, and Full Writing, there is good reason for this division.

PICTURES

The fact that pictures are quoted under the first stage, called 'No Writing', implies (1) that what we normally understand as pictures—that is, objects of art resulting from an artistic-aesthetic urge—do not fall under the category of writing, and (2) that writing had its origin in simple pictures. The case could be paralleled, for example, by calling steam the first stage in a chart showing the development of the steam engine. Steam, as it issues from a geyser or a tea kettle, is in itself not a steam engine, but it is the element around which the successive stages had to build in order to reach the ultimate development.

FORERUNNERS OF WRITING

Under 'Forerunners of Writing' are included all the various devices by which man first attempted to convey his thoughts and feelings. The all-inclusive term which I have coined for these devices is 'semasiography' from Greek *sēmasía*, 'meaning, signification,' and *graphē*, 'writing.' As the word implies, this is the stage in which pictures can convey the general meaning intended by the writer. In this stage visible drawn forms—just like gesture language—can express meaning directly without an intervening linguistic form.

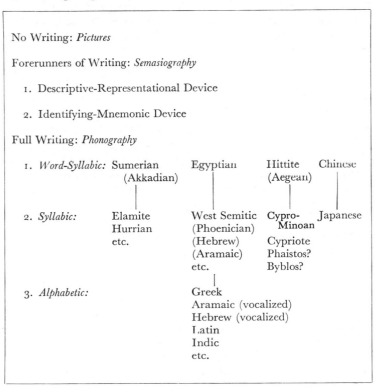

No Writing: *Pictures*

Forerunners of Writing: *Semasiography*

   1. Descriptive-Representational Device

   2. Identifying-Mnemonic Device

Full Writing: *Phonography*

1. *Word-Syllabic:*	Sumerian (Akkadian)	Egyptian	Hittite (Aegean)	Chinese
2. *Syllabic:*	Elamite Hurrian etc.	West Semitic (Phoenician) (Hebrew) (Aramaic) etc.	Cypro-Minoan Cypriote Phaistos? Byblos?	Japanese
3. *Alphabetic:*		Greek Aramaic (vocalized) Hebrew (vocalized) Latin Indic etc.		

FIG. 95.—STAGES OF THE DEVELOPMENT OF WRITING

The most primitive ways of communication by means of visible symbols were achieved by means of the descriptive-representational and the identifying-mnemonic devices. As the two devices are frequently interlocking it is difficult to assign rigorously some primitive writings to definite categories.

Under the descriptive-representational device are included means of communication similar to drawings produced as a result of an artistic-aesthetic urge, differing from the latter in that they contain only those elements which are important for the transmission of the communication and lack the aesthetic embellishments which form an important part of an artistic picture. In the identifying-mnemonic device, a symbol is used to help to record or to identify a person or an object, as in the drawing of a threaded needle which represents the proverb 'the thread follows the needle' (p. 48). The desire to record things for posterity through similar symbols used as memory aids constituted an important factor leading directly to the development of real writing.

To a superficial observer the descriptive-representational device may appear to be the more developed of the two devices discussed above because this method seems better adapted to convey communication than the device using symbols of an identifying and mnemonic nature. It is clear, for instance, that a drawing depicting a battle by the descriptive-representational device tells the story better than a sign or two helping to memorize the battle by the identifying-mnemonic device. Similar conclusions might be drawn in comparing, for example, the early specimens of the Egyptian writing like the so-called 'Narmer palette', drawn chiefly by the descriptive-representational device (see pp. 72 ff.), with the Old Sumerian ledger tablets, drawn by the identifying-mnemonic device (see pp. 63 ff.).

It is not the descriptive-representational device, however, which lies on the direct road toward a fully developed writing. Pictures drawn by this device follow the conventions of art with all of their drawbacks and limitations as a vehicle of human intercommunication. The binding traditions of art, established hundreds and thousands of years before man first attempted communication by means of conventional marks, were too strong to allow for the development of the descriptive-representational device in the right direction.

In the identifying-mnemonic device pictures are drawn as in the descriptive-representational device, but their aim is not to describe an event but to help to remember and to identify an object or a being. Thus, a complete correspondence is established and gradually conventionalized between certain symbols, on the one hand, and certain objects and beings on the other. Since these objects and beings have names in the oral language the correspondence is further established between the written symbols and their spoken counterparts. Once it was discovered that words can be expressed in written symbols a new and much better method of human intercommunication was firmly established. It was no longer necessary to express a sentence such as 'man killed lion' by means of a drawing of a man, spear in hand, in the process of killing a lion. The three words could now be written by means of three conventional symbols representing man, spear (killing), and lion, respectively. Accordingly, '5 sheep' could now be expressed by means of two symbols corresponding to two words in the language instead of by five separate pictures of sheep, which would have to be drawn in an artistic picture or in the descriptive-representational device (see p. 59). The introduction in the identifying device of a strict order of the signs following the order of the spoken words is in direct contrast to the methods of the descriptive device and of the artistic picture, in which the meaning is conveyed by the totality of little drawings without any convention as to the beginning of the message or the order in which it should be interpreted.

A device in which individual signs can express individual words should naturally lead toward a development of a complete system of word signs, that is, a word writing or logography. Against the general opinion of scholars it is my belief that such a fully developed system never existed either in antiquity or in more modern times. To create and memorize thousands of signs for thousands of words and names existing in a language and to invent new signs for newly acquired words and names is so impracticable that either a logographic writing can be used as a limited system only or it must find new ways to overcome the difficulties in order to develop into a useful system. Experience with the Alaska and Cherokee word writings, created artificially in modern times for the use of American natives, is indicative of the impracticability of such limited systems. Even Chinese, the most logographic of all the writings, is not a pure logographic system because from the earliest times it has used word signs functioning as syllabic signs. And what is true of the Chinese system is even more true of other ancient Oriental systems such as Sumerian, Egyptian, and Hittite.

A primitive logographic writing can develop into a full system only if it succeeds in attaching to a sign a phonetic value independent of the meaning which this sign has as a word. This is phonetization, the most important single step in the history of writing. In modern usage this device is called 'rebus writing', exemplified in the drawing of an eye and of a saw to express the phrase 'I saw', or in that of a man and a date to express the word 'mandate'. With the introduction of phonetization and its subsequent systematization complete systems of writing developed which made possible the expression of any linguistic form by means of symbols with conventional syllabic values. Thus full writing originated, in contrast to the feeble attempts grouped together as semasiography, which deserve no higher designation than implied in classifying them as forerunners of writing.

WORD-SYLLABIC SYSTEMS

It is to the Sumerians that we are indebted for having taken the important step leading toward a fully developed writing. The organization of the Sumerian state and economy made imperative the keeping of records of goods transferred from the country to the cities and vice versa. Records were kept in concise ledger form, of the type '5 sheep' or, with a personal name, '10 bows, X.' The choice of one sign for one word resulted in the origin of a logographic system which soon expanded into a phonographic system through the necessity of expressing personal names in an exact way to prevent confusion in the records. The greatness of this achievement lies in the fact that in creating a full word-syllabic system from the old identifying-mnemonic device the Sumerians were able to break away entirely from the hampering conventions of the descriptive-representational device. They developed writing from the former device, while they continued the latter undisturbed in their technique of reproductions on seals. The Amerindians, too, had both devices at their disposal as means of communication, but the emphasis placed upon the descriptive technique of art at the expense of the identifying device forced all their attempts in the wrong direction with the result that none of the Amerindian systems—and this includes the Maya and the Aztec—developed beyond the stage of forerunners of writing. It is possible that even the predynastic Egyptians, because they too placed too much emphasis upon conventions of art in their early attempts to convey communication, would never have developed a writing of their own without foreign influence. This influence may very well have come from the Sumerians.

The oldest of the seven ancient Oriental systems of writing is Sumerian, attested in southern Mesopotamia around 3100 B.C. From there the main principles of the Sumerian writing may have spread eastward first to the neighbouring Proto-Elamites and then, perhaps via the Proto-Elamites, to the Proto-Indians in the valley of the Indus; one of the Near Eastern writings may, in turn, have been the stimulus leading to the creation of the Chinese writing. Around 3000 B.C. Sumerian influence presumably worked its way westward to Egypt; Egyptian influence, in turn, spread toward the Aegean where, about 2000 B.C., originated the Cretan writing, and a few centuries later, in Anatolia, the Hittite hieroglyphic writing.

Since of the seven systems three—namely, Proto-Elamite, Proto-Indic, and Cretan—are as yet undeciphered or only partially deciphered, we can discuss only the principles of writing as they are found in the remaining four—namely, Sumerian, Egyptian, Hittite, and Chinese.

As far as the inner principles of writing are concerned, the unifying characteristic of the four systems is that they are all phonographic almost from the very beginning of their development and that they all contain signs of these three classes: word signs or logograms, syllabic signs, and auxiliary signs.

The formation of word signs is identical or very similar in all four systems. One sign or a combination of signs expresses one word or a combination of words. Also the principles of using auxiliary signs, such as determinatives or punctuation marks, are identical, although the various systems may differ in outer form. Only in the use of syllabic signs are the differences so prominent as to enable us to form exact subdivisions by types.

The four Oriental systems employ syllabaries of four different types[1]:

Type I.—Sumerian. Monosyllables ending in a vowel or consonant: *ta, ti, te, tu; at, it, et, ut; tam, tim, tem, tum;* very rarely also dissyllables like *ata; tama.*

Type II.—Egyptian. Monosyllables and dissyllables ending in a vowel, with differences in vowels not indicated: t^x; $t^x m^x$.

Type III.—Hittite. Monosyllables ending in a vowel: *ta, ti, te, tu.*

Type IV.—Chinese. Monosyllables ending in a vowel or consonant: *ta, ti, te, tu, to; at, it, et, ut, ot; tam, tim, tem, tum, tom.*

SYLLABIC SYSTEMS

Out of the four word-syllabic systems four syllabaries, showing various degrees of simplification, have developed in the course of time:

Type I.—Elamite cuneiform, etc. Monosyllables ending in a vowel or consonant: *ta, ti, te, tu; at, it, et, ut; tam, tim, tem, tum.*

Type II.—West Semitic. Monosyllables ending in a vowel, with differences in vowels not indicated: t^x.

Type III.—Cypriote. Monosyllables ending in a vowel: *ta, ti, te, tu, to.*

Type IV.—Japanese. Monosyllables ending in a vowel: *ta, ti, te, tu, to; (da, di, de, du, do).*

An interesting conclusion which can be drawn about the new syllabic writings is that they were all created by heterogeneous peoples. Thus, while the Mesopotamian Babylonians and Assyrians accepted almost without change the Sumerian system of writing, the foreign Elamites, Hurrians, and Urartians felt that the task of mastering the complicated Mesopotamian system was too heavy a burden; they merely took over a simplified syllabary and eliminated almost entirely the ponderous logographic apparatus. The Semites of Palestine and Syria went even farther in their tendency toward simplification; what they accepted from the Egyptians was nothing but the principle of writing monosyllables with differences in vowels not indicated. Similarly, the Cyprians created a syllabary from an Aegean system of writing, omitting entirely the use of word signs. The Japanese were not as radical. They, too, developed a simple syllabary very similar in principle to that of the Cyprians, even though it distinguishes by separate marks the voiced from the voiceless consonants; but side by side with it they use word signs taken over from the Chinese writing. In all cases it was the foreigners who were not afraid to break away from sacred traditions and were thus able to introduce reforms which led to new and revolutionary developments.

The general name of 'West Semitic syllabary'—given to the various forms of writing used by the Phoenicians, Hebrews, and other Semites from the latter half of the second millennium B.C. on—expresses clearly my belief that these writings are syllabaries and not alphabets, as is generally assumed. These Semitic writings follow exactly the pattern of their Egyptian prototype and the latter cannot be anything else but a syllabary from the point of view of the development of writing.

ALPHABETIC SYSTEMS

The question may now be legitimately asked: If these early Semitic writings are not alphabets what, then, is the alphabet? The answer is clear. If by the word 'alphabet' we understand a writing which expresses the single sounds of a language, then the first alphabet was formed by the Greeks. Although throughout the second millennium B.C. several attempts were made to find a way to indicate vowels in syllabaries of the Egyptian-Semitic type, none of them succeeded in developing into a full vocalic system. The usual way was to add phonetic indicators as helps in reading the vowels which normally were left unindicated in the Semitic systems of writing. But while the Semites employed these so-called *matres lectionis* (see pp. 166 ff.) sporadically, as in the case of m^a-l^a-$k^{(a)}$-t^i-y^i for *malakti*, 'I reigned,' the Greeks used them systematically after each syllable. Thus, following the principle of reduction (see pp. 182 f.), they were soon able to reach the conclusion that since in the writing t^i-y^i the second sign is not a syllable y^i but a vowel i, consequently the first sign must stand for a consonant t and not for a syllable t^i.

It was therefore the Greeks who, having accepted in full the forms of the West Semitic syllabary, evolved a system of vowels which, attached to the syllabic signs, reduced the value of these syllables to simple consonantal signs, and thus for the first time created a full alphabetic system of writing. And it was from the Greeks that the Semites in turn learned the use of vowel marks and consequently developed their own alphabets.

There are three types of alphabets in use, characterized by three different methods of indicating vowels:

Type I.—Greek Latin, etc. Vowels indicated by separate signs: *t-a, t-i, t-e, t-u, t-o.*

Type II.—Aramaic, Hebrew, Arabic, etc. Vowels indicated by separate diacritic marks: *t̥, t̥, t̥, t̥, t̥,* or the like.

Type III.—Indic, Ethiopic. Vowels indicated by diacritic marks attached to the sign or by internal modification.

In the last twenty-five hundred years the conquests of the alphabet have encompassed the whole of civilization, reaching to the farthest corners of the earth, but during all this period no reforms have taken place in the principles of writing. Hundreds of alphabets throughout the world, different as they. may be in outer form, all use the principles first and last established in the Greek writing.

OBSERVATIONS

In looking at the small and simple characters of our handwriting or of our book print one would hardly realize that a span of many thousand years lies between our modern characters and their original ancestors. Most of us would call our writing 'English' because it serves as a means to express the English language. Many might know that it can be called 'Latin', for even in its modern form our writing differs little from the Latin writing of more than two thousand years ago. But how many would know the steps by which the history of the Latin writing can be traced backward; that the Latin alphabet is a development from the Greek alphabet; and that the latter, in turn, is an adaptation of a writing which was developed among the Semites of Syria in the middle of the second millennium B.C.? But that is not the end. The history of our writing goes even further back. Though in outer form this first Semitic writing seems to be an original and individual creation which cannot be traced back to any other known writing, its principles are certainly those of the Egyptian syllabary. The latter is part of the Egyptian system of writing which, together with Sumerian, Hittite, Chinese, etc., belongs to the great family of ancient Oriental systems of writing. The history of the oldest of these writings, Sumerian—which may have been the mother of all the other systems—can be followed from about 3000 B.C.

In both scholarly and popular books we often meet with statements about the invention of writing. But was writing really invented? Or, speaking in more general terms, is there such a thing as 'invention'? If we consider, for example, such an 'invention' as money we will readily see the point I wish to make. It is said that money was invented by Croesus, King of the Lydians. But in reality what he did was no more than to accept the custom of using precious metals as a medium of exchange—a practice widely known for centuries all over the Near East—and to add to it his and the state's guarantee as to the exact relation of value to weight of each piece of metal. Similarly should be viewed all other achievements called 'inventions': Marconi's wireless or the radio is unthinkable without Hertz's wave theory; Stephenson's railroad is an application of Watt's steam engine on wheels; while the latter is a practical adaptation of observations of many generations made over a period of centuries.

In considering the examples just mentioned one can see that every so-called 'invention' is actually nothing more than an improvement upon something that had been known before. Writing, like money, or the wireless, or the steam engine, was not invented by one man in one certain place in one particular period. Its history and prehistory are as long as the history of civilization itself.[2]

To be sure, we must always reckon in the case of all great cultural achievements with the decisive intervention of men of genius who were able either to break away from sacred tradition or to transfer into practical form something on which others could only speculate. Unfortunately, we do not know any of the geniuses who were responsible for the most important reforms in the history of writing. Their names, like those of other great men who were responsible for the crucial improvements in the practical use of the wheel, or the bow and arrow, or the sail, are lost to us forever in the dimness of antiquity.

Before we begin with the discussion of the salient points in the evolution of writing some remarks should be made in connection with the use of terminology and definitions in the chart in Figure 95. There are no pure systems of writing just as there are no pure races in anthropology and no pure languages in linguistics. As elements retained from an older period and innovations ahead of the accepted development may be found in a language of a certain period, so a system of writing at one period may contain elements from different phases of its development. In a schematic reconstruction of a chart it is impossible to take account of all these minor divergences. Long and complicated terminologies might be introduced to include all the characteristics of a system, but that would only tend to obscure the issue. For this reason the terminology used in the chart is meant to define only the major characteristics of a writing. Here are a few specific examples. English writing, like Latin, is called alphabetic, even though it contains some word signs, as in the writing '3 lb.' or '£3' for 'three pounds'. Many more word signs are used with the Elamite syllabary and the Pehlevi alphabet. The Hittite hieroglyphic syllabary contains a few signs of the type *tra, ara*, outside of the normal development. The so-called 'Carian alphabet' consists of alphabetic signs borrowed from Greek plus a number of syllabic signs borrowed from another system of local Anatolian origin.[3] In all phonographic writings, especially in Chinese, are found elements which we normally include under the semasiographic stage of writing.

In the preceding chapters the various types of writing were organized and discussed in groups in accordance with the stages as reconstructed on the basis of the inner development of writing. The successive stages are represented first by semasiographic forerunners of writing, followed by three subdivisions of full writing which include logo-syllabic, syllabic, and alphabetic stages. The main stress given in my division to the inner principles of writing is in direct contrast to the efforts of those scholars who try to classify writings in terms of some formal or geographic aspects. The grouping of writings according to outer form—for example, pictorial and linear—or according to geographic position—for example, Oriental, African, Amerindian, etc.—is in my treatment a matter of secondary importance.

Another point which should be stressed in this reconstruction of the various phases of writing is the principle of unidirectional development. The term 'unidirectional' as used here means that writing developed in one certain direction, and it should not be confused with the term 'unilinear', which would mean that writing progressed in one direction following a straight line of development. Nothing would be farther from the truth than to argue in defence of a straight development of writing, since we know rather well that it was along the path of trial and error that writing progressed from stage to stage in the long course of its history. There is nothing unusual in arguing in favour of a unidirectional development, as a similar line of evolution can be attested in many other aspects of our culture, such as language, art, religion, and economic theory. In linguistics, for instance, we know of the tendency of languages to develop from isolating to agglutinative to inflectional stages. In a more specific case such as phonetics we can frequently observe a tendency of voiceless consonants to change to aspirates and in turn of aspirates to change to voiced consonants (see also p. 202). The gradual evolution of the definite and indefinite articles and the gradual disappearance of the old dual are further illustrations of the unidirectional development of language. [4]

What this principle means in the history of writing is that in reaching its ultimate development writing, whatever its fore-runners may be, must pass through the stages of logography, syllabography, and alphabetography in this, and no other, order. Therefore, no writing can start with a syllabic or alphabetic stage unless it is borrowed, directly or indirectly, from a system which has gone through all the previous stages. A system of writing can naturally stop at one stage without developing farther. Thus, a number of writings stopped at the logographic or syllabic stage. The saying 'natura non facit saltus' can be applied to the history of writing in the sense that no stage of development can be skipped. Therefore, if it is accepted that logography develops first into syllabography, then the so-called Egyptian 'alphabet', which developed from logography, cannot be an alphabet but must be a syllabary. There is no reverse development. an alphabet cannot develop into a syllabary, just as a syllabary cannot lead to the creation of logography. For that reason it is absurd to speak of the development of the Ethiopic (or Sanskrit) syllabaries from a Semitic alphabet. As shown in another place (see pp. 186 ff.), both the Ethiopic and Sanskrit writings are further developments from a Semitic syllabary, which, in turn, is a creation following the model of the Egyptian syllabary.

It is difficult to predict the future of our own writing, in other words, what will be the next stage into which our alphabetic system may develop in the years to come. Should our writing evolve accidentally in the direction of semasiography, that is, a system of writing without definite correspondence to spoken language (see pp. 243 f.), this could not be brought forth in favour of a reverse development. Like the parallel phenomenon in the case of languages developing through the isolating > agglutinative > inflectional > isolating, etc., stages[5] or in the case of the 'TAM-TAM rule' in Indo-European phonetics (tenuis > aspirata > media > tenuis > aspirata > media),[6] the development of writing in the direction of semasiography would only show that writing can pass through various stages along a circular, or rather spiral, line of development. Only if our present alphabet should change directly into a word or syllabic writing could a case be made against the principle of unidirectional development.

From what has been said above we should expect to find the normal development of writing from logographic to syllabic or from syllabic to alphabetic attested within one writing as used in one certain area. But *habit is always dearer to men than progress*, and consequently writing very rarely develops to this extent within one area. The trend from a preponderantly logographic to a preponderantly syllabic writing can be observed within the hieroglyphic Hittite system. On the other side, although in their earlier stages the Mesopotamian cuneiform and Egyptian systems manifested sound tendencies in the direction of syllabography, in the course of centuries they became more and more burdened with a great number of additional word signs. The retrograde evolution of individual writings was frequently facilitated whenever they fell under the control of a priestly or political caste. In such cases the systems gradually became so overburdened with various artificial and baroque deflections that they grew too difficult for large masses of people to master. The final result of such degenerated writing was frequently its total rejection by the people and its replacement by an entirely new system introduced from abroad (see also pp. 165 and 196). Such was the case with the relatively simple and easy to learn cuneiform systems of the Old Akkadians, Old Assyrians, and Old Babylonians, as compared with those of the Late Assyrians and Late Babylonians, which were finally replaced by the Aramaic script. Or that of the hieroglyphic systems of the Egyptian Pyramid and Empire periods, as contrasted with the complicated and enigmatic developments in the Ptolemaic Era, which finally resulted in the replacement of hieroglyphic by the Coptic writing. The almost unbelievable development of logography in the Chinese writing is a well known phenomenon. Due to its marginal geographic position in the Old World, China was not affected by foreign invasions to the extent that the Near Eastern areas were. For that reason, the evolution of the Chinese writing progressed through thousands of years undisturbed by foreign influences, resulting finally in a type of writing which perfectly suited the needs of a small bureaucratic clique, but was totally inaccessible to 90 per cent of the population.

The history of our writing in the course of thousands of years is closely paralleled by the history of some modern writings created under the stimulus of white men among primitive societies, for example, the Cherokee Indian and the African Bamum writings, which will be discussed more fully on pages 206 f. and 208 f. Both of these writings, starting with an unsystematic semasiography, first developed logographic systems in which individual signs expressed individual words of the language. Due to the inadequacy of pure logography both writings were soon forced to evolve syllabic systems, but while the Bamum writing in its ultimate development seems to show certain tendencies toward alphabetization, the Cherokee writing, like many other comparable writings used by primitives, stopped at the syllabic stage. This sequence of the stages of writing reflects the stages of primitive psychology. Naturally, as all primitives can grasp parts of speech, such as utterances and phrases, it is frequently with some difficulty that they can recognize individual words. The ability to divide a word into its component syllables is a great step in their understanding of speech and it frequently must be learned through outside influence. The division of syllables into single sounds usually lies beyond their capacity. That this sequence in analysing speech is the most natural one is supported by the fact that almost all the writings introduced in modern times among primitive societies stopped at the syllabic stage. The effectiveness of syllabaries and the extraordinary ease with which the ability to write and read syllabic writings can be acquired by native students—in contrast to alphabetic writings—have been pointed out repeatedly by Western observers.[7]

In going over this short sketch of the development of writing we can observe three great steps by which writing evolved from the primitive stages to a full alphabet. In chronological order they are: (1) the Sumerian principle of phonetization, (2) the West Semitic syllabic writing, and (3) the Greek alphabet.

The principle of phonetization, leading toward a fully systematized syllabary, is historically first attested among the Sumerians, later among many other writings of the Old World. The sporadic occurrence of phonetization in various parts of the Old as well as the New World (pp. 5, 41, and 54) proves that this principle could have been evolved independently in different areas.

The second important step was the creation of the West Semitic syllabary consisting of some twenty-two signs, fully identical in principle with the corresponding Egyptian syllabary of twenty-four signs. The greatness of the Semitic achievement does not lie in any revolutionary innovation but in its rejection of all the word signs and signs with more than one consonant of the Egyptian system and in its restriction to a small number of open syllabic signs. In a way this achievement is no greater than that of the Cypriote syllabary, which developed from an Aegean word-syllabic writing by discarding the word sign apparatus. Of course, the creation of the Semitic syllabary was of considerably greater importance in the history of writing than the parallel creations in other areas, simply because this writing happened to become the mother of all the alphabets, while the Cypriote system died out without leaving any direct descendants.

Finally, the third important step, the creation of the Greek alphabet, was realized by the systematic use of a device (*matres lectionis*) which was widely but sporadically employed in various parts of the Near East. The regular addition of vowels to the syllabic signs resulted in reducing the values of these syllabic signs to alphabetic signs, consequently leading to the creation of a full alphabet. As shown elsewhere (see pp. 166 ff.), many other Oriental writings were also on the way toward the development of an alphabetic writing very similar to that evolved systematically for the first time by the Greeks.

The point which needs to be stressed is that none of these three important steps is really revolutionary in the sense that it presents something entirely new. In line with what was said previously about so-called 'inventions' in general (see p. 199), the only observable development in the history of writing is the systematization at a certain stage of devices which had been known previously but had been used only in a haphazard way.

We have thus followed the evolution of writing from primitive semasiographic attempts to fully developed word-syllabic, syllabic, and alphabetic systems. Simple as this development of writing may appear at first sight, it must be strongly emphasized that it has heretofore been badly mistreated. How else can we regard the opinion of a scholar who takes for granted the successive evolution of the word, syllabic, and alphabetic writings,[8] but at the same time calls the Egyptian phonetic, non-semantic writing consonantal,[9] and elsewhere talks about the syllabic writing as being a blind alley (*Sackgasse*) which could never lead to an alphabetic writing?[10] How can we reconcile the conflicting statements of another scholar who believes that writing developed from a pictographic-ideographic through the syllabic to an alphabetic stage,[11] but at the same time takes the Egyptian non-semantic writing to be a multiconsonantal and uniconsonantal mixture,[12] and concludes that the absence of vowels in Egyptian and West Semitic writings has not been satisfactorily explained?[13] It seems to me that these conflicting sets of statements can be eliminated only if we try rigorously to draw a logical conclusion from the two basic premises:—

Premise I.—*From the point of view of the theory of writing the evolution is from a word-syllabic writing through a syllabic writing to an alphabetic writing.*

Premise II.—*From the historical point of view the development is from the Egyptian writing through the West Semitic writing to the Greek writing.*

If we accept the two premises—and there seems to be no disagreement among scholars as to the validity of these two premises individually—then we must draw the self-evident conclusion that some sort of a syllabary existed either in the Egyptian or in the Semitic systems before the evolution of the Greek alphabet. This is the crux of the problem. It can be entirely eliminated if we accept the theoretically and historically justified development of writing as proposed in this study: *from the Egyptian word-syllabic system to the purely syllabic West Semitic writing, and from the West Semitic syllabic writing to the Greek alphabet.*

VII

MODERN WRITINGS AMONG PRIMITIVES

OUTSIDE of the limited systems which have been used in recent times among primitive societies and which were discussed in Chapter II under Forerunners of Writing there is a large number of more developed writings introduced in modern times among primitive societies under the influence of white men, chiefly missionaries. In the following short discussion all these writings are grouped according to the continents on which they originated. For the sake of completeness, the writings invented directly by white men for use among primitive societies are also included. Due to the importance of the subject, literature is quoted as completely as possible.

DESCRIPTIVE PRESENTATION

The most important and apparently the oldest on the American continent is the Cherokee writing, invented by an Indian named Sikwāyi—known better in the form Sequoyah—for the use of his tribesmen living in the territory now covered by the state of North Carolina. Sequoyah received the stimulus to invent writing from white men, but, although he was acquainted with the existence of books printed in English, he could neither read nor write that language. About 1820 he began experimenting with a new writing by organizing on the basis of primitive Indian semasiography (see pp. 29 ff. and 39 ff.) a system of pictographic signs each of which stood for words of his tongue. Gradually realizing how hard it would be to persuade his fellow tribesmen to learn a difficult word writing, he gave up his initial attempt and began to work on a system in which not words but their component parts, namely syllables, were expressed by individual signs. At the same time he abandoned his original idea of expressing signs by pictures and instead decided to use the forms of the signs in his English book as the basis for the signs in his own syllabary. For example, to the sign *H* he gave the value *mi*, to the sign *A* that of *go*, etc. Other signs were either freely invented or were derived variants of the English forms. Thus he created first a syllabary of some two hundred signs, which by 1824 he simplified considerably by shortening it to eighty-five signs. This is the writing in which books and newspapers of the Cherokee nation were subsequently published.[1]

Of less importance is the syllabary invented a little after 1840 by J. Evans, an English missionary, for the use of the Cree Indians and other neighbouring tribes of the Algonquins, in Canada. The syllabary is composed of forty-four signs drawn in simple geometric form. Vowel differences are indicated by different orientation of the basic sign. An additional set of signs is used to indicate final consonants. Several systems are known.[2]

The ponderous system of word signs in the writing invented by a missionary named Christian Kauder had a limited use among the Micmac (or Megum) Indians living in eastern Canada. In 1866 a whole catechism was printed in Vienna in this writing, for which no less than 5,701 different signs, freely invented, were used.[3] The absurdity of the system is best illustrated by the fact that it contains separate signs even for such little-used words or names as Vienna and Austria.

A pure alphabet is represented by the various systems used by the Algonquin tribes of Sauk, Fox, and Kickapoo in the south-west. The alphabet consists of fifteen signs, with slight variations all taken over from a cursive form of the Latin writing. In eleven cases the sign values are approximately those of English; only in four cases the values have been changed arbitrarily.[4] Very little is known about an alphabet which was borrowed by a Winnebago tribe from the Sauk Indians. The alphabet is supposed to consist of seventeen Latin letters and two new signs, arbitrarily created. It is reported that of the seventeen Latin letters (capital or small?), ten retained their Latin values (e.g. written *m* = spoken *m*) while seven acquired new values (e.g. written *r* = spoken *s*).[5]

Of greatest interest are the various writings used among the Alaska Eskimos. Out of primitive semasiography (see p. 34.)

some time toward the end of the nineteenth century a word writing was developed with signs both pictorial or linear. In the course of time the writing acquired certain features of phonetization, although a full phonetic syllabary of the Cherokee type was never achieved among the Eskimos. Several types of the Eskimo writing are in use in different parts of Alaska, in some of which certain tendencies toward alphabetization are discernible.[6]

Turning now to Africa, the first writing to appear there was that of the Vai Negroes in the region of Sierra Leone and Liberia. According to one source, some years before 1848 a native Negro named Bukele developed from a primitive semasiographic system (see pp. 48 ff.) a picture word writing and then a syllabic system. Some syllabic signs were derived from the corresponding word signs, others were formed arbitrarily. In the course of years the pictures gradually lost their pictographic character, while the number of word signs was so reduced that in its final stage the Vai writing consists of some 226 syllabic signs plus a very few word signs.[7]

Closely allied to the Vai is a group of syllabic writings, most of which may very well have originated under the influence of the older Vai writing:—

The Mende syllabic writing consists of some 190 signs and was invented by a native called Kisimi Kamala.[8]

The Basa syllabary in Liberia is known only from general reports.[9]

The writing of the Kapelle or Kpelle, north of Basa, is still unpublished.[10]

The Toma syllabary in French Guinea and Liberia consists of 187 signs showing strong Vai-Mende relationships.[11]

The Gerze writing in French Guinea is represented by only 87 signs.[12]

Much more recent than the Vai writing is the equally important writing of the Bamum in the Cameroons, invented about 1895–96 by a native chieftain Njoya under the influence of Europeans or Hausa merchants.[13] The Bamum writing, like Vai, started first as a picture word writing composed of some 510 signs. Gradually the signs lost their original pictographic character and, at the same time, the number of signs was gradually reduced from about 510 to 437 to 381 to 295 to 205. In its ultimate development a Bamum syllabary of some 70 signs appears, showing certain tendencies toward alphabetization—a phenomenon entirely unique among writings of modern African societies.[14] The origin of this new type of writing is due to most unusual circumstances. It seems that the King Njoya became jealous of his royal colleagues in the neighbouring countries who possessed a royal language of their own apart from the common language of their subjects, and decided to create a language for the use of his royal court. The new language, composed with the help of a European woman missionary, represents a concoction of French, German, and English words, all pronounced in the native fashion but with meanings arbitrarily assigned. Because of the inadequacy of the existing syllabic system to express foreign words, a device was introduced to add vowel signs to open syllables in the form known as *plene* writing in the many systems of the Near East (see pp. 166 ff.). Thus, the word *fété* 'stuff' (from English 'fate') is written as *f(é)-é-t(é)-é,* just as *atol* 'that's it' (from English 'at all') is written as *a-t(é)-o-l(i).* But the device is not used systematically and a full alphabet has never been achieved among the Bamum. Although the alphabetic spelling of the above words as *f-é-t-é* and *a-t-o-l,* used by some scholars, does not seem to be fully justified, the Bamum development is of greatest importance for the theory of writing, proving, as it does, that an alphabet can originate not only from a syllabary of the Semitic type, consisting of signs in which vowels are not indicated, but also from a syllabary like Bamum, which consists of signs with a full indication of vowels[15] (see pp. 175 f. and 184 f.).

The only sure example of an alphabetic writing developed in modern times among African natives is the Somali alphabet. The creator of the writing, a native by name of ʿIsmān Yūsuf, was not an illiterate person since he was well acquainted with Arabic and, to some extent, with Italian. On the basis of his knowledge of these systems, ʿIsmān Yusūf evolved an alphabet of his own, composed of nineteen consonants and ten vowels. The order of the consonants is that of the Arabic alphabet. The forms of the signs were borrowed neither from Arabic nor Italian but seem to be freely invented, perhaps partially under the influence of the *ductus* of the Ethiopic writing.[16]

A unique system invented in modern times in Asia is that of the Chukchi shepherd, named Tenevil, in Siberia. The writing consists of several hundred signs, conventionally drawn, each of which stands for a certain word. As the phonetic-syllabic stage was never reached, the writing was difficult to learn and its use was, therefore, confined to Tenevil's family and acquaintances. [17]

Several syllabic systems with linear signs were devised by the British Bible Missions for use of different languages in Southwest China. Nothing is known to me about them beyond samples of writing, as given in a catalogue issued by the British and Foreign Bible Society. [18]

Finally, we should refer to a syllabic script allegedly used on one of the Caroline Islands, about which nothing is known except that—as in the Cherokee writing—the forms of Latin signs were used as the basis for the signs of the Caroline syllabary.[19] The syllabary used on the island Oleai or Uleai, in the Carolines, is said to contain signs partly developed from pictures, partly arbitrarily invented, and may therefore be a different creation. [20]

OBSERVATIONS

Even this short résumé clearly shows how difficult it is even to list all the writings which have been created in recent times for use among primitive societies. Some of these writings are known very inadequately, others are known only from hearsay, and still others must exist in obscure corners of the globe as yet unnoticed by scholars. This is a fertile ground for investigation, heretofore badly neglected in works on writing. A strong impetus to the study of these important writings has been given in recent years by the well known Orientalist, Johannes Friedrich.

The study of these writings leads to conclusions which are of primary importance for the general history of writing. Here are some pertinent points:—

(1) All the writings which have gone through an extended process of evolution, like the Cherokee and Alaska systems in North America or Vai and Bamum systems in Africa, have evolved from primitive semasiography and have passed successively through the stages of logography and syllabography, showing at times in the final stages certain tendencies toward alphabetization. Thus, the sequence of stages in writings introduced among primitives fully parallels the history of writing in its natural evolution, as discussed above, pp. 190 ff.

(2) The writings developed among primitives under the

influence of white men have passed within the span of one or two generations through a process of evolution which had taken thousands of years for writing in general to pass. Thus, we can observe the process of evolution speeded up immensely under the impact of foreign stimulus (see also pp. 219 f.).

(3) The case of the original Cherokee word writing, invented by Sequoyah and then given up by him, the limited use of the Alaska and Chukchi word writings prove the contention espoused on p. 193 about the infeasibility of word writing in general as a system of communication.

(4) Judging by the great majority of writings, discussed in this chapter, the syllabic stage is best suited for use among primitive societies. This is in line with the view expressed above, p. 203.

(5) Certain tendencies of such syllabic writings as Bamum and Alaskan to develop in the direction of an alphabet belie the statement of K. Sethe,[21] that the syllabic writing is a blind alley (*Sackgasse*) which could never lead to an alphabetic writing. The view defended in this study is that an alphabet could not develop from anything else but a syllabary (see p. 205).

VIII

MONOGENESIS OR POLYGENESIS OF WRITING

AT the outset of our discussion one point must be stressed immediately. It is impossible to speak about the monogenesis of writing if we use the term 'writing' in its widest sense to stand for all methods of human communication by means of visible markings. Writing in this sense, like pictures in general, could have been and actually was used by various people in various parts of the world, and it would be just as senseless to speak about the common origin of these writings as it would be to try to derive all art from one common source. Thus, the problem of the monogenesis or polygenesis of writing can pertain only to what we call full or phonetic writing.

We know of seven great systems of writing, all of which, theoretically, could claim independent origin: Sumerian, Proto-Elamite, Proto-Indic, Chinese, Egyptian, Cretan, and Hittite. As each of these systems represents a phonetic writing, it was thought by some scholars, like Alfred Schmitt[1] and Arthur Ungnad,[2] that all of them must have one common origin because such an important feature as phonetization could not have been independently achieved in several parts of the world. Personally, I am not much convinced as to the validity of their reasoning. Phonetization may truly be the most important step in the development of real writing, but there are no grounds for arguing that such a step could have been reached only once in one certain place (see p. 204). It was not the invention of phonetization but the systematization of this principle that was of such paramount importance in the evolution of full writing.

Before we go deeper into the problem of the monogenesis or

polygenesis of writing let us discuss briefly the conditions and the cultural background under which the seven Oriental systems developed, and see what evidence there is of cultural contact between them.

CULTURAL BACKGROUND OF THE SEVEN ORIENTAL SYSTEMS

The oldest of the seven Oriental systems of writing is Sumerian which originated in southern Mesopotamia around 3100 B.C. From a period only a few centuries later come our first examples of the undeciphered Proto-Elamite writing, discovered at Susa, the capital of ancient Elam. At least in the case of the Proto-Elamite inscriptions it is difficult to speak about an independent origin. Elam was so close to Sumer and throughout its entire history showed such strong cultural dependency on its western neighbour that the conclusion that the Proto-Elamite writing originated under the Sumerian stimulus is almost inevitable. This cultural dependency of Elam upon Sumer finally resulted in the total elimination of the Proto-Elamite writing and in its replacement by a Mesopotamian type of cuneiform (see p. 121).

The very existence of cylinder seals in the Proto-Indic civilization points definitely toward cultural borrowing from Mesopotamia. This, as well as the existence of other cultural features of probable Mesopotamian origin, leads to a probable conclusion that the Proto-Indic writing, too, owed its origin to Mesopotamian influence.[3]

From the Indus Valley our problem leads us to northern China, where about 1300 B.C., during the Shang Dynasty, the first written records made their appearance in the form of short inscriptions on bone, shell, and bronzes. The fact that the extant Chinese inscriptions are limited almost exclusively to divinatory texts should not be taken to mean that the Chinese writing was used solely for this purpose. The very occurrence in the earliest Shang inscriptions of the sign for 'book', in the form of a picture of tablets tied together by a string, testifies to the use of some perishable material like wood. This book literature is now entirely lost, but who knows whether by a stroke of luck some future excavation will not uncover evidence to prove the existence of a widely used literature in this early period. The problem of the origin of the Chinese writing is closely connected with the problem of the origin of the Shang civilization. The researches of the last few years have proved conclusively that the Shang civilization in North China succeeded painted pottery and black pottery cultures of a rather primitive character. As compared with these simple cultures, there are so many innovations during the period of the Shang Dynasty that in the opinion of some eminent Sinologists the Shang period gives the impression of being an imported, ready made civilization. Highly developed metallurgy in bronze, horse-drawn war chariots, many new weapons, domesticated animals and plants and, of course, writing—these are the main new characteristics which stand out sharply in the Shang civilization as against the general cultural poverty of previous periods.

There are two different theories which try to explain the origin of the Shang civilization: One, chiefly represented by native Chinese scholars and in America by Professor Herrlee Creel, tries to prove that the Shang civilization sprang from the native soil and should therefore be regarded as a natural development from previous cultures[4]; the other, championed chiefly by Western scholars, is in favour of explaining the sudden appearance of a fully developed civilization in the Shang period as due to foreign influences.[5] Whence exactly this influence came it is impossible, of course, even to suggest, since any of the highly developed civilizations of the Near East could be taken into consideration. Especially important in connection with the problem of cultural borrowings is the existence in China of the war chariot in a form which greatly resembles the war chariot found throughout the Near East in the middle of the second millennium.[6] This is perhaps the clearest and the surest example of the diffusion of a cultural element over the vast area extending from the shores of the Mediterranean to the Yellow Sea.

The direct derivation of the Chinese writing from Mesopotamia, suggested by some scholars on the basis of formal comparisons of Chinese and Mesopotamian signs,[7] has never been proved by rigorous scientific method. As will be seen later (pp. 217 f.), such formal comparisons are *a priori* doomed to failure.

If we return now to the Near East, our next task is to

investigate the origin of the Egyptian writing. Impossible as it may have been to give a definite answer to this question some thirty or forty years ago, our task at present is considerably facilitated by the extensive comparative material which has recently come to light from both Egypt and Mesopotamia. The new evidence shows conclusively that around 3000 B.C., at the time of the introduction of the Egyptian writing, a rather strong Mesopotamian influence is detectable in the Egyptian civilization. The existence of cylinder seals and of the potter's wheel, directly imported from Mesopotamia, as well as a strong influence in pottery making and brick architecutrc, all point to the Mesopotamian imprint upon the Egyptian civilization at this early period. The weight of these implications can be realized more easily if it is pointed out that the primacy of the Mesopotamian civilization is not propagated by Pan-Babylonists who in years past, through exaggerated ideas of the importance of the Babylonian civilization, had rendered so much disservice to Assyriology, but by eminent scholars in the field of Egyptology who, instinctively, would not be in sympathy with a plea for a secondary position for their own field of study.[8]

Finally, we should refer to the recent investigations of A. Scharff, who proved that the forms of signs representing objects in the earliest Egyptian inscriptions correspond to the forms of objects in use about 3000 B.C. in Egypt. That means, according to Scharff, that the Egyptian writing originated about 3000 B.C., i.e. in the period when the Mesopotamian influence was strongest, and thus supports the argument that the writing may have originated under the Mesopotamian influence.[9]

Considerably easier than the problem of the origin of other Oriental writings is that of the Aegean group of writings, among which we include the Cretan writing with its offshoots in Greece and the adjacent islands, the writing of the Phaistos disk, the Cypro-Minoan syllabary, the Cypriote syllabary, the Byblos syllabary, and the Hittite hieroglyphic writing.

Throughout its entire history the Cretan civilization was under strong Egyptian influence. Finds of Egyptian origin have been made in various strata of Cretan sites; in fact, the whole Cretan chronology can be reconstructed almost exclusively by correlation of the Cretan strata with the Egyptian imports.

As the Cypriote, Phaistos, and Byblos writings have been discussed elsewhere (see pp. 153 ff.), I should like to refer here only to the fact that at least from the formal point of view the Cypriote syllabary can be derived from the Cretan writing through the intermediate stage of the so-called 'Cypro-Minoan' inscriptions, that is, 'Cretan' inscriptions discovered in Cyprus.

Already the oldest Hittite hieroglyphic texts known at present, like the ones from Emirgazi, show a well developed system of writing, in the main identical with the system known in later periods. We know of Hittite inscriptions which are older than the Emirgazi texts—on seals, for example—but even these can hardly represent the earliest phases of the writing. The forms of signs are already too well developed to allow of such a possibility. We may draw two possible conclusions. Either the Hittite hieroglyphic writing was an indigenous creation with its earliest stages not available to us or this writing was borrowed from elsewhere. A totally independent origin of Hittite writing in the middle of the second millennium B.C. seems *a priori* improbable since at that time Anatolia was surrounded by high civilizations with fully developed writings, which lent themselves easily to borrowing. Of these writings cuneiform cannot be taken into consideration because it is no longer a picture writing. The Egyptian writing is geographically too far away and too different from the Hittite hieroglyphic. Therefore, by the simple process of elimination, we seem justified in looking to the West for parallels, and more especially toward the Aegean cultural area. There, the Cretan writing and the other Aegean systems offer the most fertile ground for comparison.

Back in 1931, in trying to prove the common origin of the Hittite hieroglyphic and Cretan writings I drew a table showing some forty comparable signs in these two systems.[10] As I no longer believe in quantitative comparison of forms between two different writings, this table does not appear to me any more to have such far-reaching results. Many of the picture signs found in both Cretan and Hittite hieroglyphic writings, such as those for parts of the body, animals, or geometric designs, can and do frequently occur in all pictographic or hieroglyphic systems of writing. There is, however, a small group of signs in this table which, as far as I know, occur in these two systems of writing only, and another group of signs characterized by such developments in pictorial form[11] that it would be very difficult to escape the conclusion that they ultimately must go back to the same source.

Much more important, however, than the comparison of outer forms of individual signs is the comparison of inner characteristics. Although we cannot compare the principles of the Hittite hieroglyphic with those of the Cretan hieroglyphic because the latter is undeciphered, we are entirely justified in comparing the system of the Hittite hieroglyphic syllabary with the Linear B and Cypriote syllabaries, especially since we know that nowhere else in the Near East are syllabaries of this type used. Furthermore, we know that the forms of the individual signs of the Cypriote syllabary are definitely derived from the corresponding signs of the Cretan writing. Through the connection in forms of signs between Hittite and Cretan hieroglyphic, through the connection in structure between Hittite, Linear B, and Cypriote syllabaries, and through the connection in forms between signs of the Cypriote and Cretan writings, we arrive at the conclusion that all these writings are in some way related to each other, and thus feel fully justified in bringing them back ultimately to the same source, to be sought somewhere in the area around the Aegean Sea.

POSSIBLE ARGUMENTS IN FAVOUR OF MONOGENESIS

Of the seven Oriental systems of writing, Sumerian is the oldest; but that fact in itself is no proof that it must have formed the prototype of all other Oriental writings, just as there is no reason for believing that the Chinese invention of paper money and of gunpowder should be taken as the prototype of the corresponding achievements which took place in Europe many centuries later. We must therefore search for other reasons if we intend to give to the problem of the monogenesis of writing a firmer basis.

Another possible approach would lie in comparison of outer form. As has been mentioned before, for many years some scholars have been trying to derive the Chinese writing from the Sumerian by comparing the forms of the signs. Similar deductions were suggested in a number of other Oriental writings. It has been stressed often enough in this book that I am in general very reluctant to draw conclusions as to common origin of writings based solely on comparison of outer form. The signs in all the original systems of writing are pictorial in character and are employed to represent objects of the surrounding world. As human beings all over the world, and the objects by which they are surrounded, have much in common, we should naturally anticipate that the pictures they devised for their writings would also have many points of resemblance. Thus, men and parts of the body, animals and plants, tools and weapons, buildings and structures, sky, earth, water, and fire are everywhere represented by pictures characterized by great similarity in form, because all of these things actually exist in similar forms. There is no need to claim for these signs one single origin.

More important than comparisons of outer form are comparisons of inner structural characteristics, such as phonetization or vocalization. But even here the development could take similar forms in different places As evidence we may cite the fact that several writings created among primitive societies under the stimulus of white men (see pp. 206 ff.) have gone through a similar process of development in respect to inner structural characteristics, even though they have developed entirely independently of each other.

As we view the earliest history of the seven Oriental systems of writing one important observation immediately comes to mind. And that is that while the period of development of the Sumerian writing from its primitive beginnings to a full phonetic system is rather long—it may have lasted about five centuries—the situation in other Oriental writings is quite different. Thus, we find that the earliest extant Chinese and Hittite texts exhibit almost fully developed phonetic systems which hardly differ in their main inner structural characteristics from those of the later periods. In the case of Egyptian and Cretan writings the crucial period of development seems to have been very short. And finally, while we know very little about the Proto-Elamite and Proto-Indic writings, it is clear from an even superficial glance at Figs. 45 f. and 47 that, at least from the formal point of view, these two writings give the impression of being fully developed systems. These facts can be explained in two possible ways: Either the other Oriental systems all had a long proto-history, now lost, comparable in duration with that of the Sumerian writing, or the systems developed rapidly under foreign influence or stimulus. *Argumentum e silentio* may not be a strong argument, but it would seem rather difficult to argue in favour of lost protohistory when it is noted how common this silence is in the case of all the Oriental systems outside of Sumerian.

The most fruitful approach to the problem of the monogenesis of writing is that of stimulus based on cultural contact. The problem is, of course, very difficult, since it is evident that the proofs brought forth in favour of the monogenesis of writing, based as they are solely on evidence of cultural contact, do not seem strong enough to make the point conclusive. Still, one feature stands out clearly in favour of monogenesis, and that is that all Oriental systems outside of Sumerian came into existence in periods of strong cultural influences from abroad. Furthermore, it should be noted that, although there is no clear proof for the common origin of all seven systems, there is strong evidence that at least some of the systems are derived from one source. Thus, cultural contact supported by geographic proximity makes a common origin for the Sumerian, Proto-Elamite, and Proto-Indic systems highly probable. The same considerations, in addition to formal and structural features, bring together the Aegean group of writings, including Cretan and Hittite, just as some of these considerations seem to support the theory of Egyptian influence upon the Cretan writing. As for the Egyptian writing, its origin occurred close to, and quite possibly within the period when Mesopotamian influence in Egypt was stronger than at any other period either a few centuries before or after the crucial period. Finally, the Chinese writing seems to have originated in the period of the Shang Dynasty, which is characterized by so many foreign innovations that many scholars regard it as a ready made imported civilization.

How are we to evaluate the importance of stimulus based on cultural contact? The problem, of course, is not limited to writing alone, since it affects many other aspects of our civilization. Take, for example, the problem of the origins of Greek astronomy. It is, I believe, taken for granted that many elements of Greek astronomy were borrowed from the Babylonians. And what is the evidence? First, the existence of similar elements in Greece and Babylonia; second, the chronological priority of the Mesopotamian elements over those in

Greece; and third, a probable assumption of cultural contact between the two areas. It seems to me that the arguments brought forth above in favour of the monogenesis of writing are neither stronger nor weaker than those adduced in favour of the dependency of Greek astronomy on Babylonian prototypes.[12]

IX

WRITING AND CIVILIZATION

IMPORTANCE OF WRITING

J AMES H. BREASTED, the famous Chicago historian and
Orientalist, once said: 'The invention of writing and of
a convenient system of records on paper has had a
greater influence in uplifting the human race than any
other intellectual achievement in the career of man.'[1] To this
statement might be added the opinions of many other great
men—among them Carlyle, Kant, Mirabeau, and Renan—
who believed that the invention of writing formed the real
beginning of civilization. These opinions are well supported
by the statement so frequently quoted in anthropology: As
language distinguishes man from animal, so writing distinguishes civilized man from barbarian.

How can these statements be checked in the light of history?
Is it true that writing was mainly responsible for the decisive
change that made the primitive into a civilized man? The
answer is not easy. Everywhere in the Ancient World writing
appears first at a time which is characterized by a simul-
taneous growth of all those various elements which together
make for what we usually call civilization. Whenever writing
appears it is accompanied by a remarkable development of
government, arts, commerce, industry, metallurgy, extensive
means of transportation, full agriculture and domestication of
animals, in contrast to which all the previous periods, without
writing, make the impression of cultures of a rather primitive
make-up. There is no need, however, to urge that the introduction of writing was *the* factor which was responsible for the
birth of original civilizations. It seems rather that all the
factors—geographic, social, economic—leading towards a full
civilization simultaneously created a complex of conditions
which could not function properly without writing. Or, to put

it in other words: *Writing exists only in a civilization and a civilization cannot exist without writing.*

In our modern society it is difficult to imagine an intelligent and cultured person who cannot read and write. The art of writing has become so widespread that it now forms an integral and indispensable part of our culture. We have come a long way since the time when proud but illiterate kings of the Middle Ages signed their names with crosses. Nowadays an illiterate person cannot expect to participate successfully in human progress, and what is true of individuals is also true of any group of individuals, social strata, or ethnic units. This is most apparent in Europe, where nations without any noticeable percentage of illiterates, like the Scandinavians, lead other nations in cultural achievements, while those with a large proportion of illiterates, like some of the Balkan nations, lag in many respects behind their more literate neighbours.

The importance of writing can easily be realized if one tries to imagine our world without writing. Where would we be without books, newspapers, letters? What would happen to our means of communication if we suddenly lost the ability to write, and to our knowledge if we had no way of reading about the achievements of the past? Writing is so important in our daily life that I should be willing to say that our civilization could exist more easily without money, metals, radios, steam engines, or electricity than without writing.

We can make one negative observation, however. As a result of the widespread use of writing the importance of oral tradition has definitely suffered. All we have to do is to compare what we know about our own ancestors beyond our grandparents with what an illiterate Bedouin knows about his, in order to observe the great difference. The average Bedouin has no recourse to written documents to find out about his family or his tribe; he has to keep in his memory knowledge of past happenings and he can transfer that knowledge to others only by word of mouth. The extensive use of oral tradition is an important factor in sharpening and developing the powers of memorizing. It is a well-known fact that the wise men of ancient India learned the Vedas by heart, just as the ancient Greeks committed to memory the Iliad and the Odyssey. We do not have to learn our great classics by heart. We can read them in books. The phrase 'ex libro doctus' well applies to a great many of us.

Modern knowledge consists not only in the actual *knowing*, but also in *the ability to find the facts* in books and libraries. In that sense, the Baconian distinction of these two kinds of knowledge is even more pertinent to-day than it was in Bacon's own time.

WRITING AND SPEECH

The interrelation between speech and writing and their mutual influences are very strong. It is frequently difficult to study a speech without knowledge of its writing, and it is almost impossible to understand a writing without knowledge of the speech for which it is used.

Writing is more conservative than speech and it has a powerful restraining influence on the natural development of the speech. Written language frequently preserves older forms which are no longer used in the daily language. We often employ in our writing a form of English which is different from spoken English. The difference between the literary and the everyday speech is apparent, for example, in ancient Babylonian. Not only are the historical, religious, and epic compositions written in a more archaic language than the letters, but we can even observe similar archaic tendencies in the language of the formal, royal letters as compared with that of private letters written in the vernacular. Writing stubbornly resists any linguistic change, frequently termed 'corruption'. It is probable that such popular expressions as 'ain't' (for 'is not') or 'no good' (for 'not good') would long since have been accepted as 'correct' English were it not for opposition from written tradition.

A good case for the restraining power of writing over speech can be made from observation of the phonetic and morphological development of English or, for that matter, of any other language. The fact that English has changed relatively little in the last four or five hundred years, in comparison with the strong linguistic changes previous to that time, can be ascribed in some measure to the widespread knowledge of writing in the last few centuries. On the other hand, we can observe rapid linguistic changes taking place in modern times among primitive societies which are deprived of real, phonetic writing. Some of the American Indian languages are changing so rapidly that it is frequently difficult, if not impossible, for persons of the present generation to converse with people three to four generations older. Continuous linguistic changes result in the breaking-up of languages into new languages and dialects. The existence of hundreds of languages and dialects among the Indians of America or among the Bantu of Africa is a good illustration.

Writing frequently preserves older, historical spellings, as best exemplified by modern French spelling. The writing of *sain, saine* shows us that some time ago this French word was actually pronounced something like *sain, saine*, if we read it in the conventional Latin way. The historical spelling, when systematized, as in the case of French, is, of course, of great value to linguists because it helps in the reconstruction of older forms of the language. Modern English spelling is only partially historical, as in the case of 'night' or 'knight', showing that the older pronunciation was similar to that of the corresponding German words *Nacht* or *Knecht*. But English spelling is not as systematized as French. Many of our modern spellings are left-overs from a period in which a word could be spelled in several different ways, depending on the whim of the writer. There is no rhyme or reason for the English spelling of 'height' as against 'high', 'speak' as against 'speech', 'proceed' as against 'precede', or 'attorneys' as against 'stories'. The preservation of these irrational spellings in modern English writing seems to be due to an old and inborn individualistic tendency, averse to accepting any bounds imposed by systematization. This attitude is well exemplified by the learned Dr. Crown who, in the various books he published in the latter half of the seventeenth century, spelled his name indifferently as Cron, Croon, Croun, Crone, Croone, Croune; or in more modern times, by the famous Lawrence of Arabia who, when asked by his perplexed publisher to try to spell his foreign words and names more uniformly, answered: 'I spell my names anyhow, to show what rot the systems are.'[2]

The inconsistency of English writing can be well illustrated by the fact that the system permits eleven different spellings for the long *i* sound (m*e*, f*ee*, s*ea*, f*ie*ld, conc*ei*ve, mach*i*ne, k*ey*, qu*ay*, p*eo*ple, subp*oe*na, C*ae*sar) and at least five different sounds for the alphabetic sign *a* (m*a*n, w*a*s, n*a*me, f*a*ther, *a*roma). What can be done with English spelling can be seen from the story about a foreigner whose name sounded like 'Fish' in English.

Annoyed by the flexibility of English spelling he wrote his name in English as 'Ghotiugh', deriving it souhd by sound from the spelling of the following words: *gh* = *f* sound in 'tough'; *o* = *i* sound in 'women'; *ti* = *sh* sound in 'station', and *ugh* is silent in 'dough'.

Many European writings have reformed their old spellings to make them express more nearly the modern spoken forms. Italian and Spanish among the Romance languages and Croatian and Polish among the Slavonic languages express in their spellings forms which are almost identical with those of the spoken language. The best road was taken by the Czech writing which reformed its spelling by introducing diacritic marks. The Czechs write *Čech*, while the Poles write *Czech*; in both cases the initial sound corresponds to the English *ch* in 'chess'. Observe the inconsistency of the English spelling of 'Czech' with initial *cz* and final *ch* in total disagreement with the normal English spelling of the two sounds as *ch* and *kh* respectively.

Writing frequently introduces spellings due to artificial and erroneous interpretation. Thus, our English words 'debt' and 'doubt' are and always were pronounced without the *b*. Both the French and the English words were written *dette, doute*, and the present-day spellings with *b* were invented by scribes who knew the Latin antecedents of these words (*debitum, dubitum*). In a similar way the spelling of 'isle' and 'island' (from Old English 'iegland') with *s* is due to the recollection of the Latin *insula* and not to the actual pronunciation with *s* in any historical phase of English.[3] Sometimes such wrong spellings have been able to assert themselves in the spoken language. Since the digram *th*, in transliterations of Greek words, was pronounced *t* by medieval scribes, they frequently spelled with *th* words which never had the digram. Thus originated the spelling of 'author' (Latin *au(c)tor*, French *auteur*), of 'Gothic' (Latin *Goti*, German *Goten*), of 'Lithuania' (Latin *Lituania*), and the subsequent pronunciation with *th* in modern English.[4] Similarly, the English pronunciation of *x* as *ks* in Mexico and Don Quixote, pronounced as *sh* in older Spanish and as *kh* in modern Spanish, furnishes another case of the influence of spelling on pronunciation. In the same light can be viewed the frequent modern pronunciation with *t* of the words 'often, soften', where no *t* was pronounced for centuries, or of the word 'forehead' as *foor-hed*, where tradition for some time has favoured the pronunciation *fored*.

Our vocabularies are frequently enriched by expressions taken over from abbreviated written forms. Such words are usually of technical or ephemeral character. In the speech of the American Army the word 'recon' (rhymes with 'pecan') is used for 'reconnaissance', just as 'recce' (rhymes with 'Becky') is the corresponding word in the British Army. Similarly, we find 'ammo' for 'ammunition', 'arty' for 'artillery', or 'divarty' (written 'Div Arty') for 'divisional artillery'. The Germans of the Nazi period showed great predilection for creating new words from abbreviated written forms. In spite of the official Nazi attitude toward what they called the 'Bolshevic-Talmudic' tendency, the number of written and spoken abbreviations grew so large that books and bulky appendices had to be compiled to list the abbreviations used in the various branches of political, economic, and military life. During the second world war Allied Military Intelligence issued two volumes listing the various abbreviations used in the German army alone. From among thousands of examples which have entered the language we may choose *Ari* for *Artillerie*, *Hiwi* for *Hilfs-williger*, *Jabo* for *Jagdbomber*, *Pak* for *Panzerabwehrkanone*, its twin *Flak* for *Flugzeugabwehrkanone*, and, of course, the word *Nazi* for *Nationalsozialistische Deutsche Arbeiterpartei*, with its post-war corollary *Entnazifizierung*, 'denazification.' Incidentally, a few remarks should be made in respect to the types of written abbreviations preferred in various countries. The normal type of abbreviation—cutting off the last part of a word—is shown in the American writing of 'Recon' for 'reconnaissance,' 'Div' for 'division', 'Co' for 'company', and occasionally also in German as, for example, in the use of *Muni* for *Munition*. The British, following an old medieval tradition, prefer to eliminate the middle part of a word, as in 'Recce' for 'reconnaissance' or 'Coy' for 'company'. The Germans, in turn, show pre-ference for creating words by combining the first syllables of compound words, as in *Hiwi* or *Jabo*; another type of German abbreviation is exemplified by *Pak* and *Flak*. Mixed types of abbreviations, naturally, occur everywhere. Colloquial expres-sions like 'prof' for 'professor', 'prexy' for 'president', 'varsity' for 'university', 'natch' for 'naturally' originated as the result of the English language tendency toward abbreviation of long words rather than under the influence of the corresponding abbreviated written forms.

The attachment of the people to their writing is best visible in the examples furnished by the Jews and Arabs of Spain. The former, during the Arabic domination of Spain, spoke Arabic predominantly and left a considerable literature written in the Arabic language but in their own Hebrew characters. On the other hand, the Arabs, who after the Spanish reconquest accepted Spanish as their mother tongue, left us the famous *aljamiado* literature written in the Spanish language and Arabic writing. Also pertinent is the example of the Jews in the Mediterranean area who speak Ladino (a Spanish dialect) and the Jews of eastern Europe who speak Yiddish (a German dialect) both languages being written in the Hebrew alphabet. Here belongs also the case of the Polish Tatars with their literature written in the White Russian and Polish languages but in Arabic letters.

Normally a language uses only one writing at a time. Thus, in ancient times, Sumerian, Egyptian, Chinese, Greek, or Latin had only one corresponding writing, just as in modern times English, French, or Arabic are expressed only in one type of alphabet. Similarly, the late Babylonian tablets are often inscribed in the Babylonian language and in incised cuneiform writing, with drawn or painted additions in the Aramaic language and in the Aramaic alphabet. Other examples are the bilingual inscriptions, such as the Rosetta stone, one of whose inscriptions is written in the Egyptian language and in two varieties of Egyptian writing (hieroglyphic and demotic), while the other is in the Greek language and writing; or the Behistun inscriptions written in three different languages (Persian, Elamite, Babylonian), each expressed in a different kind of cuneiform.

Cases in which one language is expressed at the same time in different writings are few and unimpressive. For example, the Aramaic records, which normally used a writing of their own, were sometimes written in cuneiform. The Hurrians of northern Mesopotamia used Babylonian cuneiform for their language, but Hurrian records at Râs Shamrah, in Syria, are preserved in a unique form of cuneiform writing developed at that site.

Of course, over a long period of time a language can employ several writings. Thus, for instance, the Persian language was expressed first in a variety of cuneiform writing, then in the Pehlevi and Avestan scripts, and finally in the Arabic alphabet. If and when Persia follows the example of Turkey, it is possible that we shall see Persian written in Latin characters. The Hebrews first had a Canaanite system of writing and later developed from Aramaic their own *scriptura quadrata*. The old Egyptian language was written in its own writing, but Coptic, the direct descendant of Egyptian, used a script developed from the Greek alphabet.

During transitional stages two different writing systems may be used at the same time for one and the same language. The introduction of the Latin alphabet into Turkey in 1928 did not entirely eliminate the older Arabic alphabet. But while the older generation can and does use both alphabets, the younger generation knows only the Latin alphabet. There is no doubt that within a short period of time the older Arabic writing will die out entirely in Turkey.

While it is true that in general a language chooses only one writing as its means of expression, there are no limitations as to the use of one writing for any number of languages. The cultural predominance of a certain country frequently results in the borrowing of its writing by its culturally less developed neighbours. In ancient times the Babylonian language was the *lingua franca* of the whole Near East comparable in its extent with the widespread use of Latin in the Middle Ages. With the Babylonian language came the Mesopotamian cuneiform writing. Many literate and illiterate peoples of the ancient Near East accepted the cuneiform writing for their languages and then developed it into a number of local varieties. Thus, the Elamites, the Hurrians, the Urartians, and the Boğazköy Hittites expressed their respective languages in cuneiform writing. In later periods the Greek, Latin, Russian, and Arabic alphabets were (and are still) widely employed by many different languages.

Just as there are occasions when the spoken word is more powerful, more expressive, than its written counterpart, so there are others when writing serves its purpose more effectively than language. We know the powerful influence of the word spoken from the church pulpit or from the political rostrum. On the other hand there are sciences, such as mathematics, so full of complicated symbolism that only writing is able to express it in a short and efficient way. The effectiveness of speech is frequently enhanced by the use of written symbols. Thus, even in the classroom we often use the blackboard to help visualize things which are hard to perceive by ear.

Writing is frequently more expressive than speech. This is especially true of the pictorial writings, that is, writings like Egyptian which faithfully preserved the form of the picture. Thus, for instance, in the spoken sentence: 'I put myrrh in the vase,' there is no indication as to the size or form of the vase. In pictorial writing this vase can be drawn large or small, in a certain colour and in a certain form to indicate its desired qualities. Sometimes further information can be conveyed by unpronounced determinatives, as in the use of the determinative for stone or metal, added to the picture of the vase.

WRITING AND ART

The study of writing from the artistic point of view has heretofore been badly neglected.[5] Although the chief aim of writing is not artistic effect but the practical recording and transmission of communication, writing at all times has had elements of aesthetic value. Writing is similar in this respect to photography, inasmuch as both have primary aims of practical value, but both can, at the same time, achieve aesthetic effect.

The aesthetic feature is sometimes so exaggerated that writing serves the purpose of ornamentation, thus neglecting its primary object of communication; consider, for example, Arabic ornamental writing, beautiful but difficult to read,[6] and some exaggerated and baroque uses of writing in modern advertising.

Writing in its aesthetic—not utilitarian—aspect is one form of art in general. As such, writing shares in the general development of art and frequently exhibits features which are characteristic of other manifestations of art. It can be observed, for instance, that the roundness of Carolingian handwriting goes hand in hand with the roundness of Romanesque architecture, while the later Gothic writing has features of angularity and pointedness characteristic of Gothic architecture.[7]

In all well-developed writings we can observe two main classes: the carefully executed formal writing used on public and official monuments, and the abbreviated cursive writing used for private purposes, primarily in letters. Aesthetic execution is, of course, more evident in the formal than in the cursive writing. Hand in hand with the development of the formal writing into cursive goes the change from a pictorial form in which pictures can be clearly perceived to a linear form represented by signs whose original pictorial character can no longer be recognized.

The aesthetic impression of an inscribed monument depends on a great number of factors: the execution of the individual signs (form, size, etc.), the relation of the signs to the inscription (position, distance between signs, spacing of lines, direction, etc.), and the relation of the inscription to the monument (relief, painting, structure, etc.).

The most important of these factors, the form of the individual signs, gives us the best opportunity to judge the aesthetic quality of an inscribed record. The aesthetic effect is evident also in the grouping of signs. If the order of the signs is xXx (x represents a small sign, X a large sign), then it can be changed to $\check{x}$X, where two small signs $\frac{x}{x}$ may be so arranged as to balance the large sign X. This also avoids the empty space below the small sign, which would exist if the signs were written in the correct order. *Horror vacui,* 'fear of the empty space,' is of great influence in the arrangement of signs.

Scribal schools, each with characteristic features, are known in all periods of writing. It is not difficult, for example, to assign to the Lagash school the small Sumerian clay tablets of the Ur III period inscribed in very minute cuneiform characters; and it is relatively easy to recognize the dominant features of the Boğazköy school of scribes in their very careful execution of Hittite hieroglyphic inscriptions. In the older periods the results of individual creativeness are little known to us, even though the scribes frequently signed their names at the end of the inscriptions. This is a fertile subject for future investigation.

WRITING AND RELIGION

The concept of the divine origin and character of writing is found everywhere, in both ancient and modern times, among civilized as well as among primitive peoples. In the main it is due to a widespread belief in the magic powers of writing.[8]

Everywhere, in the East as well as in the West, the origin of writing is ascribed to a divinity. Among the Babylonians it was the god Nabû, patron of the sciences and scribe of the gods, who invented writing, occupying thus a position which in the earlier Mesopotamian tradition was assigned partly to the goddess Nisaba. The Egyptians believed that the god Thoth was the inventor of writing, and they called their writing $m^x d^x w^x$-$n^x \underline{t}^x r^x$, 'the speech of gods.' In the Chinese legends the inventor of writing was either Fohi, the founder of commerce, or the wise Ts'ang Chien with the face of a four-eyed dragon. The Hebrews had their older 'divine' writing (Ex. xxxi: 18) besides the later 'human' writing (Isa. viii: 1). In Islamic tradition God himself created the writing. According to the Hindus it was Brahma who was supposed to have given the knowledge of letters to men. The Northern Saga attributes the invention of the runes to Odin; and in the Irish legend Ogmios is known as the inventor of writing. These cases could be easily multiplied.[9]

A very interesting case of the 'invention' of a writing under divine inspiration was recently described in connection with the introduction of a new writing by the Toma in French Guinea and Liberia.[10] Wido, the native discoverer of the writing, had a vision:—

'God takes he no pity on the Tomas? Other races know writing. Only the Tomas remain in their ignorance.' God answered him: 'I fear that when you are able to express yourselves you shall have no more respect for the beliefs and customs of your race.' 'Not at all,' answered Wido, 'we shall still keep living as in past days. I promise it.' 'If such is the case,' said God, 'I am willing to grant you the knowledge, but take care never to show anything of it to a woman.'

There are other divergent accounts of the invention of this writing, none of which, however, states the reason for this special attitude toward women. The road is open to speculation at will.

Belief in the sacred character of writing is strong in countries in which knowledge of writing is restricted to a special class or caste of priests. The ancient Near East, where normally only the priest-scribes could write, is full of mystic reconstructions about writing. On the other hand, Greece—where writing was not restricted to priests but formed a popular patrimony of all the citizens—almost entirely lacks myths of this kind. [11] The educated Greeks knew that their writing, like so many other practical achievements, came from the East and felt no need for speculating about its divine origin. To be sure, the Greeks also had some mystic interpretations about writing, like the Pythagorean reconstructions, but these originated usually under Oriental influence and were outside the normal course of Greek philosophy.

Among primitives writing and books are the subject of astonishment and speculation. [12] To them books are instruments of divination. A book can predict the future and reveal what is hidden; it is a guide and a counsellor and, in general, a mystic power. To learn to read and write is to the primitive a formal initiation into a new religious practice, a baptism into a new religion. A book is considered a living being which can 'speak'. The primitive fears the magic power of its 'words'. According to one story, a native messenger refused to transport a written message because he was afraid that the letter would speak to him while he was carrying it. In another case a messenger refused to carry a letter until he had pierced it with his lance, so that it could not talk to him during the voyage. A written message is a mysterious being which has the power to see things. We know the story about an Indian who was sent by a missionary to a colleague with four loaves of bread and a letter stating their number. The Indian ate one of the loaves and was, of course, found out. Later he was sent on a similar errand and repeated the theft, but took the precaution, while he was eating the bread, to hide the letter under a stone so that it might not see him. [13] A similar story is reported from Australia. A native who had stolen some tobacco from a package with an accompanying letter was astonished that the white man was able to find him out in spite of the fact that he had hidden the letter in the trunk of a tree. He vented his wrath upon the letter by beating it furiously. [14]

Another interesting example is cited by Erland Nordenskiöld:—

When Ruben Pérez Kantule learnt picture-writing, he recorded as we know the legends also in Latin script, which, of course, was much more complete and expressive than was possible by means of the Indian writing. The strange thing is that he troubled at all to write down the songs and the incantations with pictures when he could have done it so much easier with Latin letters. This goes to prove that picture-writing *per se* carries a magic import, or that, so to speak, the virtues of the medicinal incantations are enhanced by the fact of their being expressed in picture-writing.[15]

Belief in universal symbolism as practised by Pythagoreans, gnostics, astrologers, magicians, and cabbalists had its fountain head in mystic interpretations of the alphabet. Cf., for example, a typical quotation from a recently published book on the subject: 'Nous voulons montrer que l'Alphabet latin... est la représentation idéographique des grands mythes grecs, et qu'il nous offre de ce chef... la "signification" maniable des vérités fondamentales contenues en l'homme et dans l'Univers, vérités vivantes, "Dieux," qui manifestent la Vérité Une, créatrice et souveraine.'[16]

The power of a charm or amulet depends to a great extent on the writing which it includes. Such was the case with the Babylonian amulets with their abracadabra formulas. Even in modern times we can observe the widespread use of the magic effect of writing. Here we may mention the phylacteries with sacred writings which the Jews wear during prayer, and the inscriptions on the doorposts of Jewish houses which are supposed to protect the inhabitants from harm. The Mohammedans carry amulets with enclosed verses from the Koran. Among Christians we find the custom of fanning a sick person with leaves of the Bible, or of having him swallow a pellet of paper with a prayer written on it.

A curious left-over of the belief in the sacred character of writing is the ritual which was performed at the ceremony of the consecration of the Westminster Cathedral in 1910:—

On the floor of the spacious nave, from the main entrance to the sanctuary, were painted in white two broad paths, which connected the corners diagonally opposite, and intersecting at the centre of the nave formed a huge figure x, or St. Andrew's Cross. Where the lines converged was placed a faldstool; and here the Archbishop, still in cope and mitre, knelt in prayer, while the choir continued to sing the ancient plainsong of the 'Sarum Antiphoner'. . . . Meanwhile attendants were engaged in strewing the nave with ashes. This meant the laying of small heaps of the ashes, about two yards apart, along the lines of the St. Andrew's Cross. Beside each heap of ashes was placed a piece of cardboard containing a letter of the alphabet—

the Greek on one line and the Latin on the other. The Archbishop then went towards the main entrance, attended by the deacon and sub-deacon, and preceded by the Crucifix carried between lighted candles. Starting first from the left-hand corner Dr Bourne advanced along one path of the St. Andrew's Cross, tracing with the end of his pastoral staff the letters of the Greek alphabet on the heaps of ashes; and returning again to the main entrance repeated the process on the other path, tracing this time on the heaps of ashes the letters of the Latin alphabet. This curious ceremony is variously interpreted as symbolizing the union of the Western and Eastern Churches, or the teaching of the rudiments of Christianity, and as a survival of the Roman augurs in laying their plans for the construction of a temple, or as the procedure of Roman surveyors in valuing land for fiscal purposes.[17]

The modern Near East is full of superstitious beliefs in the power of writing; this is frequently the case even with unknown writing. From among many examples I should like to quote one from my own experience. In 1935 I visited a small village in central Anatolia called Emirgazi, where about thirty years earlier some Hittite hieroglyphic inscriptions had been discovered, which had then been transferred to the Museum in Istanbul. Inquiry revealed that there were no new antiquities in the neighbourhood, but even if there were some, I was told by the villagers, they would never give them up, because the last time, after the Hittite inscriptions had been taken away, a pestilence visited the village. The magic power associated with stone inscriptions is described frequently in reports of travellers in the whole Islamic world. The mystic power of writing—sometimes entirely incomprehensible, as in the case of the Hittite hieroglyphic inscriptions just referred to—is paralleled by the magic effect of the spoken word. There is a 'widespread custom, in magic ceremonies and even in ritual and religious ceremonies, of using songs and formulas which are unintelligible to those who hear them, and sometimes even to those who utter them.'[18]

Writing and speech are the outward symbols of a nation. It is for that reason that a conqueror's first aim in destroying a nation is to destroy its written treasures. We thus understand why Cortez, having conquered Mexico in 1520, ordered the burning of all the Aztec books which might remind the native population of their glorious past; why the Spanish Inquisition in sending the Jews to the pyre, burned with them their Talmud; why the modern Nazis, anxious to destroy ideologies adverse to their own, burned the books of their opponents, and why the victorious Allies after the second world war ordered the destruction of all Nazi-tainted literature.

X

FUTURE OF WRITING

WHILE investigating the *how* of a certain phenomenon, it is difficult not to evaluate at the same time its *why*. It is therefore natural that in reconstructing the history of our writing the following question would come up time and time again: Why did writing develop from this to that stage? The overall answer to this question might be quite simple: Writing passed from one stage to another because at a certain time a new system was deemed better suited to local needs than the one currently in use. In other words, improvement is the aim of evolution, and writing, as it develops from stage to stage, is steadily progressing in the direction of a perfect means of human intercommunication. But is writing actually progressing? Can we take for granted that any new system of writing is normally better than the one used before? Before we try to give specific answers to this question let us look first at some pertinent examples from the history of writing.

In comparing the West Semitic system of writing with the Egyptian hieroglyphic, from which it had developed, it is easy to see that the West Semitic system is simpler than the Egyptian one. Certainly there can be no argument as to the fact that the twenty-two to thirty Semitic signs are easier to learn and quicker to write than the many hundreds of signs of the Egyptian system. Also, we may agree that the introduction of vowel signs in Greek made this system more exact than its predecessor, the West Semitic writing, which was characterized by lack of vowel indication. But is the West Semitic writing, therefore, to be considered better than Egyptian or Greek better than West Semitic? In the case of Egyptian versus Semitic, one could quote certain qualities of Egyptian lacking in the Semitic system, like the expressiveness of pictorial signs.

Thus, for instance, the picture of a vase in Egyptian not only can stand for the word 'vase' but can be drawn in such a way as to suggest its intended size and form; in Semitic the word 'vase' would be written by means of phonetic, syllabic signs, while any additional information could be expressed only by additional syllabic signs. In the case of Semitic versus Greek, one could bring forth the argument that the Semitic writings can get along rather well without vowel indication, and are therefore considerably quicker and shorter than Greek or any other systems using signs for vowels. And what shall we say about the opinion of those scholars and laymen who consider the Chinese writing as the best in the world and will not even listen to any suggestions to replace the Chinese word-syllabic writing with an alphabetic system? How are we to judge the enthusiastic statement about the syllabic writing which spread like wildfire among the Cherokees because they could accomplish the feat of learning the new system within the span of a single day, as contrasted with four years required by the Cherokees to master the English writing?[1] How are we to assess the superficial conclusion that the Arabic writing is superior to the Latin because, in taking dictation, the older Turks using the Arabic alphabet for their language are much faster than their younger countrymen employing the new Latin alphabet?

Thus, we can see how delicate is the matter of evaluation of quality, and how easy it is to go astray if one bases his conclusions on single observations and neglects to weigh against each other all the inherent characteristics of a certain phenomenon. The Semitic writings may truly be easier to learn and quicker to write than Egyptian hieroglyphic, while the Egyptian picture writing may be more expressive than the Semitic systems, but surely the two characteristics are not on equal footing from the relative point of view. Of what relative value is a writing like Egyptian—beautiful and expressive—if it must remain a total mystery to a vast majority of the population because of the complexities and difficulties of its system? To an even greater extent the same is true of the Chinese system— perhaps the most difficult system in the world to master. Years and years of study must be spent by an individual before he can attempt to read the simplest classics. It is, of course, true that the Chinese writing serves rather well the needs of a selfish bureaucratic clique at the top, and that a small percentage of the population, who know how to read and write, can communicate with each other by writing even when speaking mutually ununderstandable dialects. But has anybody attempted to evaluate logically these seeming advantages of the Chinese writing as against its tremendous shortcomings? Nobody but a selfish and narrow-minded person could defend the Chinese writing on the basis of its alleged merits and neglect to observe that as a result of the difficultes of the Chinese system 90 per cent of the population remain illiterate. Which is more valuable: a system which is adequate for 10 per cent of the population or a system which is accessible to everybody? And what is more important: to keep the present writing and continue with the 10 per cent clique running the country or to reform the writing into a simple system and have 100 per cent of the population sharing in the progress of the country?

Unprejudiced evaluation of all the factors involved will show that also in other cases writings on a higher scale of evolution have definite advantages over those on a lower level. Even though the Semitic writings are faster to write than Greek, only the latter created a full vowel system and thus offered to the world the potentialities of vowel indication so important for the expression of exact nuances of language, little known dialectal forms, new words, and foreign names and words. Also, the advantage of speed of the Arabic writing as used for the Turkish language is totally overshadowed by its difficult orthography; the Latin alphabet, as introduced in Turkey, is pretty nearly phonemic, and it can be acquired by school children in half of the time required for the mastering of the older Arabic writing. And, finally, when we come to evaluate the merits of the Cherokee writing we must admit that it evidently suited perfectly the expression of the Cherokee language. But was this writing suited for a people who lived within an English speaking territory? How well suited was the Cherokee writing to express the hundreds and thousands of words and names which passed to the Cherokees from the surrounding English speaking people? This inadequacy of the Cherokee writing must have been the main reason that ultimately led to the disappearance of the Indian writing and its replacement by a Latin system which was better suited to the wider needs of the Cherokee people.

To resume the question posed at the beginning of this

chapter, is writing progressing as it passes along the course of evolution marked by the logographic, syllabic, and alphabetic stages? I should say yes, it is progressing! Looking at writing from the broadest point of view I should say without hesitation that the alphabetic systems serve the aim of human inter-communication better than the syllabic ones, just as the latter systems serve it better than the logographic or logo-syllabic systems. Still, there is nothing to brag about. The inconsistencies of English orthography as compared with the pretty nearly phonemic Greek and Latin systems, and the abnormal development of sign forms in some of the writings in modern India as compared with the simple forms of older Indic writings, show that in specific cases writing does not necessarily proceed along the line of improvement. The hampering conventions imposed by tradition, religion, and nationalism frequently stand in the path of progress, thus preventing or delaying reforms which normally would have taken place in the sound evolution of writing.

In comparing any of the alphabetic writings used in the Western civilization with the Greek alphabet one observation comes immediately to mind, and that is that from the inner, structural point of view there is no difference between the Western and the Greek alphabets. In other words, in spite of the tremendous achievements of the Western civilization in so many fields of human endeavour, writing has not progressed at all since the Greek period. Think of our modern media of mass communication, such as radio, cinema, telegraph, telephone, television, and press and look at our modern writing of DADA, Latin DADA, and Greek ΔΑΔΑ. Compare the differences in the methods of mass communication between the modern and Greek times on the one side and the essential identity of the English, Latin, and Greek alphabets on the other. It is not as if our writing were so perfect as not to need any improvement. And it is not for lack of proposals of good and practical reforms that we cling so tenaciously to an obsolete way of writing. The complex causes for this conservative attitude may very well be beyond our capacity to comprehend. Still it may not be amiss to acquaint ourselves with the present state of affairs and to speculate a little as to the possibilities which may be considered or realized in the future.

Proposals and attempts to reform writing frequently go hand

in hand with those affecting the reform of speech. This is only natural if we remember the dependence of writing on speech throughout its long history.

The simplest form of language change is that which occurs when a national language is imposed upon a foreign ethnic group. Akkadian, Aramaic, Arabic, Greek, Latin, Spanish, French, Russian, and English are some of those languages which, backed up by cultural prestige or political predominance, have imposed themselves at one time or another in wide areas outside of their mother countries. Hand in hand with the languages came the imposition of national writings, as is well attested by the wide use of the cuneiform system in antiquity and of the Semitic, Greek, and Latin writings in later times. The present hegemony of Western civilization manifests itself in the widespread proposals, more or less successful, to impose the Latin writing upon the world. The acceptance of Latin writing by the Turks, its widespreading use by African and American natives, the proposals concerning the romanization of Chinese, Japanese, Arabic, and Persian are the best manifestations of this trend.

However, the wide acceptance of the Latin alphabet in modern times has led to no unity. In many cases the signs of the Latin alphabet received widely variant phonetic values in different countries. The Turks, for instance, use the Latin sign *c* for the sound *j* as in our 'jig', a correspondence which is without parallel in any Western writing. The limitless homophony of signs is best illustrated by the spellings of the name of the famous Russian writer Chekhov, in which the initial sound can be written as *Ch, Tch, C, Tsch, Tsj, Tj, Cz, Cs*, or *Č*, the medial consonant as *kh, ch, k, h*, or *x*, and the final one as *v, f*, or *ff* in various systems of the world, all using Latin signs. For centuries the need to reform the Latin alphabet has been generally recognized and many attempts have been made to remedy the malady.[2] The best of these proposals is the alphabet known by the abbreviation IPA (International Phonetic Association), which consists of Latin symbols, supplemented by a number of artificial letters and a few diacritic marks.[3] This is the system which is now generally used by linguists. It is so simple and practical that it merits a considerably wider appreciation than is accorded to it in narrow scientific circles.

The most widespread reforms have taken place within many national writings in order to simplify spellings and to systematize the correspondences between sound and sign. Some people, like the Finns, have succeeded rather well in achieving an almost phonemic system, while others, like the Anglo-Saxons, continue to carry the burden of traditional spellings. However, the future of writing no longer lies in reforms of national writings. As Mark Twain once said, be it somewhat in irregular orthography: 'The da ma ov koars kum when the publik ma be expektd to get rekonsyled to the bezair asspekt of the Simplified Kombynashuns, but—if I may be allowed the expression—is it worth the wasted time?'[4] It is too late to preach the gospel of reform for the various national orthographies. What is needed now is one system of writing in which signs have identical or almost identical phonetic correspondences all over the world. That need is fulfilled in the IPA alphabet.

Nationalistic and religious attitudes have strongly militated against the acceptance of this or that language as the world language. The Anglo-Saxons have fought against French, the Frenchmen against English, the Protestants against Latin, the Russians against all three. Even simplified languages, such as Basic English, have met with relatively little success. Add to this fact the irregularities and inconsistencies of all natural languages and you will find the reason for the rise of the many artificial languages in modern times. Among them Esperanto, Ido, Occidental, Interlingua, Novial, and Volapük at least enjoyed a certain amount of success in their times. In general, however, we may note that the attempt to create one universal language has only resulted in adding new languages to our confused Tower of Babel. Also in the field of writing proposals have been made to replace national systems with new forms of writing. The various approaches to the problem resulted in various concrete proposals, which we shall presently examine.

Whether a writing is borrowed from outside or created within, it is used at first predominantly for public and official purposes. In such cases the forms of individual signs are frequently so chosen as to show complete disregard for economy in space and time. Only gradually are cursive writings evolved for daily, practical use, with signs showing various degrees of simplification as, e.g., in our cursive handwriting contrasted with book print. But frequently even cursive forms are not simplified enough to serve adequately the purpose of a rapid writing. For that reason ever since classical times attempts have frequently been made to create new forms of writing in which individual signs were so chosen and linked together as to produce the greatest possible saving in time and space. This is the modern shorthand variously known as stenography or 'narrow writing', brachygraphy or 'short writing', and tachygraphy or 'quick writing'. Of all the reforms in writing, shorthand has enjoyed by far the greatest success. Although some of the shorthand systems claim international recognition, in reality there is no single system accepted throughout the world. One system may be used in several countries, but even then it usually shows deviations necessitated by local needs. Practical shorthand systems are used everywhere in addition to the national popular writings. None of the shorthand systems has as yet succeeded in supplanting a local national writing in popular use.

An entirely different approach to symbolizing sounds is found in Bell's 'Visible Speech'[5] and Jespersen's 'Analphabetic Notation'. The approach starts from the presupposition that all sounds have two aspects: organic (or articulatory) and acoustic. When we speak, for example, of the sound *s* we can observe its organic articulation in the shape of the mouth and the position of the tongue by which it is produced, and its acoustic counterpart in the hiss which is the result of sending the breath through the passage thus formed.[6] The new methods attempt to symbolize the articulation of the sound rather than its acoustic side.

The device known as 'Visible Speech' was first worked out by Melville Bell, the father of the inventor of the telephone, and subsequently became popular as the reformed system called 'Organic' by Henry Sweet.[7] In this system diagrammatic signs are used to imitate the form of vocal organs in position for the utterance of various sounds. An electronic device of changing speech sounds into visible patterns that one may learn to read and analyse has recently been developed by researchers in the Bell Telephone Laboratories and advertised as 'Visible Speech'[8] but, outside of the name, the new device has nothing in common with the Bell-Sweet device to record sounds.

Another method to symbolize articulation of sound is the

so-called 'Analphabetic Notation', devised by Otto Jespersen.[9] The system is even more exact than 'Visible Speech'. While in 'Visible Speech' symbols are used to indicate simple articulations, the Analphabetic Notation tries to express the sum total of all the closely correlated movements in the organs of speech resulting in a single sound. In Jespersen's notation each sound is represented by a series of Greek and Latin letters, Arabic numbers, and some other symbols each of which has a definite meaning: the Greek letter indicates the articulatory organ (lip, tongue, etc.); the number stands for the degree and form of the opening (open, close, etc.); while the Latin letter, used as an exponent, denotes the articulatory position (front, central, back, etc.). E.g., the letter u is expressed in this notation as α3ᵃ βg γ3ʲ δ0 ε1 in a form closely resembling a chemical formula. Even more complicated is the analphabetic system devised by Kenneth L. Pike.[10] In his system the sound t, for example, would be expressed by *Ma*II*De*C*Vve*I*c*AP*paatdtltnran*sfs*SiFS*s. These two systems have certain advantages in narrow scientific usage for recording individual sounds where long definitions requiring many lines of normal writing may be replaced by a few symbols, but they are not intended for the recording of utterances and are, therefore, not acceptable as a practical system of writing.

As was shown in greater detail in Chapter III, the Chinese word-syllabic writing uses word signs to a considerably greater extent than any other writing of the same type, for instance Sumerian or Egyptian. In a country divided by a number of different and frequently mutually incomprehensible dialects this characteristic of the Chinese system serves the purpose of a kind of universal writing. In imitation of the Chinese system, proposals have frequently been made in Europe to create a universal system in which signs and symbols would be used to stand for words and grammatical formatives which could be read differently although understood in the same way in various languages of the world. The full system would thus be the result of a systematization of the device used commonly in our writing of numbers, which can stand for different words in various languages. Ever since the Middle Ages various systems have been proposed, but none has been generally accepted.[11] The shortcomings of these pasigraphic systems are those of all national word writings: Inexactness and difficulties in mastering thousands of signs for different linguistic elements. Still the possibility of creating a practical pasigraphic system cannot be entirely excluded. The successful creation of an international gesture sign language for the use of deaf-mutes, in which each gesture sign has the same basic meaning in various countries, is an indication that it may yet be possible in the future to devise a parallel pasigraphic system for certain limited purposes.

Another pasigraphic system is that known as Isotype: International System Of TYpographic Picture Education.[12] Isotype has no aspiration of becoming a universal system to replace phonetic writings. What it attempts to do is to create a number of picture signs which could be *per se* understandable without the necessity of having any established correspondences between sign and word. The system is intended for use chiefly in teaching and education, but it may also be used in limited form in some international media of communication and transportation. For instance, in writing instructions of how to use a telephone a short series of pictures could be given which would be internationally understood instead of long written instructions which would be understood only by persons acquainted with the local language.

The time is to summarize. How do we stand to-day with the reform of writing and what is its future? Let us first review the reforms which seem either inadequate or impractical. It may generally be admitted that the revision of national writings in the direction of Simplified Spellings is inadequate and not worth the effort. The time to revise our writing in the national sense was the eighteenth or nineteenth century, when nationalism was born and reached its peak, not the twentieth century, when we are striving to achieve a universal community of nations. For that reason we should not approve of the imposition of the Latin alphabet upon countries exposed to Western influence. In addition, it should be noted that from the point of view of the theory of writing there is nothing in the Latin alphabet as used in Western countries that can be considered superior to what is found, for example, in the Arabic, Greek, or Russian alphabets. The main *forte* of the Latin alphabet, namely its backing by the Western civilization, seems to overshadow entirely its apparent shortcomings. What is needed, therefore, is either one system of writing reformed for international use or an entirely new type of world writing.

From the systems to be considered in the light of universal employment we may immediately exclude the types represented by 'Visible Speech' and 'Analphabetic Notation'. Both can be used internationally within limited spheres to symbolize elements of speech. They are very exact and therefore of great help in scientific disciplines, but they are not practical enough ever to be considered for a writing of daily use. For practical reasons the various pasigraphic systems with their hundreds and thousands of different signs should also be excluded from consideration as a universal writing.

There is one writing in Latin characters which is widely employed by linguists for transcription and transliteration of many and various languages of the world, and that is the alphabet of the International Phonetic Association. The alphabet is relatively exact in its correspondence between sign and sound and is at the same time so simple that with the help of it a child can acquire the art of writing in a much shorter time than it normally takes to learn the usual type of a national writing.

Although there is a difference in purpose between the reformed alphabets and the IPA alphabet in that the former are alphabets revised for national use, while the IPA alphabet is devised for use with any and all the languages of the world, still objections of equal force can be raised against both. First, there is the reaction of the general public, so well expressed by Mark Twain[13] in a comment to Simplified Spelling as exemplified in 'La on, Makduf, and damd be he hoo furst krys hold, enuf!' He thought that 'to see our letters put together in ways to which we are not accustomed offends the eye, and also takes the *expression* out of the words. . . . It doesn't thrill you as it used to do. The simplifications have sucked the thrill all out of it'. For that reason Mark Twain himself was not in favour of reforming the existent English writing but of introducing an entirely new form of writing which would not offend the eye as much as Simplified Spelling and would therefore be better received by the general public. Such a new system would not only be more acceptable on general psychological grounds, but it could also bring with it all the valuable elements of rapidity and compactness which are so sadly lacking in our Latin writing. How many persons are aware of the amount of waste in time and space in our Latin writing; that the single signs are unnecessarily complex; that the signs usually do not run in the direction of writing; that frequently they cannot be written by one continuous motion of the hand; that there is no rhyme or reason for the present formal differentiation between capital and small letters. All these shortcomings of the Latin alphabet could be eliminated by the introduction of a shorthand system. But the simple acceptance of a shorthand system would not satisfy our need for a universal writing. There are two reasons militating against the shorthand systems as they are employed at the present. First, they are devised for utmost speed in certain practical applications and therefore they are not exact; and second, they are adapted for the use of certain languages, but not of all the languages of the world.

What we should look for is a system of writing combining the exactness of the IPA alphabet with the formal simplicity of a shorthand system. Both theory and practice could be satisfied by evolving a full and exact system of notation which could be shortened and simplified under certain conditions. The full system should contain signs for all the known sounds of the various languages within the limits of the IPA alphabet, and the signs should be expressed by forms borrowed from a stenographic system. Out of this full system smaller alphabets could be excerpted for use in individual languages. At the same time the full system should be evolved in such a way as to leave open the possibility of further simplification even within the national writings. The proposed IPA-stenographic combination would doubtless be shorter and quicker than the IPA alphabet written in Latin characters, but it might not satisfy the need for rapidity and compactness as well as the present shorthand systems. Further simplification of the IPA-stenographic system would therefore be indicated for these practical purposes. In order to keep intact the basic unity of the full and the practical systems I would not suggest that the latter should seek to achieve its aim by creating new signs for words and phrases, following the well known procedure in the stenographic systems. A practical system could very well be realized by the process of abbreviation and elimination of all those elements which under certain conditions are not necessary to achieve understanding of the record or communication. Some Semitic writings with their well-known abbreviations and arbitrary omissions of vowel signs could serve as good models for possible simplification of the proposed IPA-stenographic system. Thus, using steno-graphic forms in all cases, in a full system the word 'simplifica-tion' could be spelled something like 'simplifikeyšn', while in certain practical applications the same word could be written as 'smplfkyšn' by omission of vowels, as 'simplifik.' by abbrevia-tion, or even as 'smplfk.' by both abbreviation and omission of vowels.

We have come to the end of our speculation on the future of writing. I am fully aware how vulnerable this chapter is to criticisms from various quarters. Traditionalists will decry it as another useless proposal to change the *status quo*. Professional scholars will bemoan my cursory treatment of an important subject. I am not much affected by the traditionalistic outbursts against the reformers. Were it not for the reformers, the traditionalists, dressed in skins and feathers, would still be living in caves and would have nary a chance to talk or write about the 'pestilent heresy of reform'. More serious might be the criticisms levelled at the rather cursory fashion in which the important subject of the future of writing was treated in this chapter. In my defence I should like to state that I had no intention of making a formal proposal of a new universal writing. What I intended to do in this chapter was simply to put together certain ideas which grew out of my experience with past writings in order to see what may be learned from them in the future. Therein only lies such value as this chapter may have.

XI

TERMINOLOGY OF WRITING

THIS is the first attempt to collect and define terminology of writing. In an attempt of this kind it has been impossible to follow in the footsteps of tradition. In order to bring out the definitions in sharper typological outline, new terms had to be coined, while some old definitions had to be changed or redefined. The principles governing writing have been placed together to enable the readers to evaluate *in toto* what I regard as the most important contribution in this study. It is hoped that this first attempt will serve as a useful foundation on which, later, a firm terminology of writing can be established.

Acrophony, see *Principle of Acrophony.*

Aesthetic Convention, see *Principle of Aesthetic Convention.*

Allogram. Logographic, syllabic, or alphabetic signs or spellings of one writing when used as word signs or even phrase signs in a borrowed writing. For example, the Sumerian spelling *in-lá-e,* 'he will weigh out,' stands for Akkadian *išaqqal,* 'he will weigh out'; the Aramaic spelling *malkā,* 'king,' stands for Persian *šāh,* 'king.'

Alphabet or *Alphabetic Writing.* A writing in which a sign normally stands for one or more phonemes of the language. Thus, in English, the alphabetic sign *b* stands for the phoneme *b,* while the sign *c* stands for the phonemes *k* or *s.* See also *Logography, Syllabary.*

Associative Sign. A sign expressed by drawing a picture of a concrete object, which stands for a word connected with the picture by association only. Thus, the picture of the sun may stand for the word 'day'.

Auxiliary Mark or Sign. A non-phonetic sign, such as a non-phonetic punctuation mark, and, in some systems, a determinative or classifier, added to help in the understanding of writing.

Classifier, see *Semantic Indicator.*

Consonantal Writing. The so-called consonantal signs of the Egyptian and West Semitic writings are explained in this book as syllabic signs in which vowels were left undetermined.

Context of Situation, see *Principle of Context of Situation.*

248

Conventionalization, see *Principle of Conventionalization*.

Convergence, see *Principle of Convergence*.

Cursive Writing. A quick and superficial form of writing used for daily, practical purposes. Sometimes a cursive writing becomes monumental, developing at the same time a secondary cursive form. Opposite of *Monumental Writing*.

Descriptive-Representational Device. A semasiographic device to convey communication by means of pictures drawn and grouped in accordance with conventions of figurative art.

Determinative, see *Semantic Indicator*.

Diagrammatic Sign. A sign expressed by a geometric form, such as a circle for the words 'all, totality' or a stroke for the numeral 'one'.

Divergence, see *Principle of Divergence*.

Economy, see *Principle of Economy*.

Forerunners of Writing. Various devices, grouped together under *Semasiography*, to achieve intercommunication by means of visible marks, expressing meaning but not necessarily linguistic elements. Opposite of *Phonography*.

Grammatology. Science of writing.

Hieroglyphic. A logo-syllabic system of writing using pictures as signs, such as Egyptian hieroglyphic or Hittite hieroglyphic.

Homophony. A characteristic of several written signs expressing the same phoneme in the language. For example, the written 'too, two, to' are all pronounced *tuu*. Opposite of *Polyphony*.

Identifying-Mnemonic Device. A semasiographic device to convey communication by means of pictures or visible marks, which help to identify or to record certain persons or objects. For example, the drawing of a panther on a shield may convey some such general meaning as 'this shield belongs to the person who killed the panther'.

*Ideogram. Philologists use frequently and improperly the term 'ideogram' for our logogram.

*Ideography. A system of writing alleged to use *Ideograms.

Inner Development, see *Principle of Inner Development*.

Linear Writing. A form of writing using linear designs or non-recognizable pictures as signs. Opposite of *Pictorial Writing*.

Linguistic Transfer. Identification of signs of a system with signs of language, resulting in the former becoming a tool of the latter. Thus, when signs of writing are conventionally associated with linguistic elements, the writing becomes a secondary transfer of language.

Logogram. A word sign used in logography. Not *Ideogram. In English, for example, the signs 2 (two, second), $ (dollar), ° (degree). See also *Primary*, *Associative*, and *Diagrammatic Signs*, *Semantic Indicator*, *Phonetic Transfer*, and *Phonetic Indicator*.

Logography or *Word Writing*. A writing in which a sign normally stands for one or more words of the language. See also *Syllabary*, *Alphabet*.

Logo-Syllabic. A logo-syllabic writing, such as Sumerian or Egyptian, which uses logographic and syllabic signs.

Manual Writing. Writing done by hand. Opposite of *Mechanical Writing*.

Meaning. Mental association between a sign and a referend, that is a thing meant, such as the association between a word and a referend or between a visual sign (with or without a word) and a referend.

Mechanical Writing. Writing done with a mechanical help, such as type or typewriter. Opposite of *Manual Writing*.

Mnemonic, see *Identifying-Mnemonic Device*.

Monumental Writing. A careful form of writing normally found on monuments and used for official display purposes. Opposite of *Cursive Writing*.

Object Writing or *Object Language*. A system utilizing objects as signs, such as the *quipu* knot writing or flower language.

Outer Development, see *Principle of Outer Development*.

Pasigraphy. A system of writing proposed for universal use and using signs expressing meaning, but not necessarily linguistic elements.

Petroglyph. Primitive pictogram on rocks, incised or carved.

Petrogram. Primitive pictogram on rocks, drawn or painted.

Phonetic Complement/Indicator. A sign expressing a phonetic but non-semantic element attached to the basic sign. Thus, in Sumerian, while the basic picture of female breasts can be read as *dumu*, 'son,' *banda*, 'boy,' and *tur*, 'small,' the sign *da* added to the basic picture necessitates the reading *banda* and not *dumu* or *tur*.

Phonetic Sign. Any sign of a full writing which expresses linguistic elements by means of visible marks, such as an *Alphabetic*, *Syllabic* and *Word Sign*, and, in some systems, a *Prosodic* and *Phrase Sign*. Phonetic Signs may be subdivided into two classes : (1) Phonetic semantic signs, such as word and phrase signs, (2) phonetic non-semantic signs, such as alphabetic, syllabic, and prosodic signs.

Phonetic Transfer, see *Principle of Phonetization*.

Phonetization, see *Principle of Phonetization*.

Phonography. A full *Writing*, that is a system of signs expressing linguistic elements by means of visible marks. Opposite of *Semasiography*.

Phraseography or *Phrase Writing*. A type of writing in which a sign stands for a phrase or sentence. Although not known as a writing system, many phraseographic signs are used in stenography and in the sentential calculus.

Pictography. *Forerunners of Writing* using pictograms, that is, pictures as signs, such as are known, for example, among American Indians.

Pictorial Writing. A form of writing using recognizable pictures as signs. Opposite of *Linear Writing.*

Polyphony. A characteristic of a single written sign expressing more than one phoneme in the language. Cf., for example, the polyphonous character of the alphabetic sign *a* in the writing of 'man, mane, malt', etc. Opposite of *Homophony.*

Position, see *Principle of Position.*

Primary Sign. A sign expressed by drawing a picture of a concrete object, which stands for a concrete object or action. Thus, the picture of a man may stand for the word 'man', the picture of a man holding bread in the hand placed near his mouth may stand for the word 'to eat'.

*Principle of Acrophony. A principle by which syllabic and alphabetic signs allegedly originated by using the first part of a longer word and casting off the rest. The principle could be illustrated in English by choosing the picture of a house to stand for an alphabetic sign *h*, because the word 'house' starts with an *h*. Not counting sporadic exceptions, acrophony as a principle seems to play no part in the history of writing.

Principle of Aesthetic Convention. A principle by which form and/or arrangement of signs may be changed in accordance with aesthetic/artistic conventions. For example, the correct order of signs $\overset{xx}{X}$ (x represents a small sign, X a large sign) may be changed to $\overset{x}{x}X$, where the two small signs $\overset{x}{x}$ are so arranged as to balance the large sign X.

Principle of Context of Situation. A principle by which reading and interpretation of signs may be dependent on the context of situation. For example, the abbreviation *m* may stand for 'minute' in one context, and for 'meter' in another.

Principle of Conventionalization. A principle by which the forms and meanings of all signs and symbols are conventionalized.

Principle of Convergence. A principle by which different word signs are eliminated and replaced by syllabic spellings, as in Sumerian or Hittite. Opposite of *Principle of Divergence.*

Principle of Divergence. A principle by which new signs for new words are created, as in Chinese. Opposite of *Principle of Convergence.*

Principle of Economy. A principle by which a writing strives to achieve its maximum efficiency by the smallest possible number of signs. For example, certain syllabaries do not distinguish between voiced, voiceless, and emphatic consonants, while others do not indicate differences between various vowels.

Principle of Inner Development. A principle by which a writing develops from one inner structural stage to another, as from a syllabary to an alphabet. Parallel to *Principle of Outer Development.*

Principle of Outer Development. A principle by which a writing develops from one outer formal stage to another, as from a pictorial to a linear form. Parallel to *Principle of Inner Development.*

Principle of Phonetization. A principle, called in modern usage the *Rebus Principle*, by which word signs which are difficult to draw are written by signs expressing words which are similar in sound and are easy to draw. Thus, in Sumerian, the word *ti*, 'life', is expressed by the picture of an arrow, which also is *ti* in Sumerian.

Principle of Position. A principle by which reading and meaning of signs may be dependent on their position, as in the writing of '32' and '3²'.

Principle of Reduction. A principle by which the value of a sign may be shortened when it is followed by a phonetic non-semantic sign. Thus, the combination *ṭâb-ab*, 'good,' composed of the word sign *ṭâb* plus the phonetic complement/indicator *ab*, was conceived as *ṭâ(b)-ab* by the Akkadians, resulting in taking the first sign to stand for the syllable *ṭa* only. Similarly, the writing of the syllable *bi* by means of two syllabic signs *bi-i* was conceived as *b(i)-i* by the Greeks, resulting in the interpretation of the first sign, originally syllabic, as an alphabetic sign *b*.

Principle of Unidirectional Development. A principle of development from word to syllabic to alphabetic writing.

Prosodic Sign. A sign or mark to denote a prosodic feature, such as quantity, accent, tone, and pause, as in the writing of *dêmos* or *ku₃*.

Rebus Principle, see *Principle of Phonetization.*

Reduction, see *Principle of Reduction.*

Representational, see *Descriptive-Representational Device.*

Semantic Indicator. A sign frequently called 'determinative', expressing a semantic but non-phonetic element attached to the basic sign, as in the Chinese writing of THUMB.WOOD for the word *ts'ung*, 'village,' contrasted with the writing of THUMB alone for the word *ts'ung*, 'thumb.' In some writings determinatives became classifiers, that is auxiliary signs marking words to which they were attached as belonging to a certain class. In Akkadian, for example, all divine names were marked by a divine determinative/classifier.

Semasiography. Forerunners of Writing, including the *Identifying-Mnemonic* and *Descriptive-Representational* devices, to achieve intercommunication by means of visible marks expressing meaning, but not necessarily linguistic elements. Opposite of *Phonography.*

Sign. A conventionally used *Symbol* forming part of a system, such as a word in a system of signs called 'language', or a written mark in a system of signs called 'writing'. In a narrow sense only a written mark.

Signary. A list of signs of a writing.

Syllabary or *Syllabic Writing.* A writing in which a sign normally stands for one or more syllables of the language. Thus, in Sumerian, one sign has the syllabic value *ba*, another *ri* or *dal*, still another *bala*. See also *Logography, Alphabet.*

Syllabic Sign or *Syllabogram.* A sign used in a *Syllabary* or *Syllabic Writing.*

Symbol. Same as *Sign* but not forming part of a system, such as the symbol 'cross' for Christianity, or 'anchor' for hope.

System of Signs. Assemblage of organically related signs conventionally used for the purpose of intercommunication, such as language, writing, gesture language, etc.

Transcription. A form of graphic transfer wherein one sign (or a combination of alphabetic signs and artificial symbols) stands for each phoneme of the language we are recording. Thus, three cuneiform signs, transliterated as *i-din-nam* or *i-di(n)-nam*, may be transcribed as *iddinam*.

Transliteration. A form of graphic transfer wherein one sign (or a combination of alphabetic signs and artificial symbols) stands for each character of the writing we are recording. Thus, three cuneiform signs may be transliterated as *i-din-nam* or *i-di(n)-nam*.

Unidirectional Development, see *Principle of Unidirectional Development.*

Word Sign, see *Logogram.*

Writing. A system of intercommunication by means of conventional visible marks. See also *Forerunners of Writing* or *Semasiography* and *Phonography.*

XII

BIBLIOGRAPHY

PHILIPPE BERGER, *Histoire de l'écriture dans l'antiquité* (2nd ed.; Paris, 1892).

ALOYS BÖMER, 'Die Schrift und ihre Entwicklung' in *Handbuch der Bibliothekswissenschaft*, hrsg. von F. Milkau, i (Leipzig, 1931), pp. 27–149. 2nd ed. edited by Walter Menn (Wiesbaden, 1952).

JOSEPH BOÜÜAERT, *Petite histoire de l'alphabet* (Bruxelles, 1949).

P. E. CLEATOR, *Lost Languages* (London, 1959).

EDWARD CLODD, *The Story of the Alphabet* (3rd ed.; New York, 1938).

MARCEL COHEN, *L'écriture* (Paris, 1953).

MARCEL COHEN, *La grande invention de l'écriture et son évolution.* Three volumes: *Texte, Documentation et index, Planches* (Paris, 1958).

TH. W. DANZEL, *Die Anfänge der Schrift* (2nd ed.; Leipzig, 1929).

HERMANN DEGERING, *Die Schrift, Atlas der Schriftformen des Abendlandes vom Altertum bis zum Ausgang des 18. Jahrhunderts* (Berlin, 1929). 3rd ed. in 1952.

HERMANN DELITZSCH, *Geschichte der abendländischen Schreibschriftformen* (Leipzig, 1928).

DAVID DIRINGER, *L'alfabeto nella storia della civiltà* (Firenze, 1937).

DAVID DIRINGER, *The Alphabet. A Key to the History of Mankind* (London and New York, 1948). 2nd ed. in 1949.

DAVID DIRINGER, *The Story of the Aleph Beth* (London, 1958).

DAVID DIRINGER, *Writing* (London, 1962).

ERNST DOBLHOFER, *Voices in Stone. The Decipherment of Ancient Scripts and Writings* (London and New York, 1961). Translation of Doblhofer's *Zeichen und Wunder* (Wien, Berlin, Stuttgart, 1957).

FRANZ DORNSEIFF, *Das Alphabet in Mystik und Magie* (2nd ed.; Leipzig und Berlin, 1925).

MAX EBERT, *Reallexikon der Vorgeschichte*, xi (1927–28), 315–366: article 'Schrift' by Thurnwald, Sundwall, Roeder, J. Pedersen, F. Hiller von Gaertringen, and J. de C. Serra-Ràfols.

BEN ENGELHART and FRANS DE CLERCQ, *50 eeuwen schrift. Een inleiding tot de geschiedenes van het schrift* (Utrecht, 1956).

CARL FAULMANN, *Illustrirte Geschichte der Schrift* (Wien, Pest, and Leipzig, 1880).

254

JAMES G. FÉVRIER, *Histoire de l'écriture* (Paris, 1948). Nouvelle édition in 1959.

CHARLES FOSSEY, *Notices sur les charactères étrangers anciens et modernes, rédigées par un groupe de savants* (Paris, 1927). Nouvelle édition in 1948.

J. FRIEDRICH, *Entzifferung verschollener Schriften und Sprachen* (Berlin, 1954). Also the American edition: *Extinct Languages* (New York, 1957).

I. J. GELB, *Von der Keilschrift zum Alphabet. Grundlagen einer Sprachwissenschaft* (Stuttgart, 1958). Translation and a revised edition of Gelb's *A Study of Writing*.

WALTER JAMES HOFFMAN, *The Beginnings of Writing* (New York, 1895).

LANCELOT HOGBEN, *From Cave Painting to Comic Strip* (New York, 1949).

V. A. ISTRIN, *Razvitie pis'ma* (Moskva, 1961).

HANS JENSEN, *Geschichte der Schrift* (Hannover, 1925).

HANS JENSEN, *Die Schrift in Vergangenheit und Gegenwart* (Glückstadt und Hamburg, 1935). 2nd ed. in 1958.

FREDERIC G. KENYON, *Ancient Books and Modern Discoveries* (Chicago, 1927).

WILHELM H. LANGE, *Schriftfibel. Geschichte der abendländischen Schrift von den Anfängen bis zur Gegenwart* (3rd ed.; Wiesbaden, 1952).

C. R. LEPSIUS, *Standard Alphabet* (2nd ed.; London and Berlin, 1863).

Č. LOUKOTKA, *Vývoj písma* (Praha, 1946).

WILLIAM A. MASON, *A History of the Art of Writing* (New York, 1920).

ANNELISE MODRZE, *Zum Problem der Schrift. Ein Beitrag zur Theorie der Entzifferung* (Dissertation; Breslau, 1930).

A. C. MOORHOUSE, *Writing and the Alphabet* (London, 1946).

A. C. MOORHOUSE, *The Triumph of the Alphabet. A History of Writing* (New York, 1953).

HUBERT NELIS, *L'écriture et les scribes* (Bruxelles, 1918).

GEORGE F. VON OSTERMANN and A. E. GIEGENGACK, *Manual of Foreign Languages for the Use of Printers and Translators* (3rd ed.; Washington, 1936). 4th ed. in 1952.

WALTER OTTO, *Handbuch der Archäologie*, i (München, 1939), 147–356: articles by F. W. von Bissing, A. Rehm, E. Pernice, and H. Arntz.

HOLGER PEDERSEN, *Linguistic Science in the Nineteenth Century* (Cambridge, 1931), chap. vi, pp. 141–239: 'Inscriptions and Archaeological Discoveries. The Study of the History of Writing.'

ALFRED PETRAU, *Schrift und Schriften im Leben der Völker* (Essen, 1939). 2nd ed. in 1944.

BIBLIOGRAPHY

W. M. FLINDERS PETRIE, *The Formation of the Alphabet* (*British School of Archaeology in Egypt, Studies Series*, iii; London, 1912).

PAUL SATTLER and GÖTZ V. SELLE, *Bibliographie zur Geschichte der Schrift bis in das Jahr 1930* (*Archiv für Bibliographie*, Beiheft 17; Linz a.D., 1935).

ALFRED SCHMITT, *Die Erfindung der Schrift* (*Erlanger Universitäts-Reden*, 22; Erlangen, 1938).

O. SCHRADER, *Reallexikon der indogermanischen Altertumskunde*, ii (Berlin und Leipzig, 1929), pp. 338–353: article 'Schreiben und Lesen'.

KURT SETHE, *Vom Bilde zum Buchstaben. Die Entwicklungsgeschichte der Schrift*. Mit einem Beitrag von Siegfried Schott (*Untersuchungen zur Geschichte und Altertumskunde Ägyptens*, xii, Leipzig, 1939).

R. STÜBE, *Beiträge zur Entwicklungsgeschichte der Schrift* (*Monographien des Buchgewerbes*, vi; Leipzig, 1913).

R. STÜBE, *Der Ursprung des Alphabets und seine Entwicklung* (Berlin, 1921).

ISAAC TAYLOR, *The Alphabet* (2 vols.; London, 1883).

ISAAC TAYLOR, *The History of the Alphabet* (2 vols.; New York, 1899).

JAN TSCHICHOLD, *Geschichte der Schrift in Bildern* (Basel, 1940). 2nd German ed. in 1946 = *An Illustrated History of Writing and Letters* (London, 1946).

B. L. ULLMAN, *Ancient Writing and Its Influence* (New York, 1932).

KARL WEULE, *Vom Kerbstock zum Alphabet* (20th ed.; Stuttgart, 1926?).

H. S. WILLIAMS, *The History of the Art of Writing*. Manuscripts, inscriptions and muniments, etc. (4 vols.; London and New York, 1901–8).

HEINRICH WUTTKE, *Die Enstehung der Schrift. Die verschiedene Schriftsysteme* (Leipzig, 1877).

PRIMITIVE DEVICES

HENRI BREUIL, *Four Hundred Centuries of Cave Art* (Montignac, 1952). Translated from French.

L. S. CRESSMAN, *Petroglyphs of Oregon* (Eugene, 1937).

DANIEL S. DAVIDSON, *Aboriginal Australian and Tasmanian Rock Carvings and Paintings* (*Memoirs of the American Philosophical Society*, v; Philadelphia, 1936).

SELWYN DEWDNEY and KENNETH E. KIDD, *Indian Rock Paintings of the Great Lakes* (Toronto, 1962).

G. B. M. FLAMAND, *Les pierres écrites. Gravures et impressions rupestres du Nord-Africain* (Paris, 1921).

LEO FROBENIUS and DOUGLAS C. FOX, *Prehistoric Rock Pictures in Europe and Africa* (New York, 1937).

BIBLIOGRAPHY

W. G. HELLINGA, 'Pétroglyphes caraïbes: problème sémiologique,'
Lingua, iv (1954), 121–65.

A. T. JACKSON, *Picture-Writing of Texas Indians* (Austin, 1938).

THEODOR KOCH-GRÜNBERG, *Südamerikanische Felszeichnungen* (Berlin,
1907).

HERBERT KÜHN, *Die Felsbilder Europas* (Stuttgart, 1952).

E. LOHSE, *Versuch einer Typologie der Felszeichnungen* (Dissertation;
Leipzig, 1934).

GARRICK MALLERY, *Pictographs of the North American Indians*. A Preliminary Paper (*Fourth Annual Report of the Bureau of Ethnology*,
Smithsonian Institution; Washington, 1886; pp. 1–256).

GARRICK MALLERY, *Picture-Writing of the American Indians* (*Tenth
Annual Report of the Bureau of Ethnology;* Washington, 1893; pp. 1–
822).

ERLAND NORDENSKIÖLD, *The Secret of the Peruvian Quipus* (*Comparative
Ethnographical Studies*, 6 Part 1; Göteborg, 1925).

ERLAND NORDENSKIÖLD, *Picture-Writings and other Documents by Néle
and Ruben Pérez Kantule* (*Comparative Ethnographical Studies*, 7 Part 1;
Göteborg, 1928).

E. B. RENARD, 'Indian Petroglyphs from the Western Plains,'
Seventieth Anniversary Volume Honoring Edgar Lee Hewett (Albu-
querque, New Mexico, 1939), pp. 295–310.

HENRY R. SCHOOLCRAFT, *Historical and Statistical Information Respecting
the History, Condition and Prospects of the Indian Tribes of the United
States*, Part i (Philadelphia, 1851).

JULIAN H. STEWARD, 'Petroglyphs of California and Adjoining
States,' *University of California Publications in American Archaeology
and Ethnology*, xxiv (1929), 47–239.

JULIAN II. STEWARD, 'Petroglyphs of the United States,' *Annual Report
of the Board of Regents of the Smithsonian Institution for the Year 1936*
(Washington, 1937), pp. 405–425.

ANDRÉ VARAGNAC et al., *L'homme avant l'écriture* (Paris, 1959).

AZTEC-MAYA

T. S. BARTHEL, 'Die gegenwärtige Situation in der Erforschung der
Maya-Schrift,' *Journal de la Société des Américanistes*, n.s. xlv (1956),
219–227.

HERMANN BEYER, 'The Analysis of the Maya Hieroglyphs,' *Internationales Archiv für Ethnographie*, xxxi (1932), 1–20.

DANIEL G. BRINTON, *A Primer of Mayan Hieroglyphics* (*Publications of
the University of Pennsylvania Series in Philology, Literature and Archaeology*, iii, 2; Boston, 1895).

TH. W. DANZEL, *Handbuch der präkolumbischen Kulturen in Latein-
amerika* (Hamburg und Berlin, 1927).

257

YURIY V. KNOROZOV, 'Drevnyaya pis'mennost' Centralnoy Ameriki,' *Sovetskaya Etnografiya*, 1952, Part 3, pp. 100–118.

YURIY V. KNOROZOV, 'Pis'mennost' drevnikh Maiya, Opyt rasshifrovki,' *Sovetskaya Etnografiya*, 1955, Part 1, pp. 94–125.

YURIY V. KNOROZOV, 'New Data on the Maya Written Language,' *Journal de la Société des Américanistes*, n.s. xlv (1956), 209–216 (*Proceedings of the Thirty-second International Congress of Americanists* (Copenhagen, 1958), pp. 467–475).

YURIY V. KNOROZOV, 'The Problem of the Study of the Maya Hieroglyphic Writing,' *American Antiquity*, xxiii (1958), 284–291.

RICHARD C. E. LONG, 'Maya and Mexican Writing,' *Maya Research*, ii (1935), 24–32.

RICHARD C. E. LONG, 'Maya Writing and Its Decipherment,' *Maya Research*, iii (1936), 309–315.

SYLVANUS G. MORLEY, *An Introduction to the Study of the Maya Hieroglyphs* (Washington, 1915).

SYLVANUS G. MORLEY, *The Ancient Maya* (Stanford University Press, 1947).

P. SCHELLHAS, 'Fifty Years of Maya Research,' *Maya Research*, iii (1936), 129–139.

EDUARD SELER, *Gesammelte Abhandlungen zur amerikanischen Sprach- und Alterthumskunde* (5 vols.; Berlin, 1902–1923).

J. ERIC S. THOMPSON, *Maya Hieroglyphic Writing. Introduction* (Washington, D.C., 1950). 2nd ed., Norman, Oklahoma, 1960.

J. ERIC S. THOMPSON, *A Catalogue of Maya Hieroglyphs* (Norman, Oklahoma, 1962).

ALFRED M. TOZZER, 'The Value of Ancient Mexican Manuscripts in the Study of the General Development of Writing,' *Annual Report of the Board of Regents of the Smithsonian Institution for the Year 1911* (Washington, 1912), 493–506.

ALFRED M. TOZZER, 'Maya Research,' *Maya Research*, i (1934), 3–19.

BENJAMIN L. WHORF, 'Maya Writing and Its Decipherment,' *Maya Research*, ii (1935), 367–382.

BENJAMIN L. WHORF, 'Decipherment of the Linguistic Portion of the Maya Hieroglyphs,' *Annual Report of the Smithsonian Institution*, 1941, pp. 479–502.

GÜNTER ZIMMERMANN, *Die Hieroglyphen der Maya-Handschriften* (Hamburg, 1956).

MESOPOTAMIAN CUNEIFORM

G. A. BARTON, *The Origin and Development of Babylonian Writing* (2 vols.; Leipzig, 1913).

FRANZ BAYER, *Die Entwicklung der Keilschrift* (*Orientalia*, xxv; Roma, 1927).

BIBLIOGRAPHY

CUMBERLAND CLARK, *The Art of Early Writing. With Special Reference to the Cuneiform System* (London, 1938).

G. CONTENAU, 'Les débuts de l'écriture cunéiforme,' *Revue des études sémitiques*, 1940, pp. 55–67.

ANTON DEIMEL, *Keilschrift-Palaeographie* (Roma, 1929).

E. DHORME, 'L'écriture et la langue assyro-babyloniennes,' *Revue d'assyriologie*, xl (1945–46), 1–16.

A. FALKENSTEIN, *Archaische Texte aus Uruk* (Leipzig, 1936).

CHARLES FOSSEY, *Manuel d'assyriologie* (2 vols.; Paris, 1904–1926).

I. J. GELB, *Memorandum on Transliteration and Transcription of Cuneiform*, submitted to the 21st International Congress of Orientalists, Paris (Chicago, 1948). Mimeographed.

RENÉ LABAT, *Manuel d'épigraphie akkadienne* (Paris, 1948).

L. MESSERSCHMIDT, *Die Entzifferung der Keilschrift* (*Der Alte Orient*, v, 2; Leipzig, 1903).

M. RUTTEN, 'Notes de paléographie cunéiforme,' *Revue des études sémitiques*, 1940, pp. 1–53.

F. THUREAU-DANGIN, *Recherches sur l'origine de l'écriture cunéiforme* (Paris, 1898).

ECKHARD UNGER, *Die Keilschrift* (Leipzig, 1929).

ECKHARD UNGER, *Keilschrift-Symbolik* (Berlin, 1940).

EGYPTIAN HIEROGLYPHIC

W. F. ALBRIGHT, *The Vocalization of the Egyptian Syllabic Orthography* (New Haven, 1934).

W. F. EDGERTON, 'Egyptian Phonetic Writing, from Its Invention to the Close of the Nineteenth Dynasty,' *Journal of the American Oriental Society*, lx (1940), 473–506.

A. ERMAN, *Die Hieroglyphen* (Neudruck; Berlin und Leipzig, 1917).

H. W. FAIRMAN, 'An Introduction to the Study of Ptolemaic Signs and Their Values,' *Bulletin de l'Institut Français d'Archéologie Orientale du Caire*, xliii (1945), 51–138.

A. H. GARDINER, 'The Nature and Development of the Egyptian Hieroglyphic Writing,' *Journal of Egyptian Archaeology*, ii (1915), 61–75.

H. KEES, S. SCHOTT, H. BRUNNER, E. OTTO, and S. MORENZ, *Ägyptische Schrift und Sprache.* (Handbuch der Orientalistik, hrsg. von B. Spuler, Erste Abt., Erster Bd., Erster Abschnitt; Leiden, 1959).

PIERRE LACAU, *Sur le système hiéroglyphique* (Institut Français d'Archéologie Orientale. Bibliothèque d'Étude, T. xxv; Le Caire, 1954).

E. NAVILLE, *L'écriture égyptienne* (Paris, 1926).

A. SCHARFF, *Archäologische Beiträge zur Frage der Entsehung der Hiero-*

glyphenschrift (*Sitzungsberichte der Bayer. Akad. d. Wiss.*, Philos.-hist. Abt., 1942, Heft 3).

SIEGFRIED SCHOTT, *Untersuchungen zur Schriftgeschichte der Pyramidentexte* (Dissertation; Heidelberg, 1926).

SIEGFRIED SCHOTT, *Hieroglyphen. Untersuchungen zum Ursprung der Schrift* (*Akademie der Wissenschaften und der Literatur in Mainz, Abhandlungen der Geistes- und Sozialwissenschaftlichen Klasse*, Jahrgang 1950, Nr. 24).

KURT SETHE, *Das hieroglyphische Schriftsystem* (*Leipziger Ägyptologische Studien*, Heft 3; Glückstadt und Hamburg, 1935).

H. SOTTAS and E. DRIOTON, *Introduction à l'étude des hiéroglyphes* (Paris, 1922).

WALTER TILL, 'Vom Wesen der ägyptischen Schrift,' *Die Sprache*, iii (1956), 207–215.

HITTITE HIEROGLYPHIC

H. TH. BOSSERT, *Santaš und Kupapa* (*Mitteilungen der Altorientalischen Gesellschaft*, vi, 3; Leipzig, 1932).

E. O. FORRER, *Die hethitische Bilderschrift* (*Studies in Ancient Oriental Civilization*, No. 3; Chicago, 1932).

J. FRIEDRICH, *Entzifferungsgeschichte der hethithischen Hieroglyphenschrift* (Sonderheft 3 der Zeitschrift *Die Welt als Geschichte;* Stuttgart, 1939).

IGNACE J. GELB, *Hittite Hieroglyphs* (*Studies in Ancient Oriental Civilization*, Nos. 2, 14, and 21; Chicago, 1931–1942).

IGNACE J. GELB, 'The Contribution of the New Cilician Bilinguals to the Decipherment of Hieroglyphic Hittite,' *Bibliotheca Orientalis*, vii (1950), 129–141.

B. HROZNÝ, *Les inscriptions hittites hiéroglyphiques* (3 vols.; Praha, 1933–1937).

EMMANUEL LAROCHE, *Les hiéroglyphes hittites*. Première partie: L'écriture (Paris, 1960).

P. MERIGGI, *Die längsten Bauinschriften in 'hethitischen' Hieroglyphen nebst Glossar zu sämtlichen Texten* (*Mitteilungen der Vorderasiatisch-ägyptischen Gesellschaft*, xxxix, 1; Leipzig, 1934). The glossary was republished under the title *Hieroglyphisch-hethitisches Glossar* (2nd ed.; Wiesbaden, 1962).

P. MERIGGI, 'Listes des hiéroglyphes hittites,' *Revue hittite et asianique*, iv (1937), pp. 69–114 and 157–200.

CHINESE

PETER BOODBERG, 'Some Proleptical Remarks on the Evolution of Archaic Chinese,' *Harvard Journal of Asiatic Studies*, ii (1937), 329–372.

BIBLIOGRAPHY

PETER BOODBERG, ' "Ideography" or Iconolotry?,' *T'oung Pao*, xxxv (1940), 266–288.

HERRLEE G. CREEL, 'On the Nature of Chinese Ideography,' *T'oung Pao*, xxxii (1936), 85–161.

HERRLEE G. CREEL, 'On the Ideographic Element in Ancient Chinese,' *T'oung Pao*, xxxiv (1938), 265–294.

BERNHARD KARLGREN, *Analytic Dictionary of Chinese and Sino-Japanese* (Paris, 1923).

BERNHARD KARLGREN, *Sound and Symbol in Chinese* (London, 1923).

BERNHARD KARLGREN, *Philology and Ancient China* (Oslo, 1926).

BERNHARD KARLGREN, *Grammatica Serica, Script and Phonetics in Chinese and Sino-Japanese* (*Bulletin of the Museum of Far Eastern Antiquities*, No. 12; Stockholm, 1940).

P. PELLIOT, 'Brèves remarques sur le phonétisme dans l'écriture chinoise,' *T'oung Pao*, xxxii (1936), 162–166.

A. VON ROSTHORN, 'Zur Geschichte der chinesischen Schrift,' *Wiener Zeitschrift für die Kunde des Morgenlandes*, xlviii (1941), 121–142.

BRUNO SCHINDLER, several articles in *Ostasiatische Zeitschrift*, 1914–1918.

TAI T'UNG, *The Six Scripts, Or the Principles of Chinese Writing*. Translated by L. C. Hopkins (Cambridge, 1954).

TCHANG TCHENG-MING, *L'écriture chinoise et le geste humain* (Shanghai and Paris, no date, about 1939?).

PROTO-ELAMITE

F. BORK, *Die Strichinschriften von Susa* (Königsberg, 1924).

WILLIAM C. BRICE, 'The Writing System of the Proto-Elamite Account Tablets of Susa,' *Bulletin of the John Rylands Library, Manchester*, xl (1962), 15–39.

C. FRANK, 'Elam. Schrift' in Max Ebert, *Reallexikon der Vorgeschichte*, iii (1925), 83 f.

WALTHER HINZ, 'Zur Entzifferung der elamischen Strichschrift,' *Iranica Antiqua*, ii (1962), 1–21.

PROTO-INDIC

H. HERAS, 'La escritura proto-Indica y su desciframiento,' *Ampurias*, i (1939), 5–81.

B. HROZNÝ, 'Inschriften und Kultur der Proto-Inder . . . ,' *Archiv Orientální*, xii (1941), 192–259; xiii (1942), 1–102.

G. R. HUNTER, *The Script of Harappa and Mohenjodaro and Its Connection with Other Scripts* (London, 1934).

ERNEST J. H. MACKAY, *Further Excavations at Mohenjo-Daro* (2 vols.; Delhi, 1937–1938).

ERNEST J. H. MACKAY, *Chanhu-Daro Excavations 1935-36* (New Haven, 1943).

JOHN MARSHALL, *Mohenjo-Daro and the Indus Civilization* (3 vols.; London, 1931).

P. MERIGGI, 'Zur Indus-Schrift,' *Zeitschrift der Deutschen Morgenländischen Gesellschaft*, lxxvii (1934), 198–241.

HEINZ MODE, *Indische Frühkulturen und ihre Beziehungen zum Westen* (Basel, 1944).

MADHO SARUP VATS, *Excavations at Harappā* (2 vols.; Calcutta, 1940).

CRETAN

EMMETT L. BENNETT, *The Pylos Tablets. Texts of the Inscriptions Found 1939-1954* (Princeton, 1955).

W. C. BRICE, *Inscriptions in the Minoan Linear Script of Class A* (Oxford, 1961).

JOHN CHADWICK, *The Decipherment of Linear B* (Cambridge, 1958).

JOHN CHADWICK and MICHAEL VENTRIS, 'Greek Records in the Minoan Script,' *Antiquity*, xxvii (1953), 196–206.

FERNAND CHAPOUTHIER, *Les écritures minoennes au palais de Mallia* (École Française d'Athènes. *Études crétoises*, ii; Paris, 1930).

STERLING DOW, 'Minoan Writing,' *American Journal of Archaeology*, lviii (1954), 77–129.

ARTHUR J. EVANS, *Scripta Minoa* (2 vols.; Oxford, 1909–1952).

ARTHUR J. EVANS, *The Palace of Minos* (4 vols. and Index; London, 1921–1936).

ARNE FURUMARK, *Linear A und die altkretische Sprache, Entzifferung und Deutung* (2 parts, multigraphed; Berlin, 1956).

G. P. GOULD and M. POPE, *Preliminary Investigations into the Cretan Linear A Script* (mimeographed; University of Cape Town, 1955).

A. E. KOBER, 'The Minoan Scripts: Fact and Theory,' *American Journal of Archaeology*, lii (1948), 82–103; also *op. cit.*, xlviii (1944), 64–75, xlix (1945), 143–151, and l (1946), 268–276.

MICHEL LEJEUNE, ed., *Études mycéniennes*, Actes du Colloque International sur les Textes Mycéniens (Paris, 1956).

MICHEL LEJEUNE, *Mémoires de philologie mycénienne*, Première série (Paris, 1958), esp. pp. 321–330.

P. MERIGGI, *Primi elementi di Minoico A* (Salamanca, 1956).

LEONARD R. PALMER, *Mycenaeans and Minoans* (London, 1961).

AXEL W. PERSSON, *Schrift und Sprache in Alt-Kreta* (*Uppsala Universitets Årsskrift*, 1930, No. 3).

EMILIO PERUZZI, *Le iscrizioni minoiche* (Firenze, 1960).

G. PUGLIESE CARRATELLI, *Le iscrizioni preelleniche de Haghia Triada in Creta e della Grecia peninsulare* (*Monumenti Antichi*, xi, 4ª; 1945; pp. 421–610).

BIBLIOGRAPHY

G. Pugliese Carratelli, 'La decifrazione dei testi micenei e il problema della lineare A,' *Annuario della Scuola Archeologica di Atene,* xiv–xvi (1952–1954), 7–21.

J. Sundwall, 'Die kretische Linearschrift,' *Jahrbuch des K. Deutschen Archäologischen Instituts,* xxx (1915), 41–64.

J. Sundwall, *Der Ursprung der kretischen Schrift* (*Acta Academiae Aboensis.* Humaniora, i, 2, 1920).

J. Sundwall, 'Kretische Schrift' in Max Ebert, *Reallexikon der Vorgeschichte,* vii (Berlin, 1926), 95–101.

J. Sundwall, 'Methodische Bermerkungen zur Entzifferung minoischer Schriftdenkmäler,' *Eranos,* xlv (1947), 1–12.

Michael Ventris, 'King Nestor's Four-Handled Cups,' *Archaeology,* vii (1954), 15–21.

Michael Ventris and John Chadwick, 'Evidence for Greek Dialects in the Mycenaean Archives,' *Journal of Hellenic Studies,* lxxiii (1953), 84–105.

Michael Ventris and John Chadwick, *Documents in Mycenaean Greek* (Cambridge, 1956).

DERIVED CUNEIFORM SYLLABARIES

George C. Cameron, *Persepolis Treasury Tablets* (*Oriental Institute Publications,* lxv; Chicago, 1948).

Johannes Friedrich, *Kleinasiatische Sprachdenkmäler* (Berlin, 1932).

Friedrich Wilhelm König, *Corpus inscriptionum Elamicarum* (Hannover, 1928).

C. Lehmann-Haupt, *Corpus inscriptionum Chaldicarum* (Berlin und Leipzig, 1928—).

E. A. Speiser, *Introduction to Hurrian* (*The Annual of the American Schools of Oriental Research,* xx, New Haven, Conn., 1941).

WEST SEMITIC SYLLABARIES

W. F. Albright, 'New Light on the Early History of Phoenician Colonization,' *Bulletin of the American Schools of Oriental Research,* No. 83 (1941), 14–22.

W. F. Albright, 'The Phoenician Inscriptions of the Tenth Century B.C. from Byblus,' *Journal of the American Oriental Society,* lxvii (1947), 153–160.

W. F. Albright, 'The Early Alphabetic Inscriptions from Sinai and Their Decipherment,' *Bulletin of the American Schools of Oriental Research,* No. 110 (1948), 6–22.

H. Bauer, *Zur Entzifferung der neuentdeckten Sinaischrift und zur Enstehung des semitischen Alphabets* (Halle, 1918).

H. Bauer, *Das Alphabet von Ras Shamra* (Halle, 1932).

263

H. BAUER, *Der Ursprung des Alphabets* (*Der Alte Orient*, xxxvi, 1/2; Leipzig, 1937).

AUGUSTIN BEA, 'Die Enstehung des Alphabets. Eine kritische Übersicht,' *Miscellanea Giovanni Mercati*, vol. vi = *Studi e Testi*, 126 (Città del Vaticano, 1946), 1–35.

A. VAN DEN BRANDEN, 'L'origine des alphabets protosinaïtiques, arabes préislamiques et phénicien,' *Bibliotheca Orientalis*, xix (1962), 198–206.

FRANK M. CROSS, 'The Evolution of the Proto-Canaanite Alphabet,' *Bulletin of the American Schools of Oriental Research*, No. 134 (1954), 15–24.

FRANK M. CROSS and THOMAS O. LAMBDIN, 'An Ugaritic Abecedary and the Origins of the Proto-Canaanite Alphabet,' *Bulletin of the American Schools of Oriental Research*, No. 160 (1960), 21–26.

E. DHORME, *Langues et écritures sémitiques* (Paris, 1931).

D. DIRINGER, 'The Origins of the Alphabet,' *Antiquity*, xvii (1943), 77–90 and 208 f.

D. DIRINGER, 'The Palestinian Inscriptions and the Origin of the Alphabet,' *Journal of the American Oriental Society*, lxiii (1943), 24–30.

D. DIRINGER, 'Problems of the Present Day on the Origin of the Phoenician Alphabet,' *Journal of World History*, iv/1 (1957), 40–58.

G. R. DRIVER, *Semitic Writing. From Pictograph to Alphabet* (London, 1948). Rev. ed. in 1954.

M. DUNAND, *Byblia grammata. Documents et recherches sur le developpement de l'écriture en Phénicie* (Beyrouth, 1945).

R. DUSSAUD, 'L'origine de l'alphabet et son évolution première d'après les découvertes de Byblos,' *Syria*, xxv (1946–1948), 36–52.

JAMES G. FÉVRIER, 'La genèse de l'alphabet,' *Conférences de l'Institut de Linguistique de l'Université de Paris*, vi (1938), 21–39.

JAMES G. FÉVRIER, 'Les fouilles de Byblos et la date de l'alphabet phénicien,' *Journal asiatique*, ccxxxvi (1948), 1–10.

JOHN W. FLIGHT, 'The Present State of Studies in the History of Writing in the Near East,' *The Haverford Symposium on Archaeology and the Bible* (New Haven, 1938), pp. 111–135.

J. FRIEDRICH, 'Einige Kapitel aus der inneren Geschichte der Schrift,' *Archiv für Schreib- und Buchwesen*, n.F. ii (1935), 8–18.

A. H. GARDINER, 'The Egyptian Origin of the Semitic Alphabet,' *Journal of Egyptian Archaeology*, iii (1916), 1–16.

T. H. GASTER, 'The Chronology of Palestinian Epigraphy,' *Palestine Exploration Fund Quarterly Statement*, 1935, pp. 128–140, and 1937, pp. 43–58.

I. J. GELB, 'New Evidence in Favor of the Syllabic Character of West Semitic Writing,' *Bibliotheca Orientalis*, xv (1958), 2–7.

J. Leibovitch, 'Les inscriptions Protosinaitiques,' *Mémoires présentés à l'Institut d'Égypte*, xxiv (1934).

M. Lidzbarski, *Ephemeris für semitische Epigraphik* (3 vols.; Giessen, 1902–1915).

B. Maisler, 'Zur Urgeschichte des phönizisch-hebräischen Alphabets,' *Journal of the Palestine Oriental Society*, xviii (1938), 278–291.

B. Maisler, 'Phoenician Inscriptions from Byblos and the Development of the Phoenician-Hebrew Alphabetic Writing,' *Leshonenu*, xiv (1946), 166–181 (in Hebrew).

Julian Obermann, 'The Archaic Inscriptions from Lachish,' *Journal of the American Oriental Society*, Supplement to vol. lix, No. 2, 1938.

Vittore Pisani, 'Origini dell'alfabeto,' *Annali della R. Scuola Normale Superiore di Pisa*. Lettere, Storia e Filosofia. Serie II, vol. v (1936), 267–277.

Alfred Schmitt, 'Die Vokallosigkeit der ägyptischen und semitischen Schrift,' *Indogermanische Forschungen*, lxi (1954), 216–227.

Kurt Sethe, 'Der Ursprung des Alphabets,' *Nachrichten von der K. Gesellschaft der Wissenschaften zu Göttingen*. Philos.-hist. Kl., 1916, pp. 87–161.

Kurt Sethe, 'Die neuentdeckte Sinai-Schrift und die Enstehung der semitischen Schrift,' *Nachrichten von der K. Gesellschaft der Wissenschaften zu Göttingen*. Philos.-hist. Kl., 1917, pp. 437–475.

Martin Sprengling, *The Alphabet. Its Rise and Development from the Sinai Inscriptions* (*Oriental Institute Communications*, No. 12; Chicago, 1931).

B. L. Ullman, 'The Origin and Development of the Alphabet,' *American Journal of Archaeology*, xxxi (1927), 311–328.

S. Yeivin, 'The Palestino-Sinaitic Inscriptions,' *Palestine Exploration Quarterly*, 1937, pp. 180–193.

CYPRO-MINOAN AND CYPRIOTE

Hans-Günther Buchholz, 'Zur Herkunft der kyprischen Silbenschrift,' *Minos*, iii/2 (1954), 133–151.

Stanley Casson, 'The Cypriot Script of the Bronze Age,' *Iraq*, vi (1939), 39–44.

John Franklin Daniel, 'Prolegomena to the Cypro-Minoan Script,' *American Journal of Archaeology*, xlv (1941), 249–282.

Olivier Masson, 'Nouvelles inscriptions en caractères chyprominoens,' in C. F. A. Schaeffer, *Enkomi-Alasia*, i (Paris, 1952), pp. 391–409.

Olivier Masson, 'Les écritures chypro-minoennes et les possibilités de déchiffrement,' in *Études mycéniennes*, ed. M. Lejeune (Paris, 1956), 199–206.

Olivier Masson, *Les inscriptions chypriotes syllabiques. Recueil critique et commenté* (Paris, 1961).

Piero Meriggi, 'I primi testi ciprominoici e l'eteociprio,' *Athenaeum*, n.s. xxxiv (1956), 3–38.

E. Sittig, 'Hellenische Urkunden des 2. vorchr. Jahrtausends von Cypern,' *La Nouvelle Clio*, vi (1954), 470–490.

E. Sittig, 'Zur Entzifferung der minoisch-kyprischen Tafel von Enkomi,' *Minos*, iv/1 (1956), 33–42.

PHAISTOS

Ernst Grumach, 'Die Korrekturen des Diskus von Phaistos,' *Kadmos*, i (1962), 16–26.

G. Ipsen, 'Der Diskus von Phaistos,' *Indogermanische Forschungen*, xlvii (1929), 1–41.

Ernst Schertel, 'Der Diskos von Phaistos. Wege zu seiner Entzifferung,' *Würzburger Jahrbücher für die Altertumswissenschaft*, iii (1948), 334–365.

Benjamin Schwarz, 'The Phaistos Disk,' *Journal of Near Eastern Studies*, xviii (1959), 105–112 and 227 f.

BYBLOS

John Pairman Brown, *The Pseudo-Hieroglyphic Texts of Byblos* (mimeographed; American University of Beirut, 1962).

E. Dhorme, 'Déchiffrement des inscriptions pseudo-hiéroglyphiques de Byblos,' *Syria*, xxv (1946–1948), 1–35.

M. Dunand, *Byblia grammata* (Beyrouth, 1945), chap. iv.

G. Janssens, 'Contribution au déchiffrement des inscriptions pseudo-hiéroglyphiques de Byblos,' *La Nouvelle Clio*, vii–ix (1955–57), 361–377.

M. Martin, 'Revision and Reclassification of the Proto-Byblian Signs,' *Orientalia*, n.s. xxxi (1962), 250–271 and 339–363.

Harvey Sobelman, 'The Proto-Byblian Inscriptions—a Fresh Approach,' *Journal of Semitic Studies*, vi (1961), 226–245.

JAPANESE

Basil Hall Chamberlain, *A Practical Introduction to the Study of Japanese Writing* (2nd ed.; London, 1905).

N. E. Isemonger, *The Elements of Japanese Writing* (2nd ed.; London, 1943).

R. Lange, *Einführung in die japanische Schrift* (2nd ed.; Berlin, 1922).

Joseph K. Yamagiwa, *Introduction to Japanese Writing* (Ann Arbor, Michigan, 1943).

BIBLIOGRAPHY

PERSIAN CUNEIFORM

J. FRIEDRICH, 'Einige Kapitel aus der inneren Geschichte der Schrift,' *Archiv für Schreib- und Buchwesen*, n.f. ii (1935), 14 ff.

F. H. WEISSBACH, *Die Keilinschriften der Achämeniden* (Leipzig, 1911).

GREEK

RHYS CARPENTER, 'The Antiquity of the Greek Alphabet,' *American Journal of Archaeology*, xxxvii (1933), 8–29.

RHYS CARPENTER, 'The Greek Alphabet Again,' *American Journal of Archaeology*, xlii (1938), 58–69.

MARGIT FALKNER, 'Zur Frühgeschichte des griechischen Alphabets,' *Frühgeschichte und Sprachwissenschaft*, hrsg. von Wilhelm Brandenstein (Wien, 1948), pp. 110–133.

V. GARDTHAUSEN, *Griechische Palaeographie* (2 vols.; 2nd ed.; Leipzig, 1911–1913.)

J. PENROSE HARLAND, 'The Date of the Hellenic Alphabet,' *University of North Carolina Studies in Philology*, xlii (1945), 413–426.

F. HILLER VON GAERTRINGEN, *Griechische Epigraphik;* W. Schubart, *Papyruskunde;* P. Maas, *Griechische Palaeographie* (*Einleitung in die Altertumswissenschaft*, hrsg. von A. Gercke und E. Norden, vol. i, Heft 9; Leipzig und Berlin, 1924).

L. H. JEFFERY, *The Local Scripts of Archaic Greece* (Oxford, 1961).

W. LARFELD, *Handbuch der griechischen Epigraphik* (2 vols.; Leipzig, 1902–1907).

W. LARFELD, *Griechische Epigraphik* (3rd ed.; Berlin, 1914).

ARTHUR MENTZ, *Geschichte der griechisch-römischen Schrift bis zur Erfindung des Buchdrucks mit beweglichen Lettern* (Leipzig, 1920).

E. S. ROBERTS and E. A. GARDNER, *An Introduction to Greek Epigraphy* (2 vols.; Cambridge, 1887–1905).

WILHELM SCHUBART, *Das Buch bei den Griechen und Römern* (2nd ed.; Berlin und Leipzig, 1921).

EDWARD MAUNDE THOMPSON, *Handbook of Greek and Latin Palaeography* (3rd ed.; London, 1906).

EDWARD MAUNDE THOMPSON, *An Introduction to Greek and Latin Palaeography* (London, 1912).

B. L. ULLMAN, 'How Old Is the Greek Alphabet?' *American Journal of Archaeology*, xxxviii (1934), 359–381.

WEINBERGER and GAERTE, 'Die Schrift' in Pauly-Wissowa, *Real-Encyclopädie der classischen Altertumswissenschaft* (Stuttgart, 1921).

LATIN

RHYS CARPENTER, 'The Alphabet in Italy,' *American Journal of Archaeology*, xlix (1945), 452–464.

BIBLIOGRAPHY

H. DESSAU, *Lateinische Epigraphik;* P. Lehmann, *Lateinische Paläographie* (*Einleitung in die Altertumswissenschaft*, hrsg. von A. Gercke and E. Norden, vol. i, Heft 10; Leipzig und Berlin, 1925).

JAMES C. EGBERT, *Introduction to the Study of Latin Inscriptions* (rev. ed.; New York, 1923).

M. IHM, *Palaeographia Latina*, Series I (2nd ed.; Lipsiae, 1931).

JEAN MALLON, *Paléographie romaine* (Madrid, 1952).

J. MALLON, R. MARICHAL, and C. PERRAT, *L'écriture latine de la capitale romaine à la minuscule* (Paris, 1939).

M. PROU, *Manuel de paléographie latine et française* (4th ed.; Paris, 1924).

J. E. SANDYS and S. G. CAMPBELL, *Latin Epigraphy* (2nd ed.; Cambridge, 1927).

FRANZ STEFFENS, *Lateinische Paläographie* (2nd ed.; Trier, 1909).

MODERN WRITINGS AMONG PRIMITIVES

J. FRIEDRICH, 'Schriftgeschichtliche Betrachtungen,' *Zeitschrift der Deutschen Morgenländischen Gesellschaft*, xci (1937), 319–342.

J. FRIEDRICH, 'Zu einigen Schrifterfindungen der neuesten Zeit,' *op. cit.*, xcii (1938), 183–218.

J. FRIEDRICH, 'Noch eine Parallele zu den alten Schrifterfindungen. Eine Schrifterfindung bei den Alaska-Eskimos,' *op. cit.*, xcv (1941), 374–414.

J. FRIEDRICH, 'Schriftsysteme und Schrifterfindungen im Alten Orient und bei modernen Naturvölkern,' *Archiv Orientální*, xix (1951), 245–259.

J. FRIEDRICH, 'Alaska-Schrift und Bamum-Schrift,' *op. cit.*, civ (1954), 317–329.

ALFRED SCHMITT, *Die Alaska-Schrift und ihre sprachgeschichtliche Bedeutung* (*Münstersche Forschungen*, Heft 4; Marburg, 1951).

NOTES

NOTES to Chapter I, pages 1–23

1. Cf. Adolf Noreen, *Einführung in die wissenschaftliche Betrachtung der Sprache* (Halle, Saale, 1923), pp. 1 ff., and O. Krückmann, 'Sethe's Buch über die Enstehung der Schrift,' *Orientalia*, n.s. x (1941), 255.

2. L. A. Rosa, *Espressione e mimica* (Milano, 1929); Giuseppe Cocchiara, *Il linguaggio del gesto* (Torino, 1932); Macdonald Critchley, *The Language of Gesture* (London, 1939); J. Vendryes, 'Langage oral et langage par gestes,' *Journal de Psychologie*, xliii (1950), 7–33; David Abercrombie, 'Gesture,' *English Language Teaching*, ix (1954–55), 3–12; William P. Stokoe, *Sign Language Structure: An Outline of the Visual Communication Systems of the American Deaf* (Buffalo, 1960). A notation system for analysis of body motion and gesture can be found in the pioneering work by Ray L. Birdwhistell, *Introduction to Kinesics* (Louisville, Kentucky, 1952).

3. Lucien Lévy-Brühl, *How Natives Think* (London, 1926), pp. 158–159.

4. Cf. Dietrich Westermann, 'Zeichensprache des Ewevolkes in Deutsch-Togo,' *Mitteilungen des Seminars für Orientalische Sprachen*, vol. x, Abt. 3, pp. 1–14; George Herzog, 'Drum-Signalling in a West African Tribe,' *Word*, i (1945), 217–238; George M. Cowan, 'Mazateco Whistle Speech,' *Language*, xxiv (1948), 280–286; J. F. Carrington, *A Comparative Study of Some Central African Gong-Languages (Institut Royal Colonial Belge. Section des Sciences Morales et Politiques. Mémoires. Collection in -8°. Tome xviii, fasc. 3; Bruxelles, 1949); idem, Talking Drums of Africa* (London, 1949).

5. Marcel Cohen, 'Sur l'écriture libyco-berbère,' *Comptes rendus du Groupe Linguistique d'Études Chamito-Sémitiques*, v (1948–1951), 40, reports that young Berber lovers often use a sort of communication by tracing signs in the palms of their hands.

6. L. Leland Locke, 'The Ancient Quipu, a Peruvian Knot Record,' *American Anthropologist*, n.s. xiv (1912), 325–332; *idem, The Ancient Quipu or Peruvian Knot Record* (New York, 1923); André Eckardt, 'Das Geheimnis der Knotenschriften,' *Forschungen und Fortschritte*, xxxii (1958), 340–342; Porfirio Miranda Rivera, 'Quipus y jeroglíficos,' *Zeitschrift für Ethnologie*, lxxxiii (1958), 118–132.

7. Garrick Mallery, *Picture-Writing of the American Indians* (Tenth

Annual Report of the Bureau of Ethnology, Smithsonian Institution; Washington, 1893), pp. 228–231.

8. 'Zur Entstehung der Schrift,' *Zeitschrift für ägyptische Sprache*, xlix (1911), 2 f.

9. *West African Studies* (2nd ed., London, 1901), pp. 126 f.

10. C. A. Gollmer, 'On African Symbolic Messages,' *The Journal of the (Royal) Anthropological Institute of Great Britain and Ireland*, xiv (1885), 169–181.

11. As reported to me by Professor John Lotz.

12. Gollmer, *op. cit.*, pp. 173 f.

13. R. Stübe, 'Ein türkischer Liebesbrief aus Zentralasien in "Markenschrift",' *Zeitschrift des Deutschen Vereins für Buchwesen und Schrifttum*, i (1918), 3, quoting A. von Le Coq, *Volkskundliches aus Ost-Turkistan* (Berlin, 1916), p. 5.

14. Karl Weule, *Vom Kerbstock zum Alphabet* (20th ed.; Stuttgart, 1926?), p. 16; Hans Jensen, *Die Schrift* (Glückstadt und Hamburg, 1935), pp. 10 ff.

15. On all these expressions and many more see the article 'Schreiben und Lesen' in O. Schrader, *Reallexikon der Indogermanischen Altertumskunde*, ii (Berlin und Leipzig, 1929).

16. Cf., e.g., Alan H. Gardiner, *The Theory of Speech and Language* (Oxford, 1932); Rudolf Carnap, *Introduction to Semantics* (Cambridge, Mass., 1942), p. 3; Charles Morris, *Signs, Language, and Behavior* (New York, 1946), pp. 36 ff. On systems of communication besides speech language, cf. the programmatic article by George L. Trager, 'Paralanguage: A First Approximation,' *Studies in Linguistics*, xiii (1958), 1–12, with extensive literature.

17. For other terminology cf. Allen W. Read, 'An Account of the Word "Semantic",' *Word*, iv (1948), 78–97.

18. E.g., Leonard Bloomfield, *Language* (New York, 1933), chapters 9 and 17; *idem*, 'Language or Ideas?' *Language*, xii (1936), 89–95; *idem*, *Linguistic Aspects of Science* (*International Encyclopedia of Unified Science*, vol. i, no. 4; Chicago, 1939), pp. 6 ff.; *idem*, 'Secondary and Tertiary Responses to Language,' *Language*, xx (1944), 45–55; Edward Sapir, *Language* (New York, 1939), p. 19; B. L. Whorf in *Annual Report of the Board of Regents of the Smithsonian Institution for the year 1941* (Washington, 1942), p. 483; George S. Lane, 'Changes of Emphasis in Linguistics with Particular Reference to Paul and Bloomfield,' *Studies in Philology*, xlii (1945), 465–483.

19. On the general problem cf. also the illuminating article of Margaret Schlauch, 'Early Behaviorist Psychology and Contemporary Linguistics,' *Word*, ii (1946), 25–36.

20. C. K. Ogden, *The Meaning of Psychology* (New York and London, 1926), pp. 221 f.

21. Eduard Martinak, *Psychologische Untersuchungen zur Bedeutungslehre* (Leipzig, 1901), pp. 3 f. Cf. V. Panfilov, 'A propos des rapports entre la langue et la pensée,' *Recherches internationales à la lumière du marxisme*, No. 7. Linguistique (1958), pp. 74–93. On writing as viewed by psychologists, cf. Friedrich Kainz, *Psychologie der Sprache*, iv (Stuttgart, 1956), chapter 1, 'Das Schreiben' (pp. 1–161), and bibliographical annotations (pp. 493–506).

22. Carnap, *loc. cit.*, believes that spoken language is the most important of all the systems of signs, but recognizes that there are other systems which can be learned and used independently of speech.

23. E.g., Peter A. Boodberg in *Harvard Journal of Asiatic Studies*, ii (1937), p. 332, n. 5; and in *T'oung Pao*, xxxv (1940), p. 269, n. 1.

24. *Idem* in *Harvard Journal of Asiatic Studies*, *loc. cit.*

25. E.g., Bloomfield, *Language*, *loc. cit.*; *idem*, *Linguistic Aspects of Science*, *loc. cit.*

26. Sapir, *loc. cit.*

27. E.g., William F. Edgerton, 'Ideograms in English Writing,' *Language*, xvii (1941), 148 ff.; Herrlee G. Creel, 'On the Nature of Chinese Ideography,' *T'oung Pao*, xxxii (1936), 85–161; *idem*, 'On the Ideographic Element in Ancient Chinese,' *op. cit.*, xxxiv (1938), 265–294.

28. Bloomfield's opinion in *Language*, p. 283, that the 'picture-writing' of the American Indians is not real writing (because it bears no fixed relation to linguistic forms) seems to be in disagreement with his avowed contention that all writing is a secondary derivate of language (e.g., p. 144).

29. Even to a Chinese scholar, who lived some six hundred years ago, 'writing is pictured speech, and speech is vocalised breath.' Cf. Tai T'ung, *The Six Scripts, Or the Principles of Chinese Writing*. A translation by L. C. Hopkins (Cambridge, 1954), p. 31.

30. Strictly speaking, the use of *X* for 'cross' in the above example does not form part of a conventional system, but must be understood as a 'sportive' device on a line with the use of + for 'plus' in 'voici le + important' or with even more complicated cases of the type Ga expressing 'j'ai grand appetit' by way of 'G grand a petit'.

31. A syllabic sign normally expresses a vowel, either by itself or flanked by a consonant in front or in back of it. This definition can sometimes be extended to include a vowel or a diphthong, either by itself or flanked by more than one consonant in front or in back of it.

32. Taken from Dwight L. Bolinger, 'Visual Morphemes,' *Language*, xxii (1946), 333–340.

33. Still another example belonging to this class is found in the writing of '£3' and '3 lb.'

34. 'The Cultural Basis of Emotions and Gestures,' *Journal of Personality*, xvi (1947), 49–68, esp. p. 59.

35. Kurt Sethe, *Das hieroglyphische Schriftsystem* (Glückstadt und Hamburg, 1935), pp. 10 ff.; *idem, Vom Bilde zum Buchstaben* (Leipzig, 1939), pp. 18 f.

36. *Ibid.*

37. Garrick Mallery, *Picture-Writing of the American Indians* (Tenth Annual Report of the Bureau of Ethnology, Smithsonian Institution; Washington, 1893), p. 624. In the Egyptian hieroglyphic writing, individual signs are often distinguished by different colouring; coloured are vowel marks in early Koran manuscripts and punctuation marks (such as word and sentence division marks) in the Ethiopic writings.

38. More compounds of this type are cited in Kurt Sethe, *Das hieroglyphische Schriftsystem* (Glückstadt und Hamburg, 1935), p. 13.

39. C. K. Ogden and I. A. Richards, *The Meaning of Meaning* (2nd ed.; New York, 1927), Supplement I, pp. 306 ff.

40. I have noted further usage of PG for the Post-Gazette (in Pittsburgh), primary grade (in the Laboratory School of the University of Chicago), poison gas (on a radio broadcast), Pleasant Grove (a place in Texas), paying guest (in a novel), prison graduate (Life Magazine), Peoples Gas (a company), Procter and Gamble (a company), and Predynastic Graves (in Sumer).

41. The scientific investigation of the relationship of writing to speech has been pursued in recent years mainly by scholars with a background in general linguistics. A general treatment of the subject can be found in the respective chapters of the introductory manuals to linguistics by Leonard Bloomfield, *Language* (New York, 1933), chapter 17; H. A. Gleason, Jr., *An Introduction to Descriptive Linguistics* (New York, 1955), chapters 21 and 22; W. Nelson Francis, *The Structure of American English* (New York, 1958), chapter 8; Archibald A. Hill, *Introduction to Linguistic Structures* (New York, 1958), pp. 442 f.; Charles E. Hockett, *A Course in Modern Linguistics* (New York, 1958), chapter 62; H. M. Hoenigswald, *Language Change and Linguistic Reconstruction* (Chicago, 1960), pp. 4–12. A more detailed treatment is offered in the articles by Josef Vachek, 'Zum Problem der geschriebenen Sprache,' *Travaux du Circle Linguistique de Prague*, viii (1939), 99–104; *idem*, 'Some Remarks on Writing and Phonetic Transcription,' *Acta linguistica*, v (1945–1949), 86–93; *idem*, 'Written Language and Printed Language' in *Mélanges*, J. M. Kořínek (Bratislava, 1948?, not available to me); H. J. Uldall, 'Speech and Writing,' *Acta linguistica*, iv (1944), 11–16; Ernst Pulgram, 'Phoneme and Grapheme: A Parallel,' *Word*, vii (1951), 15–20; and Angus McIntosh, 'The Analysis of Written Middle English,' *Transactions of*

the Philological Society, 1956, pp. 26–55; *idem*, ' "Graphology" and Meaning,' *Archivum linguisticum*, xiii (1961), 107–120. While Uldall and Pulgram describe the mutual relationship between and the dependence of writing on speech, Vachek and McIntosh emphasize the largely independent character of writing. The common characteristic of all these investigations is that they are built on modern writings, and little, if any, account is taken of the pre-alphabetic systems. A thorough investigation of the mutual relationships between writing and speech in all their historical phases is badly needed.

42. I am using the term 'primitive' deliberately, though fully aware of the aversion in anthropological circles against this term. Some societies which I call 'primitive' may not be primitive in respect to elaborated rituals or ways of basket-making, but they are primitive when considered from the point of view of the total of accomplishment. The term 'preliterate', used by some anthropologists in the place of 'primitive', shows the same narrowness of approach that expressed itself in the opposition against 'primitive'.

43. G. H. Luquet, *Les dessins d'un enfant* (Paris, 1913).

44. Kurt Goldstein, 'On Naming and Pseudonaming, from Experiences in Psychopathology,' *Word*, ii (1946), 1–7; *idem*, 'L'analyse de l'aphasie et l'étude de l'essence du langage,' in *Psychologie du langage* par H. Delacroix, etc. (Paris, 1933), pp. 430–496; Adhemar Gelb, 'Remarques générales sur l'utilisation des données pathologiques pour la psychologie et la philosophie du langage,' *op. cit.*, pp. 403–420; Roman Jakobson, *Kindersprache, Aphasie und allgemeine Lautgesetze* (*Uppsala Universitets Årsskrift*, 1942, No. 9, pp. 1–83); Kurt Goldstein, *Language and Language Disturbances. Aphasic Symptom Complexes and Their Significance for Medicine and Theory of Language* (New York, 1948); Roman Jakobson and Morris Halle, *Fundamentals of Language* ('s-Gravenhage, 1956), Part 2: 'Two Aspects of Language and Two Types of Aphasic Disturbances'; A. R. Luria, 'Differences between Disturbances of Speech and Writing in Russian and in French,' *International Journal of Slavic Linguistics and Poetics*, iii (1960), 13–22.

45. David Diringer, *The Alphabet* (London, 1949), pp. 35 f.

46. Friedrich Ballhorn, *Grammatography. A Manual of Reference to the Alphabets of Ancient and Modern Languages*. Translated from German (London, 1861). The original German book does not use this term.

1. Cf. Henri Breuil, *Four Hundred Centuries of Cave Art*. Translated from French (Montignac, 1952); Herbert Kühn, *Die Felsbilder Europas* (Stuttgart, 1952); André Varagnac *et al.*, *L'homme avant l'écriture* (Paris, 1959).

2. Cf. esp. Garrick Mallery, *Pictographs of the North American Indians*. A Preliminary Paper (Fourth Annual Report of the Bureau of Ethnology, Smithsonian Institution; Washington, 1886, pp. 1–256), and *idem*, *Picture-Writing of the American Indians* (Tenth Annual Report; Washington, 1893, pp. 1–822). Among the latest publications with extensive bibliographies, cf. Julian H. Steward, 'Petroglyphs of California and Adjoining States,' *University of California Publications in American Archaeology and Ethnology*, xxiv (1929), 47–239; L. S. Cressman, *Petroglyphs of Oregon* (Eugene, 1937); A. T. Jackson, *Picture-Writing of Texas Indians* (Austin, 1938); Theodor Koch-Grünberg, *Südamerikanische Felszeichnungen* (Berlin, 1907).

3. 'Petroglyphs of the United States,' *Annual Report of the Board of Regents of the Smithsonian Institution for the Year 1936* (Washington, 1937), pp. 405–425.

4. In Max Ebert, *Reallexikon der Vorgeschichte*, vii (1926), 156 ff.

5. Mallery, *Picture-Writing*, pp. 353 f.

6. Henry R. Schoolcraft, *Historical and Statistical Information, Respecting the History, Condition, and Prospects of the Indian Tribes of the United States*, Part I (Philadelphia, 1851), pl. 57 B, opp. p. 406.

7. Mallery, *Picture-Writing*, pp. 363 f. = *idem*, *Pictographs*, pp. 160 f.

8. Mallery, *Picture-Writing*, pp. 362 f.

9. James Bonwick, *The Last of the Tasmanians* (London, 1870), pp. 83 ff.

10. Mallery, *Picture-Writing*, p. 332 = *idem*, *Pictographs*, pp. 147 f. = Walter James Hoffman, 'The Graphic Arts of the Eskimos,' *Annual Report of the Board of Regents of the Smithsonian Institution for the Year 1895* (Washington, 1897), 904 f.

11. Mallery, *Picture-Writing*, pp. 352 f. = *idem*, *Pictographs*, pp. 154 f. = Hoffman, *op. cit.*, p. 907.

12. In *Reallexikon der Assyriologie*, ii (1938), 91.

13. Karl Weule, *Vom Kerbstock zum Alphabet* (20th ed.; Stuttgart, 1926?), p. 13; Alfred Schmitt, *Die Erfindung der Schrift* (Erlangen, 1938), p. 4.

14. Mallery, *Pictographs*, pp. 174–176, and *idem*, *Picture-Writing*, pp. 419–425.

15. Mallery, *Pictographs*, pp. 176–181.

16. *Picture-Writing*, pp. 447 ff.

17. *Op. cit.*, pp. 380 ff.

18. Cf. the extensive treatment in Mallery, *Pictographs*, pp. 89–146, and *idem*, *Picture-Writing*, pp. 266–328. For additional literature and examples, cf. James H. Howard, 'Dakota Winter Counts as a Source of Plains History,' *Smithsonian Institution, Bureau of American Ethnology*, Bulletin 173 (1960), pp. 273–416.

19. As pointed out by Leslau in *Word*, xi (1955), 282, the connection between 'winter' and 'year' is indicated also by the existence of Hebrew *ḥoreph*, 'winter,' and Ethiopic *ḥarif*, 'the current year'; for South Arabic, ḤRF meaning both 'winter' (or 'autumn') and 'year,' cf. C. Conti Rossini, *Chrestomathia Arabica meridionalis epigraphica* (Roma, 1931), p. 158.

20. Collected and discussed by Mallery, *Pictographs*, pp. 82–84, and *idem*, *Picture-Writing*, pp. 231–250.

21. Mallery, *Pictographs*, *loc. cit.*

22. Mallery, *Picture-Writing*, pp. 233–236.

23. William Tomkins, *Universal Indian Sign Language of the Plains Indians of North America* (San Diego, California, 1927), pp. 79–85.

24. Cf. p. 266, n. 27.

25. 'La reconstruction typologique des langues archaïques de l'humanité,' *Verhandelingen der K. Nederlandsche Akademie van Wetenschappen. Letterkunde*, N.R. xliv (Amsterdam, 1940), pp. 120 f. A similar misrepresentation of facts can be detected in the illustration purporting to reproduce a prehistoric painting, published in Oscar Ogg, *The 26 Letters* (New York, 1948), pp. 24 f. The painting reconstructed on the basis of original finds made in Spain and France shows scenes depicting in a consecutive order a ceremonial hunt dance, leaving for the hunt, sighting the quarry, surrounding the quarry, the kill, and the return home. Alone the parallels quoted in Ogg's book (as on p. 23) belie the existence of such nicely ordered paintings in the prehistoric times. The truth is that prehistoric man painted complex scenes without either feeling the necessity or being able to represent them in any consecutive order of the actual occurrences.

26. From Carl Meinhof, 'Zur Entstehung der Schrift,' *Zeitschrift für ägyptische Sprache*, xlix (1911), pp. 1–14, pl. I h.

27. R. E. Dennett, *At the Back of the Black Man's Mind* (London, 1906), pp. 71 ff.

28. *Pictographs*, p. 17.

29. Erland Nordenskiöld, *Picture-Writings and Other Documents by Néle and Ruben Pérez Kantule* (Göteborg, 1928); David Diringer, *L'alfabeto nella storia della civiltà* (Firenze, 1937), p. 605.

30. Diringer, *op. cit.*, pp. 600 ff.; C. F. Lehmann-Haupt in *Zeitschrift der Deutschen Morgenländischen Gesellschaft*, lxxiii (1919), 58 ff.; Johannes Friedrich, *op. cit.*, xci (1937), 333 f. A vast literature is growing on these South American systems. Cf., among others, Dick Edgar Ibarra Grasso, *La escritura indígena Andina* (La Paz, 1953); Porfirio Miranda Rivera, 'Quipus y jeroglíficos,' *Zeitschrift für Ethnologie*, lxxxiii (1958), 118–132. These scripts, used to reproduce modern songs, hymns, and catechisms, are developing under Western influence into logographic systems with strong trends in the direction of phonetization.

31. Diringer, *op. cit.*, p. 600.

32. Diringer, *op. cit.*, pp. 56 ff.; Hans Jensen, *Die Schrift* (Glückstadt und Hamburg, 1935), p. 112.

33. Marcel Griaule and Germaine Dieterlen, *Signes graphiques soudanais.* (*L'Homme. Cahiers d'ethnologie, de géographie et de linguistique*, iii, Paris, 1951); D. Zahan, 'Pictographic Writing in the Western Sudan,' *Man*, l (1950), 136–138.

34. On real phraseograms, as used in stenographic systems, see above, p. 14.

35. Eduard Seler, *Gesammelte Abhandlungen zur amerikanischen Sprach- und Alterthumskunde*, ii (Berlin, 1904), 35.

36. Theodor-Wilhelm Danzel, *Handbuch der präkolumbischen Kulturen in Lateinamerika* (Hamburg und Berlin, 1927), p. 51.

37. Jensen, *op. cit.*, p. 122.

38. Seler, *op. cit.*, i (Berlin, 1902), 383.

39. As far as I can judge the situation, this is true of the more serious attempts made in recent years by the American linguist Benjamin L. Whorf and the Russian ethnologist Yuriy V. Knorozov. Whorf's work, 'Maya Writing and Its Decipherment,' *Maya Research*, ii (1935), 367–382, and 'Decipherment of the Linguistic Portion of the Maya Hieroglyphs,' *Annual Report of the Smithsonian Institution*, 1941, pp. 479–502, was criticized by J. Eric S. Thompson, *Maya Hieroglyphic Writing* (Washington, D.C., 1950), pp. 311 ff., but favorably received by Archibald A. Hill in *International Journal of American Linguistics*, xviii (1952), 184 ff. Knorozov's work, 'Drevnyaya pis'mennost' Centralnoy Ameriki,' *Sovetskaya Etnografiya*, 1952, Part 3, pp. 100–118; 'Pis'mennost' drevnikh Maiya, Opyt rasshifrovki,' *op. cit.*, 1955, Part 1, pp. 94–125; 'The Problem of the Study of the Maya Hieroglyphic Writing,' *American Antiquity*, xxiii (1958), 284–291; and 'New Data on the Maya Written Language,' *Journal de la Société des Américanistes*, n.s. xlv (1956), 209–216 (*Proceedings of the Thirty-second International Congress of Americanists* [Copenhagen, 1958], pp. 467–475), was favorably received by Tor Ulving in 'Russian Decipherment of the Maya Glyphs,' *International Journal of American*

Linguistics, xxii (1956), 184 ff., and 'A New Decipherment of the Maya Glyphs,' *Ethnos*, xx (1955), 152–158, but criticized by T. S. Barthel in 'Die gegenwärtige Situation in der Erforschung der Maya-Schrift,' *Journal de la Société des Américanistes*, n.s. xlv (1956), 219–227, and by J. Eric S. Thompson in *Yan*, ii (1953), 174–178, and 'Systems of Hieroglyphic Writing in Middle American and Methods of Deciphering Them,' *American Antiquity*, xxiv (1959), 349–364. The preliminary reports by Evreynov, Kosarev, and Ustinov on the 'Siberian' decipherment of the Maya writing with the help of computer machines are not available to me. For a criticism of their work see Knorozov, 'Mashinnaya deshifrovka pis'ma Maiya,' *Voprosy yazykoznaniya*, xi/1 (1962), 91–99.

40. Seler, *op. cit.*, i, pl. opp. p. 289.

41. J. Leslie Mitchell, 'The End of the Maya Old Empire,' *Antiquity*, iv (1930), 285–302.

42. Paul Schellhas, 'Probleme der Mayaforschung,' *Forschungen und Fortschritte*, xvi (1940), 122.

43. Cf., e.g., the writing of '3 days' with three signs for 'day' in our Fig. 9 and of '5 martens' with five signs for 'marten' on an Alaskan drawing published in Mallery, *Picture-Writing*, pp. 581 f. In the same light should be considered the writing of '51 men' in our Fig. 9, and of '$53' in Fig. 10.

44. Richard C. E. Long, 'Maya and Mexican Writing,' *Maya Research*, ii (1935), 24–32, esp. p. 31.

45. P. Schellhas, 'Fifty Years of Maya Research,' *op. cit.*, iii (1936), 129–139, esp. p. 138.

NOTES to Chapter III, pages 60–119

1. A note on these inscriptions will be published soon by the author. Cf., provisionally, R. D. Barnett and N. Gökce, 'The Find of Urartian Bronzes at Altintepe, Near Erzincan,' *Anatolian Studies*, iii (1953), 121–129.

2. The Easter Island 'inscriptions' were taken seriously as writing by H. Jensen, *Die Schrift* (2nd ed.; Berlin, 1958), pp. 334–338; James G. Février, *Histoire de l'écriture* (nouv. ed.; Paris, 1959), pp. 147–149; and D. Diringer, *The Alphabet* (London, 1948), pp. 136–40. M. Cohen, in his *La grande invention de l'écriture et son évolution* (Paris, 1958), pp. 31–33, first placed the Easter Island 'inscriptions' under forerunners of writing; then, impressed by recent works of such scholars as Thomas Barthel, *Grundlagen zur Entzifferung der Osterinselschrift* (Hamburg, 1958), and N. A. Butinov and Y. V. Knorozov, 'Preliminary Report on the Study of the Written Language of Easter Island,' *The Journal of the Polynesian Society*, lxvi (1957), 5–17, changed his mind, and in his *Documentation*, pp. 49 ff., assigned them to the 'picto-ideographic stage,' together with the Aztec and Maya writings. The plain fact is that if we were to assign the Easter Island 'inscriptions' to a stage of writing, any stage of writing however primitive, we would have to reckon with the existence of a completely unique type of writing from the point of view of the form and composition of its signary. The object of writing being communication, the forms of signs in accepted writings are construed normally in such a way as to permit easy and quick recognition of the different signs. By contrast, the great majority of the Easter Island signs look so alike and are differentiated by such minute details as to cause the greatest difficulties in the recognition of the different signs. Note further that scholars who have worked in the Easter Island field have not succeeded in providing us with a clear-cut list of different signs occurring in the texts. Barthel, for example, talks about '120 Grundbestandteile' and 'etwa 1500–2000 verschiedene Kompositionen' (*op. cit.*, p. 314), and then proceeds to group them in '790 Kennziffern' in his Formentafeln 1–8. Cf. also J. Imbelloni, 'Las "tabletes parlantes" de Pascua, monumentos de un sistema gráfico indo-oceánico,' *Runa*, iv (1951), 89–177; Alfred Métraux, *Easter Island*, translated from French (Oxford, 1957), esp. pp. 183–207.

3. Tablets published and discussed by A. Falkenstein, *Archaische Texte aus Uruk* (Berlin, 1936).

4. P. Delougaz and S. Lloyd, *Pre-Sargonid Temples in the Diyala Region* (Chicago, 1942), p. 135.

5. F. Wachtsmuth in *Archiv für Orientforschung*, xiii (1939-1941), 203, and S. N. Kramer in *American Journal of Archaeology*, lii (1948), 164.

6. *Op. cit.*, pp. 32 f.

7. *Op. cit.*, pl. 1, nos. 1-3 and 7-8.

8. *Op. cit.*, pl. 31, no. 339. The text is reproduced here in the form familiar to us in the later periods, after the orientation of the tablet had been changed by turning it ninety degrees counterclockwise.

9. E. A. Speiser, in *Studies in the History of Science*, University of Pennsylvania Bicentennial Conference (Philadelphia, 1941), pp. 57 f.; also in the *Journal of the American Oriental Society*, Supplement to vol. lix, no. 4 (1939), pp. 20 ff. and 26.

10. As justly observed by Falkenstein, *op. cit.*, p. 32, and Johannes Friedrich in *Zeitschrift der Deutschen Morgenländischen Gesellschaft*, xci (1937), 325 f.

11. The American Indians express pictorially ideas having no or limited connection with linguistic elements; the Sumerians represent words, that is, signs of language. In the Indian device, the pictures are often drawn without any clear order; in the Sumerian system, written signs are ordered in the sequence of the corresponding speech forms. In a development parallel to figurative art, Indians represent counted objects by means of as many pictures as there are objects to be counted, while the Sumerians use only two signs, one for the number and the other for the things counted.

12. C. K. Ogden and I. A. Richards, *The Meaning of Meaning* (2nd ed.; New York, 1927), Supplement I, pp. 306 ff.

13. Full phonetic transfer, often called the rebus principle, can be recognized in heraldic symbols, as in the representation of the coat of arms of Oxford, showing an ox crossing a ford, or of the Griffin family, showing a mythical griffon. Cf. A. C. Moorhouse, *The Triumph of the Alphabet* (New York, 1953), p. 18.

14. Falkenstein, *op. cit.*, pp. 33 and 38.

15. *Op. cit.*, pp. 34 and 40.

16. *Op. cit.*, p. 112, no. 408.

17. *Op. cit.*, p. 43, quoting nos. 340, 539, 594 f., etc.

18. In a recent article published in the *Journal of Near Eastern Studies*, xx (1961), 194 ff., I brought forth evidence to show that the cuneiform sign WA has, besides the values *wa, wi, wu*, also those of *aw, iw, uw*.

19. Adolf Erman, *Ägyptische Grammatik* (2nd ed.; Berlin, 1902), §§ 11 ff., later revised in the third and fourth editions. Erman's old terminology is still followed by some Egyptologists.

20. Kurt Sethe, 'Zur Reform der ägyptischen Schriftlehre,' *Zeitschrift für ägyptische Sprache*, xlv (1908–9), 36–43.

21. *Op. cit.*, pp. 37 f.; also *mēne, mīne, mno*, not clearly indicated by Sethe.

22. For practical reasons it may be advisable to continue with consonantal transliterations in the field of Egyptology, but such transliterations, if my theory is accepted, would lead to a misunderstanding in a general work on writing.

23. W. F. Edgerton in *Journal of Near Eastern Studies*, xi (1952), 288, expressed doubt about the correctness of my statement in respect to the existence of dozens of syllabic writings which developed ultimately from a logographic stage. My number is based on the evaluation of the following systems: Sumerian and the syllabic systems based on cuneiform, such as Assyro-Babylonian, Elamite, Hurrian, Urartian, Hittite, etc.; cuneiform Persian (partially); hieroglyphic Hittite; Cretan Linear B, Cypriote, and probably other systems derived from Cretan, such as Linear A, Phaistos, and Cypro-Minoan; Chinese and the derived systems, such as Old Korean, Japanese, and several little known systems used mainly in southwestern China; Indic Kharoṣṭhī, Brāhmī, and the many South Asiatic writings based on the latter; Ethiopic and the derived systems; Iberian A and B (partially); Cherokee and several systems of the Cree and Fox Indians, as well as the Alaska systems; African Vai and Bamum, and several systems developed from the latter, such as Mende, Basa, Kapelle, Toma, and Gerze.

24. The sign ꞌ stands for any glottal stop before an initial vowel; *u* in 'lngug' and 'wthut' stands for consonantal *w*.

25. Alan H. Gardiner, *Egyptian Grammar* (Oxford, 1927), § 7.

26. Cf. Curtius H. Sethe, *De aleph prosthetico in lingua Aegyptiaca verbi formis praeposito* (Dissertation; Berolini, 1892), and *idem*, 'Die Vokalisation des Ägyptischen,' *Zeitschrift der Deutschen Morgenländischen Gesellschaft*, lxxvii (1923), 144–207, esp. pp. 201 ff.

27. A powerful step forward in the decipherment of the Hittite hieroglyphic writing was achieved by the recent discovery of bilingual Hittite and Phoenician inscriptions at Karatepe in Cilicia by Bossert and his collaborators. Cf. Gelb, 'The Contribution of the New Cilician Bilinguals to the Decipherment of Hieroglyphic Hittite,' *Bibliotheca Orientalis*, vii (1950), 129–141.

28. For more examples of this type cf. O. Franke, 'Grundsätzliches zur Wiedergabe fremder Länder- und Ortsnamen im Chinesischen,' *Sitzungsberichte der Preussischen Akademie der Wissenschaften*, Philos.-hist. Kl., 1934, pp. 244–280, and Otto Maenchen-Helfen, 'History in Linguistics,' *Journal of the American Oriental Society*, lxviii (1948), 120–124. According to a story reported by Abel Rémusat, 'Remarques

sur quelques écritures syllabiques tirées des caractères chinois, et sur le passage de l'écriture figurative à l'écriture alphabétique,' *Mémoires de l'Institut Royal de France, Académie des Inscriptions et Belles-Lettres,* viii (1827), 43, a Chinese (brought to France) wrote the name of his country phonetically with a sign meaning *Thang*, 'sweet', and justified the writing by saying that China was the sweetest country in the world. Yuen Ren Chao reports in the *Journal of the American Oriental Society,* lxxxi (1961), 175, that some Chinese writers called Chicago *Shyjiagun*, 'Valley of the poets'. In the decades after 1900 several reforms to simplify the Chinese writing or to replace it by a phonetic alphabet based on Latin were proposed, none of them successful. In 1956 the Chinese commission to reform the Chinese writing published a project to replace the old Chinese writing by Latin alphabetic characters, which apparently has a good chance of succeeding. The reform of writing goes hand in hand in China with the 'reform of language', specifically with the replacement of the various Chinese dialects by one dialect, namely the so-called Peiping dialect. Cf. Wou Yu-Tchang, 'La reforme de l'écriture chinoise', *Recherches internationales à la lumière du marxisme,* no. 7. Linguistique (1958), pp. 127–135, and Lo Tchang-Pei and Liu Chou-Shiang, 'Vers la unification de la langue chinoise,' *op. cit.,* pp. 94–126.

29. A. Forke, 'Neuere Versuche mit chinesischer Buchstabenschrift,' *Mitteilungen des Seminars für Orientalische Sprachen,* vol. ix, Abt. 1 (1906), pp. 401–408.

30. Very little space can be devoted here to the discussion of the scripts developed by peoples of non-Chinese origin, such as the scripts of the Lo-lo, Mo-so (or Na-khi or Na-hsi), and Yao peoples of the Tibeto-Burmese family of languages, spoken in southwest China and beyond, in Burma and Indo-China, and the scripts of the Choitan, Niu-chih (or Jou Chen), and Tangut (or Si-hia or Hsi-hsia) peoples of the Turkic or Mongol family of languages, spoken in central and northern China. Although some of the systems show forms reminiscent of Chinese, others, such as Lo-lo and Mo-so, have developed independent forms based on fully pictographic characters. Another characteristic of these systems is a very strong development of syllabography. The writings are very little known and they are in dire need of a comprehensive study, both from the formal as well as structural points of view. Cf. Hans Jensen, *Die Schrift* (Glückstadt und Hamburg, 1935), pp. 144–152; David Diringer, *The Alphabet* (London and New York, 1949), pp. 141–148; and James G. Février, *Histoire de l'écriture* (Paris, 1948), pp. 82–85. These scripts, some dating from medieval times, have nothing to do with the scripts of the Pollard system developed by the missionaries in modern times for use of the non-Chinese populations of China, noted on p. 301, n. 18.

31. On the character of Proto-Elamite writing cf. provisionally the article by C. Frank in Max Ebert, *Reallexikon der Vorgeschichte*, iii (1925), 83 f.

32. The Proto-Indic writing is discussed by G. R. Hunter, *The Script of Harappa and Mohenjodaro and Its Connection with Other Scripts* (London, 1934). The inscriptions are usually very short, the average running to about six signs. The direction of the writing is generally boustrophedon, with the first line beginning on the right.

33. Arthur J. Evans, *The Palace of Minos* (4 vols. and index; London, 1921–1936), and *idem, Scripta Minoa*, i (Oxford, 1909).

34. Michael Ventris and John Chadwick, 'Evidence for Greek Dialects in the Mycenaean Archives,' *Journal of Hellenic Studies*, lxxiii (1953), 84–105; Ventris, 'King Nestor's Four-Handled Cups,' *Archaeology*, vii (1954), 15–21; Chadwick and Ventris, 'Greek Records in the Minoan Script,' *Antiquity*, xxvii (1953), 196–206; Ventris and Chadwick, *Documents in Mycenaean Greek* (Cambridge, 1956); Chadwick, *The Decipherment of Linear B* (Cambridge, 1958); Michel Lejeune, *Mémoires de philologie mycénienne*, Première série (Paris, 1958), esp. pp. 321–330.

35. G. Pugliese Carratelli, *Le iscrizioni preelleniche di Haghia Triada in Creta e della Grecia peninsulare* in *Monumenti Antichi*, xi, 4ᵃ (1945), pp. 422–610; *idem*, 'La decifrazione dei testi micenei e il problema della lineare A,' *Annuario della Scuola Archeologica di Atene*, xiv–xvi (1952–1954), 7–21; G. P. Gould and M. Pope, *Preliminary Investigations into the Cretan Linear A Script* (mimeographed, University of Cape Town, 1955); Arne Furumark, *Linear A und die altkretische Sprache. Entzifferung und Deutung* (2 parts, multigraphed; Berlin, 1956); P. Meriggi, *Primi elementi di Minoico A* (Salamanca, 1956); W. C. Brice, *Inscriptions in the Minoan Linear Script of Class A* (Oxford, 1961).

36. What that means in the case of the four writings discussed above is that in Sumerian and Chinese the signs of both the monumental and cursive forms are largely linear, while in Egyptian and Hittite the signs of the monumental form are largely pictorial, but in the cursive form they are largely linear.

37. Tai T'ung, *The Six Scripts, Or the Principles of Chinese Writing*, a translation by L. C. Hopkins (Cambridge, 1954), and Tchang Tcheng-Ming, *L'écriture chinoise et le geste humain* (Changhai and Paris, n.d.), pp. 5 ff. For a discussion of the classification of word signs as proposed in this book, cf. Tai Chün-Jên, 'Mr. Gelb's Six Principles of Writing,' *Academic Review Quarterly*, iv/1 (1955), 37–42, in Chinese.

38. Alan H. Gardiner, *Egyptian Grammar* (Oxford, 1927), § 266.

39. E. T. Peet, *The Rhind Mathematical Papyrus . . .* (Liverpool, 1923), pp. 25 f. Cf. also O. Neugebauer in *Zeitschrift für ägyptische Sprache*, lxv (1930), 42–48.

40. Some examples of American Indian pictographic signs derived from gestures are quoted above, in the discussion of the forerunners of writing (pp. 34, 40, and 41). For more examples of gesture and posture signs among American Indians, cf. Garrick Mallery, *Picture-Writing of the American Indians (Tenth Annual Report of the Bureau of Ethnology;* Washington, 1893), pp. 637–648. An exhaustive study of Chinese word signs derived from gestures can be found in a study of Tchang Tcheng-Ming, *L'écriture chinoise et le geste humain* (Shanghai and Paris, n.d.); he calls such signs 'dactylograms.' No account can be taken of the exaggerated opinions of Jacques van Ginneken, 'La reconstruction typologique des langues archaïques de l'humanité,' *Verhandelingen der K. Nederlandsche Akademie van Wetenschappen.* Letterkunde, N. R. xliv (Amsterdam, 1940), and *idem*, 'Die Bilderschrift-Sprachen,' *Travaux du Cercle Linguistique de Prague*, viii (1939), 247–254, who makes spoken language derivative of both gesture and pictography.

41. Alan H. Gardiner, *The Theory of Speech and Language* (Oxford, 1932), p. 122.

42. R. O. Faulkner in *Antiquity*, xvii (1943), 207.

43. The term 'Sumerogram' was introduced some years ago among the Chicago Assyriologists, but it is impossible now to ascertain its exact authorship.

44. Cf. below, pp. 207 f., and Johannes Friedrich in *Zeitschrift der Deutschen Morgenländischen Gesellschaft*, xcv (1941), 381 f.

45. This point is made quite clear by Siegfried Schott in *Hieroglyphen. Untersuchungen zum Ursprung der Schrift (Akademie der Wissenschaften und der Literatur in Mainz, Abhandlungen der Geistes- und Sozialwissenschaftlichen Klasse,* Jahrgang 1950, Nr. 24), pp. 115 f., where he says that the Egyptian 'muss lernen' and 'er muss wissen' are signs which are conventionally associated with definite words and not with vague ideas or meanings.

46. But cf. the enlightened comments in the recent book by Schott, quoted just above.

47. I. J. Gelb, *Hittite Hieroglyphs*, ii (Chicago, 1935), 3.

48. *Idem, Hurrians and Subarians* (Chicago, 1944).

49. Cf. Yuen Ren Chao in *Harvard Journal of Asiatic Studies*, v (1940), 189–191; and Franklin Edgerton in *Proceedings of the American Philosophical Society*, lxxxvii (1944), 29.

50. In *T'oung Pao*, xxxii (1936), 85–161, and xxxiv (1938), 265–294.

51. In *Harvard Journal of Asiatic Studies*, ii (1937), 329–372, and in *T'oung Pao*, xxxv (1940), 266–288. On the history of the terms 'logography' versus 'ideography' and their present usage, see the discussion by Gelb in *Language*, xxxviii (1962), 208–211.

52. Cf. Fig. 40.

53. On this problem cf. Gelb, *Memorandum on Transliteration and Transcription of Cuneiform*, submitted to the 21st International Congress of Orientalists, Paris (Chicago, 1948), §§ 80–87.

54. E.g., Alan H. Gardiner, *Egyptian Grammar* (Oxford, 1927), § 17, and Gustave Lefebvre, *Grammaire de l'Égyptien classique* (Le Caire, 1940), § 14, partly qualified by the statement in § 15.

55. *Vom Bilde zum Buchstaben* (Leipzig, 1939), pp. 28 f.

56. As justly observed by Siegfried Schott *apud* Sethe, *op. cit.*, pp. 78 f. Cf. also the masterly study of H. W. Fairman, 'An Introduction to the Study of Ptolemaic Signs and Their Values,' *Bulletin de l'Institut Français d'Archéologie Orientale du Caire*, xliii (1945), 51–138, who, in calling 'acrophony a very dead horse' (p. 52), expresses clearly doubts about the existence of the acrophonic principle even in the late Egyptian (Ptolemaic) times.

57. Cf. also the recent discussion of alleged acrophony in hieroglyphic Hittite by Gelb in *Language*, xxxviii (1962), 199, with references to Egyptian and Cretan.

58. The exceptions are those marks (strokes, dots, or spacing) which are used to indicate word division. Such marks of pauses or junctures, often termed 'suprasegmental phonemes,' are to be noted under the prosodic features of language.

59. Cf. J. Friedrich, 'Die Parallel-Entwicklung der drei alten Schrift-Erfindungen,' *Analecta Biblica*, xii (1959), 95–101.

60. See the discussion by Battiscombe Gunn in the *Journal of Egyptian Archaeology*, xxix (1943), 55–59 (reference from Professor Keith C. Seele).

61. This point is made quite clear in an old study by Abel Rémusat, 'Remarques sur quelques écritures syllabiques tirées des caractères chinois, et sur le passage de l'écriture figurative à l'écriture alphabétique,' *Mémoires de l'Institut Royal de France, Académie des Inscriptions et Belles-Lettres*, viii (1827), 34–59.

NOTES to Chapter IV, pages 120–165

1. Friedrich Wilhelm König, *Corpus inscriptionum Elamicarum*, i (Hannover, 1928), 'Schrifttafel' at end of publication.

2. F. H. Weissbach, *Die Keilinschriften der Achämeniden* (Leipzig, 1911), pp. xxxix ff. The exact statistics should be corrected in accordance with George C. Cameron, *Persepolis Treasury Tablets* (*Oriental Institute Publications*, lxv; Chicago, 1948), chapter ix.

3. Johannes Friedrich, *Kleinasiatische Sprachdenkmäler* (Berlin, 1932), pp. 8 ff. Only the introduction to the letter is written almost entirely with Akkadian word signs.

4. 'The Egyptian Origin of the Semitic Alphabet,' *Journal of Egyptian Archaeology*, iii (1916), 1–16.

5. 'The Early Alphabetic Inscriptions from Sinai and Their Decipherment,' *Bulletin of the American Schools of Oriental Research* No. 110 (1948), 6–22.

6. J. Leibovitch, 'Sur quelques inscriptions indéchiffrables,' *Bulletin de l'Institut d'Égypte*, xvi (1934), 177–183.

7. J. Leibovitch, 'Les inscriptions Protosinaïtiques,' *Mémoires présentés à l'Institut d'Égypte*, xxiv (1934), pls. iv–vi.

8. All these texts are discussed in David Diringer, 'The Origins of the Alphabet,' *Antiquity*, xvii (1943), 77–90 and 208 f., and 'The Palestinian Inscriptions and the Origin of the Alphabet,' *Journal of the American Oriental Society*, lxiii (1943), 24–30.

9. Finally, the sherd from Tell eṣ-Ṣārem and the epigraphically very important javelin heads found by a peasant from El-Ḥaḍr, a village situated in the close vicinity of Bethlehem, are dated to about 1100 B.C. Cf. Ruth B. Kallner, 'Two Inscribed Sherds,' *Kedem*, ii (1945), 11–14 and vii, and E. L. Sukenik, 'Note on the Sherd from Tell eṣ-Ṣarem,' *op. cit.*, pp. 15 and vii; J. T. Milik and Frank M. Cross, Jr., 'Inscribed Javelin-Heads from the Period of the Judges: A Recent Discovery in Palestine,' *Bulletin of the American Schools of Oriental Research*, No. 134 (1954), 5–15, and Cross, *op. cit.*, pp. 15–24.

10. For divergent opinions on the dates and readings of the different Proto-Palestinian inscriptions, cf. works by authors quoted in footnotes 8 f.; and also Frank M. Cross, Jr., and David N. Friedman, *Early Hebrew Orthography* (New Haven, Connecticut, 1952), pp. 8 f., and G. R. Driver, *Semitic Writing from Pictograph to Alphabet* (rev. ed.; London, 1954), pp. 98–103 and 198 f.

11. W. M. Flinders Petrie, 'The Alphabet in the XIIth Dynasty,' *Ancient Egypt*, vi (1921), pp. 1–3.

12. G. Horsfield et L. H. Vincent, 'Une stèle Égypto-Moabite au Balou'a,' *Revue Biblique*, xli (1932), 417–444.

13. 'À propos de la stèle du Balou'a,' *op. cit.*, xlii (1933), 353–365.

14. Maurice Dunand, in *Mélanges Maspero*, i (Le Caire, 1935–1938), pl. opp. p. 570; *idem, Byblia grammata* (Beyrouth, 1945), pp. 135 ff. Interpreted as West Semitic by W. F. Albright, in *Bulletin of the American Schools of Oriental Research*, no. 116 (1949), 12 ff., following H. Grimme; cf., however, the difficulties discussed by Frank M. Cross, Jr., in *Bulletin of the American Schools of Oriental Research*, no. 134 (1954), 22 ff.

15. *Byblia grammata*, p. 143.

16. General discussion in Hans Bauer, *Das Alphabet von Ras Schamra* (Halle, 1932).

17. Cf. the discussion by A. Herdner, 'A-t-il existé une variété palestinienne de l'écriture cunéiforme alphabetique?,' *Syria*, xxv (1946–1948), 165–168. One of the most important finds made at Râs Shamrah in recent years is the recovery of an ancient abecedary, showing the order of the signs to be the same as in later (Phoenician, Hebrew, and other) West Semitic writings, with the following qualifications: Among the first twenty-seven signs of the Ugaritic abecedary there are five signs (*Ḥ, Š, Ḏ, Ẓ, Ġ*), which disappeared in the later West Semitic; the signs Nos. 28 and 29 (*ʾi, ʾu* representing a structural evolution from No. 1, originally ʾ), as well as No. 30 (mainly in Hurrian usage) are from a local development and were placed at the end of the abecedary. Cf. Cyrus H. Gordon, 'The Ugaritic "A B C",' *Orientalia*, n.s. xix (1950), 374 ff.; W. F. Albright, 'Some Important Recent Discoveries: Alphabetic Origins and the Idrimi Statue,' *Bulletin of the American Schools of Oriental Research*, no. 118 (1950), 11–20; *idem, op. cit.*, no. 119 (1950), 23 f.; E. A. Speiser, *op. cit.*, no. 121 (1951), 17–21; Frank M. Cross and Thomas O. Lambdin, *op. cit.*, no. 160 (1960), 21–26; William W. Hallo, 'Isaiah 28:7–13 and the Ugaritic Abecedaries,' *Journal of Biblical Literature*, lxxvii (1958), 324–338; Gelb in *Bibliotheca Orientalis*, xv (1958), 6 f.

18. P. Montet, *Byblos et l'Égypte* (Paris, 1928–29), Texte, pp. 215–238, and Atlas, pls. cxxvi–cxli; S. Ronzevalle, 'L'alphabet du sarcophage d'Aḥīrām,' *Mélanges de l'Université Saint Joseph*, xii (1927), 3–40.

19. Dunand, 'Spatule de bronze avec épigraphe phénicienne du xiiie siécle,' *Bulletin du Musée de Beyrouth*, ii (1938), 99–107; *idem, Fouilles de Byblos* (Paris, 1937), Atlas, pl. xxxii, no. 1125; *idem, Byblia grammata*, pp. 155 ff. and pl. xiii, no. 2.

20. *Idem*, 'Nouvelle inscription phénicienne archaïque,' *Revue Biblique*, xxxix (1930), 321–331.

21. P.-É. Guiges, 'Pointe de flèche en bronze à inscription phéni-

cienne,' *Mélanges de l'Université Saint Joseph*, xi (1926), 325–328; and S. Ronzevalle, 'Note sur le texte phénicien de la flèche publiée par M. P.-É. Guiges,' *op. cit.*, pp. 329–358. Cross and Friedman, in works quoted on p. 285, n. 10, date the ᶜAzarbaᶜal and Ruweiseh inscriptions to a period before Aḥīrâm, in the eleventh century.

22. René Dussaud, 'L'inscription du roi Abibaʿal,' *Syria*, v (1924), 145–147.

23. René Dussaud, 'Dédicace d'une statue d'Osorkon I par Elibaʿal, roi de Byblos,' *Syria*, vi (1925), 101–117.

24. Dunand, *Byblia grammata*, pp. 146 ff.

25. As observed by W. F. Albright in the *Bulletin of the American Schools of Oriental Research*, no. 102 (1946), p. 20, who dates these two inscriptions to the early ninth century B.C.

26. The lowering of the date of the Aḥīrâm inscription to about 1000 B.C., proposed some years ago by several scholars and lately defended by W. F. Albright, 'The Phoenician Inscriptions of the Tenth Century B.C. from Byblos,' *Journal of the American Oriental Society*, lxvii (1947), 153–160, is supported by archaeological evidence as newly reconstructed in a *Post-scriptum* by Dunand, *Byblia grammata*, pp. 197 ff.

27. A. T. Olmstead, 'Excursus on the Cuneiform Alphabet of Ras Shamra and Its Relation to the Sinaitic Inscriptions,' in Martin Sprengling, *The Alphabet* (Chicago, 1931), pp. 57 ff. The West Semitic origin of the Ugaritic writing was defended by H. Buchman, 'Die Enstehung der Formen des Keilschriftalphabets von Ras Schamra,' *Przegląd Historyczny*, 1934, pp. 213–234; E. Burrows, 'The Origin of the Ras Shamra Alphabet,' *The Journal of the Royal Asiatic Society*, 1936, pp. 271–277; and B. Rosenkranz, 'Der Ursprung des Alphabets von Ras Schamra,' *Zeitschrift der Deutschen Morgenländischen Gesellschaft*, xcii (1938), 178–182.

28. E. Ebeling, 'Zur Entstehungsgeschichte des Keilschriftalphabets von Ras Schamra,' *Sitzungsberichte der Preussischen Akademie der Wissenschaften, Philos.-hist. Kl.*, 1934, pp. 10–15.

29. A. Jamme, 'An Archaic South-Arabian Inscription in Vertical Column,' *Bulletin of the American Schools of Oriental Research*, no. 137 (1955), 32–38, dates one inscription, recently discovered, to the ninth or the tenth century B.C.

30. Heinrich Schäfer, 'Die Vokallosigkeit des "phönizischen" Alphabets,' *Zeitschrift für ägyptische Sprache*, lii (1914), 95–98.

31. This theory is best represented in Martin Sprengling, *The Alphabet* (Chicago, 1931).

32. 'Ein Beitrag zur Entwicklung der Schrift,' *Archiv für die Gesamte Psychologie*, xxxvi (1917), 359–390; *idem*, 'Die Entstehung der Sinaischrift und des phönizischen Alphabets,' *Journal of the*

Society of Oriental Research, xii (1928), 131–145; *idem,* 'Les débuts de l'écriture,' *Revue archéologique,* Série vi, Tome iv (1934), pp. 109–134.

33. 'Zur Herkunft des Alphabets,' *Zeitschrift der Deutschen Morgenländischen Gesellschaft,* lxxiii (1919), 51–79.

34. 'Einige Kapitel aus der inneren Geschichte der Schrift,' *Archiv für Schreib- und Buchwesen,* n.F. ii (1935), 8–18; *idem,* 'Schriftgeschichtliche Betrachtungen,' *Zeitschrift der Deutschen Morgenländischen Gesellschaft,* xci (1937), 319–342; *idem,* 'Zu einigen Schrifterfindungen der neuesten Zeit,' *op. cit.,* xcii (1938), 183–218; *idem,* 'Noch eine moderne Parallele zu den alten Schrifterfindungen,' *op. cit.,* xcv (1941), 374–414.

35. 'L'origine de l'alphabet et son évolution première d'après les découvertes de Byblos,' *Syria,* xxv (1946–48), 36–52, and previously in *Syria,* xi (1930), 185 ff., and xix (1938), 88 ff.

36. *Der Ursprung des Alphabets (Der Alte Orient,* xxxvi, 1–2; Leipzig, 1937).

37. Cf. also Vittore Pisani, 'Origini dell'alfabeto,' *Annali della R. Scuola Normale Superiore di Pisa. Letere, Storia e Filosofia,* serie ii, vol. v (1936), 267–277; *idem,* review of Diringer, *L'alfabeto nella storia della civiltà, op. cit.,* vi (1937), 371–376.

38. Cf. the long discussion in G. R. Driver, *Semitic Writing* (London, 1948), pp. 152–171.

39. Some names of signs can be grouped together, bearing evidence that they were created following certain phonetic patterns rather than forms of pictures. We can list here the group including the names *wāw, tāw,* and even *ṣāw, qāw,* found in Isa. 28 : 9–10 (cf. Driver, *op. cit.,* pp. 89 f., 155, 167 f., 230), and the group including *ḥēth, ṭēth,* and possibly even *bēth* (if not *bêth,* 'house') and *zēth* (in accordance with the Greek *zēta*). The structure of the names of the West Semitic signs with a final consonant is familiar to us from Georgian, where we find names of the letters normally (but not exclusively) ending in *-n,* as in *an, ban, gan, don, en,* etc.

40. The difficulties affecting the interpretation of the Semitic sign names are best discussed in Th. Nöldeke, *Beiträge zur semitischen Sprachwissenschaft* (Strassburg, 1904), pp. 124–136, and Mark Lidzbarski, *Ephemeris für semitische Epigraphik,* ii (Giessen, 1908), 125–139.

41. W. M. Flinders Petrie, *The Formation of the Alphabet* (London, 1912), pls. ii–iv.

42. From Hans Bauer in *Der Alte Orient,* xxxvi, 1/2, p. 36.

43. In *Nieuwe Theologische Studiën,* xiv (1931), 137 f.

44. Cf. the discussion by S. Yeivin in *Archiv Orientální,* iv (1932), 77, and by A. Poebel, *Studies in Akkadian Grammar* (Chicago, 1939), pp. 62 f.

45. Wolf Leslau's position, expressed in *Word,* xi (1955), 281 f.,

that the inventor of the Ethiopic vocalic system considered the vowel *a* as basic because of its frequent occurrence in the language, loses its strength on the basis of statistics: in counting the occurrences in four passages in G. Bergsträsser, *Einführung in die semitischen Sprachen* (München, 1928), pp. 104 ff., I found that syllabic signs containing *a* number 126, while those with the *shewa* mark number 139.

46. Enno Littmann in *Nachrichten von der K. Gesellschaft der Wissenschaften zu Göttingen*, Philos.-hist. Kl., 1917, p. 677. Edward Ullendorff, 'Studies in the Ethiopic Syllabary,' *Africa*, xxi (1951), 207–217, argues that the Ethiopic names *hā, lā,* etc., were original in Ethiopic, while the *hōi, lāwī* type of names was probably borrowed secondarily from Hebrew.

47. Note also that the mark for *sukūn* is derived formally from the number zero.

48. Sigurd C. Ylvisaker, *Zur babylonischen und assyrischen Grammatik* (Leipzig, 1912), pp. 15 f.

49. *Op. cit.*, p. 13, and James Philip Hyatt, *The Treatment of Final Vowels in Early Neo-Babylonian* (New Haven, 1941), p. 20.

50. *Op. cit.*, p. 15.

51. In his review of Hyatt's book published in *Classical Weekly*, xxxvi (1942), 100 f.

52. Cf. the discussion in Poebel, *op. cit.*, pp. 61 f.

53. For additional points in favor of the syllabic character of the West Semitic writing, based on evidence culled from the Iberian, Etruscan, and early Greek writings, see Gelb, 'New Evidence in Favor of the West Semitic Writing,' *Bibliotheca Orientalis*, xv (1958), 2–7, esp. pp. 4–6. For the Ugaritic evidence bearing on the subject, see *op. cit.*, pp. 6 f., and William W. Hallo, 'Isaiah 28:9–13 and the Ugaritic Abecedaries,' *Journal of Biblical Literature*, lxxvii (1958), 324–338.

54. Franz Praetorius, *Über den Ursprung des kanaanäischen Alphabets* (Berlin, 1906), pp. 1 ff.

55. A. Seidel, *Sprachlaut und Schrift* (Wien und Leipzig, 1920), pp. 130 and 133.

56. 'The Sign 3 and the True Nature of the Early Alphabets,' *Archiv Orientální*, iv (1932), 71–78.

57. David Diringer in *Antiquity*, xvii (1943), 89.

58. *Griechische Grammatik*, i (München, 1939), 145.

59. *Studies in Akkadian Grammar* (Chicago, 1939), pp. 61–64.

60. *An Introduction to Linguistic Science* (New Haven, 1947), p. 22.

61. *Linguistic Science in the Nineteenth Century* (Cambridge, 1931), pp. 142 ff. and 180 ff.

62. *Op. cit.*, p. 142.

63. In addition to Praetorius, Seidel, Yeivin, Poebel, Schwyzer,

Sturtevant, and Pedersen, noted in the preceding footnotes, the following scholars argued in favor of the syllabic character of the West Semitic writing: Roland G. Kent, Donald C. Swanson, Marcel Cohen, Edmond Sollberger, Antoine Meillet, Herbert H. Paper, E. A. Speiser, Paul Kretschmer, and Alfred Schmitt, all noted in my article in *Bibliotheca Orientalis*, xv (1958), 4; add to this list also William W. Hallo in *Journal of Biblical Literature*, lxxvii (1958), 324–338, and Elizabeth Bowman in *Journal of Near Eastern Studies*, xix (1960), 46–48. For the opposite point of view, see the two articles by Stanislaw Segert, 'Charakter des westsemitischen Alphabets, eine Entgegnung an Ignace J. Gelb,' and 'Charakter des westsemitischen Alphabets,' *Archiv Orientální*, xxvi (1958), 243–247 and 657–659.

64. Last stated in his *Scripta Minoa*, i (Oxford, 1909), pp. 68–77.

65. 'Prolegomena to the Cypro-Minoan Script,' *American Journal of Archaeology*, xlv (1941), 249–282.

66. Recent discoveries of additional short texts, as well as of large tablets, containing hundreds of signs, enlarged considerably our knowledge of the Cypro-Minoan writing. Cf. Olivier Masson, 'Nouvelles inscriptions en caractères chypro-minoens' in C. F. A. Schaeffer, *Enkomi-Alasia*, i (Paris, 1952), pp. 391–409; Porphyrios Dikaios in *Antiquity*, xxvii (1953), 103 ff., 233–237; xxx (1956), 40 f.; Claude F. A. Schaeffer, *op. cit.*, xxviii (1954), 38 f. Cf. also the discussion of P. Meriggi, 'I primi testi ciprominoici e l'eteociprio,' *Athenaeum*, n.s. xxxiv (1956), 3–38, and P. Meriggi, O. Masson, and others in *Etudes mycéniennes*, ed. Michel Lejeune (Paris, 1956), pp. 193–206 and 268–271.

67. Otto Schroeder, 'Gesetzte assyrische Ziegelstempel,' *Zeitschrift für Assyriologie*, xxxiv (1922), 157–161.

68. *Byblia grammata* (Beyrouth, 1945), chapter iv.

69. Cf. *Comptes Rendus de l'Académie des Inscriptions et Belles Lettres*, 1946, pp. 360–365 and 472–479, and 'Déchiffrement des inscriptions pseudo-hiéroglyphiques de Byblos,' *Syria*, xxv (1946–1948), 1–35.

70. Following *Byblia grammata*, pp. 88 ff.

71. *Op. cit.*, pp. 85 f., 155 ff., and pl. xiii, 2.

72. In modern times a large measure of standardization of forms has been achieved.

73. As a result of the decree of the Japanese Ministry of Public Instruction in 1900 the number of word signs was greatly reduced, but still 1,200 word signs were considered the minimum required for elementary schools. On November 16, 1946, the Japanese Cabinet and Ministry of Education issued a list of 1850 *kanji* characters which were recommended for general use, presumably outlawing the use of perhaps four or five thousand other characters carried in the fonts of publishing houses. Scholars generally doubt the success of the re-

form. Cf. Joseph K. Yamagiwa, 'Reforms in the Language and Orthography of Newspapers in Japan,' *Journal of the American Oriental Society*, lxviii (1948), 45–52, and a 'Note' by F. J. Daniels in *Bulletin of the School of Oriental and African Studies*, xvi (1954), 393 f. Criticisms of the first edition of this work by Daniels (*loc. cit.*) as well as helpful suggestions of Professor Yamagiwa contributed to the improved form of the Japanese portion of the present edition.

74. S. Kanazawa, *Über den Einfluss des Sanskrits auf das japanische und koreanische Schriftsystem* (Tokio, 1907).

75. Among other less well-known writings of the Aegean group we find that Cypro-Minoan contains about sixty-three, Phaistos about sixty, and Byblos about eighty to ninety syllabic signs, while the comparable numbers for the Linear A and B syllabaries (discussed under the logo-syllabic writings) are eighty and eighty-eight, respectively.

NOTES to Chapter V, pages 166–189

1. Hans Bauer and Pontus Leander, *Historische Grammatik der hebräischen Sprache des Alten Testamentes* (Halle, 1918), p. 92; citation to be corrected in accordance with *David Ḳimḥi's Hebrew Grammar (Mikhlol)*, ed. by William Chomsky (Philadelphia, 1933), p. 12.

2. Cf., e.g., S. Yeivin, 'The Sign ʒ and the True Nature of the Early Alphabets,' *Archiv Orientální*, iv (1932), 71–78; Frank R. Blake, 'The Development of Symbols for the Vowels in the Alphabets Derived from the Phoenician,' *Journal of the American Oriental Society*, lx (1940), 391–413; William Chomsky, 'The History of Our Vowel-System in Hebrew,' *The Jewish Quarterly Review*, xxxii (1941–42), 27–49.

3. Cf. the discussion in Frank Moore Cross, Jr., and David Noel Friedman, *Early Hebrew Orthography. A Study of the Epigraphic Evidence* (New Haven, Connecticut, 1952).

4. All examples taken from Mark Lidzbarski, *Handbuch der nordsemitischen Epigraphik* (Weimar, 1898).

5. The indication of the vowel *o* by means of ʿaiin, found in the neo-Punic spellings such as $B^x c^x m^x l^x q^x r^x t^x$ (=Latin *Bomilcar*), is very instructive, as it shows that in some Semitic dialects this consonant influenced an *a* to *o* change which may have been responsible for the ultimate development of the vowel *o* from ʿayin in the Greek writing.

6. *The Vocalization of the Egyptian Syllabic Orthography* (New Haven, 1934). For recent material on the subject, cf. Elmar Edel in *Journal of Near Eastern Studies*, vii (1948), 11–24; *idem, op. cit.*, viii (1949), 44–47; W. F. Albright in *Journal of the American Oriental Society*, lxxiv (1954), 222–233; and especially W. F. Albright and T. O. Lambdin, 'New Material for the Egyptian Syllabic Orthography,' *Journal of Semitic Studies*, ii (1957), 113–127.

7. 'Egyptian Phonetic Writing, from Its Invention to the Close of the Nineteenth Dynasty,' *Journal of the American Oriental Society*, lx (1940), 473–506, esp. p. 486.

8. Albright, *Vocalization*, pp. 6–15.

9. Edgerton, *op. cit.*, pp. 486–990.

10. Even in the cuneiform writing we find such anaptyctic spellings, as in *Ki-iz-zu-wa-ta-na*, *Ki-iz-wa-ta-na*, etc. (Gerhard Rudolf Meyer in *Mitteilungen des Instituts für Orientforschung*, i (1953), 121.

11. According to Albright, *Journal of the American Oriental Society*,

lxxiv (1954), 224, the number of syllabic groups employed in the New Kingdom was about sixty, which compares well with the number of syllabic signs in the syllabic systems discussed above on p. 164 and p. 291, n. 75.

12. *Op. cit.*, p. 506.

13. Johannes Friedrich, *Phönizisch-punische Grammatik (Analecta Orientalia*, xxxii; Roma, 1951), pp. 42 f., and 'Vulgärpunisch und Vulgärlatein in den neupunischen Inschriften,' *Cahiers de Byrsa*, iii (1953), 100 f., has tried to establish two different methods of vowel indication in the late Neo-Punic (Friedrich's 'Vulgarpunisch') inscriptions: one method, in which ɔ = *e*, *o*, ᶜ = *a*, Y = *i*, W = *u*, and another, much rarer method, in which ɔ = *a*, H = *e*, ᶜ = *o*, Y = *i*, W = *u*.

14. Erich Ebeling, *Keilschrifttexte aus Assur juristischen Inhalts* (Leipzig, 1927), no. 121 a, rev. 2, and elsewhere.

15. Leroy Waterman, *Royal Correspondence of the Assyrian Empire*, i (Ann Arbor, 1930), Nos. 258:4, 263:5, 345:3, etc.

16. E. Forrer in *Zeitschrift der Deutschen Morgenländischen Gesellschaft*, lxxvi (1922), 227, 231, etc., and H. Otten in *Zeitschrift für Assyriologie*, xlviii (1944), 123.

17. Examples quoted in E. A. Speiser, *Introduction to Hurrian* (New Haven, 1941), pp. 15 ff.

18. See on this problem the discussion by J. Friedrich in *Archiv für Schreib- und Buchwesen*, n.F. ii (1935), 15. Among recent studies supporting the view of an *ad hoc* creation of the Old Persian syllabary rather than its survival from a fuller, as yet unattested, syllabary, cf. Herbert H. Paper, 'The Old Persian /L/ Phoneme,' *Journal of the American Oriental Society*, lxxvi (1956), 24–26, and, with different arguments, Walther Hinz, 'Die Einführung der altpersischen Schrift,' *Zeitschrift der Deutschen Morgenländischen Gesellschaft*, cii (1952), 28–38.

19. *Ibid.*; later modified in *Zeitschrift der Deutschen Morgenländischen Gesellschaft*, xcii (1938), 207, and xcv (1941), 414.

20. Cf. the extensive literature in M. Dunand, *Byblia grammata* (Beyrouth, 1945), pp. 189–192, and G. R. Driver, *Semitic Writing* (London, 1948), pp. 128 f.

21. *Beiträge zur semitischen Sprachwissenschaft* (Strassburg, 1904), p. 135.

22. 'Die Urgeschichte des Alphabets,' *Rheinisches Museum für Philologie*, n.F. lxxxv (1936), 347–366.

23. 'How Old Is the Greek Alphabet?' *American Journal of Archaeology*, xxxviii (1934), 359–381.

24. 'The Antiquity of the Greek Alphabet,' *op. cit.*, xxxvii (1933), 8–29.

25. *Handbuch der Archäologie*, hrsg. von Walter Otto, i (München,

1939), 195. The Greek inscriptions referred to in footnotes 25–30, as well as several other early Greek inscriptions, are republished and discussed in L. H. Jeffery, *The Local Scripts of Archaic Greece* (Oxford, 1961).

26. Ullman, *op. cit.*, p. 365, and many other scholars.

27. Carpenter, *op. cit.*, p. 24.

28. *Op. cit.*, p. 26.

29. Carl W. Blegen, 'Inscriptions on Geometric Pottery from Hymettos,' *American Journal of Archaeology*, xxxviii (1934), 10–28.

30. Agnes N. Stillwell, 'Eighth Century B.C. Inscriptions from Corinth,' *op. cit.*, xxxvii (1933), 605–610.

31. W. F. Albright, 'New Light on the Early History of Phoenician Colonization,' *Bulletin of the American Schools of Oriental Research*, No. 83 (1941), 14–22.

32. In recent times, Margit Falkner, 'Zur Frühgeschichte des griechischen Alphabets,' *Frühgeschichte und Sprachwissenschaft*, hrsg. von Wilhelm Brandenstein (Wien, 1948), pp. 110–133, came out in favour of the ninth century, while Franklin P. Johnson, 'Notes on the Early Greek Writing,' *American Journal of Philology*, lxxvii (1956), 29–37, favored the tenth century. R. M. Cook and A. G. Woodhead, 'The Diffusion of the Greek Alphabet,' *American Journal of Archaeology*, lxiii (1959), 175–178, and L. H. Jeffery, *The Local Scripts of Archaic Greece* (Oxford, 1961), pp. 1–21, favour the date of the second half of the eighth century B.C. and the middle of the eighth century B.C., respectively, and believe that the Greek alphabet was borrowed by the Greeks residing and trading in the coastal cities of Syria and Phoenicia.

33. The vase was evidently offered as a prize to the merriest dancer chosen in a contest.

34. Johannes Friedrich in the two studies quoted on p. 293, n. 13, takes for granted that the development of vocalization in the neo-Punic writing is due to the Latin influence.

35. In *Archiv für Schreib- und Buchwesen*, n.F. ii (1935), 17 f. Adolf Grohman, 'Über den Ursprung und die Entwicklung der äthiopischen Schrift,' *Archiv für Schriftkunde*, i (1915), 57–87, esp. pp. 80 ff., rejected the derivation of the Ethiopic vowel system from Indic because of differences in outer form of several vowel marks, neglecting completely the connections between the two systems based on common structure.

36. Or should we conclude that in the stenographic systems even the sign for *ka* is alphabetical and analyse it as the basic sign for *k* plus the heavy form for the indication of the vowel *a*? Similarly in the case of Ethiopic, we could analyse such vowel indication as the basic sign plus some formal modification. The case of Ethiopic and

Indic basic signs standing for a consonant plus *a* could be analysed as the basic sign plus zero to indicate the vowel *a*.

37. *Die Schrift* (Glückstadt und Hamburg, 1935) and the older edition entitled *Geschichte der Schrift* (Hannover, 1925).

38. *L'alfabeto nella storia della civiltà* (Firenze, 1937).

39. *Histoire de l'écriture* (Paris, 1948).

40. *The Alphabet*, 2 vols. (London, 1883) = *The History of the Alphabet*, 2 vols. (New York, 1899).

41. *The Alphabet. A Key to the History of Mankind* (London and New York, 1948; 2nd ed. in 1949).

42. *Notices sur les charactères étrangers anciens et modernes*, rédigées par un groupe de savants, réunies par Charles Fossey (Paris, 1927); nouvelle édition in 1948).

43. Marcel Cohen, *La grande invention de l'écriture et son évolution*. Three volumes: *Texte, Documentation et index, Planches* (Paris, 1958).

1. For the definition of a syllabic sign, see p. 271, n. 31.
2. I cannot agree with the opinion expressed in Ralph Linton's *The Study of Man. An Introduction* (New York, 1946), pp. 304 ff., where discovery is defined as 'any addition to knowledge' and invention—both basic and improving—as 'a new application of knowledge.'
3. The Coptic alphabet, borrowed mainly from the Greek, has one sign, borrowed from the Egyptian Demotic, with a syllabic value *ti*.
4. See Giuliano Bonfante's article on 'Semantics,' *Encyclopaedia of Psychology* (New York, 1946), p. 844, and 'On Reconstruction and Linguistic Method,' *Word*, i (1945), 85 ff.
5. Observe the evolution of Chinese, originally isolating, now almost agglutinative, and the trend of English, originally inflectional, now developing in the direction of isolating languages.
6. Observe Indo-European **pətḗr* (Latin *pater*): Old Norse *faðir* (English *father*): Old Saxon and Gothic *fadar*: German *Vater* or Indo-European **dheu-*: English *dead*: German *tot*: dialectal German *thot*. C. Meinhof, *Die moderne Sprachforschung in Afrika* (Berlin, 1910), p. 59, observed that 'Grimm's Law' holds good for eighteen different Bantu languages.
7. This point is emphasized strongly by scholars who have analysed the typology of systems created in modern times among such primitive societies as the Alaska Eskimos and the African Bamum. See J. Friedrich in *Zeitschrift der Deutschen Morgenländischen Gesellschaft*, civ (1954), 322, 325, 328 f.; *idem* in *Archiv Orientální*, xix (1951), 256 ff.; Alfred Schmitt, *Die Alaska Schrift und ihre schriftgeschichtliche Bedeutung* (*Münstersche Forschungen*, Heft 4; Marburg, 1951), pp. 100, 107; *idem* in *Indogermanische Forschungen*, lxi (1954), 225; Egerton R. Young, *The Apostle of the North—Rev. James Evans* (New York, 1899), pp. 181 ff.; Louis-Philippe Vaillancourt, 'L'origine des caractères syllabiques,' *Anthropologica*, v (1957), 127 f.; K. L. Pike, *Phonemics* (Ann Arbor, Michigan, 1947), chapter 16; J. Berry, 'The Making of Alphabets,' *Proceedings of the VIII International Congress of Linguistics* (Oslo, 1957), 752–764.
8. Kurt Sethe, *Vom Bilde zum Buchstaben* (Leipzig, 1939), p. 66.
9. *Op. cit.*, pp. 26 ff.
10. *Op. cit.*, pp. 44 and 52; this discrepancy was clearly observed

by S. Schott *apud* Sethe, *op. cit.*, p. 71. An opinion identical with that of Sethe is expressed by G. R. Driver, *Semitic Writing* (London, 1954), p. 138: 'Syllabic writing is a blind alley from which there is no escape.'

11. David Diringer, *L'alfabeto nella storia della civiltà* (Firenze, 1937), p. 704.

12. *Op. cit.*, p. 88; Diringer uses the term 'syllabic' in the sense 'multiconsonantal' criticized on pp. 76 ff. of this study.

13. *In Antiquity*, xvii (1943), 88.

NOTES to Chapter VII, pages 206–211

1. Hans Jensen, *Die Schrift* (Glükstadt und Hamburg, 1935), pp. 166; David Diringer, *L'alfabeto nella storia della civiltà* (Firenze, 1937), pp. 602 f.; C. F. Lehmann-Haupt in *Zeitschrift der Deutschen Morgenländischen Gesellschaft* (hereinafter referred to as *Zeitschrift*), lxxiii (1919), 60–65; Johannes Friedrich, *Zeitschrift*, xci (1937), 331 f.

2. Jensen, *op. cit.*, pp. 168 f.; Diringer, *op. cit.*, p. 604; Louis-Philippe Vaillancourt, 'L'origine des caractères syllabiques,' *Anthropologica*, v (1957), 125–129. From *The Gospel in Many Tongues Published by the British and Foreign Bible Society* (London, 1954), I learn that systems similar to those used by the Cree Indians are at home among the Eskimos of the Baffin Land (No. 199) and the Slave or Tinne in the Mackenzie River area (No. 708). Cf. also the article 'Eskimo in Print,' in *Time* magazine, June 29, 1959, p. 37.

3. Diringer, *op. cit.*, pp. 601 f.; Garrick Mallery, *Picture-Writing of the American Indians* (Tenth Annual Report of the Bureau of Ethnology, Smithsonian Institution; Washington, 1886), pp. 666–671. Nothing much can be learned from the standard manuals about the *actual* use of the Micmac writing. However, from an article by Wilhelm Schlag, 'Austrian Missionaries to American Indians,' *Austrian Information*, published by the Austrian Information Service of New York, vol. xv, no. 2 (January 31, 1962), p. 5, republished from *Österreich und die angelsächsische Welt*, ed. Otto Hietzsch (Wien-Stuttgart, 1961, not available to me), we learn the following: 'In the Austrian National Library may be found two presentation copies of a curious one volume catechism, prayer book and abridged Biblical history, printed in pictographs. The book was written by Christian Kauder for his congregation of Micmac Indians in Nova Scotia. The two copies are all that is left of the entire edition printed gratuitously by the Imperial and Royal Government Printing Office in Vienna. The ship which was to bring the books to the New World sank.' A two-line excerpt from a Micmac manuscript preserved in the Bibliothèque Nationale, Paris, reproduced in M. Cohen, *La grande invention de l'écriture*, *Planches* 86A, and discussed in his *Documentation*, pp. 123 f., apparently is written in a Micmac writing of unknown origin.

4. William Jones, 'An Algonquin Syllabary,' in *Boas Anniversary Volume* (New York, 1906), pp. 88–93. Jones calls the Algonquin writing a syllabary, not alphabet. He justifies this statement by saying that 'it is common to associate the consonants in combination with

vowels, and in learning the syllabary, the vowels are told off first, and afterwards the consonants in combination with the vowels. The order followed is not vowel and then each consonant one after the other with that vowel, but first all the vowels, and then one consonant at a time in connection with all the four vowels.' This concept of the syllabary is further supported by noting that in an evolved form of the Algonquin syllabary the row of signs for a consonant plus vowel u ($=$ ɔ or the like) is expressed by a symbol without any vowel indication, in contrast to other syllabic rows in which vowels are fully indicated.

5. Alice C. Fletcher, 'A Phonetic Alphabet Used by the Winnebago Tribe of Indians,' *The Journal of American Folk-Lore*, iii (1890), 299–301 (reference from Dr. Thomas Sebeok, of Indiana University). It is reported about another Fox syllabic system that it 'employs our ordinary Arabic numbers in place of letters or symbols.' See Truman Michelson, 'Fox Linguistic Notes. An Unknown Fox Syllabary,' in *Festschrift Meinhof* (Hamburg, 1927), pp. 405–406.

6. Alfred Schmitt, *Untersuchungen zur Geschichte der Schrift. Eine Schrifterfundung um 1900 in Alaska* (3 vols.; Leipzig, 1940); Friedrich, *Zeitschrift*, xcv (1941), 374–414; II. Dewey Anderson and Walter Crosby Eells, *Alaska Natives* (Stanford University, 1935), pp. 191 ff.; W. J. Hoffman, 'The Graphic Art of the Eskimos,' *Annual Report of the Board of Regents of the Smithsonian Institution for the Year 1895* (Washington, 1897), pp. 739–968. Much new and important information on the Alaska writing can be found in Alfred Schmitt, *Die Alaska-Schrift und ihre schriftgeschichtliche Bedeutung (Münstersche Forschungen,* Heft 4; Marburg, 1951); Friedrich, *Zeitschrift*, civ (1954), 325–329; *idem, Archiv Orientální*, xix (1951), 252–259. Owing to the inadequacy of a pure word writing, in the course of time the Alaska writing acquired certain features of phonetization applied in words which were difficult to express in pictures, as in the writing of the name Peter (pronounced *pita*) by means of a picture sign which normally stood for *pitâ*, 'he catches it.' The use of the syllabic-phonetic signs increased steadily, replacing entirely in the final stages of development the logographic spellings. At the same time the writing lost its pictorial character and acquired linear forms. The final syllabaries consist of about seventy to eighty signs, some of which are used alphabetically in a form quite similar to that achieved in the Bamum writing (p. 209). Thus the word *qánertoq*, 'he speaks,' originally expressed by means of a picture sign, is expressed first syllabically as *qa-ner-tuq*, then as *qa-n-ner-tuq*, *qa-n-ner-r-tuq*, *qa-a-n-ne-r-t-tu-q*, and *qa-a-n-ne-r-ri-t-tu-q*.

7. Jensen, *op. cit.*, pp. 115 ff.; Diringer, *op. cit.*, pp. 222 ff.; A.

Klingenheben, 'The Vai Script,' *Africa*, vi (1933), 158–171; Friedrich, *Zeitschrift*, xci (1937), 328 f.

8. Jensen, *op. cit.*, p. 118; Friedrich, *Zeitschrift*, xci (1937), 329 ff. and 505; *idem*, *op. cit.*, xcii (1938), 189–208.

9. Friedrich, *Zeitschrift*, xci (1937), p. 328, n. 2, and p. 508; Joseph Joffre, *Man*, xliii (1943), 112, quoting H. Baumann, D. Westermann, R. Thurnwald, *Völkerkunde von Afrika* (Essen, 1940), p. 380, not available here.

10. Cf. Friedrich, *Zeitschrift*, xci (1937), 331, and *op. cit.*, xcii (1938), p. 185, n. 1.

11. Joseph Joffre, 'A New West-African Alphabet: Used by the Toma, French Guinea and Liberia,' *Man*, xliii (1943), 108–112; *idem*, 'Sur un nouvel alphabet ouest-africain: le Toma (frontière franco-libérienne),' *Bulletin de l'Institut Français d'Afrique Noire*, vii (1945), 160–173.

12. Cf. Joffre in *Man*, xliii, p. 112, and A. Lassort, 'L'écriture guerzée,' *Première conférence internationale des africanistes de l'ouest, Comptes rendus*, ii (Paris, 1951), 209–215. Very little is known about the use of the Bété writing on the Ivory Coast invented in or about 1956 by a French-educated native Frédéric Bruly-Bouabré. The writing in its ultimate development consists of 401 syllabic signs, mainly of pictographic origin. The very interesting document with the hand-written description of the character of the new writing by Bruly-Bouabré was published in Th. Monod, 'Un nouvel alphabet ouest-africain: le bété (Côte d'Ivoire),' *Bulletin de l'Institut Français d'Afrique Noire*, xx (1958), 432–553. A separate monograph on the Bété writing by Monod is soon to appear.

13. Jensen, *op. cit.*, pp. 112–115; Diringer, *op. cit.*, pp. 206 f.; Friedrich, *Zeitschrift*, xci (1937), 326 ff.; Maurice Delafosse, 'Naissance et évolution d'un système d'écriture de création contemporaine,' *Revue d'ethnographie*, iii (1922), 11–36; O. G. S. Crawford, 'The Writing of Njoya,' *Antiquity*, ix (1935), 435–442; I. Dugast et M. D. W. Jeffreys, *L'écriture des Bamum, sa naissance, son évolution, sa valeur phonétique, son utilisation* (*Mémoires de l'Institut Français d'Afrique Noire. Centre du Cameroun. Série: Populations*, no. 4 (1950); Friedrich, *Zeitschrift*, civ (1954), 317–325.

14. In the new system the word *mfɔn*, 'king,' originally written logographically with one sign, is now expressed by four signs as *m-fu-ɔ-n*, just as the word *lam*, 'marriage,' is written *la-a-m*. Described by Delafosse, *op. cit.*, pp. 17 f. and 33–36, but not discussed in the otherwise admirable work of Dugast and Jeffreys cited in the preceding footnote.

15. An artificial new language and script were reported from the extreme southeast of Nigeria as being used from 1936 on by a band

of professing Christians called Oberi Okaime. According to R. F. G. Adams, 'Oberi Okaime, a New African Language and Script,' *Africa*, xvii (1947), 24–34, 'there appear to be thirty-two main symbols, most of them taking very strange forms, while diacritic marks are found as well as special letters. All the thirty-two symbols have both small and capital forms.' Adams' description is not sufficient to get a clear idea of the character of the syllabary. Two slightly differing forms of a Nubian alphabet, apparently based on Arabic, are reproduced and discussed in H. A. MacMichael, *A History of the Arabs in the Sudan* (Cambridge, 1922), ii, 328; M. Delafosse in *Revue d'ethnographie et des traditions populaires*, iv (1923), 106 f.; M. Cohen, 'Inscriptions arabes en caractères séparés recueillies en Mauritanie par P. Boëry,' *Hespéris*, xiv (1932), 17–21, esp. pp. 18 f. A writing of unknown character and origin is used among the Galla in Ethiopia. Cf. A. d'Abbadie in *Bulletin de la Société de Géographie*, 1842 (not available to me), cited by Cohen in *Hespéris*, xiv, 20 f.

16. E. Cerulli, 'Tentativo indigeno di formare un alfabeto somalo,' *Oriente Moderno*, xii (1932), 212 f.; Friedrich, *Zeitschrift*, xcii (1938), 186–189; Mario Maino, 'L'alfabeto "osmania" in Somalia,' *Rassegna di Studi Etiopici*, x (1951), 108–121.

17. Friedrich, *Zeitschrift*, xcii (1938), 209–218, referring to a Russian publication by V. G. Bogoraz, not available here.

18. *The Gospel in Many Languages*. Specimens of 665 Languages in Which the British and Foreign Bible Society Has Published or Circulated Some Portions of the Word of God (London, 1933), Nos. 286 (Kopu), 308 (Laka), 322 f. (Lisu), 387 ff. (Miao), 442 (Nosu), and 656 (Na-hsi). The recently published book by D. Diringer, *The Alphabet* (London, 1948), pp. 184 f., has a short discussion of some of these systems. These modern scripts are different from the much older scripts developed by the non-Chinese populations of China, briefly discussed on p. 281, n. 30. Very little is known about a script used in the Chin Hills of Burma, which, according to Pau Chin Hau, the leader of a sectarian movement, was revealed to him in a dream by a divinity. From about 1900 on, he experimented with several versions of the writing, the third and final revision being carried out in 1931. The writing consists of twenty-one signs, of the consonant plus *a* structure, such as *pa, ka, la*, while vocalic differentiation is indicated by seven additional signs, as in *pi* written *p(a)-i*. An unusual type is represented by nine signs of vowel plus consonant structure, such as *ab, ag, ad*. Forms of signs are all linear, apparently freely created, although some of them resemble Latin characters. See *Census of India*, 1931, vol. xi: *Burma*, part i: *Report* by J. J. Bennigon (Rangoon, 1933), pp. 194 f. and 217 f.

19. Theodor-Wilhelm Danzel, *Die Anfänge der Schrift* (Leipzig, 1912), p. 219.

20. J. Macmillan Brown, 'A New Pacific Ocean Script,' *Man*, xiv (1914), 89 ff.; *idem, Peoples and Problems of the Pacific*, i (London, 1927), pp. 117–120. The following information on this writing is found in Saul H. Riesenberg and Shigeru Kaneshiro, 'A Caroline Islands Script,' *Smithsonian Institution, Bureau of American Ethnology, Bulletin* 173 (1960), 273–333. Two types of script exist on the islands: the older, script 2, consisting of 19 signs formed on the basis of Roman characters, and the younger, script 1, consisting of at least 78 signs, all freely invented. The signs stand for syllables of the consonant plus vowel type. The two scripts, introduced on the islands between 1907 and 1909 by way of stimulus diffusion from the West, have a very limited use at the present time. I owe the information on the Caroline Islands scripts to Messrs. Eric P. Hamp and Saul H. Riesenberg.

21. *Vom Bilde zum Buchstaben* (Leipzig, 1939), pp. 44 and 52, supported by J. Friedrich in *Zeitschrift der Deutschen Morgenländischen Gesellschaft*, xcv (1941), 405, and G. R. Driver, *Semitic Writing* (London, 1948), p. 138.

1. *Die Erfindung der Schrift* (Erlangen, 1938), p. 8.

2. In *Reallexikon der Assyriologie*, ii (1938), 92, and previously in *Wiener Zeitschrift für die Kunde des Morgenlandes*, xxxiv (1927), 79 f.

3. Cf. W. Norman Brown, 'The Beginnings of Civilization in India,' *Journal of the American Oriental Society*, Supplement to vol. lix, no. 4 (1939), pp. 32–44; Henri Frankfort, in *Annual Bibliography of Indian Archaeology for the Year 1932*, pp. 1–12; idem, *Cylinder Seals* (London, 1939), pp. 304–307; Heinz Mode, *Indische Frühkulturen und ihre Beziehungen zum Westen* (Basel, 1944).

4. Herrlee Glessner Creel, *Studies in Early Chinese Culture* (Baltimore, 1937), and *The Birth of China* (London, 1936).

5. This approach is represented, e.g., by Carl W. Bishop, 'The Beginnings of Civilization in Eastern Asia,' *Journal of the American Oriental Society*, Supplement to vol. lix, no. 4 (1939), pp. 45–61.

6. According to Professor Ludwig Bachhofer; see provisionally his article 'Zur Frühgeschichte Chinas,' *Die Welt als Geschichte*, iii (1937), 257–279, esp. p. 279.

7. E.g., Terrien de Lacouperie, *Western Origin of the Chinese Civilisation* (London, 1894); idem, 'The Old Babylonian Characters and Their Chinese Derivates,' *The Babylonian and Oriental Record*, ii (1887–1888), 73–99; and C. J. Ball, *Chinese and Sumerian* (Oxford, 1913).

8. H. Frankfort, 'The Origin of Monumental Architecture in Egypt,' *American Journal of Semitic Languages and Literatures*, lviii (1941), 329–358; A. Scharff, *Die Frühkulturen Ägyptens und Mesopotamiens (Der Alte Orient*, xli; Leipzig, 1941). Cf. also Helene J. Kantor, 'The Early Relations of Egypt with Asia,' *Journal of Near Eastern Studies*, i (1942), 174–213, and 'The Aegean and the Orient in the Second Millennium B.C.,' *American Journal of Archaeology*, li (1947), 1–103.

9. Cf. 'Die Entstehungszeit der ägyptischen Hieroglyphenschrift in archäologischer Beleuchtung,' *Forschungen und Fortschritte*, xviii (1942), 172 f., with a fuller discussion in his *Archäologische Beiträge zur Frage der Enstehung der Hieroglyphenschrift (Sitzungsberichte der Bayerischen Akademie der Wissenschaften*, Philos.-hist. Abt., 1942, Heft 3).

10. I. J. Gelb, *Hittite Hieroglyphs*, i (Chicago, 1931), 81.

11. Helmuth Th. Bossert, *Šantaš und Kupapa* (Leipzig, 1932), pp. 7 ff.

12. My basic approach to the problem of monogenesis of writing

is in perfect agreement with the ideas expressed by A. L. Kroeber, 'Stimulus Diffusion,' *American Anthropologist*, n.s. xlii (1940), 1–20, which became known to me only after the completion of the manuscript. I cannot claim, however, total originality, as it is quite possible that I may have received the stimulus to write about the importance of stimulus indirectly from Kroeber by way of talks with my colleagues in the Department of Anthropology.

NOTES to Chapter IX, pages 221–235

1. *The Conquest of Civilization* (New York, 1926), pp. 53 f.
2. *Seven Pillars of Wisdom* (London, 1935), p. 25.
3. Leonard Bloomfield, *Language* (New York, 1933), pp. 292 f.
4. *Op. cit.*, pp. 448 and 494.
5. Cf. the sections on the artistic value of writing by F. W. von Bissing, Albert Rehm, and Helmut Arntz in Walter Otto, *Handbuch der Archäologie*, i (München, 1939), 174 ff., 213 ff., and 348 f.; also 'Schrift als Ornament' in *Buch und Schrift*, Jahrbuch des Deutschen Vereins für Buchwesen und Schrifttum, ii (1928).
6. Cf., e.g., Samuel Flury, 'Le décor épigraphique des monuments fatimides du Caire,' *Syria*, xvii (1936), 365–376; Ernst Kühnel, *Islamische Schriftkunst* (Berlin-Leipzig, 1942), pp. 77 ff.; Kurt Erdmann, *Arabische Schriftzeichen als Ornamente in der abendländischen Kunst des Mittelalters* (Wiesbaden, 1953).
7. B. L. Ullman, *Ancient Writing and Its Influence* (New York, 1932), pp. 118 ff.
8. Cf. the full documentation in A. Bertholet, *Die Macht der Schrift in Glauben und Aberglauben* (*Abhandlungen der Deutschen Akademie der Wissenschaften zu Berlin*. Philos.-hist. Klasse, Jahrgang 1948, Nr. 1; Berlin, 1949); for attestation in the Mohammedan tradition, see H. A. Winkler, *Siegel und Charaktere in der muhammedanischen Zauberei* (Berlin and Leipzig, 1930).
9. For more examples cf. Franz Dornseiff, *Das Alphabet in Mystik und Magie* (2nd ed.; Berlin, 1925), pp. 2–10.
10. Joseph Joffre and Théodore Monod, 'A New West-African Alphabet: Used by the Toma, French Guinea and Liberia,' *Man*, xliii (1943), 108–112.
11. As observed by Dornseiff, *op. cit.*, p. 5.
12. Lucien Lévy-Brühl, *La mentalité primitive* (4th ed.; Paris, 1925), pp. 424–433.
13. *Annual Report of the Smithsonian Institution for the Year 1864*, p. 379.
14. Baldwin Spencer, *Native Tribes of the Northern Territory of Australia* (London, 1914), p. 36.
15. Erland Nordenskiöld, *Picture-Writing and Other Documents by Néle and Ruben Pérez Kantule* (Gotebörg, 1928), pp. 18 f.
16. François Haab, *Divination de l'alphabet latin* (Paris, 1948), p. 9.
17. Described in *The Times* of 29th June, 1910, and reported by

S. H. Hooke in *Antiquity*, xi (1937), 261. This custom is known also elsewhere; cf. Guido Mazzoni *apud* David Diringer, *L'alfabeto nella storia della civiltà* (Firenze, 1937), pp. xliii f.

18. Lucien Lévy-Brühl, *How Natives Think* (London, 1926), p. 179.

NOTES to Chapter X, pages 236–247

1. Marion L. Starkey, *The Cherokee Nation* (New York, 1946), p. 85.

2. See *L'adoption universelle des caractères latins*, edited by the Société des Nations. Institut International de Cooperation Intellectuelle (Paris, 1934).

3. (Otto Jespersen and Holger Pedersen), *Phonetic Transcription and Transliteration*. Supplement to *Maître phonétique* (Oxford, 1926).

4. *What Is Man? and Other Essays* (New York and London, 1917), p. 262.

5. Professor Giorgio Levi Della Vida calls my attention to the fact that 'visible speech' is a Dantesque expression; cf. 'visibile parlare' in *Purgatorio* 10, 95, where the cinema is anticipated.

6. Henry Sweet, *A Primer of Phonetics* (3rd ed.; Oxford, 1906), p. 1.

7. Sweet, *op. cit.*, and Wilhelm Viëtor, *Elemente der Phonetik* (6th ed.; Leipzig, 1915), pp. 16 f.

8. Ralph K. Potter, 'Visible Patterns of Sound,' *Science*, cii (1945), 463–470; R. K. Potter, G. A. Kopp, and H. C. Green, *Visible Speech* (New York, 1947).

9. Otto Jespersen, *Lehrbuch der Phonetik* (2nd ed.; Leipzig und Berlin, 1913), and Viëtor, *op. cit.*, pp. 17 f.

10. *Phonetics* (Ann Arbor, 1943), p. 155.

11. Th. W. Danzel, *Die Anfänge der Schrift* (Leipzig, 1912), pp. 212–218.

12. Otto Neurath, *International Picture Language* (London, 1936), and *idem, Basic by Isotype* (London, 1937).

13. *Op. cit.*, p. 263.

INDEX

Abbadie, A. d', 301
Abbreviations, 20, 87, 97, 226 f., 246 f.
ᶜAbdaᶜa, 132
Abercrombie, David, 269
Abībaᶜal, 131 f., 177
Acoustic signals, 3, 8
Acronym, 226
Acrophony, 111, 138, 141, 143, 251, 284
Adams, R. F. G., 301
Advertising, 229
Aegean writings, 83, 92, 129, 147, 156 ff., 164, 191, 195 f., 204, 215 ff., 291
Aesthetic convention, 68, 230, 251
African writings, 4, 21, 24 f., 48 ff., 79, 200, 208 f., 256 f., 268
Aḥīrâm, 131 ff., 139, 146 f., 177, 180
Akkadian cuneiform, 61, 68, 183, 191, 252
Akkadogram, 106
Alaskan writings, 21, 32 ff., 106, 193, 207 f., 210 f., 299
Albright, W. F., 123, 168 ff., 259, 263, 286 f., 292, 294
Algonquin writing, 207, 298 f.
Allogram, 105, 248
Alphabetography, 13 ff., 16, 54, 138 ff., 147 ff., 166 ff., 191, 197 f., 200 ff., 207, 209 ff., 239, 248
Amerindian writings, 19, 21, 25 f., 29 ff., 35, 38 ff., 65 f., 68, 74, 79, 103, 193 f., 200, 206 ff., 251, 256 f., 268, 279
Amerindians, 2, 4, 13, 57
Amnesic aphasiacs, 22
Analphabetic notation, 242 f., 245
Anaptyxis, 151, 169
Anatolia, 37, 60, 68, 82 f., 110, 121, 195, 216, 236
Anderson, H. Dewey, 299
Anglo-Saxon runic, 141 f.
Animal branding, 38
Arabic writing, 122, 134, 137, 150 f., 185 f., 188, 198, 209, 227 ff., 237 f., 244
Aramaeogram, 106
Aramaic writing, 133 ff., 141, 152, 176 f., 187, 191, 198, 202, 227 f., 248
Aristotle, 1, 13
Armenia, 60, 68, 121
Armenian writing, 141
Army, 142, 226

Arntz, Helmut, 255, 305
Art, 7, 35 f., 97, 190 ff., 212, 229 f.
Artificial languages, 241
Aśoka, 187
Associative sign, 99 f., 248
Assyrian cuneiform, 61, 196
Astronomy, 51, 54, 219 f.
Athens, 178 f., 181
Auditory communication, 2 f., 8
Australians, 2, 21, 232
Auxiliary marks, 99, 103, 113, 195, 248
Avestan writing, 228
Aymara Indians, 50
ᶜAzarbaᶜal, 131, 158, 177
Aztec writing, 12, 19, 51 ff., 57 ff., 61, 66, 68, 74, 111, 194, 257 f.

Babylonian cuneiform, 61, 196, 227
Bachhofer, Ludwig, 303
Bacon, Roger, 223
Baᶜlat, 123, 147
Ball, C. J., 303
Ballhorn, Friedrich, 273
Balti writing, 144
Balūᶜah, 128, 132
Bambara, 50
Bamum writing, 21, 79, 176, 183, 203, 208 ff.
Barnett, R. D., 278
Barrākib, 135
Barthel, Thomas S., 257, 277 f.
Barton, G. A., 258
Dasa writing, 208
Bauer, Hans, 129, 138 f., 144, 263 f., 286, 288, 292
Baumann, H., 300
Bayer, Franz, 258
Bea, Augustin, 264
Bedouins, 222
Behaviourists, 9 ff.
Behistun, 227
Bell, Melville, 242
Bennett, Emmett L., 94, 262
Bennigon, J. J., 301
Berger, Philippe, 254
Bergsträsser, G., 289
Berry, J., 296
Bertholet, A., 305
Bété writing, 300
Beth Shemesh, 123, 130
Beyer, Hermann, 257
Bibliography of writing, 206, 254 ff.
Birdwhistell, Ray L., 269